Historia

NUMBER SEVEN

Rio Grande / Río Bravo

Borderlands Culture and Traditions

Norma E. Cantú, General Editor

Historia

THE LITERARY MAKING OF CHICANA & CHICANO HISTORY

Louis Gerard Mendoza

TEXAS A&M UNIVERSITY PRESS
College Station

First edition

The paper used in this book meets the minimum requirements
of the American National Standard for Permanence
of Paper for Printed Library Materials, z39.48-1984.
Binding materials have been chosen for durability.

Library of Congress Cataloging-in-Publication Data

Mendoza, Louis Gerard, 1960–
Historia : the literary making of Chicana and Chicano history / Louis Gerard Mendoza. — 1st ed.
p. cm.
Includes bibliographical references (p.) and index.
ISBN 1-58544-150-3 (cloth: alk. paper)—
ISBN 1-58544-179-1 (pbk.: alk. paper)
1. Mexican Americans—Ethnic identity. 2. Mexican Americans—Historiography. 3. American literature—Mexican American authors. 4. Ethnicity in literature. 5. Mexican Americans in literature. I. Title.
E184.M5 M47 2001
305.868'72073—dc21 2001000482

Para mis abuelos
maternos y paternos
who had the courage to migrate northward
and embrace the unknown,
as well as the *ganas* to survive.

y

Para mis padres,
Joe Mendoza, Jr.,
and Mary Concepción Martínez Mendoza,
who, in addition to their undying love,
bequeathed to their children
a sense of duty to *nuestra comunidad,*
a love for learning,
and
a belief in the realization
of social justice.

CONTENTS

ACKNOWLEDGMENTS

This study is my effort to understand representations of the past; however, the work is informed and guided by a commitment to a more inhabitable future. I have been influenced and encouraged by numerous people, but I carry my life experiences with me, my joys and sorrows—and thus I begin by thanking all the members of my family. The wisdom, guidance, and dignity of my parents deserve special notice. My sisters, Rosemary, Mary Ann, Beatrice, Margie, Cynthia, and Gilda, and my brother, Bobby, deserve credit for all their love, faith, support, and patience over the years. I love you all. Good friends in Houston, especially Cynthia Galaviz Suarez, have expressed confidence and have been good confidantes.

Students at every institution I have been affiliated with have given me inspiration as peers, friends, mentees, and allies. Struggling students and students in struggle continue to mark the experience of higher education for many Chicanas/os. May we never forget the circumstances and privileges that make our education possible nor the unfortunate fact that our access to institutions is an exception to the rule.

I am deeply obliged to early mentors at the University of Houston who provided a foundation for the study of literature and Chicana/o Studies. At the University of Texas at Austin, Wahneema Lubiano's and Ramón Saldivar's early display of confidence in my work was crucial to my pursuit and continuation of graduate studies. Members of my dissertation committee, Martha Menchaca and Charles Rossman, gave me enthusiastic feedback and support. Over the years, the mentorship, scholarship, and friendship of José Limón have been an important influence and model for my work. Likewise, this project would not have been possible without the disciplined guidance, wisdom, and camaraderie of Barbara Harlow. My intellectual development owes much to the integrity of these two scholar-teachers. Barbara's courses on colonialism and literature, Third World feminisms, and prisons and political detention were key to helping me understand the abuses and strategic uses of power and its "linkage" to political and social discourse. José's courses on Chicano criticism and cultural poetics provided the initial impetus for this project and his scholarship has been crucial to my analysis. Their support has been invaluable.

I owe an inexpressible debt of gratitude to the members of the writing collective organized by Barbara Harlow at UT-Austin for their thoughtful and provocative feedback on my work in its earlier stages. These include Purnima Bose, Laura Lyons, S. Shankar, Hosam Aboul Ela, Nandhi Bhatia, Luc Fanou, Zjaleh Hajibashi, Rachel Jennings, and Luis Marentes. In San Antonio the *compas* of our informal writing collective provided crucial support and feedback in the final stages of revision. These dedicated friends, scholars, and teachers are Rachel Jennings, Kamala Platt, Irasema Coronado, Rodolfo Rosales, Lorraine Mora, Juan Mora-Torres, and Ben V. Olguín.

I am thankful to the late Américo Paredes for his work and for taking the time to converse with me about the history of *George Washington Gómez.* I am indebted to Inés Hernández-Ávila for permission to use her excellent translations of Sara Estela Ramírez's poetry and for her groundbreaking critical work on this author. Likewise, Teresa Acosta was extremely generous in giving me access to drafts of unpublished poems and providing insightful reflections on my work. The collections staff and librarians at the Benson Latin American Collection at the University of Texas at Austin, University of California–Santa Barbara, University of California–Berkeley's Chicano Studies Collection, and the Chicano Studies Library at the University of California–Los Angeles were helpful, gracious, and accommodating. The work on chapter 2 was made possible by a 1995 Recovering the Hispanic Literary Project Grant. I am also thankful for a Summer 1998 UTSA College of Fine Arts and Humanities Dean's Circle Award that helped me work on revisions to the manuscript.

My life in academia has been complemented and wonderfully complicated by various organizations and friends who allowed me the pleasure of working with them in the universities and communities of Houston, Austin, Providence, San Antonio, and elsewhere. A special *abrazo* is owed to all of my *compas* in: Chicanos Against Military Intervention in Latin American (CAMILA), La Peña, and People Organized in Defense of the Earth and Her Resources (PODER), the Barrio Student Resource Center, MEChA (University of Houston, University of Texas at Austin, Brown University, and the University of Texas at San Antonio), the Chicana/o Graduate Students Association at the University of Texas, UTSA's Chicana and Chicano Student Union, La Despedida, The Esperanza Peace and Justice Center, and San Anto Cultural Arts. These organizations have provided me with a safe place in an often hostile context. I admire their ability and willingness to articulate a vision for change and challenge the system in order to construct a better university and society. I am happy that they have allowed me to work with them. In Austin, Raúl Salinas, *poeta del barrio y compañero en la lucha,* deserves special mention for his crucial role in keeping *poesia en la calle* alive in Austin through Red Salmon Press's sponsorship of *canto libre* readings and in keeping the doors of Resistencia Bookstore open for the last eighteen years. He, in turn, has been the recipient of my *rasquache* carpentry and poor poetry—both necessary exercises in maintaining sanity during these crazy times.

The La Raza Faculty and Administrators Association at UTSA deserve special thanks for defining and advocating a vision of higher education in San Antonio. This work would not be realizable without the crucial support of community organizations and individuals who initiated this struggle. *Colegas* such as Ellen Riojas Clark, Arturo Vega, Yolanda Leyva, Bernadette Andrea, Juan Mora-Torres, Juan Rodríguez, Rodolfo Rosales, Josephine Mendez-Negrete, and Ben Olguín have been especially important sources of strength.

Thanks to my friends, Greg Cancelada, Dana Maya Maynard, Martine Torres-Aponte, and Emiliano Compean for their editorial and technical assistance at various stages of this work. An extra special debt of gratitude is owed to my dear friend Sandy Soto, for her intellectual insights, encouragement, and most of all, for her friendship. For her support, friendship, love, and understanding, Marianne Bueno deserves a special thanks. I look forward to your intellectual transformation and the many *historias* you will produce. I need also to acknowledge the late great Nina, who accompanied me throughout all my travels and educational endeavors. If I have omitted anyone, it is not because of my ingratitude but my own frailties of memory. To all, mentioned and not mentioned, thank you.

Finally, while so many have contributed to this work in various ways, its limitations, omissions, and faults are all mine.

¡Mil gracias a todos!

Historia

Prologue

Cuando reclamamos nuestra historia, afirmamos nuestro futuro

In the study that follows, I examine the personal and political motivations of historians and creative writers and suggest that in their work we see the role that imagination and desire play in how they tell their stories. It is only fair that as I begin this work I offer readers some insight into my own motivations for why I do what I do and for whom I would like to imagine that I do it. In doing so, however, I am aware that the representation I offer here is just that: a self-portrait available for critique.

When I left my hometown of Houston for graduate school more than a decade ago, I was very unsure about the profession and the institution I was entering. I was wholly unable to imagine myself as a literary and cultural critic. All I knew was that I was committed to literature and to the study of Mexican Americans. I was not even sure that it would be possible to pursue these interests simultaneously. Sixth-born in a family of eight children (six sisters and one brother), I was the third to receive a B.A. and the first to pursue graduate studies. I knew almost nothing about graduate school or research, much less literary criticism, teaching, multicultural debates, or postcolonialism. At twenty-eight years of age and coming from Denver Harbor, an oddly named barrio in East Houston, I had only relatively recently heard the term "Chicano," much less understood the complexities of the "Chicano Movement."[1] What I did know as I left to pursue an advanced degree was that I carried within me a love for Mexican American literature that had remained with me from the first Mexican American–studies class I took at the University of Houston–Downtown in the spring of 1985. Tomás

Vallejo, my professor in that class, was inspiring, knowledgeable, enthusiastic, and wholly supportive and interested in my work. Unlike my experiences in other literature classes, in his the writing came easy and seemed "important"; I was learning about myself in a multitude of ways and finding validation of everyday experience for the first time, in books. Tomás died of an AIDS-related illness in 1991. In an odd twist of fate, I was hired as his replacement at the University of Houston–Downtown when I sought my first job. The literary and historical, the familial and communal—this quartet of concerns are interrelated and signify for me the past and the present. It is through literature and history that I have come to better know and understand my family and the Chicana/o community, not just the barrio I grew up in but the larger community of *mexicanos* and Chicanas/os living in barrios and small towns all over the United States. To be sure, there are real limits to what I mean—and a certain amount of imagination being exercised—when I say I "know" that larger community, but I think one can grasp a sense of the general based on clear insight into the particulars. I agree with Hayden White that the study of history (and literature) produces a paradoxical relationship to the past—the more you know about it, the more difficult it is to generalize about it. While this is certainly true of my understanding of the greater Mexican community in the United States, it is also true of my familial history, about which I often feel I know much less. We owe a great debt to writers, historians, storytellers, journalists, poets, and individuals who, in their letters and diary entries, have not let the past slip away—who have interrupted the process of forgetting that is sanctioned, supported, and promoted by the government and by the difficulties and demands of everyday life. It took me so long—well into my adult years—to realize that I even had a history worth recovering. As a product of the educational system, as a "good" student, I had come to believe that the only history worth remembering was that of certain "great men" and their so-called great deeds as marked by the official commemoration of them on holidays and accompanying public ceremonies. As a second-generation Mexican American whose *abuelas* and *abuelos* had migrated northward to avoid the ravages of war in Mexico, I am a product of an ongoing war. My siblings and I have been cut off from our past by the international boundary, the economy, the time, and the cultural differences that separate Houston from the villages in Coahuila and Chihuahua our *antepasados* left behind. It is true that none of these distances should seem insurmountable or even very great, especially today; yet unlike many *mexicanos* who frequently traversed the distance between *este lado y el otro lado*, mine did not and does not. Why that is so is one of the particulars of my family history that must explored.

I think I understand some of the reasons for this distance between places that produces a gap in our family history. Travel is never easy for those without resources. When my grandparents came to Texas on foot it was a one-way trip; to return home for a visit to maintain relations was an unaffordable luxury. This problem persisted into the next generation. My parents made rare and infrequent visits to Mexico to meet relatives, but as our family grew in size, travel became more and more difficult. We made, I believe, one trip to Coahuila when I was very young, our entire family of ten crammed into our pinkish Oldsmobile station wagon. The distance between generations and nations was also exacerbated by language. Like so many other *mexicanos* in the States, my parents experienced the pain and humiliation of physical, psychological, and verbal punishment and abuse for speaking Spanish at school. In an effort to spare us the pain of having our language beat out of us, they did not encourage their children to learn Spanish. Now I continue, like many of my generation, to retrieve what was stolen through the force of violence and intimidation. This too explains the gap we experienced with our grandparents, who spoke primarily Spanish. It kept us from listening, questioning, responding to, and comprehending the full force of their stories and from fully benefiting from their experiences.

What the members of my family know about our Mexican past is only what is remembered; therefore it is fragmented and at times inconsistent. Over the years, though, I have come to the realization that this fractured and fragmented past is not unique to our family. Moreover, the harsh experiences of migration and struggling to work, live, and love with dignity is another common thread that binds my familial history to the tapestry of experiences that compose the history of the *mexicano* community in the United States. It is an odd thing to feel comfort in knowing that one is not alone in experiencing discrimination, social animosity, rejection, and so on. But that is a consequence of the violence of race and class domination. Along with the stories of pain, however, are stories of resistance and endurance; these are stories that often get told only as an afterthought, the stories that only some members of the family remember. Consequently, much as in the last vignette of Tomás Rivera's *. . . y no se lo tragó la tierra,* only when all the pieces are put together and recalled do we see the commonalities of experience and survival. One of the things that gives me comfort about my education is that it provides me with a framework in which to listen to and speak with my family, friends, and students about shared experience in a way that accounts for the contradictions and gaps in our lives.

Even as Chicana/o historians produce well-calculated and well-researched accounts of the past, with which much of the community can identify, much of our organic memory tells a different story. My parents were born into large families in Houston during the late 1920s and thus were children of the Great Depression. Fixed in my mother's memory of those years are the many Sundays when they would lie quietly with the shades drawn, hiding from the landlord, whom they could not pay—this after my grandfather labored as a mason all week building the homes located adjacent to Rice University. My father's family lived off the money my grandfather earned working on the docks at the Port of Houston.

Because I am aware of the critically important role that writing, reading, and teaching alternative histories and literatures plays in cultural negotiations, I find myself wanting most to speak to those with shared or similar experiences. For this reason, teaching in Texas public institutions of higher education is both a tremendous opportunity and a huge responsibility, one that I could not have foreseen nor taken for granted in this profession, but it also produces mixed feelings.

The road to my future is the road to my past. This is what I have learned after my literal and metaphorical sojourns. A year at Brown University in Providence, Rhode Island, one of the most prestigious universities in the country, taught me that a "sense of place" is integral to my "sense of purpose." Living at "home," in Texas, a state that doesn't let you forget who or where you are, means that I also constantly confront myself as a changed person, especially in contrast to who I was and my relationship to the barrio culture that made me who I am. Why should this produce ambivalence? I think this is so because now, more than ever, I know that knowledge demands responsibility. My parents practiced *compadrazgo,* and in this cultural concept that is my inheritance I know that I cannot write and teach about Mexican culture without considering my own social status in relation to the status of *mexicanos* in general, not as a cultural group but as a people who live and learn and love and struggle and fight every day to survive in a society that still thinks we are inferior when we proclaim our *mexicanidad* and wear it on our sleeves and our faces.

My familial and communal histories are intertwined, but there are also discontinuities and inconsistencies. As with many families, the process of remembering and recovering the past is informal and often occurs around family gatherings, holidays, and rituals. This is best exemplified by examples from three visits home I made as I neared the end of my career as a student—one was a Christmas visit, another was for my sister BB's (Beatrice's) wedding, and the third was for the funeral for my uncle Jesse.

Very little seems to be known about the particulars of our familial ancestors. The mystery surrounding my paternal grandfather's history and genealogy perhaps best exemplifies this. The day before Christmas, 1993, my father showed me his parents' 1919 marriage certificate from Our Lady of Guadalupe Church in Houston. It lists the names of my great-grandparents and their hometowns in Mexico. My father mentioned that he was fairly certain that the information about his grandparents was incorrect, because he did not think his father knew his parents. Prior to this, all my father had ever said he knew about my grandfather was that he had crossed over as a young boy at the turn of the century. As far as he knew, my grandfather had been an orphan and had been living and working at a tin factory before coming to the States. The following day I initiated a conversation with my aunt Margaret, my father's sister, who gave me a very different and very detailed history of my grandfather. She told me that as a child she acted as translator between my grandfather and a lawyer he had hired to help him document his birth in Mexico so he could file for U.S. citizenship. According to her, my grandfather had been born a twin; his brother and mother had died at childbirth. My great-grandfather, whom they never knew, had emigrated from Spain. When his wife and one of his children died, he turned over my grandfather to his wife's parents, who were living in Mexico City. How my grandfather became separated from them is unclear. When my grandfather came to the United States, my aunt said, he traveled with a family named García and assumed their last name to make the border crossing easier. He kept that name for approximately fifteen years until he married my grandmother, when, to her surprise, he revealed and reclaimed the name Mendoza. My aunt recalls that my grandfather's birth certificate listed the name of my great-grandfather and the town in Spain where he was born. She does not recall the town, but she does remember that my grandmother wrote a letter to the Mendoza family in that town in Spain and received a reply that included photographs. The letter and the photographs have since been lost. She also told me stories about her childhood visits to Mexico, during which, against her mother's wishes, she renewed familial ties with relatives that my grandmother had forbidden her to see. The day after my conversation with my aunt I told my parents what she had told me, and they both did not believe it! Their only response was to say that she "tends to make things up."

This story is significant to me because it exemplifies the slippery nature of history and memory, and the significance of documentation. If my aunt had produced the letter and photographs, or even documentation (from the Immigration and Naturalization Service, for example) to support her claims, then her version of the story would be irrefutable.

A somewhat similar event occurred at my sister's wedding in April, 1994. This time it involved a creative representation of my own making, one that presented a perspective that caused enough discomfort to one of my cousins that she decided to let me know about it as we passed each other on the dance floor. In the spring of 1988, Arte Público Press sponsored a writing contest called "Being Hispanic in Houston." The parameters were wide open. A bit unsure about what genre they were looking for, I submitted a hybrid of essay, dialogue, and historical and personal narrative that detailed some of my impressions and thoughts on the history of Mexicans in Houston. I was awarded an honorable mention, and the essay has since been passed around to various family members. In trying to describe the ambivalence I carried about the social geography and history of our neighborhood, I wrote in one passage:

> Interstate 10 slices through Denver Harbor like a swollen scar of an improperly cared for wound. Railroad tracks surround it—they are the sutures holding our wounds together. The healing process is never ending. People are contained within by the less visible barriers of poverty and *comunidad.* In our house on Zoe Street I used to lie awake at night in one of the upstairs bedrooms my father and his *compadres* had added on to better house our large family. There, the painful squeaks and moans of rusty freight cars passing in the night would sing me to sleep. Those eerie sounds both haunted me and made me hunger—they seemed to call, to dare me to hop on and take off to new, unknown places. Their motion was persistent—shhh, shhh, shhh, all roads lead out shh, shh, shh, they whispered. In the dark, in my bed, I let them take me away—to happier, unreal places. During the day these cumbersome caterpillars crawled rudely through our world. Doug and Larry and I used to wait for them on Wallisville or old Clinton Road: out of defiance we jumped on them, only to hop off after a few blocks. The ride was always disappointing, falling far short of our expectations.

It was these images that stuck in my cousin Kathy's mind and made her want to confront me as we paused between dances. She asked, "Why did you describe the freeway as a scar and the tracks as stitches? I never thought of them like that, they were just there." I found myself unable to offer a quick or coherent answer. I said something to the effect of, "Well, I always saw them as dividing us from each other and from those on the other side of the tracks"—Fifth Ward, Settegast, Port of Houston, and Clinton. I then invoked what I thought was common sense by adding, "You know how everybody on one side of the freeway fought with others on the other side," to which she responded, "No, I didn't know that, at least that's not the way it was with people I knew." As the music started, our brief exchange ended. I was left feeling dissatisfied with my answers and wanting to talk with her some more. We did not resume our conversation that evening. Her remarks were simply casual and honest, yet I realized that in many ways she had pinpointed the limitations and inability of a single narrative to capture everyone's sense of things. As I thought more about it afterward I realized that in no way could my recollections, told from the perspective of a young boy, represent her experience. Again, what stuck out the most to me was the dissimilarity of perspectives that existed in the same time, region, and family. Since then I have realized that I need to seek out a longer conversation with this cousin, not to discuss my narrative of the past, but to listen to hers—perhaps to discover where we agree and where we do not.

This issue extends beyond differences I have with family and friends in how we remember and represent the past; it is also connected to my "status" as the Ph.D. in my family. On May 12, 1994, my uncle Jesse died. When my mother called me in Austin to tell me that the Rosary would be the next evening, I wasn't sure I could afford to take a break from my writing to go to Houston. I hung up the phone without committing myself. As I thought about whether or not to go, I realized I could not recall precisely when I had last seen my uncle. He died a slow death from a lifetime of hard work at the shipyards and many, many an hour in Houston barrio icehouses. Recalling the fond memories of my uncle and my cousin, I decided to take the trip the next day. I drove straight to the funeral home to see my aunt, her children, and the rest of my extended family and friends. After the services my cousin, my brother, their spouses, and some other friends and I went to a *taquería* to talk. I had seen my cousin Jesse and our friend Roy hardly at all in the six years since I had been in graduate school. As we talked about how things had changed, or not, they teased me about my soon-to-be-acquired status as

"Doctor" and asked if they could sit in my classes for free and get A's, still call me "Jerry" (my middle name and family nickname), whether or not I was going to get a haircut ("you're about ten years behind the times, man"), and if I would prescribe their favorite "medicine" for them. Joking along with them, I said no to everything, of course. When I left there that night I realized with certainty that going back home to my family and friends was never the problem—the "problem" was how to manage what I perceived as tension between living and working in two sometimes very distant social spheres.

This was a tension that I would not necessarily have to confront at such a personal level if I were to teach elsewhere—somewhere far away from home, far from an urban Chicana/o-Latina/o setting. Expressed another way, one that situates the question of representation and community at its center, is the challenge scholars often face in applying critical reading skills, writing, and scholarship to everyday life. It is an enduring question faced by many "minority" and working-class-origin scholars about the relationship between scholarship and activism. What is our responsibility to our community when we have learned the skills necessary to assess the social status of people's living and working conditions and their place in the cycle of economic and cultural production? This is not a question that can be easily answered nor easily dismissed. I proposed no easy answer for myself then or now; rather I believe the tension itself is constructive as I strive to retain old friendships, initiate new ones, and constantly negotiate my relationship to higher education and my barrio, first in Houston and now in San Antonio.

I must say that after returning home I found that Denver Harbor had changed enormously. Very few of my extended family and only one of my sisters continue to live there. After investing in private school for all of their children for so many years, my parents left the barrio in the mid-1980s. It was a move they sometimes regret. They did not find *comunidad* in the suburbs. My sisters live in neighborhoods that are not neglected and where the schools are fully supplied with textbooks and are not overcrowded. Like the changing conditions of barrios described by Rubén Martínez and Teresa Acosta, Denver Harbor is a mixture of residents from my generation and many newly arrived *mexicanos* as well as *salvadoreños.* The neighborhood *tienditas* have mostly been replaced by Stop-N-Gos, and the locally owned hamburger stands and *taquerías* are overshadowed by Burger King and Popeye's Fried Chicken. The intense patrols by the police cars and helicopters remain the same, however, as does the traffic of drugs and trains.

As part of an ongoing battle for social justice that will lead to social reconciliation, the evocation of the past is strategic and necessary. This is why I strive to bring together fact and fiction, the real and the imagined. I believe that in understanding what was, we can begin to see more clearly what is and know what yet can be. What we recall as our history surely participates in the determination of our future, and it is that process and its products that we must negotiate in order to make the future an inhabitable social space—one worthy of our everyday struggle to live and love.

Introduction

Literature as History, History as Literature, and Cultural Poetics

The passage from memory to history has required every social group to redefine its identity through the revitalization of its own history.
—Pierre Nora

The most important aspect however, for those who are Chicano, is that in writing the history, they will contribute modestly to the heritage and self-knowledge of the community, and perhaps contribute a structural analysis for positive action on behalf of the community.
—Juan Gómez-Quiñones, "Toward a Perspective on Chicano History"

In her powerful exploration of the role of imagination in the construction of historical paradigms, Norma Alarcón asserts in "Traddutora, Traditora" that the reason so many Latina intellectuals and writers have been fascinated with Malintzín Tenepal, (aka "La Malinche"), the indigenous translator and mistress of Hernán Cortes, and have subsequently produced imaginative and historical revisions and recuperations of her life is because "it is through a revision of tradition that self and culture can be radically reenvisioned and reinvented" (Alarcón 71). Alarcón astutely points out that such revisions are more imagined than historical because Tenepal herself had no access to self-representation in the historical record—her voice has always been mediated by others. The extensive examination of the historical representations of

Tenepal and the imagined reconstruction of her as both subject and object of this formative period in history have done little to clarify her individual history, but it enables a contemporary critical discourse on gender relations, sexuality, and *indigenismo* that has had a profound impact on Chicana/o constructions of "community" and subsequent political practices. The recovery and revision of history, then, often reflect the political exigencies of the context from which that history emerges and can be mobilizing ideological forces.

In a provocative example of the intersection between the imagined and the historical, Teresa Palomo Acosta's poem "Preguntas y frases para una bisabuela española" explores her complex cultural history—her relationship to her Spanish and Amerindian *antepasadas.* Separated from them by time, different cultural and linguistic practices, and a different relationship to the ruling class, the poet finds it difficult to imagine her Spanish heritage. This difficulty is articulated in the opening lines:

> Sabe, bisabuela, *I just barely thought about you tonight.*
> *For the first time considered I might be related to you.*
> *Because we mestiza cafecitas con high cheekbones believe*
> *We're almost ninety-nine percent Indian*
> *And we may be ninety-nine percent right.* (*Nile*, 75)

But however much she identifies with her indigenous heritage, the poet also knows she is marked both genetically and linguistically by her "Spanish" inheritance. This recognition is rife with ambivalence. Disinherited from her past because of colonial racism, she does not know whether her knowledge of Spaniards is based on stereotypes or fact. Nor does she know the relationship to power that her grandmother maintained. She can, however, identify two possible attitudes that a Spanish woman might hold toward indigenous women. She asks:

> *Were you haughty and arrogant?*
> *Ready to do in la india*
> *Clutched by el soldado español*
> *As he crossed your path?*
> *Or did you also hide from him*
> *In a corner of your hacienda?* (75)

Aware that the strongest possibility for reconciliation with her Spanish heritage is shared experience, she considers that not all Spanish women were complicit in the subjugation of indigenous peoples, especially because they, too, suffered under colonial patriarchal relations. In this poem Acosta recreates the possibility of alliance between indigenous and "elite" women. This imagined alliance allows her to address the stereotypes about Mexicans in the United States held by Spanish and Mexican elites in order "To set some crooked things en nuestra historia / At least at a slant, / If not straight," between them (76). It is this "writing" of historical wrongs that is at the heart of Acosta's poetics.[1]

Like "Preguntas y frases," much of Acosta's poetry addresses specific historical female antecedents; therefore it is instructive to examine the meaning of history for this poet who disagrees with a monolithic construction of history produced by both mainstream and Chicano historians. Born in the rural community of McGregor, Texas, in 1949, Acosta has said that media exposure to the Chicano and black civil rights movements "greatly inclined" her to study her people and to document their history through creative forms. Acosta's poetry links her present-day reality to the past and in so doing contributes to the documentation of the history of women of Mexican descent. Informed by what is lacking in written histories, many of her poems challenge textbook history.

Acosta's work has received scant attention from literary critics. In her desire to recuperate women's voices in history, her implicit message about women is twofold: first she insists that women *have* been political—both within and outside their homes and home cultures; second, the narrow notions of power that inform historical narratives have simultaneously elided women's cultural production. Having emerged from the Chicano Movement, Acosta's poetry first appeared in the Austin-based literary journal *Tejidos,* and then in an anthology produced to commemorate the First Annual Chicano Literary Festival, *Festival de flor y canto, An Anthology of Chicano Literature* (1976). Since then she has published three collections, *Passing Time* (1984), *Nile Notebooks* (1994), and *Nile and Other Poems* (1999), and numerous other selections in anthologies, literary journals, and magazines. Much of Acosta's poetry addresses two concerns that are germane to my study: the articulation and recuperation of women's voices in history and a critique of "official" history produced by institutional historians. In addition to giving her work long-overdue attention, this study will use her poetry as contrapuntal evidence to the generational paradigm that underwrites much Chicano historiography. I will use Acosta's writing and the creative work of other authors to facilitate a rereading of Chicano historical texts. Women's historical and literary voices will be an integral part of the analysis of the historical dimensions of literature and the literary dimensions of history in this book. Rather than performing an extended reading of her work in only one chapter, however, a reading of Acosta's poetry will be woven throughout to serve as a critical prism and counterbalance of gender and genre. Treating her work in this manner best captures the broad historical range of her poetry, which covers the lives of Mexicans, primarily women, from the nineteenth century to the present.

Acosta's poetry seeks to reconfigure our understanding of the present through the past. She blurs both historical and geographical boundaries in her writing by combining concerns about movements (political and geographical), conflict, and intellectual leadership. Informed by a feminist, post–Chicano Movement analysis, her poetry shifts some of the focus away from public institutions toward other sites of power—the family, the body, and real and metaphorical boundaries that shape identity—while nevertheless maintaining a material analysis of Chicana/os' lived reality. Providing a counterhistory is central to Acosta's poetics. Her poetry of reconciliation is not dependent on replacing one perspective with another, but it explores possibilities of the past and future that have been left unexamined. In this manner her work is exemplary and offers a powerful revision of the past and present. In "Tejana History as a Poem" Acosta says that she wanted to document the "emotional facts of *[tejanas']* lives [that] are not available in archives and [that] history cannot express . . . for us. They must find their voices in imaginative literature to become part of Tejana history" (13). Acosta's work is testimony to the creative and empowering relationship between the literary and the historical.

Historical Literature and Literary History

In this book I will challenge conventional notions of the relationship between historical and literary narratives by examining the literature of people of Mexican descent in the United States as they have chosen to represent their past through "factual" and "fictional" narratives. In the chapters that follow, I conduct an ideological analysis of the poetics and implicit politics of genre and discipline. More specifically, I examine how style, purpose, and context function to facilitate and/or constrain our understanding of the past.

To render a more complex understanding of twentieth-century literature by Chicano men and women, I read "imaginative" literature "against the grain" of recent political histories written by Chicano historians and social scientists. I deconstruct the generational paradigm that often prevails in Chicano historiography through a reading of Chicana/o prose and poetry. My method exposes the tendency of this model to present Chicana/o culture monolithically. Creative literature, I argue, enables readers to better see the role culture plays as a historical force, one that is often disregarded in historical narratives that are shaped by approaches to the past that privilege particular sites and agents of social contestation. Imaginative reconstructions of daily life examine the particulars of identity formation as they are shaped by ritual, emotional relations, spiritual beliefs, and relations of power outside the traditional domain of political and economic relations. This study of the relationship between writing, political processes, and the formation of "minority" identities is guided by a larger interest in the role of culture in retaining and refashioning identity in colonial and postcolonial contexts, particularly when it occurs at contested sites of struggle, whether that space is designated as the workplace, the home, the academy, the barrio, or along/across national borders. For Chicana/o historians, the complex forces surrounding national and racial identity are exacerbated by the desire to have their work contribute to the consolidation of group identity and struggle. Often this interest manifests itself in their work through certain periodization schemas that skirt the issue of group complicity in the domination of Native Americans and intracultural struggles against race, class, and gender oppression.

Since the late 1960s historians and literary critics of Chicana/o culture and politics have been engaged in critical revisionist projects that examine the presuppositions underlying the relationship between dominant and subordinate cultures in the United States and throughout the Americas. Many of these critiques question the validity of widely accepted analytical paradigms. This book is motivated by the same critical impulse but looks at the limitations and contradictions of revisionist studies that also reproduce what Gayatri Spivak has called cognitive gaps or historical blind spots. I utilize an interdisciplinary cultural-studies approach to investigate the links, parallels, and junctures between historical and imaginative literature as sources of political vision. Because much of the literature of people of Mexican descent in the United States addresses geographical and social movement, this study will also examine the ways in which Chicana/o literature engages in a nontraditional form of travel literature. For people of Mexican descent, movement is usually generated by social, economic, or military forces that result in displacement or mobility. In politics the word "movement" refers to the organized mobilization of people for the achievement of shared goals or resistance to a perceived assault on a way of life. This attention to the causes, consequences, and conflict generated by geographical and social movements situates this study in relation to postcolonial studies' attentiveness to the geopolitics of identity and nation.

Significant book-length studies of Chicana/o literature, such as Ramón Saldívar's *Chicano Narrative* (Wisconsin University Press, 1990), Hector Calderón and José Saldívar's *Criticism in the Borderlands* (Duke University Press, 1991), Tey Diana Rebolledo's *Singing in the Snow: A Cultural Analysis of Chicana Literature* (Arizona University Press, 1995), Teresa McKenna's *Migrant Song: Politics and Process in Contemporary Chicano Literature* (University of Texas Press, 1997), Jóse Saldívar's cultural-studies analysis, *Border Matters* (University of California Press, 1997), and, most recently, Leticia Garza-Falcón's *Gente Decente* (University of Texas Press, 1998) have made important contributions to this rapidly growing field, but none has interrogated the relationship between Chicana/o history and literature with the methodology I practice here. The status of history in these studies of Chicana/o literature varies depending on the national history against which it is measured. On the one hand, when placed in relation to narratives traditionally sanctioned by the United States, Chicana/o literature is often perceived as presenting a counternarrative that functions as a corrective to the effaced or misrepresented history of Mexicans in the States. In these cases, as Ramón Saldívar has noted, history is the narrative battleground upon which the literature is based—the writing and rewriting of Chicana/o history thus becomes an important subtext of the literature. On the other hand, in most Chicana/o literary criticism, Chicana/o historical narratives are integrated uncritically into an analysis of the literature to establish a context or background for reading. In these cases Chicana/o historical writings are invoked as a representation of the "real," a presentation of historical facts as a counternarrative intended to complement or substantiate the imaginative subject matter of the literature. This use of history merely reinforces a polarity in which history is seen as "factual truth" and literature as "imaginary." In both instances, historical works serve as secondary sources in Chicana/o literary criticism to enable a revisionist critique of U.S. history and culture. An important objective of this study, therefore, is to interrogate the common assumption that the goals of Chicana/o literature, criticism, and history are always identical because of their shared critique of the U.S. master narrative.

Method and Paradigms Engaged

In foregrounding a critique of Chicana/o historiography, this study targets the constructed nature of historical narratives and reveals blind spots that have diminished, if not effaced, culturally specific ways of conveying knowledge of past events and truths that enable survival. I am motivated by a recognition that many Chicana/o-studies scholars who engage in interdisciplinary work are predisposed by their politics and the limits of their training to assume an inherent commonality with the work done in their discipline and that done in other disciplines due to a common subject matter and shared goals. As practitioners of a still emerging and contested field of study, Chicana/o-studies scholars have relied on each other's work for guidance, inspiration, and example. And while there has been some contestation among Chicana/o scholars about the ideological implications of various theoretical paradigms, there has also been much interdependency on each other's work, especially across the disciplines.

One of the goals of this study was initially encountered as a problem: Could I reconcile the role of a primarily masculinist history in a project that sought to uncover the significant political and cultural power of women and men whose "typical" lives were often not the subject of revisionist history? While I found texts like Rodolfo Acuña's *Occupied America,* David Montejano's *Anglos and Mexicans in the Making of Texas,* Mario García's *Mexican Americans: Leadership, Ideology, and Identity,* and Carlos Muñoz's *Youth, Identity and Power: The Chicano Movement* tremendously insightful, they offered me little assistance in conceptualizing the relationship between culture and power, especially as it affects the formation of individual subjectivity and its relationship to collective identity. Absent in these counternarratives was a critical approach to intracultural relations. What I have developed in this study is a method for enhancing the insight and potential of different disciplinary approaches and paradigms of Chicana/o studies. Thus, even as I critique the limits of certain paradigms, I strive to retain the valuable insight they yield. What I propose here is a method of reading Chicana/o literature so as to reconceptualize agency in a manner that accounts for individual and collective experiences. This study goes beyond previous work on Chicana/o literature by juxtaposing the literary and the historical in such a way as to offer new insight on culture, agency, and experience. Central to my methodology is the claim that seeing literature as valid historical evidence enables a new way of conceptualizing the nature of power and its negotiation with more complexity and accuracy; bringing the literary and the historical into a dialectical relationship with one another promotes an interpretive practice that enables the reader to imagine possibilities for intervention and produce new strategies for social change. I also argue that seeing history as a literary genre is similarly enabling: while there is a different and necessary relationship to "truth" and "facts," *how* we make history, as well as *what* we consider worthy of recording, is continually revised according to what we deem important. What this study does, then, is offer an incipient theory of reading literature and history, one that asks us to consider the epistemological nature of cultural practices as viable sources of historical knowledge and as strategies for empowerment and survival.

The principal objective of this study is to examine the different understanding of history produced by literary narratives when they are read against historical narratives. This analytical approach will entail an investigation of how Chicano social scientists, many of whom were also involved in *el movimiento,* have chosen to depict the political history of the Chicana/o community and to analyze the consequences of their historical perspectives. Although they have different emphases and structures of periodization, three book-length studies of Chicana/o political history published since 1989 have foregrounded the issues of identity, ideology, and leadership. The different approaches to the history of people of Mexican descent in the United States that we see in Mario Garcia's *Mexican Americans,* Juan Gómez-Quiñones's *Chicano Politics: Reality and Promise, 1940–1990,* and Carlos Muñoz's *Youth, Identity, and Power* are representative of different paradigms that have in common a generational approach to history. Not coincidental, I argue, is the fact that these (counter) narratives are written by males. In general, these grand narratives provide a synthesis of preexisting work and thus carry with them the biases, blind spots, and limitations of early work; most significantly, they do not adequately address women's history. Chicana historians have refused to embrace the patriarchal structure of the generational paradigm and the macroscopic, master-narrative approach to history. In studies like *Cannery Women, Cannery Lives* (1989) by Vicki Ruiz, Patricia Zavella's *Women's Work and Chicana Families* (1987), Cynthia Orozco's forthcoming book on the early Mexican American civil rights movement, or the works in collections like *Essays on La Mujer* (1977) and *Between Borders: Essays on Mexicana/*

Chicana History (1990), Chicana historians have consistently chosen to conduct focused, discrete studies of particular work sites, organizational affiliations, or social institutions many of which rely on oral histories—thus giving primacy to female self-representation.

As political historians have discovered, there is no essential or singular form of leadership or ideology that can adequately characterize the way in which power relations between Chicanas/os and Anglos have been negotiated. Political processes never, or hardly ever, involve an entire community of people, even though the entire community may suffer or benefit from the consequences. An important component of writing political history is sensitivity to the ideological underpinnings of one's approach. Given the importance of the 1960s as an era of intensified political activity and the focus by Chicanas/os on achieving access to knowledge vis-à-vis educational institutions, it is important to focus on the conceptualization of leadership, identity, and ideology by the intellectuals who emerged from this period. Elite institutions often perpetuate rather than problematize notions of "universal progress" by promoting linear narratives of development and underdevelopment, which sustain social hierarchies based on race, class, and gender. Therefore, the sanctioned history of the political and social conflict between Chicanas/os and the dominant U.S. culture is relatively "new" and sparse. Elite histories operate on assumptions about the perceived "weak" and the assumed "powerful" in order to "naturalize" unequal social relations between the dominant and the subordinate; this occurs both on a national and global scale. Prior to the 1960s, Chicanas/os had limited access to the educational institutions that had the power to make Chicana/o history a "legitimate" research topic. Consequently, for many years there were relatively few book-length narratives available to counter Euro-American bourgeois histories that had denigrated or neglected people of Mexican descent. Since the '60s however, a critical mass of Chicana/o historians have received their Ph.D.s in history and have made critical advances in recovering, rewriting, and revising the history of people of Mexican descent in the United States.

Inasmuch as Chicana/o literature also narrates the historical experiences of Mexican men and women in the United States, it offers us yet another way of imaginatively reconstructing historical, cultural, and social relations. Moreover, the emergence of a cultural-studies model of analysis has provided us with a framework for interrogating the relationships of power between social institutions and culture. In its attention to the production of meaning in everyday life, cultural-studies and ethnic-studies practitioners have examined the distinctions between official and unofficial cultural practices and discourses. Culturally distinct negotiations about the relationship between the past and the present are only one of many important areas of exploration addressed in this study. Chicana/o writers and historians recover history in different forms. On the one hand, "fiction" writers reconstruct the past imaginatively. Historians, on the other, utilize their knowledge and evidence of "factual" events to tell us the "truth" about the past. These two seemingly very different tasks have a similar end, however—to create a narrative of the past in such a way as to offer a simultaneous representation and interpretation of some discrete dimension of time, space, and experience. In reference to the perceived difference between, and status of, the fields of history and literature, Hayden White has noted that "history can be set over against "literature" by virtue of its interest in the "actual" rather than the "possible," which is supposedly the object of representation of "literary" works. Thus within a long and distinguished critical tradition that has sought to determine what is "real" and what is "imagined" in the novel, history has served as a kind of archetype of the "realistic" pole of representation" (White 89). The relationship between "literary" and "historical" projects is no longer as clear nor as easily accepted as it once seemed. The disciplinary boundaries between history and literature have been blurred; a text can be both literary and historical.[2]

Integral to the thesis of this study will be an argument about the relationship between culture and history. The historical experiences of Chicana/os and their accommodation to or conflict with the dominant culture are consistently articulated within Chicana/o literature. By and large, histories written by Chicanas/os have challenged the academy as a whole and the presuppositions that have allowed traditional "American" historians either to ignore the history of Mexicans in the United States or to subsume it within the racial discourse on manifest destiny and racial inferiority. This study of twentieth-century Chicana/o literature will examine both intracultural and intercultural conflict—but not as unrelated phenomena. The relationship between politically dominant and dominated cultures is complex, dynamic, and interactive. A politically subordinate group is often dependent upon the educational and cultural institutions of the hegemonic group. This dependence is often a hindrance, especially when the perspective one adopts is critical of the dominant group; analytical paradigms sanctioned by the culturally dominant can be limiting, if not debilitating. Official Chicano histories—that is, those produced within elite educational institutions that facilitate the reproduction of social relations—provide good examples of this; many contemporary analytical paradigms are unable to escape "universal" notions of history that are exclusionary and elitist in focus. These studies often sustain the gatekeeping standards of academia, which maintain models of history that privilege top-down, male-dominant, and economic, political, or military approaches that efface the everyday lives and cultural relations of disempowered women, children, and men.

Identity and the Generational Paradigm

Much historical and creative literature by people of Mexican descent in the United States is characterized by the significance placed on certain "defining" moments in history that have had a significant impact on their citizenship status, ethnic identity, and racial classification as Mexicans or Americans. In the continuum between the cultural poles "Mexican" and "American" lie varying degrees of cultural and political identity, as the multiple identifiers available for representing cultural identity attest.[3] A survey of historical literature suggests that the most significant defining moments in the history of people of Mexican descent who live in the States are the U.S.-Mexican War, the Mexican Revolution, the Great Depression, World War II, and the Chicano Movement. These particular historical moments notwithstanding, the pervasive, everyday, shared historical experiences of economic exploitation and racial and sexual discrimination have also helped shape the lives of Mexicans in the United States (Gómez-Quiñones, *CP* 15; Montejano, *AM* 5). These "moments" of social conflict and the resulting political consciousness and practice are taken up as theme, plot, and form in Chicana/o literature.

Recent historical narratives are an important resource for providing context and informing any analysis of twentieth-century Chicana/o literature. It is important, however, to be critically aware of the limitations of these sources and their guiding premises. This is especially true for histories that assume a generational approach to political history. The generational approach presupposes "a group of people who have undergone the same basic historical experiences during their formative years" (Rental, qtd. in García, *MA* 3). According to Mario T. García, political generations are "shaped by historical changes—usually convulsive ones, such as wars or revolutions—specific to a certain period, which trigger a particular political response or responses by a collection of individuals who come of political age during this time" (García, *MA* 4). The generational distinctions that many Chicano historians identify and use in their analyses are both limited and useful. On the one hand, they are usually temporally and geographically well focused and delimited studies; on the other, they rarely acknowledge their own limits and tend to devalue the events and people that exist outside of their immediate scope. At the very least they are shared chronological schemas that reflect the ways in which ethnic and political identity have played a significant role in the politics of people of Mexican descent.[4] Further, these generational constructions have a rough correspondence to the defining moments in the history of Mexicans in the United States identified earlier. For instance, the beginning of the Migrant Generation (1900–30) can be said to correspond with the Mexican Revolution; the Mexican American Generation (1930–60) encompasses the experiences of the Great Depression, World War II, and the cold war; the Chicano Generation (1960–75) is linked to the U.S. civil rights, antiwar, and feminist movements; and the Hispanic Generation (1976 to the present) brings us to the contemporary period, an era characterized by the consolidation of global capital through hemispheric trade agreements.[5]

Each chapter of this study will include a survey and analysis of historical writings about a particular generation. Although the generational schema serves as an organizational framework for this study, the goal is not to affirm the framework but to illustrate its limitations.

Conflict and Containment: History as Ideology and the Emergence of an Alternative Master Narrative

The legacy of conflict that marks Anglo-Mexican relations in the United States has been central to Chicana/o histories. It must be said, however, that the critical paradigms generally used to examine and revise the dominant culture's representation of these relations have not always been sufficient. Referring to the different theoretical models used to interpret Mexican political practice, Gómez-Quiñones has noted that "one stresses order, the maintenance of stability, while the other stresses conflict or contradiction in the existing society. In the case of Mexican history, the concept of order would stress accommodation, assimilation, rewards, and mobility; the concept of conflict would stress resistance, assertive negotiation, exploitation, and insurgent culture" (*CP* 220). As frameworks for comprehending political practice, historical analyses have their parallel in cultural practice. The economic and political domination of Mexicans in the United States provided the preconditions for the emergence of bodies of historical and imaginative literature that are, by and large, critical of ethnic and class relations in the States. The primary literary texts selected for this study of Chicana/o literature will represent different aspects of Chicana/o history that are unaccounted for in the generational paradigm.

Traditional beliefs about the "purity" of history or literature are questionable. As Hayden White has said, "The older distinction between fiction and history, in which fiction is conceived as the representation of the imaginable and history as the representation of the actual, must give place to the recognition that we can only know the *actual* by contrasting it with or likening it to the *imaginable*" (White 98). Histories are not comprehensive. They are composed of selected materials that are gathered and informed by the focus and interests of the historian. Both Anglo-American and Chicano historiography attest to this. As a cultural manifestation of experience, literature can offer imaginative reconstructions of possible events, occurrences, and interactions that are historically informed. Just as the writing of history and literature presupposes certain interpretive schemas, so too do their reading and the conditions of their production. White has noted that "our explanations of historical structures and processes are thus determined more by what we leave out of our representations than by what we put in. For it is in this brutal capacity to exclude certain facts in the interest of constituting others as components of comprehensible stories that the historian displays his tact as well as his understanding" (91). More will be said on the excluded aspects of Chicana/o history shortly. For now, let us examine the development of an alternative master narrative within Chicana/o studies.

In his 1987 appraisal of Chicano-related historical writings, Alex Saragoza points to a still unresolved debate occurring in Chicana/o historiography surrounding the "lack of clarity in the definition of Chicano history" (Saragoza 25). One of the debates that emerged from the early years of Chicana/o historiography was whether to emphasize themes of resistance and conflict or to focus on the processes of accommodation and assimilation. Presumably, this debate was shaped around the premise that the two approaches were mutually exclusive and thus irreconcilable. One of the early, and certainly most popular, attempts to construct a counterhistory of Mexicans in the United States was Américo Paredes's *With His Pistol in His Hand* (1958). José Limón, Renato Rosaldo, José David Saldívar, and Leticia Garza-Falcón, among others, have analyzed the importance of Paredes's pioneering work as an intervention in the racist discourse on Mexicans produced by esteemed U.S. and Texas historians. Limón and Rosaldo have noted the highly patriarchal and masculinist nature of this counternarrative as a struggle for interpretive power that privileged male bravado, confrontation, and armed resistance to the exclusion of female agency. These two critics have also observed that the development of the Chicano warrior-hero allowed Paredes himself to be inscribed as one: the Chicano scholar uses words, not bullets, to defend his people. Paredes's paradigmatic figure and rhetorical identification with the hero served as a model for the work of Chicano anthropologists and literary critics who emerged in the 1960s. The resistance narrative, with its attendant gendered limitations on the definition of resistance and sites of struggle, became the dominant paradigm in Chicana/o studies for many years.

Rodolfo Acuña's *Occupied America* (1972) greatly facilitated the popularization of a "great man" approach to Chicano history, one that found its greatest appeal among students who were organizing for social and curriculum changes. Pervasive in Chicano Movement historical and creative literature we see a focus on the "Big Four" organizational and political leaders: César Chávez with the United Farm Workers; José Angel Gutiérrez, cofounder of the La Raza Unida Party; Rodolfo "Corky" González with the Crusade for Justice; and Reies López Tijerina of *La Alianza Federal de Mercedes.* This approach encourages a lack of critical analysis of Chicana/o leadership. Mario García, for example, identifies "exemplary" people and organizations that existed prior to *el movimiento* and must be seen as intellectual, political, and organizational predecessors of the '60s. And though these individuals and organizations were important, this approach "runs the risk of reducing history to anecdotes or brief sketches about the ruling classes or to vignettes of famous women [or men]," as Rosaura Sánchez has noted ("The History of Chicanas" 13). Not enough comparative analysis of the styles, methods, and messages of individuals and organizations has been done to offer a synthesized, comprehensive perspective of Chicana/o politics of this era. In partial agreement with García, Gómez-Quiñones says that leadership changes "according to internal changes within classes, but generally it has been drawn from the three major classes and predominantly from the middle. . . . Autochthonous leadership was internal and organic to the local community; but under domination increasingly leaders were externally imposed, and frequently chosen because of their loyalty to the grantor . . . [Thus] accountability is a continual problem" (*CP* 10). By virtue of their status as acknowledged leaders, individuals find themselves struggling with competing concerns and discourses surrounding "their own interests, the interests of the community, and the demands of the dominant power" (10–11).

The different emphases placed on race, class, or ethnicity by political scientists and historians emerged from the real and sometimes contradictory political practices that *mexicanos* have engaged in over the years. Nationality is a signifier that serves multiple functions; it can be a marker of one's citizenship status or of one's national origin, or it may reflect one's political ideology or consciousness. Ethnicity, on the other hand, usually functions as a marker of one's social position in a racialist society. The tenuous nature of identity for Mexicans in the United States across various class and political interests has affected the way Chicana/o intellectuals have theorized and written about social change. It has also, as Gómez-Quiñones points out, led to an "ideological conundrum—reformism versus utopianism" in political practice (*CP* 21). Whichever political goal was forwarded, one thing was certain: "Within this interplay [of political struggle within the Mexican community] lies a historical memory as well as a partial vision of the future—the negation of what was oppressive in the past" (30).

Why Cultural Studies?: On Gender, Genre, and Alternatives to the "Great Man" Approach to History

How, then, can an against-the-grain reading of literary texts benefit us? Since the generational paradigm privileges the activities of one sector of a community (usually men), we should feel compelled to ask, What was occurring among other members of that group? What sectors of the community are being privileged, and why? What sites of power are being ignored? Who occupies those arenas? Even in a framework that examines resistance, what limitations to our understanding of a people are produced by privileging certain forms of resistance over others? Many historians have been unable to escape traditional social-science frameworks. For instance, it has been notoriously difficult for theorists to incorporate and reconcile the study of gender within existing bodies of theory. This difficulty has itself been productive because it problematizes intellectuals' approach to knowledge. Joan Scott has pointed to the current epistemological turmoil in the social sciences. She notes a shift in focus from an emphasis on "cause" to an emphasis on "meaning" (from a scientific to a literary paradigm) as being especially significant because it opens a space that brings together the scholarly and the political (Scott 93). One of the chief limitations of the generational paradigm that a cultural-studies approach to literary analysis can challenge is this historical inability or refusal to address gender as a category of analysis.

Scott has also noted that as categories of analyses, neither race nor gender, unlike class, has a history of theoretical inquiry or alternative master narratives. If Scott's observation that epistemology is currently undergoing a shift from a scientific to a literary paradigm is correct, then the interpretation of meaning and power as they are produced socially and linguistically assumes prime importance.

Scott's concern about the significance of interpretation is corroborated by White, who says that ". . . considered as a system of signs, the historical narrative points in two directions simultaneously: toward the events described in the narrative and toward the story type or mythos which the historian has chosen to serve as the icon of the structure of the events" (88). An insistence on the role of gender in narrative and analysis can potentially alter disciplinary paradigms of study because it opens up new avenues of inquiry by giving voice and value to "personal, subjective experience as well as public and political activities" (82). What this means is that women's literature and women's history can shift the grounds of discussion about the past and will alter and complicate our understanding of it. Power is not simply a feature of social institutions and a dynamic between majority and minority cultures. The privileging of a warrior-hero paradigm to the exclusion and underdevelopment of others has posited limited notions of power, violence, and resistance; consequently, this has depreciated or denied the role of women in politics, inhibited an analysis of the family as a gendered site of social power, and maintained a focus on institutions and practices that, through de facto or de jure segregation, excluded women's participation. Such an approach in historical writing has meant that exemplary figures (Chicano heroes) were almost always male, because public space was given primacy over private or domestic sites.

The struggle for interpretive power is not limited to historians. The importance of discovering, remembering, and revising understandings of the past is also a preoccupation with critical theorists and poets. And, as this study demonstrates, interpretive power is also an imperative for social activists, lawyers, laborers, and many others working for social change. Chicana/o literary scholars confront the scarcity of primary sources from periods when the publication of literature was impeded, if not determined, by conflictual social relations. Contemporary literature about the past is more prevalent. This includes both "historical" narratives and "imaginative" literature. The problem with this, however, is that the production of an understanding of history through historical or literary narratives is affected by different disciplinary obligations, expectations, and paradigms, including exigencies of the current moment. Moreover, although literature is often regarded as a historical resource, histories are rarely considered for their imaginative and sometimes fictional qualities. Reading disciplinary texts against the grain of one another contrasts two different ways of transmitting knowledge, culture, and beliefs about power relations.

Can literature help in recovering the political/social history of Chicanas/os without distorting it or reducing it to "mere fiction"? Can it render the past differently—that is, more complexly—than "history" can? What can it add? Is it better able to capture the nuances of intercultural relations and intracultural conflict? These are the questions this book will address.

The guiding methodology for this study is based on cultural-studies and privileges an analysis of lived experience, class, ethnicity, and gender. I move from historical representations of periods that are structured around specific notions of ideology, identity, and political power to fictional representations of individual lives that often subvert fixed notions of identity and power. Each chapter proceeds with a deconstruction of a historical period and juxtaposes foundational historical texts with literary ones either from or about the period under scrutiny. Because I find it important to decenter privileged sites of power and politics, I show how cultural practices shape community, domestic space, subjectivity, and collective identity in Chicana/o literature. I attempt to resist privileging idealized forms of identity, subjectivity, and class position. My analysis of gender is informed by feminist criticism and is not relegated to a chapter on women's literature but is persistently applied to all authors, texts, and cultural practices under discussion.

My objective in analyzing a wide range of literature is to illustrate that people of Mexican descent in the United States do not have simply a history on the one hand and a literature on the other; we also have that history expressed in literary form. Moreover, we have a history of that literature that is continually being rediscovered and that, in order to be properly understood, needs to be contextualized in and seen as emerging from a specific set of social relations that have affected its production and circulation. Chicana/o literary production, whether as a national, minor, or ethnic literature, exists independent of the formation of Chicana/o historical narratives and often contests the representation of a historical generation by shifting the focus of concern away from narrow definitions of power and identity. These texts are both historical and literary artifacts; they are art as well as historical evidence; they speak to the political economy of social relations within Chicana/o culture and between Chicana/os and Euro-Americans. As the breadth and scope of Chicana/o literature continues to grow, I argue that scholars must recognize the ways that historical and literary narratives complement, contradict, and complicate one another, with the intent of altering our prior understanding of the past for the insight that such a reconstruction can offer to the present moment.

Chicana/o Literature as Postcolonial Literature of Diaspora and Discovery: Migration, Movement, and Mobilization in Chicana/o Literature

The cultural position of Chicanas/os as mestizos, as immigrants, and as a defeated nationality has given rise to tensions that have uniquely influenced the production and thematics of Chicana/o literature and will thus have significant impact on any interpretation of it. fihile certainly not identical, the political and social conditions of most U.S. Mexicans and Third World writers are similar enough that one can say they share a subordinate status with respect to the First World that signifies their postcolonial condition. The relationship, however, between the Third World and Chicanas/os needs clarification. The geopolitical status of other Latinos as members of the Third World is rarely questioned; yet it is wrong to make too easy an alliance between ethnic groups residing within U.S. borders and the Third World, as the debate surrounding the limitations of an internal colonial model has shown. However, within the United States the real, measurable differences in economic, social, and political power between Euro-Americans and certain ethnic groups, in this case people of Mexican descent, suggests that something very much like a colonial experience manifested itself in the U.S. Southwest after 1848. Even though it is important to acknowledge structural differences between the status of Chicanas/os and Third World peoples, comparisons can also be instructive. The fact that the definition of the U.S. colonial era has been largely controlled by mainstream historians contributes to the confusion surrounding colonial experience in the States. For the most part, colonialism in the United States has been articulated as a historical process that refers to the relations between the emerging nation of immigrant Europeans and the construction of a mythic "homeland" of England. This is an ahistorical assertion that effaces the conquest of North America and the suppression of the indigenous population by disassociating the European settlers/colonizers from the colonialist enterprises that were occurring concurrently in Africa and Asia. On the other hand, one basic difference between the political condition of a deterritorialized group like Mexicans in the United States and that of Third World peoples is that as a consequence of Mexico's complicity in ceding lands to the United States, a territorial solution was almost never considered a viable political goal. Whatever aspirations existed for (re)claiming "Aztlán" as a homeland were tenuously grounded at best, resting on a narrowly conceived construction of origins that would legitimate claims to prior possession of the land, regardless of the Mexican nation's position. Nationalist claims for independence are further complicated because Greater Northern Mexico, currently the southwestern U.S. states, was never an independent nation, and the "mother" country has never attempted to reclaim the territory lost by military defeat. Nevertheless, theories of the nation as a territory, a historical reference, and a metaphor for liberation will be useful for understanding the political strategies and goals of Mexicans in the United States.

Many contemporary writers are influenced by a Third World perspective that cannot easily be overlooked or assimilated into paradigms of U.S. literature. This is especially true of much feminist literature. Accordingly, many feminist writers have found U.S. or European feminist critical paradigms inadequate for representing Chicana feminism. A Third World feminism has been developed by women of color who consider themselves occupants of that geopolitical position both outside and within the First World. Like Chicano historians, Chicana writers have found it useful, albeit limiting, to identify with critical models outside the First World. Consequently, there has been a growing trend toward the adaptation of Third World models of critical discourse that also account for the specific influence of First World culture.

Considered together, three recent book-length studies on Chicana/o literature reproduce this synthesizing approach to Chicana/o critical discourse. In *Chicano Narrative: The Dialectics of Difference* (1990) Ramón Saldívar argues that Chicana/o narrative could, potentially, serve as a pattern for a "dialogical model for a new American literary history" (*CN* 218). In *The Dialectics of Our America: Genealogy, Cultural Critique, and Literary History* (1991), José Saldívar, following José Martí, argues not for a reconstruction of the American literary canon but for a redefinition of "America." In yet a third vein, José Limón argues for a specificity of social and historical influence within Chicano poetry in *Mexican Ballads, Chicano Poems*

(1992); as the title of his book suggests, a steady focus on the simultaneous historical, national, and cultural heritage of Chicanos is maintained. My approach acknowledges the value and complexity of each of these studies and does not see them as mutually exclusive. From an international perspective, the literature of people of Mexican descent in the United States is both an integral part of U.S. literature and—as a diasporic literature produced by exile, migration, and displacement—a vital but rarely acknowledged component of Latin American literature. Neither language nor nationality can serve as distinctive markers between colonial and postcolonial literatures. In fact, colonialism has served as a "precondition for the birth of world writing in English" (Jussawalla and Dasenbrock 4). It is, as Feroza Jussawalla and Reed Way Dasenbrock point out in their introduction to *Interviews with Writers of the Post-Colonial World,* the use of multilingual and multicultural traditions and forms in the context of and against political and economic domination that ally "ethnic minority" writers with postcolonial ones.

A secondary objective of this study is to examine how Chicana/o literature constitutes an atypical form of travel literature. Much of Chicana/o literature participates in this theme of movement or "discovery." But unlike European and Euro-American travel literature, most of which narrates bourgeois travel experiences complicit with colonialism, movement in Chicana/o literature is not about geographical relocation for the purposes of pleasure, adventure, or as an agent of colonialist expansion. For people of Mexican descent, movement is usually generated by social, economic, or military displacement, yet another shared experience that manifests itself as a characteristic of postcolonial literatures. In sharp contrast to imperialist travel literature, movement in Chicana/o literature is not synonymous with conquest and cultural superiority. In their literature of social conflict Chicana/o writers articulate an awareness of the process of cultural and political domination of themselves as "other." The majority of Chicana/o texts, therefore, are decidedly anticolonialist. As I mentioned earlier, the word "movement" can also be used as a reference to the organized mobilization of people for the achievement of shared goals or in resistance to a perceived assault on a way of life. This is one more feature of their writing that places Chicanas/os and their literature in the postcolonial context—the mapping out and response to an antagonistic relationship between their culture and the dominant one, which seeks to marginalize their existence and diminish their worth.

Organizational Structure

The book's organization reflects the periodization schema popularized by the generational paradigm. As noted earlier, my goal is not to affirm this model but to illustrate its fallacies and limitations by reading against the grain. The five historical "generations" that have predominated Chicana/o histories are the Creation, Migrant, Mexican American, Chicano, and post-Movement Hispanic/Latino Generations. This last generation is a projection on my part that follows the progressive formation of generational periods whose identifiers are guided by perceived notions of leadership, identity, and ideology.

Chapters 1 through 5 will be arranged chronologically to match the generational framework; however, this chronology is one that privileges the historical context over the publication dates of the works discussed. This broadly chronological structure provides a framework for the study and is complemented by the use of a comparative structure within each chapter—one that places representations of ideology, history, and identity by Chicano scholars in critical relation to "creative" texts (primarily historical novels), as well as in relation to the poetry of Teresa Acosta, whose work functions as a touchstone for the application of my theory to nonnarrative forms throughout the book.

Chapter 1, "Refashioning Resistance: Jovita González, Historiography, and Chicana/o Literature," serves as a grid for demonstrating how the central questions of this project will be addressed. According to Rodolfo Alvarez, the Creation Generation corresponds to the period between the U.S.-Mexican War and the turn of the century. In this chapter, I critique historical representations of this generation by Alvarez and Americo Paredes by arguing that the privileging of a racialist political analysis over other modes of domination was attractive for the first generation of Chicano scholars because "messy" intracultural strife could be subsumed—temporarily at least. But from the perspective of the late twentieth century, not only has the meaning accorded to Chicana/o narratives changed to meet the exigencies of the moment, so has the very substance of past narratives. The world of Jovita González and Margaret Eimer's *Caballero* differs markedly from other representations of this era, whether the personal narratives of nineteenth-century men and women of the formerly elite or those of contemporary historians, in that there is a remarkable absence of pre-American nostalgia in the majority of its characters. The "domestic hierarchy" of the patriarchal system that Paredes presents in *With His Pistol in His Hand* undergoes a sustained critique in this novel. I argue that the novel eschews modernist visions of cultural unity and instead anticipates a postmodern practice of depicting the cultural negotiations that occur whenever multiple subjects occupy the same space. It is a culturally specific system of power that is critiqued without pathologizing or universalizing the cultural subject. By giving voice to and depicting the agency of women and *peones* through their informal networks of communication (letters, notes, gossip, *dichos,* etcetera), Eimer and González provide insight into a world of experience that had not been represented in historical representations of this period. Moreover, I argue that the authors' use of the romance genre for conveying the history of this period, like the rendering of the Creation Generation by Chicano Movement scholars, is motivated by exigencies that shape the political status of women in the 1930s.

Chapter 2, "Migration Literature as a Foundation for a National(ist) Literature," examines fictional and historical writings about the Migrant Generation, a period that encompasses the first three decades of the twentieth century. My goals in this chapter are to challenge those social scientists who have represented this generation as prepolitical and to explore how gender, national identity, and cultural practices were utilized to articulate and advance political claims. This chapter will focus on authors whose works confront, problematize, and write the history of this period in different ways. Literature by Alejandro Morales and Sara Estela Ramírez, as well as Acosta's poetic musings on Ramírez, will function as the contrapuntal narratives to the works of scholars of this era, such as those of Rodolfo Alvarez and Ricardo Romo, who largely classify the Migrant Generation as either apolitical or prepolitical.

Chapter 3, "Shifting Identities, Harsh Realities: Accommodation, Capitulation, and Subversion in the 'Mexican American Generation,'" examines the ambivalence and contradictions produced by ingroup class tensions before and after World War II. This chapter will examine the writings of Mexican Americans in relation to the notions of leadership, ideology, and identity set forth in Mario García's history of Mexican Americans in the years 1930–1960 and Juan Gómez-Quiñones's *Chicano Politics: Reality and Promise, 1940–1990.* Emerging from the era of border conflict and the Great Depression, Américo Paredes's novel *George Washington Gómez* is exemplary as an extended narrative of this period. It is different than the ensuing novels of immigration and migration that document movement from south of the

Rio Grande to Greater Northern Mexico. *GWG* is one of the few novels about the pacification of the border from the point of view of a *tejano.* Thus it is a novel about the occupation of the homeland, but unlike *Caballero* this novel shows the shifting terrain of struggle from a war of maneuver to a war of position and the concomitant social and psychological trauma. The primary texts for the post–World War II era of the Mexican American Generation will be Juan Gómez-Quiñones's historical narrative in *Chicano Politics* and Tomás Rivera's account of the lives of migrant workers in his novel . . . *y no se lo tragó la tierra.* These texts will sharply contrast with García's perspective of Mexican Americans. This section will look at the construction of Mexican identity and agency by Tomás Rivera and Gómez-Quiñones. Rivera's attempt to resolve the problem of alienation in the life of Chicanas/os by inspiring them with a historical consciousness of their oppressive conditions links him politically with the writers of the *movimiento* era. However, his vision of intellectual leadership for deterritorialized people is fraught with contradiction, as it is articulated in *Tierra*'s simultaneous presentation of a modernist utopian vision and postmodern dystopia.

Focusing on the Chicano Generation, chapter 4, "Identity, Memory, and Self-Representation in El Movimiento," illustrates how the movement toward cultural nationalism as a counternarrative was partially informed by the political and literary activity occurring in other regions of the world. The limitations of nationalism as an ideology, its chauvinistic and often reactionary stance toward culture, gender, race, and class, have since been identified (Gómez-Quiñones, *CP* 19; Muñoz 153–55), but its effects on cultural production continue to be seen. One of the most popular and controversial novels that took the Movement in Southern California as its subject was Oscar Zeta Acosta's *The Revolt of the Cockroach People.* Carlos Muñoz's history of the movement, *Youth, Identity and Power: The Chicano Movement,* is a provocative counter/complementary narrative to take into consideration for modes of self-representation. Both Muñoz's and Oscar Acosta's ability to represent the activists and activism as well as the political conditions in which they were working is complicated by their involvement in the Chicano Movement. To help contextualize *Revolt* I examine the state's response to the actual political activities that Oscar Acosta fictionalized. Like Sara Estela Ramírez, who died in exile in the United States, Acosta's exile in his imaginary homeland of Mexico leads to his disappearance and, presumably, his death. Their political activities and writing, culminating in their deaths in "foreign" lands, illustrate how much of Chicana/o literature should be situated in a postcolonial context. A discussion of the transnational dimension of this literature and Chicana/o identity formation is further developed in the closing chapter.

Chapter 5, "Redefining Political and National Borders: The Construction of Identity in the Post-Movement Postmodern Period," operates under the premise that many "post-Movement" writers are expanding the boundaries of Chicana/o identity established by the Chicano Generation. The literature examined in this chapter will counter the dismal appraisal of the current Hispanic Generation given by Alex Saragoza in his appraisal of Chicano-related historical writings. By confronting more directly the nature of ingroup differences based on gender and sexuality as well as national identity, these post-Movement/postmodern writers have helped expand and complicate contemporary notions of Latinos in the United States. Cultural processes and social relations are interlocking forces in the production and maintenance of power, especially in the formation of social divisions based on gender and sexuality. This chapter will examine the reconfiguration of historical and geographical boundaries by Cherríe Moraga, Guillermo Gómez-Peña, Rubén Martínez, and Teresa Acosta. In different ways these authors refute and refuse the move toward cultural homogenization and raise important concerns about movements (political and geographical), conflict, and intellectual leadership. Gómez-Peña's *Warrior for the Gringostroika,* Martínez's *The Other Side: Fault Lines, Guerrilla Saints, and the True Heart of Rock 'n' Roll,* Moraga's *The Last Generation,* and the poetry of Teresa Acosta challenge narrow notions about ethnicity, community, and ideology in this "Era of the Hispanic" by positing a Chicana/o-Latina/o identity that is at once both locally engaged and internationalist in scope. In this period, a feminist-informed critique has shifted some of the focus away from public institutions and toward other sites of power—the family, the body, and real and metaphorical boundaries that shape identity—while still maintaining a material analysis of Chicanas/os' lived reality.

The book will conclude with a brief conclusion titled "On Paradigms, Movements, and Borders." I close the study by asking why unsettled questions of identity and nonuniform treatment by dominant cultures and institutions have made it difficult for Chicana/os to come to terms with their history. It is not the intent of this project to privilege imaginative literature over historical narratives. Rather, the goal is to investigate and identify the historical and fictional value, as well as the limitations, of each. This conclusion examines narrative and other forms of literature and historical texts as generic devices for the recounting of the past and "real" or "imagined" possibilities. Furthermore, lest there be any doubt about my intentions here, people have, and will continue to have, different expectations of imaginative literature and historical texts. This study is not meant to conflate the two, nor is it an attempt to suggest that they should become more like one another. Rather, this is an exercise in reading, one that suggests that the final arbiters of any text are both individual readers and the collectivity of readers produced by the dialectical process that occurs in the writing and the reading of a text. The study will be concentrically broadened by a concern with the implications of genre for conveying and "making" history—that is, of genre as a tool for intervention.

Finally, I would be remiss if I did not openly identify what may seem to be an egregious gap in this book. I am referring to the emphasis placed on Texas and California, which has resulted in a "neglect" of integral regions of the Southwest, including New Mexico, Colorado, and Arizona. To be sure, this gap is not intended as a statement regarding the legitimacy or merit of writers from those regions and the historical contexts from which they have emerged. I selected authors and texts that lent themselves to a comparative analysis with the historical master narratives I call into question. Though I recognized this gap, I consciously sought to resist the impulse to fill it in for the sake of comprehensiveness. The structure and organizing principle of this book are chronological, not regional. A clear principle of the selection of texts was the degree to which they fit within the generational structure I meant to deconstruct. Finally, my interest in resisting the urge to be comprehensive is also part of my analysis. The desire, inclination, and impulse to comprehensively render Chicana/o history (including literary history) are a masculinist tendency to shape the generational paradigm and write master narratives that seek to tell it *all.* In the end, what I hope to offer here is a methodology—not a panacea, and not a new master narrative.[6]

CHAPTER 1

Refashioning Resistance

Jovita González, Historiography, and Chicana/o Literature

She recalled in an interview in 1983 that when she conducted her research for her 1930 Master's thesis . . . she had taken care to defer to the tenets of a patriarchal society. She kept her hair long, solicited a letter of introduction from the Archbishop of San Antonio, and knitted as she interviewed her subjects. [Jovita] Gonzalez de Mireles knew that despite her intellectual prowess and a Rockefeller Grant, she must resort to traditional assurances to the pueblo that she was, as she put it, "gente decente."

In her many accounts of life and lore along the borderlands, Gonzalez de Mireles focused on the Texas Mexican community as a whole. And the stories she collected were grounded in an ethnic sensibility which incorporates the ideals that governed gender roles of aquel entonces. This suggests that her work made men the center of her Tejano repertoire. In fact, most of it presents women in conditions ascribed to females throughout human history in such domains as the sacred or therapeutic. Though narrowly drawn depictions of women of our pueblo, they provide us the opportunity to discern from them our generation's desire to reinvent Tejana history from female-inspired notions of femaleness.

—Teresa Acosta, 1991 tribute to Jovita González de Mireles and Américo Paredes by the Texas State Historical Association

As I began this extended analysis of the link between historical narratives and the representation of the historical in fictional narratives and poetry, I was reminded of Renato Rosaldo's observation that "narrative analyses told or written from divergent perspectives . . . will not fit together into a unified summation" (Rosaldo 147). Nor will a diversity of narratives offer us a complete vision of a time and place; to acknowledge the heterogeneity of experience among Mexicans in the United States is also to accept the existence of diverse forms of knowledge. From the perspective of the early twenty-first century, not only has the meaning ascribed to Chicana/o narratives changed to meet the exigencies of the moment, but so has the very substance of past narratives. Archival searches and personal collections are shifting the ground—once thought to be stable—upon which we make claims about Chicana/o literary history. The meaning of culture shifts, then, not only according to our changing analytical frameworks and changing audiences, but also because new-found material expands the universe of knowledge through which we make meaning. This continuing disturbance to our old ways of seeing calls into question any effort to discuss the origins of Chicana/o literature. The focus of this study, however, is Chicana/o literature's ends, not its origins; this is an exploration of the ideological formations that underwrite and motivate creative and historical works. In examining a broadly defined historical literature that has been relatively unknown and unexamined by literary studies, I would point to this literature's particular sites of emergence for insight into that particular world. Moreover, as Rosaldo reminds us, much like an astronomer who suspects the presence of other celestial bodies and universes, we must try to account for the absent voices and ways of knowing to avoid participating in and perpetuating the imposition of an unjust discourse of silence on those whose lives are already marginalized.

The "History" of Chicana/o Literature

Before beginning this study on the relationship between "historical" and "imaginative" literature of people of Mexican descent in Greater Mexico, the tenuous status of a project that seeks to make any claims on the history of cultural production by a subaltern group must be declared at the outset. As recently as 1990, the most common point of departure for discussing the origins of Chicana/o literature was Américo Paredes' "seminal" text, *With His Pistol In His Hand* (1958).[1] Although this book was a formal study of the *corrido,* its discussion of balladry and folklore was conveyed in a narrative style that defied classification as a strictly scholarly text.[2] Infused with humor, sarcasm, and understatement, Paredes's narrative of Mexican history and song in South Texas reads more like a story than official scholarship. For those who resisted classifying Paredes's book as literature, there was always Antonio Villareal's *Pocho* (1959), published at approximately the same time. Paredes's book was once the preferred foundational text for Chicana/o literary history because it facilitated a historical move that identified the "folk" origins of Chicana/o literature in the oral tradition. Whichever text was designated as the "first" piece of Chicana/o literature, one thing was thought to be clear: Chicana/o literature as written text did not have a long history. In this schema, the emergence of Chicana/o literature was correlated with the burgeoning Chicano Movement of the 1960s.

In the last decade, however, much has happened to change the landscape of Chicana/o literature. Literary historians Genaro Padilla, Rosaura Sánchez, Erlinda González-Berry, Tey Diana Rebolledo, and Juanita Luna Lawhn, among others, have recovered and rediscovered narratives, letters, and at least one late-nineteenth-century novel (*The Squatter and the Don* by Amparo Ruiz de Burton), that have challenged accepted notions about the literary production of people of Mexican descent in the United States. Although the scope of this study is limited to literary production of the twentieth century, it is not unaffected by the recovery project currently underway.[3] In 1990, Arte Público Press published *George Washington Gómez;* Américo Paredes wrote the novel in the 1930s but did not, at least initially, attempt to publish it due to the hostile social conditions in South Texas during the first half of the century. In the summer of 1993, after the papers of E. E. Mireles and Jovita González de Mireles were made available by Texas A&M–Corpus Christi University, having been deposited there the previous year, a long-time quest by José Limón to locate *Caballero* was completed. Prepared for publication by Limón and María Cotera, the novel was published in 1996 (González and Eimer, ix). There are many interesting parallels between Paredes and González that deserve notice. Although South Texas contemporaries, Paredes and González apparently knew little about each other and their respective creative work. Yet Paredes's assessment that it would be futile to seek actively the publication of his novel was born out by González and Eimer's experience; they were unable to secure a publisher for their books. Both novels are situated in moments of social and military strife between Mexicans and Anglos in South Texas. There is, however, one important difference: *Caballero* narrates the years of the 1846–48 U.S.-Mexican War, while *George Washington Gómez* spans the years 1914 through the late 1930s. (I undertake an extended examination of Paredes's novel in chapter 3.) Although they both document periods marked by war, because these novels narrate different historical periods they will be examined apart from one another. The authors' relationship to each other is not limited to these two texts, however. The social history of pre-1900s South Texas that Paredes narrates to introduce the importance of *corridos* in *With His Pistol In His Hand* is important for this study. Although *Pistol* was written after Paredes's novel, it preceded *George Washington Gómez* in publication and is widely considered an important canonical text in Chicana/o studies. Many creative writers and Chicana/o-studies scholars from across the disciplines have noted its significance as an influence on their work. To varying degrees, *Pistol* and *Caballero* describe social relations among people in South Texas during the period that has come to be known as the Creation Generation by historians using a generational approach to writing history.

The recovery and publication of *Caballero* strongly invites a comparison to *The Squatter and the Don,* since they are both woman-authored historical romances that center on Mexican landowning families and "inscribe and interpret the impact of U.S. power and culture on the former Mexican northern provinces as they were being politically redefined into the American Southwest" in the mid- and late nineteenth century (González and Eimer xii). The novels do differ regionally and socially; the territorial struggle depicted in the former is steeped in the South Texas military conflict of the U.S.-Mexico War and the latter is set in the "relatively peaceful though coercive legal disputation over land in California of the 1870s" (González and Eimer xii). Clearly the authors were committed to documenting the historical fact of dispossession as it is nuanced by gender and race. I will not, however tempting it may be, conduct an extended comparison here, because the nature of this study is not one that emphasizes different styles of literary representation; rather, my primary goal is to examine the difference in disciplinary and generic forms of representation. *Caballero*'s geographical and temporal location, as well as González and Eimer's self-conscious reconstruction of this era from a later period, offers rich insight into the means and ends of the making of history through fiction. *The Squatter and the Don* is no less compelling, especially in the rhetorical richness with which Ruiz de Burton articulates her nostalgia for the pre-American era, but its narrative structure is not as highly nuanced, nor does it contrast as sharply with historical representations of this period. My goal in privileging

Caballero's dissonance with the histories of this era is to unmask the authors' didactic purpose, especially in their critique of intracultural class and gender relations.

Before proceeding to an examination of Paredes's and González and Eimer's historical perspectives, the issue of authorship and authenticity should be addressed. The recovery of *Caballero* affects our understanding of Chicana/o literature in at least three ways: it presents a new dimension to our understanding of the historical boundaries of Chicana/o literature in Texas and the Southwest; its bicultural authorship problematizes our understanding of "authentic" Chicana/o literature; and the saliency of the historicity of literature by women of Mexican descent who articulate a critique of gendered relations of power is more firmly established. I will pay particular attention to this third dimension, but it is important to address the first two, if only briefly.

The pre-1990s paradigm of Chicana/o literature posed a significant problem regarding the "absence" of Chicana writings. Although *Pistol* located a precursory literary tradition in the *corrido,* the construction of this "origin" only exacerbated the problem of female absence and literary agency because the epic *corrido* was primarily a male genre that provided only very limited representation of women, as has been noted by José Limón and others.[4] The "discovery" of written texts by women of Mexican descent has thus not only altered the historical boundaries of this literary tradition, it has also allowed for a more complex understanding of the literal and figurative containment of women's writing.

One of the problems confronted by Limón and Cotera in their preparation of *Caballero* for publication was how to account for its dual authorship. While literary critics readily acknowledge the collaborative nature of much literature, actual attribution to more than one author is extremely rare, so much so that literary criticism has no existing framework and scant vocabulary for discussing multiple authorship. The problem of authorship is exaggerated when we examine ethnic literature because the notion of difference that shapes much ethnic literary criticism relies upon an oppositional relationship between the author and the dominant culture. The case of *Caballero* has been confounded by Margaret Eimer's social status as an Anglo woman.[5] Jovita González, on the other hand, is a well-known figure in Chicana/o studies whose work on the folklore and history of South Texas has received much attention in the last few years.[6] Since the 1960s, there have been several literary texts published as Chicano literature by non-

Chicanos.[7] These books have received mixed reviews but have called attention to the political significance of representation by people who have a history and lived experience as members of a particular ethnic group. The dual authorship of *Caballero,* along with the lack of certainty about the nature of Eimer's collaborative relationship with González, raises questions that are not easily answered but nevertheless force us to confront purist and racialist notions about Chicana/o literature. If we accept that *Caballero* is undoubtedly a work of Chicana/o literature, this assessment must be based on two criteria: its subject matter and the known identity and reputation of Jovita González.

Born in Roma, Texas, in 1904, Jovita González was a fifth-generation descendant of land grantees. As a graduate student at the University of Texas at Austin in the 1920s, she conducted research on the folklore and history of Mexican Americans in the Rio Grande Valley. Her 1930 Master's thesis, "Social Life of Cameron, Starr, and Zapata Counties," continues to be a primary source for historians of this region. In 1931, under the tutelage of J. Frank Dobie, González became the first Texas Mexican president of the Texas Folklore Society.[8] José Limón has written astutely about the ambiguity, contradiction, and doubt that inform González's writings about "her people." In "Folklore, Gendered Repression, and Cultural Critique: The Case of Jovita González," Limón asserts that González was strongly influenced by J. Frank Dobie's "ethnographic style, his ideological vision, and . . . his cultural contradictions" (458). Limón suggests, however, that despite Dobie's strong influence and González's elite status and inclinations, her later work reveals a nascent critique of gender, class, and race domination (458). From an economically privileged class of people, González conducted field work on those who worked in the fields. Limón notes that though she wrote "with a superior, often condescending and stereotyping colonialist tone," there is a tension present in her writings that "appears to be repressing a certain sense of admiration for these classes and an acknowledgment of social conflict" (459). The theme of a 1930 essay by González, "America Invades the Border Towns," which implies that Texas Mexicans had to adopt American values if race relations were to improve, even though they had suffered injustice at the hands of Americans (Limón 461), seems also to be one of the central themes of *Caballero.* Yet this theme is complicated by a gendered critique of relations of power within the Mexican community, as Limón surmises in the essay's conclusion, written when he had just discovered González's novel.

If, in her early work, González neglected to write about women in intracultural as well as intercultural social conflict; the same cannot be said for her collaborative work with Eimer. A portrayal of Mexican life far removed from the simple, pastoral, and idyllic lifestyle rendered by González in her early work in folklore is given in *Caballero.* In this novel, a complex vision of social divisions along several different axes—racial, gender, class—is depicted. *Caballero* demonstrates the stark contrast between the way historians and writers of historical novels represent the Creation Generation. González and Eimer's imaginative representation of this time alters our understanding of the history of this period as well as our understanding of the history of Chicana/o literature.

Constructing the Past: Ideology, Ethnicity, and Unexamined Class Nostalgia

Paredes's influence on Chicana/o studies has already been noted above. The nostalgic tone he adopts in *Pistol* toward pre-1900 pastoral life in the Rio Grande Valley is left unproblematized by generational historians. Referring to the post-1775 period, Paredes fosters the myth of a "bloodless" conquest of Indians by the Spanish. "In succeeding generations the Indians, who began as vaqueros and sheepherders for the colonists, were absorbed into the blood and the culture of the Spanish settlers" (*Pistol* 8). In the section of his introductory chapter where Paredes describes the lifestyle of the Mexican American community and their relations with the Anglo community in the postwar period, the author presents the Mexican American community as cohesive even while recognizing the patriarchal order that dominated social life in the countryside:

> The simple pastoral life led by most Border people fostered a natural equality among men. . . . There was almost no gap between the owner and his cowhand, who often was related to him anyway. The simplicity of the life led by both employer and employee also helped make them feel that they were not different kinds of men, even if one was richer than the other. . . . Sheep and goats were also raised in earlier days. For these more menial, pedestrian tasks the peon was employed in earlier days. The peon was usually a *fuereño,* an "outsider" from central Mexico, but on the Border he was not a serf. . . . The peon . . . could and did rise in the social scale. (10–11)

Here Paredes's description of the social order stresses harmony; he informs us, though, that in a patriarchal system of power the eldest male of the family exercised "more real power than the church or the state" (11). This absolute authority, according to Paredes, "made the Border communities more cohesive, by emphasizing its clanlike characteristics, but it also minimized outside interference, because it allowed the community to govern itself to a great extent" (13). Paredes's uncritical stance toward patriarchal governance sustains rather than questions the contradictory notions of unity and domination within the same cultural/national/ethnic group. Moreover, in his nostalgia-filled description of this time prior to Anglo economic and racial domination, Paredes does not acknowledge or problematize the already existing racial order through which elite Mexicans, the *patrones* of haciendas in particular, built and sustained their social and economic power. The *fuereños* from central Mexico were almost certainly dark-skinned indigenous or *mestizo* people who were often violently displaced from their land. In addition, under the Spanish system of colonization, people indigenous to the area were either exterminated or assimilated into the culture and economy at the lowest level as *peones.* The landed elites of Northern Mexico, in contrast, were families of privilege who often claimed a "Spanish" identity in a caste system.

Rodolfo Alvarez posits that the Creation Generation corresponds to the period between the U.S.-Mexican War and the turn of the century, the same period that Paredes uses to foreground his discussion of social relations at the turn of the century. The defining experience that binds this generation, according to Alvarez, is "economic subjugation, followed by race and class prejudice" (Alvarez 37). Alvarez defines a generation as "a critical number of persons, in a broad but delimited age group, [who have] had more or less the same social experiences because they lived at a particular time under more or less the same constraints imposed by a dominant U.S. society" (33–34). Alvarez's analysis is premised on the notion that Mexican Americans are "a creation of the imperial conquest of one nation by another through military force" (34). Such a definition is severely limiting because it defines Mexican Americans ontologically as a subjugated group, thereby creating an inherently racial and essentially antagonistic binarism between Mexicans and Anglos. This schema enables historians to neglect preexisting intracultural class, race, and gender divisions. Equally important, it prohibits the construction of an identity independent from subjugation.

The question of ethnic, national, racial, and cultural identity has long been at the center of Chicana/o critical discourse. The varied and contradictory social positions that Mexicans have written about and occupied in U.S. society has led Genaro Padilla to make an observation about the role of identity in nineteenth-century autobiographical literature that is relevant here: "In autobiographical literature, we see again and again a narrative ground (often a battleground) upon which an individual is contending with social, cultural, and ideological forces that simultaneously so disrupt identity as to unfix it yet, paradoxically, in disrupting identity, establish identity as a de-stabilized condition" (Padilla 10–11). For Padilla, the question of Mexican identity in the nineteenth century is linked to the traumatically shifting social order and led the writers of post-1848 personal narratives to

> exhibit an almost obsessive nostalgic tendency to re-create "los días pasados" as a means of divesting the second half of the nineteenth century of its absurdity. However idealized the pre-American cultural community may appear in these narratives, the autobiographical reconstitution of life before the occupation was less a self-deluding compensation, or naive wish-fulfillment fantasy, than what I consider a strategic narrative activity—conscious of its general social implications—for restoring order, sanity, social purpose in the face of political, social, and economic dispossession. Dispossession was often articulated in an autobiographical sigh of deep sadness and longing for another socio-cultural life, but there is always a barely suppressed rage running within the narrative. (11)

Padilla's observations are about a different time period and a different genre of writing than Paredes's or Alvarez's, yet they have in common a nostalgic deference to a pre-U.S. social and political order. I point out this shared nostalgia because it exemplifies a peculiar problem and contradiction in Chicana/o studies. Clearly, most of the narratives about which Padilla writes are those of the formerly elite, many of whom benefited from domination before and after conquest by the United States. Unlike Paredes, however, Padilla acknowledges and accounts for his ambivalent stance toward the elite, whom he notes may well have been complicit in the domination of his ancestors. Padilla's work, along with that of Tey Diana Rebolledo, offers a way to understand the oppositional nature of nostalgia as a site of "embryonic resistance" and forces us to account for the complex variables that make up experience and domination.

One of the reasons the paradigm of the warrior-hero Paredes postulates in *Pistol* has had such power of endurance is because the experience of racial domination is itself so enduring and all encompassing—in his narrative about Gregorio Cortez and his discursive life vis-à-vis the *corrido,* Paredes's Chicana/o readers have identified with the domination and the heroism he wrote about at the turn of the century as well as at the moment they read his words. The privileging of a racialist political analysis over other modes of domination was attractive because messy intracultural strife could be subsumed—in the realm of the imagined, at least. As Padilla points out, nostalgic narratives evoke "a harmonious cultural domain while occluding the social fragmentation of the present" (21). Thus, the creation of a history of only one form of domination privileges it as the primary source of domination.

An Alternative Historiography: Romance and the Limits of Cultural Nationalism in Caballero

This attention to the popularity and function of what Padilla calls the "utopian imagination" that informs narrative reconstitutions of the world provides a good point of departure for discussing González and Eimer's novel. The world of *Caballero* differs markedly from other representations of this era in that there is a remarkable absence of nostalgia in the majority of its characters. Instead, with the exception of Don Santiago and Alvaro, his heir, who are portrayed as authoritative, stubborn, and abusive *patrones,* most of the characters in this novel either initially or eventually embrace the change in the social order. Upon such an observation, and informed with the knowledge of González's ambivalent representations of Mexicans in her folklore, one might be tempted to think that this novel is simply a testimony to the superiority of the "American" way of life. However, rather than simply racializing the conflict, this novel marks it as only one of many sources of social conflict and offers a depiction of this era when social harmony among Mexicans was elusive because of preexisting hierarchies of privilege based on social status, gender, and race. A closer reading of the text reveals how this historical novel complicates traditional conceptions of this period by eschewing nostalgia and illustrating the role that intracultural strife played in the emergence of a new social order.

"This book is neither biographical nor autobiographical, but it gives a correct and exact atmosphere of the people and the period it deals with. . . . Without prejudice or palliation for race or religion, seeing the need to cover a phase of history and customs heretofore unrecorded, this book is offered." In this excerpt from the note that precedes *Caballero,* Margaret Eimer (pseudonym Eve Raleigh) and Jovita González declare their motivation for writing a historical novel that covers the period of the U.S.-Mexican War.[9] Written in the 1930s, an era that predates sustained academic inquiry into the culture and history of Mexicans in the United States, the novel is focused on the effects of the war on the residents of Rancho La Palma, the South Texas hacienda of the Mendoza y Soria family.

One of the early scenes of the novel depicts Don Santiago, the *patrón* of the ranch, surveying his property from atop a bluff the night before the family is to depart for a visit to Matamoros. This scene is preceded by one in which Don Santiago's "greatest fear" is expressed: "'Rather would I bury my girls,' he had told his friend, 'than see them married to an Americano.' And he had meant it" (González and Eimer 29). The *patrón*'s fear of the imminent change in the social order is manifested as a threat to his ability to retain control over his land and his family—especially the women in his family. Thus, from the outset of *Caballero,* women and land are intimately linked as the spoils of war, over whom control signifies power.[10] Standing on the bluff, Don Santiago reflects on the power accorded to him as the family patriarch.

> Don Santiago's pride spread and burst in his chest and he flung his arms wide. "Mine," he murmured. "All this that I can see, and far beyond, is mine and only mine."
>
> "Mine!" He brought his hands together, and cupped them into a bowl, and flung them wide again. . . . Power was wine in his hands. Power was a figure that touched him, and pointed, and whispered. Those dots on the plain, cattle, sheep, horses, were his to kill or let live. The peons down there were his to discipline at any time with a lash, to punish by death if he so chose. His wife, his sister, sons and daughters, bowed to his wishes and came or went as he decreed. (33)

Throughout the novel, as is apparent in the above passage, Santiago's absolute authority over and relations of power with members of his family, the *peones* who work on the ranch, and his fellow *patrones* on other haciendas are questioned and altered as a direct consequence of the changing social order precipitated by the war. These relations, and the culture, economy, and ideology they rest upon, provide a useful grid upon which to assess concerns of representation and history, concerns that are integral to this project.

If Don Santiago, the *patrón* of the *rancho,* is identified as the protagonist-hero of *Caballero,* then the novel reads as a tragedy narrating the loss of the traditional values and way of life of one social order to another as a result of military conquest. Through the course of the narrative, Don Santiago experiences a loss of stature and power in his community; the loss of two sons (one dies in a violent confrontation with Texas Rangers, the other he disowns when he chooses to pursue a career as an artist in Baltimore); the loss of his daughters through marriage to Anglos in strict defiance of his wishes (one he disowns when she marries an army officer; the other marries a Texas Ranger); and the loss of formerly faithful *peones* as a consequence of his abuse and/or refusal to pay them wages as his new Anglo neighbors do.[11] Subsequently, at the end of the novel he dies alone, dispirited and unreconciled with his wife, sister, daughters, and only surviving son.

The novel is structured around the U.S.-Mexican War, the ensuing battles, and the historical figures who appear as referents or characters: Zachary Taylor, Juan Cortinas, and Antonio Canales. The novel begins with the news announcing the advent of the 1846 war. The *patrones* of the *ranchos* in South Texas who reside in contested territory between the Nueces River and the Rio Grande have refused to believe the rumors that some Anglo and Mexican Texans had declared their independence from Mexico in 1836. Until this time they have been unaffected by the change in territorial boundaries. As the social and political world of Mexicans is altered, it becomes apparent that there is no unified agreement among the *rancheros* on whether to relocate into Mexico, accept and accommodate the Anglos, or resist them. Initially, at least, Don Santiago makes no clear choice from among these alternatives and decides that his family will avoid all interaction with Anglos, even if it means isolating themselves on the ranch. However, after a meeting is called in Matamoros by other *patrones,* he decides that militant resistance is a viable alternative; thus, he is pleased when his eldest son joins a guerrilla group fighting against the U.S. Army.

The reactions of the rest of the residents of Rancho La Palma to the news of the imminent change in the social order reveal a range of concerns that offers some insight into their degree of satisfaction with the old order. Doña María, the timid matriarch of the household, is immediately concerned for her own well-being because her husband is incensed at the news, and when he had a certain look in his eyes " . . . it boded evil for all of them. Particularly for her, his wife, buffer of his wrath" (10). Her daughters, on the other hand, have a different response. Susanita, for instance, wonders if being *Americano* would "take some of the dullness out of her life." Her brother, Luis Gonzaga, an aspiring artist, recollects stereotypes of the Americans as barbarians; thus, he despairs that they "would know nothing of art" (11). Old Paz, the cook, relays the news of the change in governance to the other *peones.* As they contemplate their future under the new system, they do not anticipate any change for themselves: "A peon is a peon, from birth to death, as the master remains the master" (12). Each of these responses maps out a different set of concerns and shifts the focus away from the family patriarch to the different levels of his domain. In their contemplations on the potential impact of this change on their lives, a degree of dissatisfaction with the present order is articulated by the patriarch's charges. The wife, the son, the daughter, and the *peones* each represent a different dimension of the patriarch's power. Their dissatisfaction with the present state of things deromanticizes any notion of a homogeneous, unified society under the hacienda system; instead, early on in the novel we are made aware that fragmentation and repressed desires exist among the workers and family members. The "domestic hierarchy" of the patriarchal system that Paredes refers to depends on obedience to the father's will. The *patrón* determines relations within and outside the family, and deference to his wishes is expected and customary. Such a system of authority depends on absolute respect and regard for male authority. Under this system the familial and cultural order are idealized, as is the master-peon relationship. In its romantic ideal, absolute deference to the patriarch requires that his subjects believe in his wisdom, guidance, and benevolence. There is both a racially based element to this belief and a pragmatic one; the familial ties made with other families through marriage are viewed as necessary to ensure that the blood line is not diluted by mixing with "inferior" peoples and to secure financial security. But, if we trace the different perspectives of the characters in this novel as they negotiate their relationship with the Anglos and each other, our understanding of the Creation Generation is altered.

Such a shift in focus, facilitated by the authors' complex construction of characters, decenters the patriarch and facilitates a redefinition of the novel's form and a reinterpretation of the meaning of these historical events. The relationship between the disempowered classes of people on the hacienda (the women and the *peones*) and the Anglos could be described as a romantic one. The newly formed relationships of love and power across cultures—

between the Anglos, the *peones,* and the Mexican women—are depicted as emerging from mutual admiration and respect, not as a result of imperial conquest. This attraction is given added force because alliances are made by choice, not through ideological or physical coercion. The extent to which this attraction may have been naive is not fully explored in the novel. The betrayal of a system that promised full citizenship and equal democratic participation is not, and possibly cannot, be fully explored in these nascent moments of incorporation; however, the violence associated with resistance and the casting of all Mexicans as suspect nationals is depicted in the novel. The novel's plot, structured as a romance between Mexicans and Anglos, reduces Don Santiago to a tragic figure who feels betrayed by his people but who ultimately is responsible for his own demise. Finding his insular world threatened by outside forces, Don Santiago asserts his control over those below him to the point of abuse, thereby weakening their loyalty to him.

The *peones* are exploitable labor who have no chance for social mobility in a rigidly defined hierarchy that is sustained by genealogy and filial alliances as well as religious ideology. These racial and class divisions are sustained by force when necessary, but they are "naturalized" within the hacienda system. In *Caballero* the *peones* become the object of physical abuse by Don Santiago when he perceives a threat to their allegiance to him. When the goatherd Victorino, for example, gives a lame sheep to some Texas Rangers after they assist him in resisting coyote attacks on the herd, Santiago accuses him of lying and questions his loyalty. His anger is exacerbated when Victorino reminds him of his long history of loyalty to "the house which I have loved next to God alone" and professes shame in Santiago for doubting him. Santiago is outraged by Victorino's boldness and lashes him with a whip. Santiago's actions are seen as out of bounds by the *peones* and his own family members, especially because they were directed at a peon whose loyalty had been proven. His sister, Dolores, reminds him that his actions do not fit those of a "good" master: "The servants and peons are shocked and angry and I need not tell you that it is wise to keep them docile and happy," she says (172). But in his rage, Santiago reveals the racist and class-invested foundations for his feelings of superiority over *peones* and his disregard for women: "Should I run my affairs by the feelings of a creature like a peon? A thing with the body of a man and without his soul? You women—pah!" (172). In dismissing his sister's comments as unwarranted sentimentality, Santiago ignores her understanding of a central tenet of the master-peon relationship: the need for a benevolent master. His own fears and insecurity about the encroachment of Anglos lead him to displace these anxieties onto Victorino.

In this reconstruction of the Creation Generation, the *peones* and the elite women view the coming of a new civil, political, and economic order as an opportunity to improve their social position because it presents opportunities for asserting agency that do not exist under the hacienda system. Under the Spanish system of settler colonialism, the peones are assimilated into the culture and economy of the haciendas in a relationship of dependency; no longer members of an indigenous tribe, they become colonial subjects with few if any options for meeting basic needs. The *peones* are attracted by the possibilities of change when they discover that they will have the opportunity to earn wages for their labor, to vote, and to acquire an education. The arrival of the Anglos exacerbates preexisting tensions and inequalities in the master-peon relationship. Many of the *peones* want to remain loyal to Santiago; for their loyalty, however, they expect to be respected and treated fairly. Consequently, when Santiago beats Victorino, refuses to protect the female *peones* from sexual assaults by Alvaro, and rejects Victorino's advice to pay them a nominal wage, their loyalty to him dissolves. His stubborn adherence to tradition is depicted critically by the authors as pride and a defense of honor.

The change in economic and social systems not only creates new opportunities for the workers, it also places them in strategically important positions as liaisons in the romantic affairs of the Anglo men and Mexican women. While the Mendoza y Sorias are in Matamoros, Manuelito, the grandson of Old Paz, the cook, delivers written messages between Robert Warrener, the army officer, and Santiago's daughter Susana. In another instance, the woman who sells flowers on the plaza outside the church is paid for delivering notes. The *peones* willingly assume the role of liaison; though they are motivated by the pay they receive for this task, they also know the notes they pass on have important meanings, even if they are unable to read them. "Ay, if only I could read, what a tale I could tell. For many notes have I passed with flowers in the years I have stood here at the church" (86). They are aware of the power and privilege associated with the written word. "Jose had never heard that the pen was mightier than the sword but the point of the long feather, black with ink, was potent with mystery and he regarded it with awe. That a man could have a piece of furniture made only to hold writings was another thing that put people into two classes: the hidalgo and the peon; and only the hidalgo and his family could have the privilege of the written word" (175). The status accorded to the written word as a sign of power and privilege is important in making Anglo society appear more democratic and thus containing more opportunities for social mobility. This is an observation that Manuelito converts into opportunity by opting to stay in Matamoros when the Mendoza y Sorias leave. He is then taught to read and write by the Anglo army officers. By constructing a benign if not mutually beneficial relationship between the Anglos and the *peones,* González and Eimer's narrative suggests that the American civil and economic order was more democratic and deserving of allegiance than the atavistic network of power under the old order.

The role the *peones* play as cultural brokers in romantic affairs is based on an identification with Mexican women that rests upon their shared status as dominated subjects and a common source of domination—Don Santiago. The facilitation of these affairs by the *peones* subverts both the master-peon and the patriarch-family relationship. Manuelito's assertiveness is admired not only by his grandmother, but also by Susanita, who reciprocates his favors to her by relaying a message for him to his grandmother. As "one who had courage to take what he wanted, and he still a child," Susana sees in him a necessary model for asserting agency (275). The alliance between the *peones* and the Mendoza y Soria women is fully realized when some of the *peones,* including Old Paz, decide to leave Rancho La Palma when Susana is disowned by Don Santiago because of her professed love for Captain Warrener and the "dishonor" she brought to the family by going to Brownsville accompanied only by a peon, even though she went to save her brother from execution. The *peones* provide Susanita safe passage to Matamoros, where she will marry Warrener; they, in turn, secure employment with an Anglo entrepreneur.

The romance with the Anglo world is thus both literal and figurative, and it articulates a critique of oppressive cultural practices. Romantic love is used to subvert romantic notions about Mexicans' pre-American history. The patriarchal system of authority depends on a belief in the integrity, sanctity, and privileging of the family as an institution and a web of cultural and social practices to keep it intact. The status of women and their lack of agency within a narrowly defined, culturally specific social order is heavily critiqued by González and Eimer. Gender roles in general, and masculinity in particular, are also questioned through the presentation of contrasting paradigms of "manhood" in the two sons; thus, the authors of *Caballero* prefigure contemporary gender analysis of the construction of the individual subject.

The members of the Mendoza y Soria family are presented as idiosyncratic characters who exhibit a complex array of responses to the imminent change in the social system, responses that emerge, however, from their existing social order. María Petronilla and Dolores, the wife and sister of Don Santiago, respectively, are contrasting characters. María is an obedient, dutiful, and silenced wife who, we learn, cried on the eve of her arranged marriage with Santiago. Dolores, by contrast, is strong-willed and outspoken. She constantly challenges her brother's narrow-mindedness and stubbornness, as well as her sister-in-law's passivity. She tells María, "That's all you can talk about, duty, duty, duty, to all but yourself! A wife has rights too and if *I* were in your place, Petronilla, the orders would not come from only *one* pair of lips, I can tell you that!" (25). As the novel progresses, María becomes more assertive and critical of her husband, although she does not express it to him but to Dolores: "I do not know, but it seems at times as though it is not right that my husband should dictate our lives" (238). The daughters, Angela and Susanita, are also very different. Once she is forbidden by her father to enter a convent, Angela, a pragmatist, is attracted to Red McLane, an entrepreneur and political opportunist who views Angela as a refined woman who will advance his social status. Neither one of them believes love is either necessary or desirable; both wish to forge a harmonious new social order, and Angela sees in marriage a religiously sanctioned structure that will allow her to do "God's work." Angela's sister Susanita, on the other hand, is attracted to Anglo men as well as to the idea of a relationship built on mutual love and respect, qualities that play no role in the Mexican elite's system of arranged marriages, in which women have no say. The narrator notes the powerlessness of the women of the house: "They were alone. A group of four living at a time when, indeed, their only destiny was to serve man and bow to the master of the house" (254). The daughters' refusal to obey their father and to maintain absolute allegiance to their culture is ultimately perceived as a cultural betrayal by Don Santiago and further signals his decline.

The eldest son, Alvaro, is depicted as the true heir to Santiago's legacy. He exhibits brashness, bravado, and hunger for authority in his exercise of power. He calls for war against the Anglos and earns a reputation as a fierce and fearless guerrilla fighter. By portraying him as the heir to the traditions Santiago values, González and Eimer suggest that those traditions cannot be reconciled with the new order. His sexual assault of the women *peones* and Santiago's refusal to stop him causes a family of longtime hacienda workers to leave.

After Alvaro is killed in the Rio Grande at the hands of the Texas Rangers, Santiago is unable to continue actively resisting change.

Luis Gonzaga, the second-born son, represents a type of man altogether different from Santiago. Luis's desire to be an artist, his dislike of ranch work, his politeness, and his lack of a raw, crude, and abusive conflation of sexuality and power set him apart from his father and brother. His artistic abilities are feminized in Don Santiago's eyes: "Painting pictures like a woman, and he a Mendoza y Soria! An artist—insult to a father's manhood! A milk-sop, and his son!" (6). His father's worries about the relationship between his masculinity, his sexuality, and his art are more explicitly linked at still another point: "Luis Gonzaga, the marica! Eighteen and without an affair, never even kissing the servant girls he sketched" (38).[12] Thus his gender betrayal occurs even before the isolated world of the hacienda is challenged by the Anglos. Like his sisters' pursuit of fulfillment outside of Mexican culture, Luis's pursuit of his artistic interests in Baltimore is perceived as both a sexual and a cultural betrayal. Unable to be the man his father wants him to be, Luis decides to leave South Texas with a captain of the U.S. Army who shares his interest in art. He does so at the cost of being disowned by his father, who later thinks to himself, "Luis was in a faraway world and lost to his home. Luis Gonzaga was a gringo now" (309). The authors' descriptions of the interactions between Luis and Captain Devlin are highly erotic and suggestive of a sexual attraction that complements their cultural and intellectual attraction to one another. "And on the striking black-maned dun pony, sitting the elaborately trimmed saddle with the ease of long familiarity with it, [Luis] made a picture which thrilled Devlin thru and thru" (48). And from Luis' perspective: "This was the Good Eve when all was peace and all men were brothers, and more than anything else in the world Luis wanted to give [Devlin] greeting, and touch his hand. . . . So happy was Luis to see his friend and so eager to greet him that he saw Warrener more as an object than a person, and when the fat Señor Montoya and his fatter wife moved so that they formed a screen, Luis hurried the few steps to be face to face with the man for whom he felt such deep affection (117). *Caballero* is remarkable for the complexity of its articulation of gender, race, and class domination and negotiations. The novel eschews modernist visions of cultural unity and instead anticipates a postmodern practice of depicting the cultural negotiations that occur whenever multiple subjects occupy the same space. It is a culturally specific system of power that is critiqued without pathologizing or universalizing the cultural subject.

History as Narrative Grounds for an Emerging Battle

Preceding the body of writings that constitute the (counter)history of Mexicans in the United States, González and Eimer's novel was not informed or influenced by "official" narratives written by Chicana/o historians.[13] Their historical vision does not ignore the role that racism played as a pretext for violence, nor does it ignore the legal and extralegal means by which Mexicans were displaced from their land in the period following conquest. Their depiction of this era does document the multiplicity of variables that inform social change. We are left to ask a series of questions: What variables influenced their vision and portrayal of this era? To what extent is their critique of gender, race, and class relations as expressed in this novel an accurate depiction of the historical consciousness of elite women and the South Texas subaltern class of the mid-nineteenth century? The narratives and letters of Mexicans in the nineteenth century currently being uncovered by literary historians do little to corroborate González and Eimer's portrayal. In fact, they often contradict it by demonstrating nostalgia for the pre-American order. Other than these sources, there is scant evidence available with which to document the historical accuracy of an embrace of the new social order by *peones;* although we do know that many of the elite class did, in fact, comply with, and in many cases facilitate, the change as a means of advancing and protecting their economic interests.[14] Furthermore, as is clearly depicted in the novel, *peones* had little motivation to remain bound to a system of debt peonage. *Caballero* can be seen as both a Mexican American historical novel and a women's novel that documents cross-cultural collaboration. Such an observation might well identify the authors' willingness to address the messy intracultural strife I noted earlier. Moreover, it may also serve as grounds to suggest that González and Eimer, writing in the postsuffrage 1930s, sought to *imagine* a genealogy of discontent and possible dissent by women in the Mexican community who, with few exceptions, were often rendered powerless by social and cultural ideas and practices.

The ideologically loaded nature of this historical novel is made all the more apparent when one considers how the presentation of events, attitudes, and social relations contrasts with Jovita González's characterization of these in her scholarly work, such as in her Master's thesis. With González's thesis as his primary resource, David Montejano informs us that "tactical marriages" were an important instrument for Mexican elites in the forging of a structure of accommodation between themselves and Anglo elites. He notes: "It was customary among the Mexican elite, as Jovita González has noted, that daughters were 'married at an early age, and not for love, but for family connections and considerations'" (*AM* 36). In the novel, González and Eimer undermine any concern about the possible self-serving ulterior motives of Robert Warrener and Red McLane by depicting them as economically self-sufficient, though McLane's motives are clearly political. Moreover, nowhere do González, Montejano, or other Texas historians claim that *peones* experienced a period of hope that Americanization would lead to new social, political, and economic opportunities, as do the *peones* on Rancho La Palma. This is not to say, however, that the desire for better opportunities and more self-determination by Mexican elite women and the *peones* was nonexistent. What *Caballero* provides us with is a mechanism for imagining the conditions and form of an emerging oppositional consciousness in this transitional period. The authors call attention to the politicized nature of social, economic, and domestic relations.

My primary intent in this brief analysis of *Caballero* has been to point to the historical relationship between literary texts and the rendering of history in a text that is both a literary and historical artifact. Further critical readings will need to consider multiple interpretations of this period that are not easily reconciled with González and Eimer's poetic vision.

Giving Voice to the Subaltern Tejana

The epigraph that opens this chapter is from a tribute to Jovita González de Mireles by Teresa Acosta on the occasion honoring González and Américo Paredes, an event sponsored by The Texas State Historical Association in 1991. Acosta has said that she has in her own work a "very strong interest in retelling historia through poetry, partly to recover and partly to discover what is in our Chicana/o alma. And, very seriously, to take our 'stories' back and away from the purview of a select few."[15] She is keenly aware of the important role González played in producing, documenting, and maintaining the history and culture of Mexicans in the United States. Of González's role as a folklorist, she said, "González de Mireles took the stories she heard in Spanish and shaped them into forceful English versions, thus also becoming one of the first Texas Mexicans to record our literature in English" ("Jovita González" 1).

González's significance as a literary precursor with a feminist sensibility is not lost on Acosta. Her tribute to González was written before *Caballero* was recovered, yet the information about the posturing that González was forced to assume in order to legitimize herself as the scholar of her community offers insight into the social climate in which González produced *Caballero.* Further, as Limón makes clear in his introduction to the novel when he writes of the events that transpired in a mid-1970s interview by Marta Cotera with Jovita González in the unyielding presence of González's spouse, E. E. Mireles, the constraints on free expression González experienced as a woman were real and persistent—in the 1930s and in the 1970s. Through the sheer force of his presence, Mireles enforced silence on González regarding the existence of *Caballero* in manuscript form; significantly, González, though unwilling or unable to break that silence verbally, nevertheless asserted her agency and signaled to Cotera that her husband was wrong in his proclamation that the manuscript no longer existed.

In her tribute Acosta asserts that though González's representations of females in the folklore she gathered are "narrowly drawn depictions of women of our pueblo, they provide us the opportunity to discern from them our generation's desire to reinvent Tejana history from female-inspired notions of femaleness" (5). Clearly, the novel became the vehicle for González to represent her Texas Mexican female antecedents in a different light. Clear, too, is the fact that Acosta and her generation's "desire to reinvent Tejana history from female-inspired notions of femaleness" was also a desire for González and Eimer. It was a desire realized in *Caballero.*

But it is not the strict purview of the novel or other narrative forms to make history. As a Central Texas Chicana poet writing from the perspective of the late twentieth century, Teresa Acosta *imagines* a voice for those women of the subaltern class whose lives and deaths were marked by violence and yet of whom little historical documentation exists. "Chipita" is one such exercise in imagination. While *Caballero* gives its readers insight into the nuances of gender domination among the elites, it does not present an extensive depiction of the many sources of domination encountered and the many forms of resistance practiced by economically and socially marginalized women.

A parenthetical author's note precedes "Chipita": "(Author's note: Chipita Rodriguez's life is clouded in mystery, as is her death in 1863, when she was hanged by the state of Texas. On June 13, 1985, over a century later, Gov.

Mark White signed Senate Concurrent Resolution Fourteen, absolving her of murder.)" (*Nile* 90). This note reminds us that official state records can be challenged, changed, and reinterpreted even if the "truth" can never be known in its entirety, and this is possible even for those people whose history has mostly been assigned to a footnote. Like many of her poems, this one discursively recreates a *mexicana* predecessor and imagines a conversation with her to give voice and saliency to a repressed history.

Including an author's note and a preface, "Chipita"'s structure simulates that of a historical text even as it contests the limitations of the discipline. The author's note informs readers that the past is still contested terrain and that past "mysteries" often mask officially sanctioned injustices. The poem documents the difficulty encountered by Acosta in constructing an understanding of a historical figure about which little is known except her dubious status as, until the spring of 1998, the only woman ever executed by the state of Texas.[16] Her poem breaks the discourse of silence imposed by histories that ignore state violence against citizens. Her poetics are invested, then, in "writing political wrongs."[17] Because written documentation about this subaltern Mexican American woman living in antebellum Texas is sparse, knowledge of the unknown past is depicted as ethereal matter by the poet; thus, past betrayals by justice systems are instantiated in "mocking birds" and "Crooked trees." In its ever present and naturalized state, a dialogue between the past and the present is established—one that, in this case, evokes a reminder to the reader that Texas holds the distinction of being the state that enacts the death penalty more often than all other states in the nation combined. The difference between a tradition of lynching and one of hanging is, to borrow from Paredes's words in another context, "the ceremony of a trial—a refinement, one must conclude, belonging to a more civilized age and a more enlightened people" (*Pistol* 18–19).[18]

The effacement of injustice from written histories is, for the poet, paralleled in the absence of poetry in the library by writers with a shared poetic sensibility. And as with so many of her poems, "Chipita" does not attempt to construct martyrs or heroes but everyday people who do everyday things like drink coffee and eat apples. For Acosta, the truth of a person's life should not be reduced to a single act or event that can then be judged as good or bad, right or wrong. The first stanza illustrates her awareness that Chipita's life has been reduced, not enhanced, by "Myth, Legend, Lie. All." The poet is keenly aware that Chipita has been made into a symbol. "Yes, all of us hating the slayers. / Wishing them dead also." Yet she knows that this construction of Chipita as a symbol of injustice is itself unjust. "But all the truth / Is buried deeper still." She does not claim to articulate Chipita's truth; rather she wants present-day Tejana/os to be accountable for the complexity of the past, especially the way it continually informs the present—even if the continuity is not readily visible.

Acosta inscribes a critique of history in Chipita's words: "'I loved my son. Some of the legends say I died / Because of him. Ah, what they'll say / To put you into history." It is a critique of history that limits our knowledge of Chipita to her role as mother and her status as victim of civil law. Official history, then, becomes the sign of another abuse of power that haunts those who, because they have individual privilege and "walk / The air-conditioned corridors" in "three-piece suits," think they "have outlived the past." In constructing a dialogue between Chipita and herself, the poet realizes that the dignity and significance of her subject lies in "who you were alive," not as a dead symbol of justice or injustice. Acosta's construction of Chipita's subjectivity does not neglect the harsh social context in which she lived, one that overdetermined relations of power between men and women, between Anglos and Mexicans, between the elite and the subaltern classes. This is evident in stanza thirteen:

> *—Eran bolillos,*
> *Los que me mandaron a matar.—*
> *"they knew which levers to pull,*
> *Were in the circles where you can order*
> *Someone to die.*
> *—Oh, maybe sometimes*
> *They have their reasons,*
> *I know. But me?"*

Chipita's warning and challenge to the poet in the final stanza is meant for all readers as well. It is a caution against believing that the past alone is what constitutes history, or that history is only about past relations. Rather, it suggests that superficial markers of "progress" mask the ugly reality of continuing injustices.

In speaking of her goals and poetics at work in "Chipita," Acosta has said that that she was

> not trying to speak anyone else's truth but only what I sense or feel and in "Chipita," for instance, which I wrote in the cold, cold library surrounded by people, students, all of us (Chicana/os included) who are privileged, I had to write "them/us" in because the surrounding of the library was a metaphor for 1. a monolithic Amerikan culture in which Chipita's history is lost to the "Hispanic Generation," (some reared by the Chicana/o Generation) and 2. for why the "Hispanic" generation thinks they are beyond "Chipita." I don't think they/we can abandon her without losing their/our souls. And, just as importantly, even if they/we do abandon her and lose their/our souls, they/we can't escape her. And that's important for me to say. The way the poem is structured is the way it "came to me." That is, I could literally see and feel Chipita present in that cold, cold library, trying to break through and speak to me directly about herself. I know this sounds mystical, but it is the case that such things occur to poets.[19]

Acosta's reflections on this poem offer verification of her investment in rewriting history. History's value to Acosta has many dimensions, but it appears that foremost is maintaining the integrity and idiosyncrasy of the lives and culture of people of Mexican descent, as distinguished from the "monolithic Amerikan culture." Here, her decision to spell America with a *k* functions as an indictment of U.S. fascism. The irony of generational values regarding political and cultural awareness is not lost on her. But for Acosta, I would argue, the differing degrees of historical awareness account for generational, political, and identity differences among people of a shared culture. Experience shapes consciousness, and privilege dulls consciousness of injustice. Here, the context of the comfortable and placid air-conditioned library contrasts sharply with the rage and violence that fuels people's sense of injustice under "Corpus Christi's sun / In agosto."

Acosta confirmed her intentions regarding what she hoped the poem would achieve:

> I guess I didn't consider myself contesting "official state records," but that's part of what happens in this poem. I am, however, very committed to giving some voice—however tinged with my perspective—to Chipita and to other unnamed people in history. I certainly intended to suggest the possibility that Chipita could speak her piece, without the heavy weight of the ill-begotten history surrounding her (refer to the

> "footnotes"—which I consider part of the poem). Also, I wanted her to "speak" directly to all the generations—whatever we were named en todos los "aquel entonces"; to what we more recently named ourselves: Chicano/; to the current state-imposed Hispanic/; to lo que nos llamen en el futuro. Partly because Chipita left us so brutally, I felt that I had a responsibility to return her to her Chicana/o hermanidad. At the same time I wanted to speak to her and have her speak directly to me, thus allowing her to become the one who challenged the authorities and who cautions the succeeding generations against becoming comfortable with a middle-class existence that is sterile and unmindful of a past so filled with extraordinary wrongs against many, many people throughout the world, because in many ways the "evils" of the past are always with us—whether as the oppressed or the oppressors or the ones who challenge their hold over us.[20]

Acosta's poetics remind us that historical memory can function as a form of resistance to cultural homogenization and individuality; for the neglected, excluded, or forgotten, it requires a sense of accountability to time and place as well as to the well-being of others. What we choose or are "taught" to forget or remember has decisive consequences for how we conceive of ourselves in the world. The fictional texts of this chapter challenge narrow notions of truth and historical value by unmasking the multiple forces and interests at work in the process of representing the past.

Conclusion

My objective in the preceding discussion of Eimer and González's novel and Acosta's poem has been to illustrate that people of Mexican descent in the United States do not simply have a history on the one hand and a literature on the other; we also have history expressed in literary form. Moreover, we have a history of literature that is continually being rediscovered and that, in order to be properly understood, needs to be contextualized within and seen as emerging from a specific set of social relations that have affected its production and circulation. Traditions are both found and invented. The recovery of *Caballero* assists in the main argument being formulated here, the argument that guides my methodology; Chicana/o literary production, whether as a national, minor, or ethnic literature, exists independent of the formation of Chicano historical narratives and often contests the representation of a historical generation by shifting the focus of concern away from narrow definitions of power and identity. The publication of works like *Caballero* have changed the corpus of Chicana/o literature. As the process of recovery and reconstruction of our literary heritage continues, scholars must address not only the different functions, methods, and objectives of historical and literary narratives; we must also be willing to recognize the ways in which their reconstructions of the past complement, contradict, and complicate one another, with the intent of altering our prior understanding of a period for the insight that such a reconstruction can offer to the present moment and to the future.

CHAPTER 2

Migration Literature as a Foundation for a National(ist) Literature

It is true that, by birth, we are Mexicans, but our minds are not so narrow, our vision not so pitifully small as to regard as aliens or enemies those who have been born under other skies. . . . The Revolution in Mexico is, however, not a political but a social and economic revolution and it is necessary to educate people, to teach them the real causes of their misery and slavery, and to point out to them the way to freedom, fraternity and equality.

This is why our hands, instead of being armed with muskets are armed with pens; a weapon more formidable and far more feared by tyrants and exploiters.

—Enrique Flores Magón, *Anarchism and the Mexican Revolution,* 1916

Constructing the Migrant Generation

Following Rodolfo Alvarez's construction of the generational paradigm, Ricardo Romo and Dale McLemore identified Mexicans who remained in the United States after the 1848 war against Mexico as the "Creation Generation" (McLemore and Romo 9). Their political, legal, and national status was "transferred" to the United States through the Treaty of Guadalupe Hidalgo. Formerly Mexican citizens, they constituted a new ethnic group within the United States. Moreover, many historians argue that after the turn of the century a Migrant Generation emerged. The labels used to classify these two generations come close to contradicting one another. The label "Creation Generation" overdetermines the national identity of the people involved in the processes and consequences of a military conquest by privileging the territorial claims of the conquering nation. Consequently, the preconquest history of the newly created ethnic minority group, Mexican Americans in this case, is often effaced as the conquest is subsumed under a progressive national history of the conquering nation. On the other hand, the label "migrant," unlike "immigrant," resists a specific national orientation in favor of emphasizing movement within or across boundaries as a mode of survival. Most historians explain the intense wave of northward migration in the first quarter of the twentieth century as a combination of economic pulls from the United States and political and economic pushes from Mexico. The pull was a consequence of growth in the agricultural, mining, transportation, and communication industries in the U.S. Southwest, which required a pool of unskilled laborers. The push arose within Mexico, where social and political turmoil preceding and accompanying the Revolution resulted in a mass exodus.[1]

Rodolfo Alvarez stresses the migrant rather than immigrant status of Mexicans. According to Alvarez, it is reductive to define immigrants solely on legal grounds. He argues that both culturally and sociologically, the peculiar psychohistorical experience of Mexican Americans in the Southwest prior to 1900 was such that they provide the basis for viewing pre–World War I new arrivals as "'migrants' who simply expanded the number of people who had more or less the same consciousness of lower caste status as those Mexican Americans who were here prior to 1900" (Alvarez 40). Mexicans entering the United States did not come into a fresh situation where they were meeting the host society for the first time. "Their experience upon entering the United States was predefined by the well-established social position of the pre-1900 Mexican Americans as a conquered people (politically, socially, culturally, economically, and in every other respect)" (40). Mexicans entering into the States viewed themselves and were viewed by the dominant society as the same as those Mexicans who had been there for many generations (43). Prior to the emergence of the industrial agricultural system in the U.S. borderlands, the similarity of the terrain north and south of the border did not require a cognitive reorientation as it did for many other immigrant groups (41). In fact, according to Oscar Martínez, the development of a foreign-based border economy in Mexico at the turn of the century occurred as a result of a simultaneous disruption in the local economies by external forces and the need for a safe haven by Anglo investors for their "vice-driven" businesses as a result of moral reforms in the United States (O. Martínez 114). Border towns, such as Juarez, Mexicali, and Tijuana, functioned as springboards for border crossers because many U.S. businessmen used those cities as labor pools for recruiting workers. A third set of reasons Alvarez gives for defining pre–World War I Mexicans as migrants rather than immigrants is the proximity and similarity of their land of origin to their land of destination and the relative permeability of the border. At the turn of the century access to and crossings of the border were not intensely regulated; the physical border between the United States and Mexico was not as clearly demarcated with fences and the presence of quasimilitary forces as it is now.

For Mexicans at that time, migration did not require that a substantial psychological and economic investment be made, as was required of immigrants from Europe or Asia (Alvarez 42). The fact that the southwestern United States had been part of Mexico in the recent past was not forgotten by migrants, a great many of whom came from the northern Mexican states. Furthermore, a move to the United States was not a vertical but a horizontal move in terms of class. Migrants "assumed the already established lower-caste position [in the States] . . . as a consequence of the prior established social structure."[2] The newly arrived as well as the U.S.-born Mexicans were treated as conquered people and foreigners by Euro-Americans. The forced deportation of Mexicans during harsh economic times, regardless of their U.S. citizenship status, testifies to their tenuous social and political status in the United States.

Most historians describe this era of intense migration in terms of Anglo response rather than viewing it as an assertive attempt for survival on the part of Mexicans. In *Occupied America,* Rodolfo Acuña notes otherwise. He says that "given the population boom in Mexico and the flight of capital Mexicans did what people have always done—they followed the resources. Migration in search of food, clothing and shelter is a basic behavior pattern which certainly predates the relatively recent concept of national borders" (Acuña 127). The border assumes significance, however, when it is used as a signifier of identity. It plays a role in defining Mexicans as "others" because it demarcates their national and ethnic identity as well as citizenship status in relation to the U.S. mainstream. In his study of Mexican immigrants in El Paso, Mario García identifies national orientation and identity between settlers and immigrants as a source of political tension within the Mexican-descent community:

> Although a key to the Ring's [Democratic machine's] success, Mexican-American politicians were no mere lackeys of the machine. Instead with their ability to deliver the Mexican vote they helped organize a Mexican-American pressure group within the Ring that assisted in obtaining jobs as well as ethnic protection. Ironically, most Mexicans had little interest in American politics. Living close to their homeland and hoping to eventually return, they saw no reason to give up their Mexican citizenship and to actively participate in local politics other than by accepting much needed money for their votes. For the majority of Mexicans one's country still meant Mexico, not the United States. (*Desert Immigrants* 7)

The labels given to the Creation Generation and the Migrant Generation are both limiting. The former exemplifies the problems associated with defining a community of people from the perspective of the dominant group in a society, while the latter defines a people's history based exclusively on the experiences of only one sector of that community. The designator "Creation generation" refers to the making of Mexicans into a subordinate ethnic group and the concomitant rise of anti-Mexican sentiment in southwestern United States. In this schema, history prior to the 1848 Treaty of Guadalupe Hidalgo is insignificant; consequently, any understanding of Mexican-descent communities in the United States is bound to a subjugated socioeconomic and political status. The application of labels that are reflective of social and political processes to an entire generation fails to take into account elite elements of this ethnic national group who were complicit with and benefited from the change in citizenship status, as well as many other situations in which social relations were different. Similar problems are inherent within the category of "Migrant Generation." The most obvious is that a focus on this group during the first two decades of the twentieth century neglects to examine the activities of people of Mexican descent who lived in the region prior to and following the U.S.-Mexican War. This is one problem that is inherent in the generational approach to history: it privileges the experiences of one sector of the community at the expense of others.

Chicano historians have not shied away from the significance of conflict in their material approaches to history; writing from a post–Chicano Movement perspective, however, they have often been too quick to judge *mexicano* resistance to economic, political, and cultural domination as "unsuccessful" in some generalized way. The following quote from Rodolfo Alvarez exemplifies this: "During the period designated as the 'Migrant Generation,' there were many isolated instances of great conflict between groups of Mexican Americans trying to alter their lower-caste status, but they were locally over-powered, and *a general state of acquiescence became the state of collective consciousness*" (Alvarez 41, emphasis mine). These notions of the Migrant Generation characterize the Mexican community as passive and prepolitical. This attitude toward pre–Chicano Movement political history prevails in historical literature; indeed, even though the generation that follows the Migrant Generation, the Mexican American Generation, is commonly perceived as assimilationist, it is also known as the first overtly political generation of Mexican Americans.[3] In explaining his approach to the Mexican American Generation, Mario García reveals something of his perception of the Migrant Generation:

> The problem . . . for this study concerns the role that ethnicity plays in the transition from either first-generation immigrants or those Mexican Americans native to the Southwest *who had been mostly isolated from mainstream currents* to a second, U.S. born generation . . . that on the whole began to understand that it was part of U.S. society and that it had to compromise between its ethnic roots and full incorporation and assimilation into American society. (*MA* 10, emphasis mine)

Political practice is thus validated only in relation to U.S. electoral politics. Little effort is made by proponents of the generational approach to understand diverse forms and articulations of political identity. Consequently, the significance of Mexico-oriented political practices and nonelectoral political struggles are often minimized or effaced.

In *Desert Immigrants,* Mario García argues that the Mexican nationalist consciousness was so pervasive in El Paso that *mexicano* political activism was strongest and most unambiguous in relation to the Mexican Revolution (7). However, so strong is his distinction between politics and class interests that he can claim the following:

> In all these strikes Mexicans attempted to improve their economic conditions. Although these actions did not involve a class consciousness,

> they did involve an ethnic one. Mexican immigrants did not see themselves as members of a proletariat class but as Mexicans temporarily in a foreign land; hence, they organized and protected themselves along ethnic lines. Furthermore, the issues in these strikes concerned disputes over wages and did not include a class ideology such as that articulated by the IWW [Industrial Workers of the World]. . . . Adjustment not resistance characterized their stay in the United States. (108–109)

García's rigid distinction between ethnic and class politics, as well as the consistent comparisons he makes between Mexican immigrant cultural, social, and organization activities and those of European immigrants, reveals the assimilation framework that characterizes much of his work.

There is, however, another school of thought that has a very different interpretation of the Migrant and Mexican American Generations' interaction with mainstream U.S. society. Chicano labor historians such as Juan Gómez-Quiñones, Emilio Zamora, and Luis Leobardo Arroyo have contributed to a more complex understanding of the role of Mexican workers in labor organizing during these periods. Their research presents Mexican workers as active agents, not as passive and submissive laborers.[4] Gómez-Quiñones's 1972 essay on Chicano labor history marks an important moment in Chicano historiography because it examines the significance of labor as a site of resistance that illuminates intracultural as well as intercultural divisions and alliances.[5] Moreover, by critiquing and expanding the field of labor history, feminist historians such as Antonia Castañeda, Adelaida R. del Castillo, Vicki Ruiz, Emma Pérez, and Deena González, among others, have successfully integrated an analysis of gender, labor, ideology, and culture that eschews elitist notions of power, space, and political participation by writing a subaltern history of those excluded from political institutions and leadership positions.[6]

The Migrant Generation is, by definition, characterized by geographical movement across national borders. For the thousands of Mexicans who migrated northward during the first two decades of the twentieth century, their movement across geopolitical boundaries helped them gain relief from the social and economic upheaval that preceded, accompanied, and followed the Mexican Revolution. It is commonly acknowledged by historians and sociologists that many of these migrants viewed their move to the United States as a temporary hiatus from the military and economic turmoil of Mexico.[7] Mexicans in the States are able to maintain their national identity with relative ease. This has been primarily due to the proximity of their nation of origin and the formation of close-knit communities that have reinforced their cultural and national identity. The consequences of their move across a loosely policed national border and their interactions with a decisively different economic, political, and social life were not determined or homogeneous. Their experiences, responses, and reactions to U.S. society varied widely. Unlike the settler community of the eighteenth and nineteenth centuries, these migrants voluntarily entered into a relationship with the United States. Their complex motivations and intentions and the effects of these on their national and political orientation are left unexamined by a generational approach that, notwithstanding its resistance to a particular national identity, universalizes their experiences across ideological and gender axes. A more complete and complex history lives within the "blind spots" and generalizations produced by the generational paradigm.

The historiography of women of Mexican descent is one such blind spot that has been created by the racialist and sexist paradigms of historians and the institutions that have produced and supported them. A lack of analysis of the impact of gender in political, social, and intellectual history exists in both canonical and Chicano revisionist historiography. This lack of analysis is usually explained as a result of insufficient data or primary materials. What has often resulted is what Gayatri Spivak calls "cognitive failure," which, in the case of revisionist histories, produces an ethnic version of elite historiography: a history that assumes a "great man" approach to writing Chicano history. The effect of dominant methods of organizing knowledge and the contradictions it entails for subalterns can be seen in the emergence of the field of Chicano history. In its early years much effort was devoted to searching for a proper paradigm or periodization schema. While new modes of analysis were tested with the intention of producing a subaltern history of Chicanas/os, they often contained limitations that were inherited from traditional paradigms. Much Chicano history privileges conflict with and resistance to domination as a means of moving away from a modes of production master narrative. The benefit of this analytical approach, as Gayatri Spivak has pointed out, is that "the agency of change is located in the insurgent or 'subaltern'" (Spivak 3). Within the framework of elite historiography, the ethnic, class, and immigrant status of Mexicans in the United States converge. One way to overcome the supposed lack of evidence of subaltern history is to examine the production and definition of "evidence," its management in the production of truth, and its interpretation.

The process of uncovering Chicana/o history is still underway. The point to be made here is that many Anglo and Chicano histories have neglected Chicanas' active participation in the making of history.[8] Analyzing the fictional representations of and by women of Mexican descent will be one of the ways that this chapter will read against the grain of established histories. Though contemporary fictional reconstructions of the past are not historical evidence per se, they reveal an author's understanding of the past and often depict dimensions of experience that formal histories neglect. Emma Pérez's recently published study, *The Decolonial Imaginary,* is an excellent polemic that incisively details how and why Chicanas have been systematically written out of history. Pérez proposes the notion of a "decolonial imaginary" as a "theoretical tool for uncovering the hidden voices of Chicanas that have been relegated to silences, to passivity, to that third space where agency is enacted through third space feminism" (xvi). In so doing, she asserts that gaps in Chicana historical discourse may be filled by exploring the historical imagination in a way that breaks down the binary between the "real" and the "imaginary," between artistic and realistic historiography (xvi–xvii).

The historical literature produced by and about the Migrant Generation foregrounds issues that continue to inform the production and critical analysis of Chicana/o literature because a material analysis is inextricably bound to a historical understanding of this period of Mexican and American history. A dialectical approach to history and culture should disallow any effort to separate neatly the impact of one nation-state and its people upon another. Under close scrutiny, the contentious relationships within and between these two bordering nations can potentially have a profound effect on our notions of nationality, nationalism, labor, leadership, and political engagement.

Representing the Migrant Generation

The two fiction authors that are central to this chapter use their writing to confront, complicate, and write the history of the Migrant Generation in different ways. The writings of Alejandro Morales and Sara Estela Ramírez also help us to better understand the dynamic and sometimes dialectical relationship between historical and creative literature. On the one hand, historical novels like Morales's *The Brick People* present a seemingly comprehensive and seamless vision of the past whose construction as art and history in narrative form must be interrogated and whose limitations need to be identified. On the other hand, a "real" historical figure, political activist, and writer like Ramírez poses the problem of the relatively limited amount of historical documentation of *mexicanas* and Chicanas and their extant cultural production, and also exposes that the process of making and representing history are intertwined and consciously fabricated. Morales, a contemporary author, situates his historical novel *The Brick People* (1988) in turn-of-the-century California. Morales's novel foregrounds the dual status of Mexicans as both settlers and immigrants. He has the benefit of hindsight and the sweeping historical vision that one can exploit from a temporal distance in his portrayal of this era. In a novel about the role Mexicans played as laborers in the manufacturing industry, Morales is able to reconstruct imaginatively the social and cultural milieu of the time.

Morales's contemporary perspective on the historical events he writes about enables him to construct a novel that spans several decades and involves dozens of characters. However, a historical narrative like Morales's contrasts sharply with the writings of a figure like Sara Estela Ramírez. Like Morales, Ramírez was concerned with the dispossession of land from *mexicanos* by capital investors, both in Mexico and in South Texas. Not only was Ramírez concerned with documenting the era she lived within, she also tried to effect social and political change for Mexicans on both sides of the border. Reading Ramírez's work presents a problem different from that of juxtaposing Morales's historical vision with other histories. With Ramírez, one of the problems is the lack of availability of all of her writings. Though she was a prolific journalist, essayist, poet, playwright, and publisher, only a fragment of the total body of her work is available. When left with only a portion of an author's work, one must read around the gaps to make meaning of the missing record, as both Emilio Zamora and Inés Hernández-Ávila make clear. Sara Estela Ramírez's involvement in political organizations, newspapers, unions, and mutualist societies helped her acquire a reputation among her peers, several of whom committed their thoughts to writing in the form of eulogies upon her death. Following the extensive and pathbreaking work of Hernández-Ávila, I also draw on these eulogies to illustrate the powerful impact and influence she had on her community.

While Ramírez should be seen as an exemplary figure of this era, she was not an anomaly. As I stated previously, within the United States at the turn of the century many Mexicans maintained the national identity of their country of origin in their cultural and political practices. For many this entailed political involvement and support of one or another political faction of the anti-Díaz *revolucionarios*. Mexican political activists used a nebulous international boundary to their advantage. Aware that residency in the United States was in many cases perceived as a temporary condition of exile by the Mexican population north of the border, some political activists exploited the border by establishing organizational bases that were, initially at least, out of the reach of Mexican officials who were trying to crush resistance against the Díaz regime. Organizations like the Partido Liberal Mexicano (PLM) tapped into the national sentiments of Mexicans residing in the southwestern United States. Sara Estela Ramírez was one such organizational representative, who became an important spokesperson for the PLM in Texas. Furthermore, chain migration from Mexico resulted in the maintenance of communal ties across the border and also provided the groundwork for labor and political organizing, a phenomenon depicted in *The Brick People.*

The process of migration, that is, the movement of a people from one region to another, is a popular theme in Chicana/o literature. Morales's *The Brick People* is one of many novels that take the migration experience from Mexico to the United States as its theme. Other well-known novels are *Pocho* by José Antonio Villareal, *Rain of Gold* by Victor Villaseñor, *Barrio Boy* by Ernesto Galarza, and *Diary of an Undocumented Immigrant* by Ramón Pérez. With the exception of *Diary of an Undocumented Immigrant,* most of the novels of this genre share certain plot features and narrative structures.[9] For instance, the plot usually follows one man's journey (usually solo, but sometimes with a family) from his country of origin to his newly adopted home. This migration is usually provoked by the civil unrest and economic instability resulting from the Mexican Revolution. The conflict of the novel often centers around his or his progeny's difficulty in fitting into U.S. society, an experience often characterized by encounters with racism and cultural isolation. Another common feature of this genre is that many of these novels follow the structure of a *Bildungsroman;* they map out the development of a male character who is obliged by social circumstance to come to terms with life under less than favorable conditions. By the novel's end, the protagonist has usually resolved the source of conflict and has become integrated into U.S. society. In Chicana/o literature, this genre is primarily a masculinist one. Its proliferation among male authors has had interesting consequences for our understanding of the period. And it is here that the relationship between imagined and historical narratives of this era is most interesting and most limited, for many contemporary novels about this era either inherit or duplicate a limited understanding of the period that privileges male experience, often to the exclusion of female experience. Yet unlike official histories, in their imaginative reconstruction of people's daily lives, the fictional literature does not restrict its focus to institutions, organizations, or leaders. As a result, women and children, extended family, and members of the community are presented as part of the social milieu. It is this added dimension that opens up the possibility of gaining a more complex understanding of power and inter- and intracultural relations of an era.

In this chapter I investigate fictional and historical writings about the Migrant Generation not only with the purpose of challenging definitions of them as prepolitical, but also with the goal of illustrating the ways in which gender, national identity, and cultural practices are utilized to articulate and advance political claims and give meaning to everyday life.

The Brick People *and the 'Proletarianization' of Mexicans in the United States*

> *Because it confronts history and makes history central to the text,* The Brick People *is both a literary and historical document and hence one in which both literary critics and historians (a division which in some circles such as New Historicism and intellectual history is becoming nonevident) have an obligation to review critically.*
>
> —Mario García, "History, Literature, and the Chicano Working-Class Novel"

This reading of the Migrant Generation through *The Brick People* will examine how Mexicans became "proletarianized" as laborers in the U.S.-sponsored expansion of capitalism. Such a reading will not necessarily offer us a different reading of the era from that offered by Chicano counterhistories, because many historians acknowledge the integration of Mexicans into the capitalist system of labor as a process that fundamentally differentiates the nineteenth and twentieth centuries. However, Morales's reconstruction of the migrant era moves the focus away from economics and shows how *mexicanos* in the United States were able to survive culturally and socially as a coherent group despite bitter intra- and intercultural battles. Morales's narrative suggests that one of the ways that Mexican culture retained a distinct identity was through the use of folk legends and practices that were informed by a sense of social justice and offered an alternative master narrative through which oppressive social relations might be eradicated. In "History, Literature, and the Chicano Working-Class Novel: A Critical Review of Alejandro Morales's *The Brick People,"* Mario García claims that Morales is basically on the mark in terms of his interpretation of the history in his novel; he does, however, criticize Morales's depiction of women and the middle-class ambitions of the main character. Ironically, this middle-class sector of the Mexican-descent community is the focus of García's best-known study, *Mexican Americans: Leadership, Ideology, and Identity, 1930–1960.*

In interesting ways, the Mexican liberal anarchist group, the Partido Liberal Mexicano (PLM), ties the contexts of Morales's and Ramírez's work together. In the time period documented by their writings, the PLM was important in both South Texas and Los Angeles. Certainly the leaders of the PLM, the Flores Magón brothers as well as other members of the *junta,* recognized the importance of establishing a base in regions that were populated by large numbers of *mexicanos.* According to Emilio Zamora, the large *mexicano* population in Laredo assured the PLM of some measure of native political and social control, which in turn produced a relatively stable work environment ("Chicano Socialist" 222). Although Los Angeles had a sizable Mexican-origin population, it was very different from Laredo in terms of its history and social relations. At the turn of the century, Los Angeles was undergoing a period of intense social, economic, and political change. Between 1900 and 1920 the city experienced a 500 percent increase in population. With the demand for cheap labor to facilitate economic growth, the Mexican-descent population increased ten-fold in that same period. Nevertheless, Mexicans constituted only about 10 percent of the overall population (Escobar, "Mexican Revolutionaries" 3–4). Moreover, in addition to being overrepresented in low-paying, menial jobs, many Mexicans actually suffered from downward mobility at this time (5). This is the social context of Morales's book.

According to Mario García, *The Brick People* is a "combination of the exhaustive historical novels of James Michener with their casts of hundreds and the Latin American Boom novel with its stress on magical realism" ("History, Literature" 189). Moreover, he asserts that this novel "represents one of the most serious efforts by a Chicano novelist to come to grips with the historical evolution of Chicanos, especially as working-class people" (189). The book does place labor, labor conflict, and working-class culture at its center, but García is unable to appreciate fully the multiple ways that *The Brick People* challenges both official histories and Chicano (male) counterhistories.

The Brick People is centered around the families—and primarily but not exclusively on the patriarchs—who chain migrate from Guanajuato to Southern California at the turn of the century seeking refuge from the turmoil of the Mexican Revolution. The jacket of the novel proclaims its historical basis with a 1930s sepia-toned photograph on the outside and a black-and-white photo of the Simons Brickyard workers on the inside.[10] Yet this is not a strictly linear account of events, with characters responding to political and social forces. The novel's epigraph, taken from Carlos Fuentes's *Terra nostra* (1975), reads, "The world dissolves when someone ceases to dream, to remember, to write." Carl Gutiérrez-Jones argues that Morales uses this epigraph "to frame his novel's project because he wishes to emphasize the recovery of an alternative history: that of the Simons brickyards in Los Angeles during the first half of this century" (82–83). I agree but take this idea further by noting that the epigraph provides a blueprint for how history and stories are made—imagination and memory precede inscription. By necessity we must have an active relationship to texts; otherwise history or literature can assume a tyrannical role in our lives. And indeed one can argue that canonical texts across the disciplines do serve an oppressive function. Morales's book illustrates how the coexistence of events, memory, and myth all shape what we call reality, though no singular reality exists.

The novel's plot traces the arrival and interaction of two groups of migrants into Southern California from the 1890s until World War II: Anglo capitalists seeking opportunities to expand their fortunes in an emerging industrial economy and Mexicans searching for an alternative to the explosive and exploitative living conditions of an economically and politically unstable society undergoing "modernization." The success of Walter and Joseph Simons's brick factory depends on the labor, knowledge, and leadership acquired from the almost exclusively Mexican work force they hire to help them build their business. In the novel, the rich and powerful Simons brothers and their families are the *patrones* who rule over the Mexican work force with the assistance of Mexican foremen. Many *mexicanos* are introduced into the plot as newly arrived immigrants who have learned about work being available in Simons town from family and friends who preceded them from Guanajuato. Composed of twenty-three untitled chapters, the events of the novel are related by an omniscient narrator and from the point of view of members of the Simons family, various foremen, and the laborers and their wives and children, who become a stronger presence as a company town is developed to accommodate and contain the factory's workers and families. Encompassing fifty years, the historical period presented by the novel is vast; it covers historical events such as the Mexican Revolution,

World War I, the Great Depression, and World War II, as well as natural disasters like the San Francisco earthquake of 1906, the 1933 Long Beach earthquake, and social catastrophes like the brutal 1923 kidnapping and murder of a young girl by William Edward Hickman, and the 1943 Zoot Suit riots. Although these events form the context of the novel, it is the day-to-day interactions and social relations of the main characters during and after these historical moments that provide the impetus for the novel's plot.

The success of the Simons's brick factory is dependent on the management of the cheap and efficient labor of Mexican migrants. With the exception of the Depression, the natural disasters and tumultuous global events marked by war all prove beneficial to the brick industry and require more work by more workers to meet the rising demand for bricks. Significantly, the global unionist movement provides a persistent challenge to the Simons Brickyard as many workers become involved in making demands for better wages and safer work conditions. Ultimately, class interests pit the proprietors and their managerial representatives against the workers, providing the central conflict of the novel. The conflict is infused with racial tension, but this dimension is complicated by the Mexican foremen who remain loyal to the Anglo businessmen during strikes.

The novel covers two generations of the *mexicano*/Mexican American community. Some of the central characters, however, are U.S.-born; thus, it extends beyond the parameters of the period known as the Migrant Generation and into the so-called Mexican American period. The decision to examine this novel in a chapter about the Migrant Generation is not entirely arbitrary: it is the workers' status as newly arrived foreign migrants that makes them a convenient source of exploitable labor for the Simons brothers, an experience that is both formative and continuous because mass migrations into the United States continue to this day. The Simons brothers, and Walter in particular, believe that as long as they offer a positive alternative to conditions in Mexico they can create a more benign form of slavery than that which existed on the haciendas in Guanajuato that Walter toured. The Simons brothers attempt to control their workers through the re-creation of a familiar labor economy of debt peonage, complete with a *tienda de raya.* There are some distinctions between and among the different generations of *mexicanos* regarding their economic status and identity, but these emerge from their experiences as workers, not from varying notions of national and cultural orientation that can be seen as a result of inherent generational differences. This is an additional reason why neatly defined generational distinctions are insufficient. Furthermore, *The Brick People's* focus on laborers requires that a different analytical framework be used to understand the way power relations are negotiated from the limited notions of politics and power privileged by the generational paradigm. Referring to the research conducted by labor historians, Gómez-Quiñones says that their work provides insight into "the impact of economic changes on the community, the degree of tension between the Chicano and the larger society, the pattern of resistance, the degree of politicization and cohesion, the role of government in regard to the community, the attitude toward and possibility of inter-minority cooperation, the state of class consciousness and how in given circumstances it transcends national antagonisms" ("The First Steps" 13–14). These concerns are integral to the plot of *The Brick People* as well. Underlying such an observation is a premise that acknowledges the different interests, concerns, and methods of labor historians in relation to historians whose work primarily focuses on elites and leaders within the mainstream.

There is a question of genre to be explored here. Labor history focuses on specific sites of struggle; historical narratives, on the other hand, make an attempt to be all encompassing, to define the zeitgeist of an era (as Mario García says), and in the process they lose specificity, especially in regards to class- and gender-differentiated experience. Moreover, these historical narratives assume a quasi-master narrative status in academia because of the supposed breadth of their scope in covering substantial portions of the history of a people. In contrast, fictional narratives do not necessarily inherit the limited scope of experience posited by historical ones. In fact, one criterion often used to gauge the success of a fictional narrative is the multidimensional development of its characters. The exploration and development of interior as well as exterior motivations often requires that main characters are understood in a communal context, not just as individual members of civil society and citizens of a nation-state.

The Historical and Political Vision of The Brick People

In his review of the novel, Mario García says that the Chicano saga is characterized by their "central experience as workers dispossessed from their lands both in the Southwest and in Mexico" ("History, Literature," 189). The historical events of the novel are told in episodic fashion with a blend of fact, fiction, legend, folklore, and myth. In the context of significant global economic and political changes, the narrative tells the story of Mexicans in what has been referred to as Greater Northern Mexico. García's essay offers insight into Morales's historical vision as well as his own. To understand fully how Morales's historical view shaped *The Brick People,* the narration of events that coincides with traditional notions of history—that is, story elements that are empirically based, including specific times, dates, names, causal factors, and consequences, as well as the meanings they convey—must be reconciled with the alternative conceptions of time, space, and power that are also an integral part of the novel. Competing epistemologies are integral to the narrative structure; Morales's historical vision has at least two dimensions, the factual and the folkloric, which coexist in an uneasy relationship to one another but cannot be reduced to an individual or to an individual's story.

What meaning is given to the lives of the characters of *The Brick People*? What is its prevailing plot structure: romance, satire, comedy, or tragedy? In assessing the literary elements of historical writings, Hayden White has argued that the historian relies on the archetypal, pregeneric plot structures, identified by Northrop Frye and others, to emplot meaning into a historical narrative (85). If, as White says, historical situations are not inherently tragic, comic, ironic, or romantic, how has Morales embedded the meaning of history in his narrative? García responds to these questions by noting the influence of Morales's intellectual generation on his understanding of Chicano history. He states that Morales's historical vision is "largely consistent with the historical themes propounded by the Chicano Movement with its stress on internal colonization, a historical but lost homeland, and *La Reconquista.*" Yet he also suggests that *The Brick People* deviates from "this more collectivist interpretation of history to posit a somewhat more individualist conception of that history" (190). Based on the characterization of Chicano history in this review, García believes the prevailing structure of Chicano histories is that of the romantic tragedy; it involves the story of a people tied to their land who find that relationship threatened by the indomitable forces of capitalism, power, and greed. García argues that this notion of history provides the framework for Morales's narrative. Consequently, in his view, the book is shaped by three key historical periods: the Anglo conquest, the capitalist expansion period of the late nineteenth and early twentieth centuries, and *La Reconquista.* Moreover, he uses this structure to gauge the historical nature of the novel and to form his own critique. And though García gives much attention to what he calls aspects of "magical realism" in the novel, he never comments on the significance of these alternative perspectives and the narrative they emplot. For García, the inclusion of myths, folklore, and the fantastic in the novel is to be understood solely as a creative use of symbolism by Morales, a mere literary convention, not as a genuinely alternative way of relating history and interpreting the meaning of events that is utilized by marginalized communities.[11]

Myth, folklore, and the fantastic are woven into the novel's plot and appear in the context of other events, usually in times of crisis and usually in response to oppressive social relations between Anglos and Mexicans. In a fashion similar to David Montejano's in *Anglos and Mexicans in the Making of Texas, 1836–1986,* albeit on a smaller geographical and temporal scale, Morales structures his narrative to illustrate the sustained impact of these two groups on one another. The opening scene sets the stage for a story of colonialism, the displacement of people, and the social contradictions that accompany the emergence of capitalism.

As Rosendo Guerrero waits outside the office of the *patrón* Joseph Simons, he recalls the crazed man who slaughtered his family in search of Emperor Maximilian, and he contemplates the juridical and managerial authority he holds over Mexican laborers in his capacity as foreman of the Simons Brickyard. "He, Rosendo Guerrero, did not labor; he directed and ordered. He, the privileged foreman, felt powerful" (Morales 8). Inside the office, Joseph Simons recalls another story of displacement, a story about the extralegal means of terror used to seize land from Californio elites. The postmortem transformation of doña Eulalia Pérez de Guillen into hundreds of "indescribably large brown insects" foreshadows the horrific deaths of members of the Simons family, through which they will pay retribution for their role in the subjugation of Mexicans. The insects and the land are metonymically connected to doña Eulalia and by extension to other Mexicans when she tells her husband, "Juan, I am this oak. It will grow as certain as my love for you and the land. The day they chop it down I will die and I'll become an insect of the land" (9). This connection between doña Eulalia and the land is reinforced by the waiter who tells the legend of the matriarch to Joseph Simons: "It's unbelievable that she turned into millions of brown insects, and yet people saw it happen. She understood the earth in a special way and possessed powers of the earth. She is the soil and those insects are her" (11). This linking of the deterritorialization of Californios and the exploitative labor relations that follow with the "magical" and often violent appearance of insects recurs throughout the novel.[12] Before further exploring the function of myth in *The Brick People,* let us consider the consequences of ignoring the implications of myth by examining the view of history that Mario García finds embedded in the novel.

By foregrounding what he sees as Morales's use of the prevailing historical periods constructed by Chicano Movement historians, García validates the novel as a counterhistory to Anglo American mainstream histories. In this novel the "Spanish Fantasy" and manifest destiny are deconstructed as the role of Mexicans in the building of California is illustrated. The violent displacement of people, as well as the proletarianization of Mexican labor and the suppression of labor movements, is central to the plot. García states that "It is [these] historical relationship[s] . . . which Morales seeks to recapture and in doing so correct what he calls the 'historical amnesia' of California which has all but swept Mexicans off the pages of history" ("History, Literature," 192). Yet, though he appreciates the historical framework of the novel, García finds that the novel "lacks commitment to acting as a political weapon" and conveys middle-class values (196). In a section of his essay titled "Working-Class Literature Versus Proletarian Literature," García's penchant for using the generational paradigm as the framework for understanding the class interests and ideological motivations of Mexicans emerges. He states that the central Mexican protagonist of the novel, Octavio Revueltas, "possesses not the Mexican dream of immigrants—the hope of return to a better life in Mexico—but the mythical American Dream of individual success and a good life for himself and his family in the United States. . . . Like most children of immigrants—the Mexican-American Generation—Octavio recognizes that his future is in the United States" (195). García's judgment of this character is based upon his desire for a home and his break with the union organizers.[13] Because he considers Octavio's "ambition" to rise above his status as a brickworker to be "the drama for the lesson Morales weaves from history" (195), García identifies the novel as nonproletarian and anti-Movement in its outlook.

In suggesting that the book fails as a proletarian novel, García contradicts himself and takes the novel out of the context from which it was written. If, as García states above, the protagonist's outlook is shaped generationally, then one should *expect* him to be assimilationist, individualistic, and striving to be upwardly mobile, for this is the characterization of the Mexican American generation that many Chicano historians, García among the most adamant, have constructed. García wants Morales's protagonist to defy this generational zeitgeist despite his own earlier acknowledgment in the essay that the author's historical vision has been shaped by Movement historians. Instead, by utilizing the genre of the proletarian novel to gauge the extent two which *The Brick People* is proworker, García applies an aesthetic paradigm shaped in the 1930s to a 1980s novel, and thus fails to appreciate the extent to which the generational paradigm of Chicana/o history has acted as a quasi-master narrative and posited limited notions about the past. He thus fails to consider the intellectual climate the author operates within. This is not, however, meant to concede to García's evaluation of the novel as a vehicle for the promotion of individualism. Rather, it is meant to raise a question about the relationship between literature and history and the degree to which one can expect a novel to prescribe reality rather than to describe particular events as they may have occurred. By asserting that the novel "lacks a revolutionary vision" in failing to provide a model for social change based on the collective interest of all workers, one that would help them prepare for the next stage of history, García projects *his desire* that this novel and its characters fit into a construction of history in which each successive stage necessarily marks progress against race and class domination.

Morales's novel does offer a critical view of history; it does so by resisting a romanticization of race and class struggle and resistance, and examines the complicity of Mexicans in the subordination of others. Undeniably, one of the virtues of fictional narratives is that they have the potential to articulate a vision that is at odds with reality—that is, they can serve a prescriptive function. There is, however, a virtue to realistic depictions of past social relations. To deny the complicity of Chicanas/os in economic, racial, and gender subordination is to create a revisionist myth that fails to examine the complex web of ideologies and material conditions that have shaped the experience of Mexicans in the United States. Class struggle has been, and continues to be, a basis of intracultural division. Perhaps a greater failure would have been to suggest that the past is characterized by the success of labor. As García points out, unionism has won gains, but it ultimately has failed for a number of reasons, including its inability to develop leadership and organizing strategies that respond to the specific ways that nativism and racism are used to defeat unions by characterizing them as antinational. When the brickyard foremen recruit African Americans from Watts to break the strike, the Mexicans of Simons gamble on their inability and unwillingness to perform the work. They discover, however, that wage laborers are replaceable and that their union dues have been used to help other strikers.

Upon discovering this, Octavio accuses the union leaders of being the same as Walter Simons: "Your only interest is in what you're going to gain. You're thieves and exploiters," he tells them (Morales 226). And his accusation is partially supported by the response of one of the organizers, who threatens to "blacklist" him.

The critique of Octavio's sense of individualism and desire for mobility is taken out of the context of the role he played as labor organizer. The sense of betrayal and disillusionment that Octavio experiences in collective struggle is heightened by a series of events, including the failure of the workers' co-op and the scapegoating, xenophobia, and violence directed toward nonwhites in the United States during World War II, despite their role in the armed services. After losing his job at the Simons Brickyard and being blacklisted because of his role as a labor leader, Octavio and his family are unable to find a place to live because of racist housing covenants against Mexicans in Anglo neighborhoods. And even though there were exceptions, Octavio notes that these people were "lighter complexioned than the Mexicans who resided in Simons. . . . the Anglo world did not reject his labor or the blood of his relatives or neighbors. For work or war the Anglo world needed him, but it refused to allow him to live among its citizens. Mexicans had to be pushed away and kept at the periphery of Anglo-American society" (270). Octavio's decision to purchase land and build a home is a last option that García characterizes as an embrace of the American dream of individual homeownership and a rejection of the collective struggle against poverty, inferior housing, racism, and worker exploitation. But García's critique appears misplaced. If individuality is a product of the ensemble of social relations, as he carefully notes, then Octavio's need for a home and the means to acquire it must be seen in the context of his role as an organizer and as a resident of Simons, whose homes the fire department refuses to aid. Why are his actions interpreted as a failure to the collective and not as a result of the collective's failure to him?

The sickness that consumes Octavio as he begins to build the house is diagnosed by a *curandera* as a *susto* (fright) that came upon him as a great shock on the night his family's house was burnt down. Since that night the family has been homeless and experienced the full force of racism. He is forced to come to terms with his place in society when the fire department refuses to enter Simons town. Octavio's pursuit of better living quarters is not validated as a heroic act; rather, it is a source of ambivalence for the community. Some are resentful because they see it as a "sign of success" and an "ostentatious show of uppitiness and money," as well as a sign of independence from an exploitative relationship with the Simons Brickyard. Milagros Revueltas, Octavio's mother, on the other hand, believes that as builders his family should see his actions as a model, for they should be able to enjoy the fruits of their own labor.

In the Simons Brickyard, workers' labors, and thus their lives, are transformed into brick. Just as they are alienated from the products of their labor, so, too, is their collective history and role as laborers mystified in the commodification process. The brickyard becomes a site of many layers of violence. Early in the narrative, when the workers uncover a mass grave of Chinese who have been massacred in the recent past, the amnesia that had allowed residents of the area to forget the brutal and indiscriminate slayings of people is challenged. What had been reduced to a Chinese legend or myth is shown to be historical fact. Only after they are faced with the indisputable evidence of bodies with bullet holes, stab wounds, and crushed craniums are people willing to accept the legend as truth. Before the empirical evidence is uncovered, "most people believed that the Chinese were apt to spin tales against the Anglo Americans and that the story of the massacre was a legend brought from China" (15). The workers are forced to exhume the mass grave, which stands in the way of the brickyard's progress. This episode represents an intersection of the different histories of the Chinese and the Mexicans, including the complicity of some Mexicans in the massacre. It is the weaving together of different histories and different means of relaying them that makes Morales's novel an important historical testimony.[14] *The Brick People* departs from Chicana/o historical narratives, especially those that fail to recognize the heterogeneity of experience within and across generational distinctions, in its willingness to illustrate contradictions and ruptures in Mexican identity and political ideologies. This is partially achieved by narrating the conflicting actions and thoughts of the central characters; furthermore, notwithstanding García's condemnation of Morales's historical vision as one that is supportive of bourgeois individualism, the novel suggests that there is another master narrative operating here, one that is imbued with a recognition of race and class domination as well as a belief in the ultimate triumph of the Mexican workers. This narrative occupies the secondary status of folklore and myth in relation to official histories. Like the Chinese "myth" about the massacre, these stories are representative of historical events. When we examine the role that these elements of Mexican culture play in *The Brick People,* we discover that they contribute to a different understanding of history and the role of culture in constructing the past and the present.

Folklore and Gender: Alternative Narratives in The Brick People

Folklore must not be considered an eccentricity, an oddity or picturesque element, but as something which is very serious and is to be taken seriously.

—Antonio Gramsci

Woven throughout the narrative of *The Brick People* are stories, myths, and communal interpretations of historical events that add a different dimension to the novel's historical character. It is in these cultural practices that the imaginative possibilities for critiquing present and past circumstances, as well as constructing future possibilities, reside. Although Morales represents these narrative and interpretive practices as an integral part of everyday life and experience, they are neither extraordinary nor sensational. In contrast to official historical narratives, oral histories present a dialogical model of history that resists notions of universal progress and individual success; in folklore, no individual or group acts in isolation. Instead, a dialectical process of power and negotiation is presented. Gramsci says that folklore should be seen as

> a "conception of the world and life" implicit to a large extent in determinate (in time and space) strata of society and in opposition (also for the most part implicit, mechanical, and objective) to "official" conceptions of the world . . . that have succeeded one another in the historical process. . . . This conception of the world is not elaborated and systematic because, by definition, the people (the sum total of the instrumental and subaltern classes of every form of society that has so far existed) cannot possess conceptions which are elaborated, systematic, and politically organized and centralized in their albeit contradictory development. . . . Folklore can be understood only as a reflection of the conditions of cultural life of the people, although certain conceptions specific to folklore remain even after these conditions have been (or seem to be) modified or have given way to bizarre combinations. (*Gramsci Reader* 360–61)

For the purpose of this analysis of *The Brick People,* two observations are important: folklore exists in opposition to official narratives, and, in this novel at least, folklore is primarily articulated by female characters. Not only, then, will an examination of the "folkloric" in this novel add a different dimension to our understanding of this period and give us insight into Morales's multilayered narrative strategy, it will also foreground his representation of the gendered dynamics of power embedded in different ways of living in and conveying other "conceptions of the world." Folklore, legend, and myth are not always associated with the feminine in this novel. They do, however, become an important means for the women to articulate alternative and oppositional interpretations of events. The linking of women and folklore by Morales risks reducing, essentializing, and reinforcing gendered divisions of space and power, which mandate that men operate in the "public" sphere of work and politics and women in the "private" domain of home and culture. This narrative strategy has potentially liberating consequences, however. If Morales's project is to write a subaltern history, as has been my thesis, we must bear in mind that "subaltern" is an adjective that connotes inferior rank not as an ontological term but as a general attribute of any form of subordination, including gender-based oppression. The relationship between women and folklore expressed in this novel is an empowering one; it both acknowledges the multiple levels of subalternity experienced by women of Mexican descent and recognizes their assertion of agency within specific material and cultural boundaries. Before proceeding to a discussion of the function of folklore and its empowering relationship to women's narrative strategies, let us examine the representation of women in the novel independent of folklore.

The *mexicanas* in the novel are shown to be the primary caregivers and managers of the domestic economy. Most of the men work twelve-hour shifts at the brickyard, and other than holidays they spend their free time with other men, pursuing pleasures outside the home. Although most of the women in the novel are given identities in relation to men, as wives and daughters, their own desires and labors are often shown to be achieved in spite of their husbands. The domestic economy has double standards for men and women. There is no division between work and home for women as there is for the men; thus, domestic space is a site of work and pleasure.

Just as García believes Morales fails to represent the successes as well as the failures of the labor struggle, he believes that the novel also fails by not depicting women as members of the work force who participate in the labor movement. He does acknowledge that the women of Simons town are shown to be strong and important contributors to familial and communal well-being as well as the transmitters of cultural traditions. In his desire for a representation of women in the labor struggle, García fails to recognize that there is value in representing the struggle against oppression in domestic space. Such an analysis privileges the site of labor as the only terrain of class struggle and fails to appreciate the ideological relations of family and culture. Nana Revueltas, like her husband, also desires a home of her own where she can be the domestic head of the family, determine priorities of work and arrangement of space within the household, and raise her children without being under the watchful eyes of her in-laws. For her, Octavio's concern that she be "protected" in his absence is patronizing and oppressive. As a young woman her duties include tending to the needs of all of her extended family as well as her immediate one. There is nothing romantic, convenient, or quaint about living in overcrowded conditions where her work responsibilities are increased quantitatively and her time with her own children is decreased and diminished qualitatively.

Morales depicts these women as survivors who face the cultural double standards that allow men privileges that are not extended to women and who sacrifice their values and needs for the sake of their family's. They also demonstrate agency in determining certain aspects of their future and in resisting oppressive conditions at home. Milagros Revueltas and Pascuala Pedroza are married to men who are sexually unfaithful but who are good providers nonetheless. Although Morales does not explore the consequences of male infidelity, he does hint at the internalized social pressure women face to be silent about their unhappiness. Pascuala, for example, remains silent about her husband's infidelity even though she knows he has children with another woman: "When she contemplated the pride and excitement her children had for their father, she did not complain" (Morales 120). Her tolerance, as well as Milagros's, is neither ennobling nor degrading but demonstrates the economic and social dependence fostered by sexist double standards and a gendered division of labor. Nana, on the other hand, voices her complaints about Octavio's nighttime soirees in the gambling world, and she takes bold initiatives to achieve what she wants. For instance, when Octavio refuses to rent an available home in Simons town, Nana speaks to the company foreman and moves the family into the house without consulting her husband. The women of *The Brick People* are not portrayed as protofeminists, but in depicting sexism in the home, women's awareness of it, and the limitations with which they are confronted, Morales makes these conditions and inequalities available for critique.

There are other female characters portrayed in the novel, including the Anglo women of the Simons family, Mexican elites who are dispossessed of their land, and a *curandera.* The Simons women, the wives and mother of the *patrones* of the brickyard, belong to a different social and class order that is reinforced by notions of a racial order, which adds to their feelings of superiority over Mexicans. They, too, operate in a world that has different roles for men and women, but with the financial resources of their husbands available to them, they cultivate themselves as "benevolent" social elites. Though they are by no means primary characters in the novel, in their construction of a paternalistic social order over Mexicans they are complicit in the perpetuation of racial domination even as the world is "modernizing." Their social status allows them to affect the social discourse about Mexicans. Edit Simons, known for organizing the orchestra of Simons Brickyard workers, agrees to be interviewed by a sociologist who "had heard of the wonders which the Simons had accomplished with housing for *their* Mexicans," the subject of the sociologist's work (124, emphasis mine). Edit's comments to the sociologist reveal her patronizing outlook even as she attempts to challenge stereotypes about Mexicans and historicize their social status:

> Our Mexicans are not those heavy-lipped, sleepy-eyed Latins reclining in the sun, too lazy to seek the shade. . . . You must consider that behind those dull eyes lies the tragedy of the nation. I agree, the Mexican is basically lazy. Their idleness is caused by a lack of mental development resulting from decades of violence and oppression. . . . We do not approve of unscrupulous landlords who provide only one toilet for an entire court which may house five families or more. . . . Simons housing, on the other hand, is excellent. . . . The Mexicans are childlike in their desires and accept what they are given. Seldom do they question their situation. . . . Mexicans, like cockroaches, are extremely adaptable. They will survive anything. Many might perish but there will always be survivors to propagate the race. They're just like cockroaches. (125–26)

The comparison of Mexicans to cockroaches is a recurrent reference in the novel that has a double meaning: it is both a pejorative and an enabling term.[15]

Moreover, this referent is the primary link to the folklore in the novel, which serves as a critique of the construction of history as merely a series of events; this reference emphasizes the significance of interpretative authority. As an element of the folkloric, cockroaches represent the subalternity, resistance, and agency of Mexican men and women and provide a more comprehensive and enabling depiction of their collective history. Folklore functions as an alternative way of interpreting the "public" events privileged by historians.

"Indescribably large brown insects," spiders, and especially cockroaches appear throughout the novel. When "cockroach" is used as a noun, it usually functions as a pejorative reference to Mexicans, often to imply a supposed lack of hygiene or to justify treating them as inferior beings. For example, when the Montebello city council is trying to demonstrate the harm being caused its citizens by the brick dust, a doctor testifies that "Mexicans were able to breathe the red dust and survive. The presentation provided the necessary convincing evidence to allow everyone in the council chambers to conclude that the Mexicans were subhuman creatures, cockroaches equipped by nature to be unconsumed by such horrible living conditions" (257–58). It is also used as a simile to describe their living conditions and social status. In these cases it may refer to the subhuman conditions in which Mexicans are forced to live. When the Revueltas were homeless, Octavio "condemned himself for bringing his wife and children to living like cockroaches of the earth" (272). Moreover, in addition to functioning as a semantic term, cockroaches are a ubiquitous presence in the novel at key moments of crisis—deaths, sicknesses, and legal and extralegal land transactions. As was mentioned earlier, cockroaches are metonymically connected to Mexicans and land as one of the "magical" elements of the story. Their presence at these times of crisis is a signification that extends beyond the metaphorical level and must be seen, instead, in the context of the ongoing power struggle between Anglos and Mexicans. At times, the roaches are seen by only one person; other times they are a grotesque element of scenes of violence and death. The multiple levels of meaning the referent assumes in this novel suggest that interpretive authority is central to the history being conveyed here.

In his essay "Dancing with the Devil: Society, Gender, and the Political Unconscious in Mexican American South Texas," José Limón explores the relationship between folklore and the political economy of race, class, and gender relations. The vehicle for his analysis is a collective narrative that emerges from different perspectives of people in relative positions of power and privilege to one another. Limón's essay is based on field work about an ongoing cultural phenomenon and the different interpretations people have of its significance. The subject of his work, then, is a discursive event that requires critical interpretation, not an empirical one that requires verification. His mission is to "understand how . . . folkloric phenomena could be integrated into an interpretive account of political economy, an account of race and class domination" (DD 228). The same concerns are germane to a reading of the folkloric elements in *The Brick People,* but they raise a different set of issues. Morales introduces folklore in the form of "fantastic" elements of the characters' historical and contemporary narratives and of cultural practices, such as *curanderismo.* The author recognizes folklore as a practice of people living in opposition to those who have the resources and social power to produce official histories. He does not, however, attempt to lay bare its significance or offer an interpretation to the reader; rather, he presents it as one more element of a larger narrative that must be reconciled with other versions of history, of cause and effect. Such a democratic presentation of official and unofficial histories privileges neither one and promotes multiple readings of the same text, what Limón calls a shared, collective model of reading (and narrating) that "produces and enhances [a community's] collectivity even while allowing their different perspectives" (234). Morales, I would argue, is thus simultaneously representing and participating in this narrative phenomenon.

Fredric Jameson's theory of the political unconscious and its relationship to the master narrative of world history is central to Limón's theory of a collective narrative. Limón relies on but revises Jameson's three-fold model of analysis that identifies various horizons of reading: political history, social classes, and the ideology of form. In addition to proposing a collective model of reading, his revision of Jameson's theory dehierarchizes the horizons of reading by placing greater emphasis on the value of political history because it is in the everyday lived experiences of people that we find the stories of those who are most susceptible to the "degrading experiences of the social contradiction of capitalism" (232). This double revision of Jameson's model allows us to better appreciate the value of the social nature of folklore and its significance as a site of meaning.

As a recurrent referent the roach becomes an important component of a collective narrative that suggests an awareness of Mexicans' subordinate status and a reminder that an alternative narrative to the prevailing model of social relations exists. The metamorphosis of doña Eulalia into thousands of insects after her family is terrorized defending their land is echoed when doña Santa Bartolo decides to sell her family's land after her husband is killed. On the day the contracts are signed between Bartolo and the Simons brothers, Joseph and Walter notice two large brown insects on her dress. The connection between the change in land ownership from the Mexican elite to the Anglo capitalists and the presence of these insects is made clearer as the narrative progresses. Though they may be transformed into bugs or reduced to living in conditions of squalor, the Mexicans of the novel are not harmed by the insects. In contrast, the Simons family, representing the new social order, are plagued by insects. Each death in their family is accompanied by the presence of roaches. The males of the family all die horrendous deaths in which their bodies are contaminated by roaches. Joseph Simons goes insane after he witnesses millions of brown insects devour a family of street people. From that point on, he wants to eat only insects. He dies after a fall in his backyard. Like his brother, Orin Elmer, the first Simons brother to die after his body is invaded by insects, Joseph is found with thousands of insects emerging from underneath and within his body. Walter Simons, the last living *patrón,* chokes to death on insects while he is sleeping. Each of these deaths is written in the same tone as other events of the novel; there is no attempt to explain them as extraordinarily bizarre. Interpreted as the "ordinary" consequences of other events, the continuing reappearance of the cockroach as a signifier of the folkloric assumes an equally important status as "official" history. Furthermore, each time roaches appear in the narrative, it is after the Mexican community has been affronted by the power of the Anglo *patrones.* They are thus by association emplotted as a sign of moral retribution and vengeance by Mexicans. Orin Elmer dies after the local priest solicits the help of the Simons to replace the original granite cornerstone of the Catholic church. Because it was dated May 1, 1913, the priest orders it removed; he does not want the church to support any Bolshevik dates "for fear that it might inspire subversive activities among the Mexicans of Simons" (Morales 76). Rosendo Guerrero, one of the Mexican foremen, attributes his death to a telluric-human curse; his is the first death resulting from contamination by insects and thus establishes a pattern of cause and effect. Joseph is overtaken by insects immediately after the onset of the Depression, when Mexicans become the targets of racial violence, scapegoating, and deportation policies because they are seen as the cause of the United States' economic problems. By the time Walter dies, the bizarre circumstance of his death is mentioned almost as an afterthought. "Walter Robey Simons had choked to death by a plague of brown insects that had inundated his mouth while he was calmly sleeping in his bed in a hotel in Paris. That morning the workers heard the news unperturbed, for after all Walter Robey Simons was just another *patrón*" (280).

This casual acceptance of the absurd is understood by Walter as one of the conditions that accompanies modernization and capitalism. When his mother dies a strange death after choking on a kernel of rice, puncturing her esophagus, and turning her head 180 degrees without moving her body, Walter tries to console the family by saying, "We simply have to accept these occurrences. The more technologically advanced we become, the stranger the happenings" (137). Walter promotes modernization and who attempts to recreate the hacienda system of labor in Simons after he visits the Hearst ranch in Mexico. His visit to Mexico is filled with encounters that reinforce the literal and metaphorical connection between Mexicans and roaches, beginning with the roach that scurries across the floor as he makes travel arrangements to Guanajuato. When Simons arrives at Rancho Mexicana USA, Hearst explains that the name signals that even though the ranch is on Mexican land, it is all American. Outside the ranch house the *peones* are condemned to live in squalor and feed on dead animals. Walter witnesses the subhuman conditions they live in and the brutal treatment they receive at the hands of the ranch authorities and can think only that the *peones* must not be human. His description of what he witnesses from that point on portrays them as insects. When he later confronts Hearst about the brutal treatment of hungry women and children, the events are denied and a narrative of people being caught stealing is constructed to justify what he witnessed, a story he knows is not true. Walter views two models of the hacienda system in Mexico and chooses to model the Simons Brickyard after the more benevolent one. He realizes, however, that central to both is the idea of absolute power.

When the Simons employees receive a photo of all the workers, they are proud because they see it "through the filter of company ideology" (Gutiérrez-Jones 89); living under Walter's system of benevolent patronage, they believe it captures "the sense that they were part of a great working family" (Morales 119). Photos are not objective. Indeed, as John Berger and his co-authors argue in *Ways of Seeing* (1972), photographic images unmask the ideology behind the organization of visual imagery. With the invention of the camera people came to realize that "what you saw depended upon where you were when. What you saw was relative to your position in time and space" (Berger 18). Two women, Milagros Revueltas and Pascuala Pedroza, share an alternative interpretation of the company photo that illustrates their economic, cultural, and social situation. These women notice the repression, tiredness, and overall state of unhappiness of the workers. Their insight also suggests a wariness of the technology of the camera as well. Ostensibly, this wariness is based upon a folk belief about the ability of cameras to capture the spirit of the object of its gaze and enslave it; however, a critique of modernization is also a direct critique of capitalism and the alienation of workers. In terms that echo Marx, Milagros makes her critique at two levels of production: "It is a photograph of sad prisoners, of tired slaves. Of men angered for being where they are at. As if they are forced to do what they do, not want to do. . . . I don't like the photograph because it is a result of a machine that reduces men. It makes them tiny; it squashes them and smears them on a piece of paper. And that way we cannot embrace them" (Morales 119). Pascuala's reaction is a similarly high-charged emotional response that has multiple levels of meaning. She says to her husband, "Gonzalo, you look tired, completely drained. It's because you work day and night. That is not right, Gonzalo. The children miss you at home. . . . You can have your photography; it is an exercise of another world. I'm afraid that someone, if they want to, could burn it and you too would burn" (120). The women's critical reactions to the photograph, informed by folk beliefs about "black magic" that can be performed to harm someone through a representation of them and cast in terms that are critical of the political economy at work, are articulated as concerns about the violence and mystery of technology. Their reactions also entail a critique of the inequalities of the domestic and cultural economy in operation. It was noted above that the husbands of these two women were having extramarital affairs. It is this aspect of the home economy, shaped by the larger context of the workplace and the social divisions of labor it produces, that they critique when they complain that their husbands are men "we cannot embrace," "who work day and night," and whom "the children miss." In their interpretation of the photograph, they make a social and moral critique that is informed by insight into the interrelatedness of economic and gendered relations of power. These women's critical insight into the multiple levels of the economy of meaning enables Morales to depict the contestatory relationship of representation between folklore and official history.

Elsewhere in the novel, females display an interpretive power that links a moral economy with a conception of history. El Eco, the daughter of one of the brickyard laborers, experiences a vision on the night of the 1906 San Francisco earthquake. In her vision she sees a great serpent whose body runs underground throughout the state as the cause of the tremors. The moral of her vision, she says, is "that the great serpent would twist and turn until we as a people would have the necessary children to reconstruct a homeland here in this place" (55). Some of the men suggest she is crazy; others derogatorily reduce her vision to a "story": "earthquakes are earthquakes and nothing more. You act like a bunch of superstitious Indians!" García claims, and here I agree with him, that "the dream relates the theme of reconquest through the employment of Pre-Columbian religious symbolism, in particular the figure of Quetzalcoatl—the Plumed Serpent and the symbol of the greatness and humanity of the Pre-Columbian world" ("History, Literature" 194). This biological reconquest and recapturing of the lands will rectify the historic wrongs of deterritorialization and conquest. El Eco's dream is modernist in its projection of cultural reunification and wholeness based upon a glorious past; however, although it is informed by a belief in a homeland, it is cast not as the desire for a nation-state but the belief that a homeland, and the degree of political and economic self-determination that implies, are necessary for a peaceful coexistence with the world.

El Eco's vision is a culturally informed phenomenon, an interpretation of a single event. *Curanderas,* on the other hand, operate as readers of everyday life. Their work is not limited to the physical well-being of their patients; rather, they believe in a holistic approach to communal and individual health. The first reference to a *curandero* in the novel is made when one of the foremen declares that Orin Elmer Simons's contamination by insects is the result of a curse, not an illness that a modern doctor can cure. Rosendo suggests to Walter Simons that a *curandero* be called. Walter listens and is willing to concede to Rosendo's wisdom, but Joseph Simons cannot be convinced. He considers *curanderos* quacks who thrive on the superstitions of Mexicans. He uses what Limón calls, in a different context, the racist and "delegitimizing language of evolutionary discourse" (*DD* 183) to reject the suggestion: "Damn you, Walter, neither Orin Elmer, nor I, nor mother believe in witches, in stupid Mexican superstitions! I will never allow my brother to be treated by ignorant Mexican Indian witch doctors" (Morales 81). Thus traditional communal medicine is juxtaposed against the modern, and the modern fails.

In "Culture and Bedevilment," the concluding chapter of *Dancing with the Devil,* Limón explores the significance of a well-known healer in South Texas at the turn of the century who "became a symbolic figure of dissent from the new social order and its value" (*DD* 193). And as Limón astutely notes, when one historicizes the place of healers in a society under transition, their real and symbolic status can tell us much about the role of culture as a site of resistance to a new hegemony. Unlike modern doctors, healers function by prescribing natural herbs, not synthetic medicines; their motivations are not monetary but entail healing as an end in itself. They strive to provide their charges with a meaningful point of stability in a changing world. Moreover, drawing on Macklin's research on female healers, Limón notes that they are "powerful figures of androgynous critical difference" (194). "The role demands an androgynous combination of nurturing compassion and openness along with a willingness to exercise the power, authority, and decisiveness necessary to confront and conquer spiritual and existential dangers. In these senses . . . healing constitutes a role that transcends gender" (Macklin, qtd. in *DD* 194). Limón asserts that in a "multivocalic reliance on and transformation of a range of material and non-material resources . . . the *curandera* eschews any singular model of rationalistic, distanced, objectivist discourse. Rather than singular rationalism and empiricist representation of ills and cures, the *curandera,* it might be said, works by evocation . . ." (205).

Limón's work is extremely useful here because Morales's own narrative strategy and the role of *curanderas* in his novel illustrate the value of evoking culture and its contrasting values against a source of domination. Doña Marcelina Trujillo Benidorn is the most prominent and the only named *curandera* in the novel. She makes three appearances: she attempts to cure Edward Hickman before he commits a kidnapping and murder, but she is unable to change his destiny; she foresees Maximiliano Revueltas's imminent death from lung disease caused by the dust from the brickyard, but he comes to her too late for her to intervene; and lastly, she successfully treats Octavio Revueltas for the *susto* mentioned earlier. It is important to mention doña Marcelina's limitations here, for Morales is not attempting to exaggerate or romanticize her abilities. Her work does play an important symbolic function for the community, though, and for Octavio in particular.

When Milagros takes her son to visit doña Marcelina, she thinks of "the narratives of their life that they had often repeated to each other" (Morales 283). In this instance, the *curandera's* curative, therapeutic powers are introduced to us in her role as interlocutor. She is not just a passive listener who counsels by trying to readjust her patients' interpretation of events. She communicates as an equal, sharing the narrative of her own life. Besides the herbal remedies she gives him, doña Marcelina invokes the spirit of her ancestors to assist her in the healing ritual. Octavio's sickness is psychological and spiritual, not physiological. After a series of disappointments in the labor strikes, his disillusionment with the lack of commitment and discipline of his peers in making the cooperative store a success, with his inability to find housing, and with the confirmation of his subordinate social status as marked by the fire department's refusal to save his house, Octavio is spiritually devastated. Throughout these events he does not accept the condemnation of the Anglos, nor does he scorn his community and culture. He is disillusioned with collective action, but there is nothing to suggest that this is a permanent attitude. The series of crises he faces destabilizes his world. His willingness to see a *curandera* demonstrates faith in cultural practices and is a sign of his desire to achieve well-being within the community. According to Octavio Romano, the act of entering into a relationship with a healer signifies a desire to maintain tradition; the act of healing "provides a meaningful point of stability during a moment of instability which has been brought about by an illness or incapacitation of some kind" (Romano, qtd. in Limón, *DD* 191). Octavio's visit to doña Marcelina constitutes a desire to anchor and solidify his identity against the ongoing siege against his economic, cultural, and psychological well-being.

Octavio's crisis is precipitated by his defeat as a worker and by a loss of faith in his community. The alienation he experiences, which is eating away at his life from within and manifests itself as malnourishment, has brought him to doña Marcelina. This alienation, his sickness that has left him feeling out of touch and to some extent out of control of his world, is depicted in the healing scene by the painting that hangs in the room where he will be treated by the *curandera.* As Octavio enters the house he feels he is "about to step into a photograph" (Morales 285). This feeling is confirmed when he sees a painting with two praying figures, a man sitting on a wheelbarrow in front of a woman, that mirrors the setting of the room. To reinforce the notion of Octavio's sickness as a form of alienation, Eric Fromm's distinction between the mental state of insanity and alienation is particularly fitting for a reading of this scene: "the person who is in touch only with his inner world and who is incapable of perceiving the outer world in its objective action context is insane, the person who can only experience the outer world photographically, but is out of touch with his inner world, with himself, is the alienated person" (Fromm 183). Doña Marcelina does not attempt to speak to Octavio about the cause of his illness; her treatment consists of invocations and a struggle with the octopuslike form it has assumed in his body, which she ingests into her own. When she is finished, a nine-day follow-up treatment is prescribed, and Octavio notices that the man in the painting is no longer present. He is on his way to being cured.

In referring to the economy of meaning embedded in histories, Hayden White makes an analogy between history and psychoanalysis: "The problem is to get the patient to 'reemplot' his whole life history in such a way as to change the *meaning* of those events for him and their *significance* for the economy of the whole set of events that make up his life. As thus envisaged, the therapeutic process is an exercise in the refamiliarization of events that have been defamiliarized, tendered alienated from the patient's life history, by virtue of their over-determination as causal forces" (White 87). Grounded as it is in a culturally specific ritual of healing and occurring in the penultimate chapter of the novel, Octavio's perception of history takes on additional importance. The last chapter of the novel presents Octavio's effort to reconcile the present with the past by focusing on his family's life in Mexico, their motivations for leaving, and their journey to the United States. The violence and social turmoil resulting from the Revolution is only one factor; many relatives had already moved to Simons under a labor-contract agreement before the Revolution. It is the modernization campaign of Diaz's regime and the infiltration of U.S. capitalism that precipitate his family's migration. His memories reveal not just economic violence but injustice and inequality that existed in the home as well. Just as Gonzalo Pedroza justified his absence from home when he was having an extramarital affair, so too did Octavio's grandfather. His recollection of his mother's discovery of the affair and her "wailing along that lighted road to [their] house" echoes the legend of *La Llorona,* about women's pain and abandonment. (In the next chapter, the enduring impact of the legend of *La Llorona* is discussed at length.) His memories and the narrative he re-creates of their relocation is also full of instances of kindness and generosity by other displaced and disenfranchised people. His narrative ends when he recalls the reunion of the entire family in Simons, and his son brings him back to the present moment by suggesting they begin the construction of their home. In the context of this narrative of displacement and horrors suffered at the hands of the revolutionaries in Mexico, Octavio's house should not be seen as selfish, individual desire but as a testimony to survival and endurance in the face of a political history in which allegiances are not simply about identity but about the abuse of power and capitalism. A strict reading of the political history of *The Brick People* would fail to account for the full range of power and its abuses, as well as the multiple sites of resistance to class, race, and gender domination. There can be no single comprehensive narrative of a people. As Hayden White wrote, "The more we know about the past, the more difficult it is to generalize about it" (89). And, indeed, this appears to be one of the objectives of Morales's narrative. The past has to be continually rethought from different perspectives if we are to make sense of our own lives on an individual and collective level. We should be skeptical about the forms in which knowledge is transmitted, since neither official histories nor folklore will provide a full account; taken together, however, they can enable us to piece together a fuller account and begin the process of reconciling the tension we experience when the past appears irreconcilable with the present, or the experiences of different communities appear to tell different stories with varied emphasis on one's gendered, racialized, or national status. The experiences of migration, deterritorialization, and exploitation that characterize descriptions of the Migrant Generation are not a phenomenon of the past; they continue today in the ongoing process of northward movement by Mexicans and other Latinos. Judged against the written history and ideology imposed on the Migrant Generation, *The Brick People* gives us a more fragmented prism through which to examine the multiple levels of experience, oppression, and resistance by migrants. It has been said that "Central to the idea of immigrant worlds is the idea of nation—not the nation as a bounded geographical unit but the nation as an ideological force" (Bhattacharjee 19–20). The consequences and strategies involved in retaining or rejecting a Mexican identity are multilayered and cannot be understood by political histories alone, for in the context of a political economy that permeates all aspects of life, domestic politics and everyday cultural practices assume added significance as sites of resistance. We now turn our attention to an activist, significantly a woman, who refused to live her life in the private sphere of home but instead helped to forge a larger sense of community and validated the intellectual and political capacities of women.

Sara Estela Ramírez: "Una Rosa Roja en el Movimiento"[16]

We need newspapers that awaken the public spirit; the patriotism of the people is entangled in a terror with no name.

—Sara Estela Ramírez, 1903

As a journalist her reputation was such that a Mexican writer, on learning of her premature death, exclaimed: "The most illustrious Mexican woman of Texas has died."

—anonymous (from Sara Estela Ramírez's funeral oration. Printed in *La Crónica,* August 27, 1910)

I have often proposed to my colegas *our need to seek out the precursors to contemporary Tejana writers. . . If we continue to remain indifferent to them, the world will never read their words, nor will we know the contentment of their literary companionship as Tejanas.*

—Teresa Acosta, "Sara Estela Ramírez and Me," 1991

The prevailing scholarship on the Migrant Generation characterizes them as a group whose primary intentions were to live and work free from the turbulent political and social climate of the Mexican Revolution. Many scholars acknowledge that some of these migrants viewed their relocation to the United States as a temporary condition. For these people, a return to their native country was imminent as soon as more peaceful conditions emerged. According to historians, the political sentiments of this generation, whether they intended to return to Mexico or not, were negligible to nonexistent; their chief concern was to survive, not to actively participate in political life. Such a perspective characterizes these Mexicans as politically passive, meek, naive, and isolated. What scholars have often overlooked is that migrants were not, and are not, an homogeneous class of people who necessarily share a common identity, ideology, degree of education, or vision of the future. Among migrants are people who see their relocation as a temporary inconvenience, others who may consider their move as permanent, those who are worried about their immediate survival and who have no predetermined long-term goals, and others who, in the first quarter of the century especially, considered themselves political exiles. This last group is often not considered officially "migrant" because they remain oriented to their nation of origin. However, I would argue that this orientation is always mediated and affected by the specific context in which they are living and working. Just as those migrants who saw their move to the States as a temporary hiatus, so too did exiles believe that they would return to Mexico when conditions improved. For a variety of reasons, many people who once thought they would return did not, including such a notable figure as Ricardo Flores Magón, who died a political prisoner in Los Angeles. We will now turn to one of his contemporaries, an exceptional figure of this period of migration.

Born in the state of Coahuila, Mexico, in 1881, Sara Estela Ramírez moved by herself to Laredo, Texas, at the age of sixteen. A journalist and poet, Ramírez's concern with issues affecting Mexicans on both sides of the border demonstrates the ambiguous nature of national borders and identity. As an eloquent and outspoken woman, Ramírez can be found to have a filial relationship to contemporary feminists, an assertion that is central to Hernández-Ávila's dissertation and essays on the author. Teresa Acosta has written an essay that investigates the relationship between herself as a contemporary Chicana poet and Ramírez as one of her most significant political and poetic precursors. This essay, "Tejana History as a Poem: Sara Estela Ramírez and Me," explores the relationship between the political and the personal in both Ramírez's and Acosta's poetry. Writers like Ramírez serve as inspiration and reminder to the contemporary Chicana poet of the significance of "historical foundations." Acosta wrote:

> Even though I had grown up in conservative McGregor, Texas, my early exposure to the Chicano and Black Civil Rights movements through the media had greatly inclined me to study my people. Once this tendency matured, I realized that my family's stories—often transmitted through my grandfather—reverberated in my imagination and memory and I could not abandon them. The Chicano movement also echoes in my ears with words like: Raza Unida, Chicanas, bronze power, Crystal city, "Mexico Chico." It also resounds for me as a history that needs to be told through poetry, fiction, and drama. (12)

Acosta's intent is to historicize not only her political consciousness, but also her poetic one: "I have often proposed to my *colegas* our need to seek out the precursors to contemporary Tejana writers. I sense that our *abuela cuentistas* are hiding in family archives but could end their silence with our help. If we continue to remain indifferent to them, the world will never read their words, nor will we know the contentment of their literary companionship as Tejanas" (3). Acosta ends her short essay by offering two original poems that she says connect Sara Estela Ramírez to her and her generation. One of them is a particularly good example of the historical poems that Acosta is so adept at writing. "Apparition (ca. 1896)" articulates Acosta's relationship to history and to her Chicana precursors, and her felt obligation to insert historical memories into her poetry. The fact that she was motivated to pen this poem soon after reading David Montejano's *Anglos and Mexicans in the Making of Texas: 1836–1986* testifies to the complementary nature of these forms of documenting history.[17] The apparitions that haunt her are those of her Chicana/o predecessors:

> *Now*
> *each day*
> *they talk to me on my walks—*
> *wondering when I will put them in my poems.*
> *They insist on whispering in my ear*
> *how things were*
> *on their ranchitos*
> *and*
> *how they lost their land in sales*
> *"fair 'n square" under somebody's law.*

Acosta's identification with Ramírez is based not only upon gender and ethnicity, but upon shared notions of justice and resistance and a common way of responding—through the written word. Acosta's sense of affiliation and camaraderie with Ramírez thus symbolically and materially connects contemporary Chicanas/os to past and present Mexicans on both sides of the border. This poetic essay on Ramírez reminds us that the legacy of racism and land dispossession still affects people of Mexican descent today. Contemporary multinational issues, like the North American Free Trade Agreement (NAFTA) and the environmental degradation that devastates both sides of Texas's southern border, remind us too that there is a continuing need to practice a politics that transcends the border. Thus the writing and the reading of the poetry and political practices of the present and the past assume added significance.

My objectives in this section are multiple: I am particularly interested in viewing the writings of Sara Estela Ramírez as a point of departure for further study on the relationship between culture and power in turn-of-the-century South Texas. By examining this feminist writer's articulation of a politicized cultural identity in the first decade of the twentieth century I hope to illuminate strategies of subversion and containment surrounding gender and national identity. I argue that Ramírez's work revises our understanding of this period. Her activism and her writing testify to the conditions that gave rise to a complex performance of gender and ethnic identity and ideology; consequently, Ramírez defies common misconceptions of women that existed in her own time and persist today due to historical neglect. Unlike Morales's, however, her work emerges from this era and is deeply invested in an interventionist, not just revisionist, making of history. Reassessing her work in light of how this generation has been represented does, however, revise our understanding of it, because it illuminates areas of the cultural, political, and social life of this era that are often overlooked. My work is deeply indebted to and follows the important groundbreaking recovery of her letters, as well as her journalism and poetry that originally appeared in *La Crónica* and *El Demócrata Fronterizo,* by Emilio Zamora, Jr., and Inés Hernández-Ávila, whose 1984 dissertation, published under the name of Hernández-Tovar, is the most extensive analysis of Ramírez yet, and without which my own work on Ramírez would not be possible. As is clear from the analysis that follows, this study not only utilizes Hernández-Ávila's translations of Ramírez's poetry and prose, but is influenced by her feminist historical framing of the life of this important Tejana poet. Hoping to expand the known corpus of Ramírez's work, I followed their lead.[18] It is clear from Zamora and Hernández-Ávila's work that a large body of Ramírez's pre-1908 journalistic and artistic endeavors are yet unrecovered. Ramírez's literary work is best appreciated if understood in the context of the times.

Sembradores: *The Role of the Alternative Press in Sowing the Seeds of Change*

The significance of writing, in all forms and genres, at the turn of the century cannot be overstated here. In *Sembradores, Ricardo Flores Magón y El Partido Liberal Mexicano: A Eulogy and Critique,* Juan Gómez-Quiñones has pointed out the important role that newspapers played as organizing vehicles in the Southwest between 1904 and 1910 (*Sembradores* 23). Furthermore, the binational leadership of the PLM considered it important to foster transregional solidarity with Mexicans in the United States and Mexicans in Mexico, as well as with Anglos. This strategy stemmed anarchists' refusal to accept the legitimacy of national borders or corrupt nation-states. The role of the alternative press in turn-of-the-century South Texas was significant and is a necessary context for our specific discussion of Sara Estela Ramírez. In her dissertation on the life and literature of Ramírez, Hernández-Ávila contextualizes Ramírez's work by noting the multiple reasons why there were hundreds of Spanish-language and bilingual newspapers established in the Southwest after the U.S.-Mexican War: "Experiencing linguistic and cultural alienation from the dominant society's media organs, finding its reality misrepresented or omitted completely from those organs, taking into consideration that whenever the Anglo media did report ostensibly radical Chicano activities that those activities were misrepresented or inaccurately reported, the Mexican community had ample reason to initiate its own means of journalistic efforts" (Tovar 110). Some of these papers were written for a specialized audience. *El Defensor del Pueblo,* for instance, was an organizing tool for the federal labor union established in Laredo in 1905. *Lucha de Clases,* published out of San Antonio in 1915, was overtly ideological, while *La Lira,* distributed in Laredo around the same time, was a musical news sheet.

The alternative press thus fulfilled a variety of needs, both general and specific. As Hernández-Ávila has said, Mexican-owned newspapers served as a "cultural arm by which to respond to historical circumstance" (108). For instance, unlike English-language newspapers, many of the publications in Spanish commonly offered a literary page (Richard Valdés, qtd. in Tovar 111). The inclusion of cultural sections in addition to local, national, and international news items as well as editorials suggests an awareness of the importance of cultural cohesion to work against the forces of racial domination. Furthermore, it is important to note that the newspapers addressed to a Mexican-origin audience throughout the Southwest emerged only in areas of high concentration of that population; economic viability was an important consideration. According to Richard Valdés, Mexican communities developed literary associations and debate societies to encourage and refine their linguistic skills and maintain their culture, as well as to provide a means for ingroup education in response to exclusion from the Anglo-dominated educational system (qtd. in Tovar 111–12).

The proliferation of politically oriented alternative newspapers in the Southwest at the turn of the century can also be seen as yet another organizing practice carried over from Mexico. In Mexico, anti-Díaz propagandists were frequently jailed and opposition presses shut down by the Mexican government in efforts to silence resistance. James Cockcroft reports that in 1901 and 1902 at least forty-two anti-Díaz newspapers were shut down and fifty journalists imprisoned (*IP* 102). In 1908, Ricardo Flores Magón showed John Kenneth Turner a list of fifty papers founded and suppressed and one hundred journalists jailed for their support of the Liberal Clubs founded by the PLM (Duffy Turner, qtd. in *IP* 102). The threat to the nation-state posed by journalism was not unique to Mexico but it does point to the powerful role of the press in facilitating a national vision that was at odds with the state apparatus and ideology. In the U.S. context, however, the form that popular Mexican nationalism assumed was of a different sort, requiring an "imagined community" that, in contrast to Benedict Anderson's definition, was not inherently limited and sovereign (Anderson 6).

In turn-of-the-century South Texas, independent newspapers fomented a cultural nationalism that transcended national borders by creating a sense of community that extended wherever Mexicans resided—in this instance the idea of the nation was *not* geographically bounded but culturally and linguistically specific, as well as cognizant of the widely shared experience of political, economic, and racial domination. The role of the Spanish language in bilingual and Mexican-owned newspapers that reported on and to the Mexican community was crucial in facilitating the imaginable alternatives to a different social order. Anderson states that by creating a unified field of exchange and communication, printed language has historically helped lay the bases for a national consciousness (44). Mexicans' place in the shifting social order of the first decade of the twentieth century, along with a common language and culture, defined their sameness, and newspapers provided them with a sense of community by articulating their shared experiences. Simultaneously, then, these same factors defined them as different than the Anglo community. Newspapers geared toward the Mexican community not only engaged the imagination of their audiences, they were also deeply historical. In producing a debate and challenging dominant discourse some journalists proposed other alternatives as possibilities; domination and subordination were denaturalized. Sara Estela Ramírez's poetry and prose is a prime example of this; in her work race and class domination were posited as perversions of another, "national" history. By engaging and fulfilling the needs of a specific audience, Mexican-oriented journalism in the United States participated in what Anderson calls a new way of linking "fraternity, power, and time," because it encouraged large numbers of people to think about themselves and others in new ways. Much of this journalistic activity was subjective, interventionary, and proactive.

Ramírez's role in advancing the alternative press movement as a feminist, a writer, a teacher, and a political activist points to her recognition of the power of the written word. Indeed, given the paucity of biographical information on her, it is primarily through her contributions to and associations with various journalistic enterprises that we know anything of her at all. Upon arriving in Laredo, Texas, in 1881, Ramírez was befriended by Clemente and Jovita Idar, the publishers of *La Crónica,* an independent Spanish-language newspaper that was an advocate for the *mexicano* community. The Idars were key players in organizing and sponsoring El Primer Congreso Mexicanista, an important statewide political conference for Mexicans held in Laredo in 1911. Through *La Crónica* the Idars led a campaign of journalistic resistance to the process of "incorporation" into the hegemony.[19] In fact, the school for children of Mexican descent where Ramírez taught was a collaborative effort with which the Idars were involved. From 1908 until her death in 1910, just a few months before the official beginning of the Mexican Revolution, Ramírez was a regular contributor to *La Crónica,* publishing essays, poetry, and literary articles frequently. However, she began writing for them soon after she arrived in Laredo. In her first letter to Ricardo Flores Magón in 1901, Ramírez thanks him for "undeserved praises" that she had received in the PLM's official newspaper, *Regeneración.* According to Inés Tovar, the *Regeneración* staff had seen her work in the pages of *La Crónica.* Ramírez also wrote for *Vesper: Justicia y Libertad,* a four-page weekly with a circulation of eight thousand published by Juana Gutiérrez de Mendoza, an early supporter of the Magón brothers. This involvement with the alternative press was to characterize Ramírez's political work for the remainder of her life.

Besides revealing the tense political climate of Laredo in 1901, which made it difficult to organize, Ramírez's first letter to Magón makes an explicit link between political and journalistic work:

> There are faint hearted spirits, conquered by terror, who refuse to support a cause, no matter whether they understand that cause to be just and noble. That is happening right now here in Laredo, where the woman is the mobile and the most powerful lever . . . it has been impossible . . . to form the liberal club to which I refer in my "Convocatoria". . . . We shall form the club without any doubt, besides it is necessary to prepare the terrain; for which, with the help of my esteemed friend, Mr. Vidal Garza Pérez and other liberal enthusiasts we shall form a small liberal newspaper which will have as its name "La Corregidora" and which will appear the Wrst day of June; as of today, its director and proprietor [Ramírez] is honored to place it at the unconditional orders of "Regeneración" and of all the clubs and liberal parties of the Republic.[20]

As Ramírez suggests in this letter, the hostile social conditions at the turn of the century situated women in a unique position to facilitate social change. According to Zamora, harassment of political organizers by local police often forced the men to be less conspicuous and prompted the women to fulfill the more public roles. Gómez-Quiñones quotes a woman observer as saying that, in Texas at least, "women had to continue the work men were now too intimidated to do" (*Sembradores* 36). Harassment of PLM members in the United States was persistent in Texas, Missouri, and California. Under the direction of the Mexican Consulate, Pinkerton men and Furlong detectives kept them under surveillance, launched raids, and assaulted Party members (25). Police repression only further highlights the risks assumed and the dedication of women like Ramírez. This was not a position that went unnoticed by the PLM leadership, who, in a time and place when it was rare, actively solicited the participation of women in political and social change. This is not to say, however, that their gender politics were radical or without contradiction. Women's strong participation was used as a means of highlighting men's weaknesses in an obvious attempt to shame men who would be bothered by this "unusual" reversal of patriarchally sanctioned gender roles. An example of this is the praise given to Juana Gutiérrez de Mendoza by *Regeneración* upon the appearance of *Vesper:* "Now when many men grow feeble and through cowardice withdraw from the struggle, considering themselves insufficiently strong to recover our liberties . . . there appears a spirited and valiant woman, ready to fight for principles which the weakness of many men has permitted to be trampled and spat upon . . ." (qtd. in Mirandé and Enríquez 204–205). The women activists were not above appealing to certain notions of manhood, either. In her 1977 dissertation on the participation of women in the Mexican Revolution, Shirlene Soto reports that in a July, 1903, issue of *Vesper,* Gutiérrez de Mendoza and Elisa Acuña y Rosetti "scorned Díaz's fear of them and taunted him as being the first man afraid of women" (qtd. in Tovar 20). For their opposition to the Díaz regime, they too would spend time in jail and find it necessary to go to Texas for temporary relief from official harassment. In the construction of the Migrant Generation as we know it, the work and lives of these women have not found a place. It is only in the specialized histories of labor, journalism, and "women" that these women's work is acknowledged. That people like Sara Estela Ramírez are not included in historical narratives attests to the limited notions of identity and leadership that inform that genre of historical literature.

Hernández-Ávila has suggested that the name Ramírez chose for her independent newspaper, *La Corregidora,* signifies her commitment to fostering feminist ideas by acknowledging the important role that Doña Josefa Ortíz de Domínguez played in the 1810 Mexican War for Independence.[21] Doña Josefa is one of the few, if not the only, women in the pantheon of heroes of Mexican independence. As Hernández-Ávila has noted, Ramírez's decision to honor her legacy illustrates her ongoing effort to combine nationalism and feminism. Although no copies of *La Corregidora* are known to exist today, Ramírez's second letter to Magón informs us that she is going to suspend its publication in order to collaborate with two other PLM supporters to publish another paper, *La Verdad,* which would be produced in Austin. In this letter, dated September 25, 1903, Ramírez further elaborates on her role as a journalist and her conception of Mexican history. Lamenting the fact that she did not go to Mexico City, she wrote, "[Elisa] should have told you the reason for my staying in this city instead of realizing my trip to the capital. We need newspapers that awaken the public spirit; the patriotism of the people is entangled in a terror with no name. . . . We need to educate the people and awaken their energy. Our race is a race of heroes, a worthy race and it will know how to make itself respected" (qtd. in Tovar 121). Besides pointing to the significance of newspapers as an organizing medium, this passage also illustrates the racialized climate of the turn of the century that characterized social and political relations. Furthermore, it also points to the early PLM strategy of promoting cultural nationalism as a means of generating support. According to Tom Nairn, the concept of nationalism as a necessary stage of development for all societies is common to both materialist and idealist philosophies: "It denotes the new and heightened significance accorded to factors of nationality, ethnic inheritance, customs, and speech" (Nairn 333). Thus, in their writing and organizing, PLM proponents depended on a *mexicano* identity to promote awareness of shared struggle. Nationalism was perhaps easier to promote than class consciousness, for it had a fully developed and accessible culture that enveloped a larger number of people whether or not they had a class consciousness. The promotion of a national identity was a convenient organizing strategy that left the primary contradiction of the world economy and class interests unresolved (335). And yet Mexican nationalism in the United States had a dual focus that makes it idiosyncratic. Most theorists of nationalism would agree that "it is an internally determined necessity, associated by Marxists with, for example, the creation of a national market economy and a viable national bourgeois class" (333). Yet the rallying cry around a national identity, exemplified by Ramírez's invocation of a "race of heroes," was not directed solely at those interested in transforming the Mexican state, but also at Mexicans in the States who were being affected by unequal development in the process of expanding capitalism. As an ideology, Mexican nationalism need not be Mexico-specific but, rather, a response to a transborder capitalism that simultaneously prompted migration from Mexico and forced people into a new relationship with capital in a land that was both foreign and familiar. In their writings, Ramírez, the Magón brothers, and other associates of the PLM did try to address the concerns of a changing global economy, class interests, and national identity as well as gender. We will take a look at some of these writings shortly, but first we should once again question why a prominent international activist has proven so difficult to fit into a single national history or literature.

Very little documentation of Ramírez's role in the PLM exists. Although she is briefly mentioned by James Cockcroft in *Intellectual Precursors of the Mexican Revolution,* she is not included in most historical accounts of the Mexican Revolution or PLM histories (*IP* 118).[22] To date, her work has received only minimal attention from Chicana/o social and literary historians, Hernández-Ávila's 1984 dissertation was pathbreaking in contextualizing Ramírez's life and making her work available to a larger audience. Her active membership in feminist organizations like *Hijas de Cuauhtémoc* and *Regeneración y Concordia,* as well as the liberal anticlerical organization *Club Redención,* show her to be aware of the value of using multiple and specialized organizational strategies to address different ideological problems. *Regeneración y Concordia* evolved from *Hijas de Cuauhtémoc,* which was originally formed in prison by Elisa Acuña y Rosetti and Dolores Jiménez y Muro, two other independent journalists and ideologues who were important precursors to the Mexican Revolution. *Hijas* was formed with the intention of guiding the struggle of the Revolution toward the radical transformation of women, while the stated goals of *Regeneración y Concordia* were "the betterment of conditions for Indians and the proletariat, elevation of the economic as well as moral and intellectual status of women, and unification of all revolutionary forces" (Mirandé and Enríquez 206). Hernández-Ávila has suggested that these women incorporated *Regeneración* into their name, aware that it was the title of the official PLM newspaper, as a way of "suggesting to the men that the other necessary element for national regeneration was the harmony that could lead them to unity and to triumph in their resistance to Porfirio Diaz's regime" (Hernandez 18). Although, in print at least, the PLM was progressive in its attitude toward the inclusion of women in political struggle, the *junta* was composed solely of men.[23] Inasmuch as these women were obliged to accommodate preexisting political organizations in order to maximize their efforts, they did not allow their critiques of those organizations to go unheard. In like manner, it is through the vigilant and insightful recovery work of scholars like Hernández-Ávila and Zamora that the contributions of these intellectuals are not lost and through which Chicana feminists can discover their intellectual antecedents throughout the southwestern United States.

The PLM's Insurgent Politics

During the first two decades of this century, the Texas-Mexico border was a hotbed of political unrest. Not only was there a steady increase in the number of people migrating northward, but many Mexican nationals were using the Texas side of the border as a base of operations for political and military actions in Mexico. In addition, many Texas Mexicans were launching irredentist guerrilla warfare against U.S. state and federal governments. Historian David Montejano has said that this was a period of transformation between two different economies that "assumed a sharp racial character" and "undermined the accommodative 'peace structure' which for two generations had contained the sentiments and politics of race antagonism" (*AM* 104). Montejano's characterization deserves further scrutiny for a number of reasons, not the least of which is the assertion that prior to this change in the economy social relations were more benignly racist and less violent. Considering the very violent process of "incorporation," the period preceding reconstruction, to describe it as a peace structure is misleading. By "peace structure" Montejano means "an accommodative arrangement between the leaders of the victors and those of the defeated—through which the commercial goals of Manifest Destiny could be pursued" (8). In this instance Montejano conflates class interests with leadership, a conflation that also occurs frequently among historians who utilize a generational schema in their interpretive analysis. Specifically, "peace structure" refers to the way the Anglo and Mexican elites were able to work together without threat to one another's class interests, an arrangement that was altered to the detriment of the Mexican elite in the first quarter of the twentieth century. This narrow definition of who and what constitute leadership elides the violence and territorial displacement experienced by the subaltern classes and ignores any notion of leadership other than that exercised by the landed elite. Furthermore, the creation of a new hegemonic order on the frontier was not established without formidable resistance on the part of Mexican subalterns. The violent nature of life in South Texas during the reconstruction period is only an extension of the same process of incorporation.

The importance of turn-of-the-century South Texas's changing economy should not be dismissed here. The rise of commercial agriculturalism devastated the ranch economy of South Texas, and the violent or otherwise coerced displacement of Mexican landholders that had occurred in other parts of Texas finally occurred along the border as well. On April 10, 1910, *La Crónica* took note of the sudden transfer of land: "The Mexicans have sold the great share of their landholdings and some work as day laborers on what once belonged to them. How sad this truth!" (qtd. in *AM* 113). The hostilities between Anglos and Mexicans reached their zenith in 1915 during the aftermath of the thwarted *Plan de San Diego*.[24] Sara Estela Ramírez worked and lived in the period immediately preceding these events in Texas, it is then that she performed her organizing and educational work on behalf of the PLM with the hopes of launching a revolution against Díaz in Mexico.

So unstable was the situation between Anglos and Mexicans in Texas in October of 1915 that approximately one half of the entire reserves of the U.S. Army were stationed along the U.S.-Mexico border between Laredo and Brownsville. This situation also marked one of the only times U.S. military aircraft were deployed to quell civil unrest within its own national borders. According to Colin MacLachlan, Mexican president Venustiano Carranza used the situation to his advantage by bringing charges against Ricardo Flores Magón and the PLM's newspaper, *Regeneración*, in an effort to have the blame for the unrest along the border placed upon the PLM. This explanation seemed plausible to American officials because PLM members had been arrested several times before for launching raids against the Mexican state from the U.S. side of the border. Moreover, many editorials condemning violence and social injustice against Texas Mexicans, especially against the abuses endured at the hand of Texas Rangers, appeared in *Regeneración* (MacLachlan 58).

The link between the PLM's agendas in Mexico and the United States is relevant here because the literature of this generation of *mexicanos* cannot be defined on the basis of national citizenship. There was a working relationship between *mexicanos* on both sides of the border for social justice, especially around issues of labor. Juan Gómez-Quiñones says that "through PLM activity Chicanos contributed to the Mexican Revolution and concurrently participated in the radical movement in the United States. Through PLM propaganda Chicanos were provided with a relatively modern revolutionary ideology and a radical critique of liberalism" (*Sembradores* 1). While there has been acknowledgment of the role Mexican Americans played in the radical movement of the first quarter of the century, few historians besides Gómez-Quiñones have acknowledged the international dimensions and mutual support that existed between the two communities across the border. The PLM organized and propagandized extensively throughout the Southwest on behalf of trade unionism. Moreover, in addition to the PLM, there were many other organizations that Mexicans used to articulate their demands for fair and just treatment. The major labor unions affecting Mexicans in the United States were the American Federation of Labor, its affiliates, and the Industrial Workers of the World. The AFL was the conservative alternative to more radical unions; consequently, it had a limited appeal to those trapped at the bottom of the laboring class. The IWW, on the other hand, had a major impact on the Mexican population in the States. Its organizational focus was the semiskilled and unskilled workers, many of whom were immigrants. The IWW often worked with the PLM ("The First Steps" 16). However, by 1920 the IWW had collapsed due to harassment by the government and also due to management's decision to deal with more conservative unions, such as the AFL, thus determining their workers' union themselves.

In 1900 the Flores Magón brothers, Ricardo and Enrique, joined the call issued by the wealthy reformer Camilo Arriaga for the formation of liberal clubs. In June, 1903, Ricardo was prohibited from publishing in Mexico. Having already been sent to prison three times, he chose exile in the United States. On January 4, 1904, Ricardo and Enrique crossed the Texas border and were temporarily hosted by Sara Estela Ramírez. Out of necessity, they took jobs as farm laborers and dishwashers in Laredo. According to an associate, the negative treatment of Chicanos had a strong impression on Ricardo (*Sembradores* 23).

Regeneración was reestablished in San Antonio and first published on November 4, 1904. It maintained a subscription list of twenty thousand, with distribution in Mexico and the U.S. Southwest (25). Almost immediately Mexican and U.S. officials in San Antonio began harassing the group. The group moved to St. Louis, where local police, along with Pinkerton men and Furlong detectives hired by the Mexican government, held them under constant surveillance. When Mexican officials succeeded in convincing the U.S. government to charge several of the PLM organizers with violating the Neutrality Act, a defense effort was put together that created the conditions for collaboration with non-Mexican radicals such as Emma Goldman and Mother Jones (MacLachlan 22–23). According to John Hart, Ricardo Flores Magón served as a catalyst for union organizing among farm and industrial workers. Flores Magón was considered an internal threat to U.S. security because of his ability to rouse the human and political resources of Mexicans and Mexican Americans (Hart, "Foreword" ix).

For many years, the PLM was a positive factor in inspiring nationalism among Mexicans, but it abandoned this position after 1911 and was among the first to transcend it in its embracing anarchism (Gómez-Quiñones, *Sembradores* 2). Flores Magón lived in the United States for eighteen years, from 1904 until his death in 1922. Throughout this time the PLM propagandized, recruited, and organized among Chicanas/os and from within the Chicana/o community. Their activities stretched across all the southwestern states from Texas to California. According to Gómez-Quiñones, the PLM was strongest along the Texas border, the mining areas of New Mexico–Arizona–El Paso, and in the urban center of Los Angeles (27).[25] The turn of the century was an important time in Mexican labor history. Despite government repression of unions, there were 250 strikes in Mexico in the years 1877 to 1910. This legacy of organizing is an important component of the personal and collective experience that migrants to the United States carried with them in their move northward. This experience helped provide the groundwork for their interaction within the U.S. economy.

The newspaper/propaganda arm of the Federal Labor Union in Laredo, *El Defensor Del Obrero,* reveals a dual impulse within the union that further illustrates the ideological context in which Ramírez wrote. On the one hand, according to Zamora,

> *El Defensor* often served notice of an impending socialist millennium, [but] it also followed a reformist course. It generally favored a trade unionist movement to prepare the Chicano masses for the class struggle, essentially within the existing racially antagonistic order. . . . While a strict application of socialist trade union principles did not meet the needs of Chicano workers, *El Defensor* never fused nationalist and working class principles into a common ideology. . . . Ethnic tensions indigenous to the Texas environment prevented an exclusive application of socialist thought to conflictual situations. ("Chicano Socialist" 223–26)

Zamora adds that trade union ideals and working-class ideology "were kept alive by Chicano socialists such as Sara Estela Ramírez and José María Mora through mutualist and social action organizations." Zamora credits Ramírez with being the "principal local propagandist" for socialism in Laredo (226). The PLM actively supported the empowerment of women and encouraged them to assume proactive positions in the revolution. Several of the male leaders, including Práxedis Guerrero and Ricardo Flores Magón, made public statements on the PLM's position on gender equality. Perhaps the best-known statement on this position is Ricardo Flores Magón's editorial "A La Mujer," which appeared in *Regeneración* on September 24, 1910. In an essay entitled "'A La Mujer': A Critique of the Partido Liberal Mexicano's Gender ideology on Women," Chicana historian Emma Pérez has examined the complex relationship women members of the PLM were obliged to negotiate even as they challenged demands that the nationalist struggle be privileged over resistance to gender oppression. For the *junta* leaders, Emma Pérez argues, a woman's role in social change was "to nurture men" (*DI* 465).[26] Ramírez chose to ally herself with one of the most important revolutionary groups of her time, yet she also had to struggle against their limited conceptions of gender. Moreover, she chose to act autonomously—both organizationally and socially. Her strongest alliances and allegiances appear to have been with like-minded women. Considering her own outspokenness and association with autonomous feminist organizations, Sara Estela Ramírez can be seen as an intellectual and ideological precursor to Chicana feminism and Chicana/o literature. Although she eventually began working with a different faction of the PLM than that led by Ricardo Flores Magón, it is evident in her letters to him that she felt absolutely comfortable expressing her consternation over what she considered the petty and personalized nature of the quarrels between some of the male leaders, especially Camilo Arriaga and Magón. In a letter dated March 9, 1904, she tells Magón:

> I've been sad and weary, Ricardo, of so many struggles and mutual antagonisms. I will tell you frankly, that I am disillusioned with everything, absolutely everything. . . . I don't want to analyze the causes of your quarrels with Camilito, I believe you both are right and both to blame. . . .
>
> I am going to cause you great pain with my frankness and also with my resolution: I am separating from the group of my dear brothers and associated with Camilito I will continue the struggle. I don't believe my

decision, absolutely spontaneous, will make me deserving of your enmity. . . . that should not be, on the contrary, with groups working in this way, separately and in distinct places, we will be in harmony and we will get along better. (qtd. in Tovar 141)

According to Cockcroft, "Although deep ideological and social differences underlay the division between Arriaga and Ricardo Flores Magón, apparently neither one of these men wanted these points to be emphasized at such an early stage in the struggle against Díaz. Unity, even in the face of their own personal quarrel, seemed preferable" (*IP* 119). Arriaga was a member of the Mexican bourgeoisie, and though he funded many of the activities of the PLM, he was often unable to resolve the contradictions that emerged from his shifting class interests. Though he was adamantly anti-Díaz, he guarded his family fortune. Cockcroft suggests that ideologically he was between Guerrero on the Left and Madero on the Right (64–71). Though it was with this group of the PLM that Ramírez eventually aligned herself, this may have been more a function of geography than an ideological split with Magón. In 1905, Arriaga was working out of San Antonio, while the Magón brothers had moved their base to St. Louis.

In Ramírez's letters to Magón it is obvious that they developed a close friendship. Although most of the letters convey questions and explanations regarding organizational logistics or news, they also contain family news and personal thoughts and feelings on the social climate and political situation in which she lived. In a letter dated October 21, 1903, Ramírez asks Magón if he would be willing to undertake the sale of her pamphlets of poetry to an editorial house in Mexico:

You know better, much better, these matters and can advise me or tell me what would be best for me to do. I would like for you—and to this end I will send you soon a copy, to consult with some editorial house. The number of poems that you sell and the price will be unconditionally accepted by me.

Don't forget that this will be always only if you have the time; I know you are weary of work and in no way would I want to disturb you. (qtd. in Tovar 129)

In the next known letter to him we find out a bit more about her poetry and Magón's response to it. She writes, "Was my little volume of poetry a bundle of memories for you? I find in each page a memory and sometimes it hurts me to remember the beloved period of heroic struggle. Why did it end? eh? When will it return?" (qtd. in Tovar 132). Although Ramírez's words suggest that the poems she refers to are about an earlier period of Mexican political history, it is difficult to tell from these lines whether her poems are about their contemporary struggle or that of a preceding era. The personal pain and confusion she expresses suggest that she is lamenting a change in their present political activities. By the time of this letter the PLM had been driven underground in Mexico, so their financial difficulties had increased. The organization was also undergoing internal conflict as well as being the target of government repression. Later in this same letter Ramírez refers to what sounds like another collection of poems: "My 'Rhymes' have suffered, like their author, a series of unspeakable contrarieties. It is time they rested in a sealed box. As soon as they come I will send you the promised gift; I will choose the color, thank you for leaving it to my choice and thank you also because my little volume will accompany your favorite books. I will add one for our brothers" (qtd. in Tovar 133). The limited circulation of Ramírez's poetry and her own diminutive adjectives in the above two references to her "little" volumes of poetry refer to an economy of production and consumption that not only reveals her humility in regards to her creative work, but is also, perhaps, indicative of material limitations. A consistent concern and problem the PLM faced was a lack of funding. This, too, is prevalent in her letters, as are the emotional ups and downs of political activity, which were made all the more difficult by the repression they faced, both inside and outside Mexico: "Arriaga wrote yesterday with the alarming news, to complete our misfortunes, that assassins abound and our associates are in danger . . . and do you know how that danger traps them? Destroyed by the lack of resources! My black hours increase, my beloved Ricardo, with the sad situation we are all in. I think about my dear imprisoned, ill sisters, and my heart hurts not to be able to help them" (qtd. in Tovar 137).

Through the PLM liaison to the northern region Ramírez was deeply involved in local events in Laredo. In a brief newspaper article titled "Yesterday and Today," which appeared on the front page of *El Demócrata Fronterizo* on March 27, 1909, Ramírez demonstrates her unflinching stand with workers by pointing out that it was the inefficiency of management and poor working conditions that were the source of local labor problems, not unionized workers who went on strike. Her prolabor stance did not go unacknowledged by workers. On April 17, 1909, *El Demócrata* published a speech she delivered to the Society of Workers on its twenty-fourth anniversary celebration the previous evening. The speech is structured around a central proclamation of "Combatants, forward!" The intent of her speech is to celebrate the work already done and to inspire its continuation, as the following excerpt illustrates:

> For such a simple expression I need no elegance of language, rhetoric, nor any wisdom. To call a worker my brother, I need only my heart, and to tell him "Forward!" I need only, like him, a soul swollen with the desire to struggle. . . . That is mutualism, a noble mission of truth, sublime and holy mission, mission of charity that nations ignore or have forgotten; nations, whose workers are dispersed, segregated, strangers to each other, and . . . how many times, sad to say, more than strangers, subject to ruinous enmities. . . . Mutualism needs the vigor of struggle and the firmness of conviction to advance in its unionizing effort; it needs to shake away the apathy of the masses, and enchain with links of abnegation the passions that rip apart its innermost being; it needs hearts that say: I am for you, as I want you to be for me . . . . That is how it is. The worker is the arm, the heart of the world. And it is to him, untiring and tenacious struggler, that the future of humanity belongs. (qtd. in Tovar 189–90)

In this speech Ramírez articulates her anarchist and revolutionary perception of the world. The fundamental "problems" she identifies are the divisive and insidious nature of the nation-state and the intra- and interclass divisions that keep workers separated from realizing a more equitable and just existence. Significantly, she makes no distinction between mutualist and unionist functions.[27]

The Poetry of Sara Estela Ramírez

Of Ramírez's surviving poems, few address overtly political themes. They divide into three general categories: occasion pieces dedicated to friends or family on their birthdays, poems of unrequited love, and philosophical poems about beauty and nature. Of the third category, many are informed by despair and an awareness of unequal social conditions. Hernández-Ávila has noted that "the impulse that provoked and urged these activists to continue was the same that often caused them to despair, that is, the reality of the social conditions which they witnessed and experienced" (265). It is primarily in her philosophical poems that Ramírez embeds political critiques and conveys her understanding of Mexican history and her vision for social change. Given her role as an activist and organizer and the intensely political nature of her letters to Magón, one might expect Ramírez's poems to be more overt calls to political action and explicit criticisms of oppressive conditions. Keeping in mind that many of her journalistic and creative works remain unavailable to contemporary readers, we are left with the task of interpreting the form, style, and content of those writings that are available.

Ramírez's writings on nature, love, and philosophy share qualities with the romantic style. The political relationships she comments on are masked by references to nature. In one way this acts as a geographical strategy of containment through which she can articulate her ideas. Given the intense repression that her political affiliates experienced, she may have utilized this style as a means of deflecting the attention of authorities. The repressed content is, nevertheless, still there as an allegory to be interpreted by the discerning reader. In *The Political Unconscious,* Fredric Jameson states that ideology, production, and style interact to create multiple levels of meaning; a reader must see through these interactions before he or she can discern the ostensible subject of a literary artifact and its ideology (Jameson 214). Thus far, much detail has been provided to help us interpret Ramírez as a historical figure; following Jameson, what I would like to suggest is that her style and form of writing also needs to be historicized, with the understanding that she was aware of her own poetic strategies.

In her poetry and essays Ramírez utilizes a rhetoric of pathos to inspire sympathy for her subjects. For instance, the following lines are taken from a poetic essay entitled "The Kiss of an Angel," a eulogy for an eight-year-old girl named María.

María was an orphan and very poor,
so poor, that her humility made a pain-
ful contrast beside the other educated
girls with rich clothes, sovereign
haughtiness, smiling cheeks and looks
always lively and mischievous.

More than once I accompanied
María to her house. Such humility, such
poverty, better said, such misery!

> *The little work her mother did was*
> *barely enough to prolong the agony of*
> *the life of four little ones.* (qtd. in Tovar 172)

Hernández-Ávila suggests that María symbolizes "Mexico, the nation, the people, the poor and suffering masses whose liberation was so urgent for these [PLM] revolutionaries" (Hernandez 14). Much of Ramírez's writing bears strong stylistic resemblance to essays in *Regeneración* written by Enrique and Ricardo Flores Magón. The following excerpt is from a piece entitled "Bread!" written by Enrique Flores Magón in the February 28, 1913, issue of the party newspaper:

> Don't cry my child. Some day a good man will give you bread. . . . His mother, a young woman, with pale and trembling lips from hunger and brilliant eyes with the fever of weakness, walked the streets of the city of Mexico, searching in vain for work.
>
> Nobody wanted to employ her. Of what good was a weak girl? . . . The night now had been closed a long time, and still the unhappy woman, with her feet sore from the unceasing walk, still hunts a piece of bread for the hungry child.
>
> Such is the life in Mexico.

Sentimentality in their writings subsumes class consciousness with nationalist sentiment. Tom Nairn suggests that political mobilization of people of underdeveloped nations often resorts to commonplace sentiment as well as cultural and racial identities because the insurgent group does not have access to economic and political institutions or "high" literature. Accordingly, though nationalism exploits difference, it is also invariably populist. "For kindred reasons, [nationalism] has to function through highly rhetorical forms, through a sentimental culture sufficiently accessible to the lower strata now being called to battle" (Nairn 340). The claim that nationalism has a cultural base that can be manipulated rhetorically, as in the above excerpts by Flores Magón and Ramírez, is buttressed by Benedict Anderson's assertion that nationalism is a cultural artifact (Anderson 4).

The titles of other poems provide insight into Ramírez's philosophical disposition, which kept her motivated despite the harshness of life. Further, they illustrate that her poetry and poetics, her very identity as a politically engaged artist, are integral to her life as she documents and makes history.

"Rise Up!," "Flee!," "A Sigh and a Tear for You," "Black Diamonds," "Before the Threshold: In an Album," "How I Love You: For María on Her Day," "The Blank Page," and "The Struggle for Good" are all poems that, as their titles suggest, are both socially and personally reflective and action-oriented. "Rise Up!" and "Flee!" suggest two contrasting responses to imminent danger—rebellion and retreat. "Black Diamonds," "The Blank Page," and "The Struggle for Good" invoke the process of addressing contradiction, uncertainty, and resistance in the creation of something tangible and meaningful. "How I Love You: For María on Her Day" is dedicated to her little sister. The first two stanzas are sufficient to glean the manner in which she embeds her outlook on life in poems to others, even on occasions that were meant to be celebratory:

Last shadow of my family,
Of my loves the supreme ideal,
Faith that strong winds do not sweep away,
Light that lasts with an eternal ray
Over the ruins of my hope
and the despoiling of my dreams,
How I bless your sweet name
and your existence. . . . How I love you!
In my darkness you are a star,
For my sorrows you are consolation,
You have lullabies for my tears,
your caresses are as a mother's,
For this, sister, I bless your love
And in you I condense
All the world of my immaculate
and lasting love. (qtd. in Tovar 146–47)

Other poems, such as "Only to the Stars: for Celvia's Album," express a cynicism that appears to be born from a betrayal of confidence:

Do not confide, beauty, your secrets,
to anyone on this earth;
Neither to the souls, that are nests for lovers,
Nor to the waves, that are nests of pearls,
Guard stubbornly from everyone your secrets,

> *From the mischievous breezes,*
> *From the light, from the arpeggio, from the roses,*
> *—your twin sisters—*
> *Because all of them, thus . . . roses and souls*
> *In colloquies of love are indiscreet.*
>
> . . .
>
> *Only to the stars!*
> *Do you know why? Because they will not profane*
> *The sublime confidence of your love . . .* (qtd. in Tovar 154–55)

The reality of the world, of the human condition and human failures, took its toll on Ramírez. She was unable, even for the sake of momentary celebration, to offer someone illusory hope that she can find happiness in the present condition of the world. Hernández-Ávila has said that "if in her poems to men, Ramírez expresses torment and disappointment, in her poems to young women, she finds cause for hope, in the midst of her despair" (244). The despair and disappointment are clear, but the "celebration" of sisterhood that Hernández-Ávila wants to ascribe to her writings is harder to discern. In "Black Diamonds: For Yuly (on her day)," Ramírez seems bitter when she writes, "I have searched in my heart for something beautiful, one ray of sun for your sad and eternally orphaned soul. . . . I have found nothing there worthy of you. I want to speak to you of life, and death knots up my throat; I want to speak to you of laughter and dreams, and tears choke me." The only positive insight she can offer Yuly is strength drawn from harsh experience and the knowledge of their condition that comes from it, but this is enough. As women living in a world that constrained their actions, they were forced to come to terms with their situation. She ends her essay by trying to identify some aspect of their experience that can represent hope. "How many times have you said it . . . 'it is prohibited' it is true! Prohibited pleasure is prohibited, love is prohibited, illusion, hope, it is true! But, on the other hand, beloved Yuly, there is something that no one or nothing can prohibit us. . . . That the darkness of our souls like diamonds give out light. . . ." Through this intensely emotional piece we see her succeed in describing dimensions of female experience, indeed of all of human experience, which here is specifically situated in a time and place often not accounted for in historical narratives. "The Struggle for Good" uses the metaphor of a journey to emphasize the path to political consciousness that must be informed by communal experience so as to minimize the pain of mistakes, hardships, or defeats:

> *The stumblings hurt much, but*
> *they teach much; they make light,*
> *and in the struggle for good light is*
> *necessary, much light, to dissipate*
> *the darkness of the path and to pre-*
> *serve its austerities.* (qtd. in Tovar 179)

As Ramírez's membership in an anticlerical association attests, she was an opponent of institutional religion, yet much of her poetry utilizes the rhetoric of faith, if only to subvert it. Her faith was secular. She believed in people's ability to overcome adversity. To this end, those experiences that strip people of their illusions are seen as valuable, even when they are painful. Her aesthetics regarding beauty and nature are often informed by power dynamics. These concerns are apparent in the opening lines of "Reef."

> *If the reef does not cause anger, if it does*
> *not discourage*
> *To be wounded twice on the same rock;*
> *If not two times, then not a hundred; the*
> *arena of combat*
> *Provokes triumph and not surrender.*

The anarchist tendency toward martyrdom, or the "heroic stance," as Gómez-Quiñones calls it, is also apparent in the above lines. Hernández-Ávila compares Ramírez's views on traditional religion and spirituality with Ricardo Flores Magón's as expressed in his essay "Vamos Hacia la Vida" (July, 1907). In these writings, both Ramírez and Magón express a philosophy of praxis, in which combat and opposition solidify and clarify one's determination. As with much of her work, Ramírez's embrace of struggle testifies to women's activism in military and cultural struggles occurring on both sides of the border. While soladera images and iconic figures have been recuperated to work against the effacement of female participation in the Mexican Revolution, little work has been done to illustrate the role of women in ideological struggle, debate, and cultural practices.[28] Here we see the poet articulating an active relationship to struggle and pain, not as victim but as a warrior-philosopher. Thus her use of pain as a metaphor for political struggle both documents and revises our limited understanding of women activists.

As is apparent in the above lines, "Reef" begins by privileging adversity. The last four lines, however, suggest that the struggle is a learning process in which metaphysical illusions must be overcome:

> *Blessed be the reef that relieves pain!*
> *Blessed be Lucifer for the rude assault!*
> *Blessed be the obstacle that teaches us*
> *To struggle and always to climb higher!* (qtd. in Tovar 183)

In firm opposition to the church, Ramírez aligns the struggle for good with Lucifer, the rebel angel who in Christian belief is thrown out of heaven for not accepting his preordained place in the hierarchy of heaven. Written in 1908, her lines echo Magón's 1907 essay, wherein he proclaims, "Submission is the cry of the vile; Rebellion is the cry of men! Lucifer, rebel, is more dignified than the henchman, submissive Gabriel" (qtd. in Tovar 234). Hernández-Ávila notes that in their writings both Magón and Ramírez claim resistance as a sacred act that demonstrated that "the spirituality of the Magonista and other revolutionary movements (like Zapata's) was grounded in a faith in the people and in the possibility of radical change" (234). In positing secular change in spiritualist terms, the Magonistas sought to engage the imagination of their audience in culturally familiar forms. Flores Magón's essay grounds revolutionary practice in the material world and aligns the Mexican Revolution with democratic struggles occurring elsewhere:

> Nations no longer rebel because they prefer to adore one god in place of another. The great social commotions that had their genesis in religions, have been left petrified in history. The French Revolution gained us the right to think; but it did not gain us the right to live, and the winning of this right is what the conscious men of every country and every race intend to do.
>
> Here is why we revolutionaries are not in pursuit of a chimera. We do not struggle for abstractions, but rather for material things. We want land for everyone, and for everyone bread. Since perforce blood must be shed, may the conquests gain benefits for all and not just for a particular social caste. (*Sembradores* 100)

As one of the chief propagandists for the PLM, Magón wrote more lengthy and developed essays than Ramírez's in *El Demócrata Fronterizo* or *La Crónica.* Although her own writings often remained abstract and less explicit in their analysis, Magón's influence upon Ramírez is evident.

One of Ramírez's occasional poems is an explicit call to political action. "21 of March: To Juárez" was written during a trip to Mexico in the spring of 1908 to commemorate the anniversary of Benito Juárez's birthday.[29] "21 of March: To Juárez" is one of four poems dedicated to Juárez published by various poets in *El Demócrata Fronterizo* and *La Crónica* from 1906 to 1910.[30] In these poems the authors praise Juárez's traits as a "true" leader of the people for the political reforms he initiated. This poetic tradition, imbued with nostalgia for better social and political times, I would argue, is informed by a critique of the Díaz regime, for all that it was not. In "21 of March" Ramírez's nationalism is clear, as is her belief in the ultimate liberation of Mexico and the long, painful nature of political struggle and the human frailties that impede social progress. Ramírez celebrates the history of resistance to domination that is Mexico's legacy. In "21 of March" she invokes songs of liberation:

It is true that the deeds of my homeland,
which I adore,
As well as her heroes
Number in the thousands.
How many pages of gold
In that history of epic songs! (qtd. in Tovar 159–61)

According to the poet, Mexico's redemption will lie in the fulfillment of its destiny, a destiny to which past wars of liberation have served only as a "prologue sublime and irresolute." And though the poem is in honor of a historical figure, Ramírez wants her evocation of to rouse political action in the present. Ever the pragmatist, Ramírez knows that victory is not easily won but is the culmination of a long process requiring dedication:

All those feats,
Cheers that the mountains repeat
Like an echo of the Creator, drive us mad:
And it is for this that on going from mouth to mouth,
From heart to heart, it is forgotten

That the glory of the present is little,
And the work for the good is unfinished.
. . . It is only the fault of human effort
Which will forgive me if I find it to be the culprit.
(qtd. in Tovar 159–61)

Ramírez continued to be associated with the PLM throughout the first decade of the twentieth century. Although ostensibly written on March 21, 1908, "21 of March: To Juarez" wasn't published in *El Demócrata Fronterizo* until May 9, 1908, after her return from Mexico. A planned revolt against the Mexican government was scheduled for that summer and involved forty to sixty-four PLM groups. The date set for the rebellion was June 25, 1908. The signal for the different PLM groups to begin their revolt was to be an attack on Ciudad Juarez launched from El Paso, Texas. Six days before the scheduled rebellion the El Paso headquarters were raided by U.S. authorities. The raid seriously impeded the effectiveness of the overall rebellion, although it did not stop it completely (Gómez-Quiñones, *Sembradores* 33). The raid at El Paso was a result of infiltration by the U.S. government (MacLachlan 18). It was particularly damaging—a large cache of dynamite that had been provided by the miners of Arizona was captured.

It cannot be unmistakably proven, but it seems quite probable that the proximity of the publication of Ramírez's "21 of March: To Juarez" to the date of this offensive was not entirely arbitrary. The call to action and the prophesy in the poem anticipate future actions even while commemorating a glorious past:

I am happy, because I feel my heart
Shout like a prophet:
You, the indomitable Mexican people,
Look at the past and think of tomorrow,
You are yet most distant from your goal. (qtd. in Tovar 159–61)

The intersection of Ramírez's poetry and politics is nowhere more evident than in the above lines. A firm nationalist who believed that Mexico could win self-determination only through a popular revolution, Ramírez also believed that inspiration for the future must be drawn from the past: "Oh pages of yesterday, blessed, holy, / You are the pedestal of glory / To which our feet direct us." "21 of March: To Juarez" is exemplary of Ramírez's poetry because in it she utilizes the natural and the metaphysical to buttress her explicit political claims.

Ramírez as Chicana Poetic Precursor

In her last known poem, "Rise Up!: To woman," Ramírez urges women to action with words that echo contemporary gender analyses and establish her as a precursor to politically engaged Chicana feminist writers. In the following excerpt from "Rise Up!" she urges action that is based on an awareness of one's agency and informed by a demystified sense of self and not limited by constructions of gender that privilege or empower either males or females.

> *One who is truly a woman is more than goddess or queen. Do not let the incense on the altar, or the applause in the audience intoxicate you, there is something more noble and more grand than all of that.*
> *Gods are thrown out of temples; kings are driven from their thrones, woman is always woman.*
> *. . . Only action is life; to feel that one lives is the most beautiful sensation.* (qtd. in Tovar 194)

Ramírez does not specify an objective to which women should aspire; what she privileges is action as an end in itself. In his essay on Ramírez, Emilio Zamora suggests that based on her life and writings we might conjecture that she is urging women to "struggle for democratic rights," and certainly there is ample basis for this. Hernández-Ávila, on the other hand, links Ramírez's purpose in this poem with the philosophy of life proclaimed by Ricardo Flores Magón. Magón says that in addition to basic needs of food, shelter, and clothing, "the man of our times [needs] intellectual sustenance that will illuminate his understanding" (qtd. in Tovar 255). Hernández-Ávila points to Ramírez's feminist critique of the narrow, preconceived roles allowed women. In response to Ramírez's encouragement to women to "be a mother, be a woman," Hernández-Ávila comments that this is possibly "a compensation for her own lack of maternal guidance as well as her own realization that women can be 'mothers' for their sisters and fellow human being [*sic*] by caring for and sustaining them" (256). Zamora's and Hernández-Ávila's interpretations of this poem are not mutually exclusive. The poem urges activity: "Only action is life; to feel that one / lives is the most beautiful sensation." The poet's own life was a model of political, social, and intellectual activity. At times, she, in the company of other women, adopted a gender-specific strategy for addressing the concerns and problems particular to women involved in political movements in South Texas and northern Mexico. In this way, these women were able to influence the political activity and program being developed. In addition to the feminist critique, which rejects the position of the pedestal as objectifying, Ramírez also comments on the constructions of other forms of power that hierarchize human relations in the social and political realm. Her admonition that there is a choice to be made and that "before Goddess or Queen, be a mother, be a woman" is a call to embrace those positions that are more innately human rather than positions of relative power. Goddesses are seen in relation to gods, queens in relation to kings. A woman in one of these positions is dependent upon a relationship to a male for her power. Ramírez does not see woman as a function of the position of man. Despite the fact that her call for women to be mothers is a valuation of a social position that may be seen as limiting, it may also be read abstractly as a call for individual and collective regeneration, a continual process in the struggle for social change.

The eulogies written on both sides of the border in Ramírez's honor testify to her impact and her reputation as a committed social activist and respected individual. Eulogies are laudatory by nature and purpose; the ones published in *La Crónica* and *El Demócrata Fronterizo* after Ramírez's death in 1910 reflect her strong influence as a binational poet, journalist, and teacher. They also tell us much about her history and the hardships she faced. For instance, although it is never specifically identified, we learn from these eulogies, as well as from some of her letters, that Ramírez suffered a lifelong, painful physical ailment. *El Demócrata Fronterizo* published on its front page the eulogy from which the following is excerpted:

> The writer of exquisite taste, of easy and correct pen; the poet of feeling and of genius; the one who had just put on the double laurel of Moliere, with her precious drama "Noema," applauded enthusiastically in our theaters; the self-sacrificing teacher who distributed prodigiously the light of her intelligence, fertilizing thousands of young minds; the noble and generous friend, Sara Estela, descended to her grave at the fullness of her life, at twenty-nine years of age. . . . (qtd. in Tovar 198)

La Crónica published two eulogies on August 27, 1910, and the funeral oration given by Clemente Idar on September 5. The anonymously written eulogy of August 27 provides us with much biographical information. Its byline reads: "The Texas Muse is in Mourning! Sara Estela Ramírez The Favorite of the Texas Muses, Has Died!" The first two paragraphs are dedicated to establishing her relationship with *La Crónica:*

> With profound grief we deliver the news of the death of our collaborator and beloved friend Sarita, as we lovingly called her in this office, having occurred on the 21st of this month at twelve midnight.
>
> *La Crónica* has more than enough reason to dress this page in mourning, since the gentle and spiritual poet was a constant collaborator of our weekly and in these same columns her first poetic essays appeared, some twelve years ago, as well as her beautiful literary articles. (qtd. in Tovar 200)

This eulogy proceeds to tell her life story: her education, her relocation to various Mexican cities, and her move to Laredo, Texas, at the age of sixteen, where she taught Spanish at the *seminario* of Laredo. Her literary history is also documented, and we learn that *La Crónica* published her "first poetic compositions and literary articles which she produced when she was barely fifteen or sixteen years old," and of her editorship of "the strong literary newspaper *La Corregidora,*" published in Laredo and Mexico City, as well as the founding of *Aurora,* a literary journal whose publication she was forced to suspend due to her illness. *La Crónica* asserts her significance as a binational border poet and journalist in the following lines: "As a profound thinker and forceful writer, she deserved the respect and admiration of the entire Texan press and a large part of the Mexican press, especially in the states along the border, where she was considered the most noble, most sentimental and first of the woman poets of the region" (qtd. in Tovar 201). The eulogies written by Jovita and Clemente Idar celebrate her dedication, creativity, and intelligence and further testify to the impact Ramírez had on border communities.

Ramírez's writing belongs to a literature of political and social movement that saw the limitations of rigid notions of national identity. For her, geographical movement across national borders was strategic, part of a larger purpose of political education and propagandizing. The Mexican diaspora to the United States has been spurred by the economic, political, and physical violence that accompanies capitalism and colonialism, and it should be seen as part of the continuing legacy of transnationalism.

Conclusion

In 1915, shortly after receiving recognition from the U.S. government, Carranza issued an antistrike decree. The PLM's response was to issue a statement in the form of an appeal. With "To the Workers of the United States" the PLM leadership was trying to illustrate the interconnectedness of their labor struggles with those of U.S. workers. This statement examined the relationship between immigration and labor interests and asserted that "unless Mexican labor received economic justice in its own land, it would depress the wage level in the United States. . . ." Looking even further ahead, the PLM's leadership warned that eventually American industrialists would "transfer their operations south of the border to exploit cheap Mexican labor, leaving closed-down factories in the north" (MacLachlan 55). The insight of the PLM into the workings of capitalism is remarkable; they were able to anticipate a time in which the border could be constructed as a way to further the interests of capital to the detriment of workers, in much the same way that NAFTA was constructed before its passage. Such a discourse allowed for foreign investment of capital without an extended discussion of its responsibilities to workers or the environment.

In focusing on the international dimension of labor, the PLM transcended the limitations of the nation-state despite their acknowledgment of the value of nationalism as an organizing strategy. As an intermediary between the PLM leadership; a devoted activist, teacher, and propagandist; and a host for some of the most important and ardent intellectual precursors to the Mexican Revolution who were forced to flee their homeland due to repression, Sara Estela Ramírez must be seen as part of a political avant garde that refused to accept or respect restrictive notions of gender roles and national identity, national borders and citizenship status. Ramírez and the PLM viewed nationalism as a stratagem for living with the contradictions produced by class struggle in the racist context of the United States. As such, for the PLM and others, nationalism functioned as a "morally and politically positive force" (Nairn 331). In Mexico it assumed an added significance; for the class struggle it meant regaining control over the natural resources that were being dominated by foreign capital. Seen as part of the world political economy, the resurgence of Mexican nationalism before and during the Revolution represents the uneven development of history (335). For Ramírez and her cohorts, geographical movement across national borders was only incidental, part of a larger strategy of political education and propagandizing.

For Morales, on the other hand, the movement of Mexicans is characterized by the process and consequence of entering into a capitalist mode of production. He differs from Ramírez in that he is looking backward to reconstruct history. This form of representation requires that he be self-conscious of the way his perspective may be shaped by a current understanding of the past and by the form and structure of the novel as a genre. Writing from the perspective of the present, Morales opts to empower the often ignored subjects of history by locating, identifying, and representing their alternative mode of expressing oppressive social relations through folklore.

Mobility of Mexicans into the United States has been spurred by the economic, political, and physical violence that accompanies capitalism. However, rather than fleeing the source of violence, Mexicans and other Latinos have run into its vortex. This phenomenon of continuous migration of Latinos to the States has produced a historical problem (in social, political, and economic terms) that continually vexes dominant notions of the course of history and the place of migrants in generational constructs. In idiosyncratic yet similar ways, the insurgent activities and gendered deconstructions of power and politics that Morales and Ramírez articulate defy notions of the Migrant Generation as prepolitical and passive. The activities and concerns they represent in their literature reverberate today and are still germane for trying to comprehend the cultural and national identity of Mexicans in the United States. In their literature, these writers demonstrate that history does not belong to any single nation and cannot be contained by national borders; nor can it be understood in segmented, discrete, and otherwise arbitrary periods of time in which a given national and political identity is rendered as universal for an entire generation.

CHAPTER 3

Shifting Identities, Harsh Realities

Accommodation, Capitulation, and Subversion in the Mexican American Generation

Growing up in this country, Mexican Americans were increasingly more acculturated, bilingual, and, as a result, more politically functional. Formally educated to a greater extent than ever before, they became better socialized to their rights as U.S. citizens. Mexican Americans expressed pride in both their U.S. citizenship and Mexican heritage, although not without degrees of insecurity regarding identity.

—Mario T. García

The secular politicized aesthetics of Sara Estela Ramírez's poetry and journalism, as well as the subversive narrative strategies of Alejandro Morales in *The Brick People,* defy accepted notions of the Migrant Generation. The political activities of Mexicans in South Texas and in Los Angeles, California, documented by these writers not only undermine the dominant historical perspective that has characterized them as prepolitical, but also demonstrates that they had complex and shifting notions of national identity that were affected by their relationship with elites both within their community and within the Euro-American community. This chapter will examine literature of an era that has been labeled as the "Mexican American Generation" in relation to the notions of leadership, ideology, and identity set forth in Mario García's *Mexican Americans: Leadership, Ideology, and Identity, 1930–1960* (1989) and Juan Gómez-Quiñones's *Chicano Politics: Reality and Promise, 1940–1990* (1990).

As the title of García's historical narrative indicates, the Mexican American Generation is commonly considered to extend from the period simultaneous with the Great Depression to the emergence of the civil rights movement.[1] The two novels that will serve as texts exemplary of this period are Américo Paredes's *George Washington Gómez* and Tomás Rivera's *. . . y no se lo tragó la tierra;* the first is situated near the era's beginning, the second near its end. Within this thirty-year period, most Chicana/o historians acknowledge a distinct division between the pre– and post–World War II eras. It is the experience of Mexican Americans during and after the war that marks this intragenerational distinction. As Ramón Gutiérrez puts it, Mexican Americans, like other U.S. citizens,

> fought in World War II to make the world safe for democracy. Fighting beside other assimilated immigrants, they believed the national promise that when they returned home, the American Dream of social mobility and middle-class status would be theirs. . . . It was in this period, between 1945 and 1960, that America's global economic hegemony was truly consolidated. For white American men the dream was indeed realized. The GI Bill helped educate many of them. The consumer goods, the cars, the stocked refrigerators, money to spare, and government loans to educate their children soon followed. But the benefits, the dreams, and the cash were not equitably distributed. Blacks, Mexicans, and persons of Asian ancestry, all legitimately Americans, had been left out. (Gutiérrez 44–45)

The failed realization of social and political inclusiveness in the postwar period reminded many Mexican Americans that their subordinate social status was systematically affected by a racialized social order. This situation prompted many educated Mexican Americans across class divisions and political affiliations to organize on a mass scale and use the judicial system to challenge social, political, and economic inequities.

The literature of the Mexican American Generation contains the ambivalence and contradictions produced by ingroup class tensions, concerns that actually are integral to any era of Mexican American history. *George Washington Gómez,* like *Caballero,* was originally written in the mid-1930s. Paredes's novel was not published until 1990, but it stands as one of the few Mexican American novels of the first half of the twentieth century. Written almost simultaneously with Eimer and González's novel but set three-quarters of a century later in the same region of South Texas, *GWG* is one of the few novels about the pacification of the border from the point of view of a *tejano.* Thus, if Eimer and González's novel is about the occupation of the homeland, Paredes's narrative speaks to its hegemonic consolidation. Furthermore, because of Paredes's insight into the importance of identity and the insidious nature of institutionalized hegemony, this novel offers a useful prism for examining social conflict prior to World War II. In these several respects, it is different than later novels of immigration and migration that document movement from south of the Rio Grande to Greater Northern Mexico.

In addition to García's and Paredes's books, important texts for the post–World War II period are Juan Gómez-Quiñones's historical narrative *Chicano Politics: Reality and Promise, 1940–1990* and Tomás Rivera's account of the lives of migrant workers in . . . *y no se lo tragó la tierra* (1971). These texts sharply contrast with García's perspective on Mexican Americans. The second section of this chapter will contrast the construction of Mexican identity and agency by Gómez-Quiñones and Tomás Rivera against that posited by García and Paredes. Rivera's imaginative resolution to the problem of alienation in the life of Mexican farm workers in the United States serves to provide them with a historical awareness of their oppressive conditions and links him politically with the writers of the *movimiento* era. Unlike many other historians of Mexican American history, Gómez-Quiñones does not use a generational paradigm. As a Marxist labor historian, he problematizes the role of elites within the Mexican community and emphasizes the significance of their class interests as part of U.S. capitalism, a crucial factor in ideological orientation and political organization.

I begin with a delineation of García's and Gómez-Quiñones's perspectives on identity, ideology, and leadership. These concepts are central to their depiction of the Mexican American Generation by informing their analysis as well as orienting their research toward particular sectors of the Mexican community in the United States.

Identity

The historians examined in this chapter primarily address identity as a function of ethnicity. They each acknowledge the complexity of ethnicity, but they address it differently and place different emphasis on it as a factor in the political and economic history of Mexicans in the United States. Mario García, for instance, acknowledges that "ethnicity in a capitalist society with its class-race-gender divisions that are fundamental to its survival assumes a role in the distribution of power and wealth" (*MA* 10). Furthermore, he identifies the focus of his book in the following way: "The problem—to put it in more social scientific terms—for this study concerns the role that ethnicity plays in the transition from either first-generation immigrants or those Mexican Americans native to the Southwest who had been mostly isolated from mainstream currents to a second, U.S. born generation or a generation . . . that on the whole began to understand that it was part of U.S. society and that it *had to compromise* between its ethnic roots and full incorporation and assimilation into American society" (10, emphasis mine). The above quote is significant for several reasons, not the least of which is the emphasis on the role of ethnicity. Here, García also casts the "problem" as being generational and developmental; consequently, a primary source of social, political, and economic alienation is located within the Mexican American community. For García, the onus is on Mexican Americans to achieve social and political integration through compromise. Elsewhere, García's presentation of the problem is cast in a series of provocative questions. He asks, "How does ethnicity . . . manifest itself in class terms both outside and inside an ethnic group? How does ethnicity influence political movements aimed at narrowing the gap between the haves and the have nots? . . . And what is the relationship between ethnicity and identity in a society that upholds equality but uses ethnic and race differences to assure class divisions?" (10–11). His questions, unfortunately, are neither fully explored nor answered. The case studies he presents provide only very tentative, indirect answers.

His recognition of a heterogeneity of ideas and political strategies within the Mexican American community notwithstanding, García tends to impose shared perspectives and intent on his subjects. Even while he refutes a stereotype, he attempts to present a monolithic picture of the Mexican community: "Despite a common stereotype of Mexican Americans clinging selfishly to their own separate culture and way of life, in fact, Mexican Americans have, with other ethnic groups, expressed pride in their U.S. citizenship and have desired to be accepted as first-class Americans" (8). Rather than arguing for the specificity of the Mexican experience in the United States in all its variations, García strives to show its ideological and political commonality with the immigrant experience of Euro-Americans, an interpretive move that overlooks the specific circumstances of U.S. Mexicans as a defeated nationality. Though he is ostensibly concerned with the material effects of ethnicity, García is also obviously interested in the way U.S. history is perceived, especially by contemporary historians: "Revisionist historians rebelled against the hegemony of the consensus approach embraced during the cold war years of the 1950s which stressed 'nonideological' consensus in American life. Instead, revisionists—sometimes referred to as the New Left—saw conflict, including race and class warfare, rather than consensus as the driving force in the history of the United States" (8). Interestingly, his own ideological position in relation to revisionist and consensus historians remains unstated. However, considering that he views compromise as a necessary component of the political process, his perspective is clearly inclined toward pluralism. García's implied critique of the New Left is two-fold. On the one hand, he thinks the New Left is too static regarding the role of ethnicity in continued social change beyond the pioneer immigrant generations (9). Using the work of John Higham, he suggests that, as with European immigrants, a synthesis occurs between assimilation and ethnicity.[2] On the other hand, García is critical of Chicana/o-studies scholars for "failing" to focus on ethnic leadership because this approach is perceived as being similar to the established "great man" tradition that generally ignores the politics of the community (12). Contrary to García's assertion, many Chicano historians have written about important leaders, especially those associated with protest politics; thus they have indeed replicated "great man" paradigms, albeit in the service of a counternarrative to mainstream "official" histories. Despite Chicano historians' conventional attention to leaders, García laments their lack of focus on middle-class leaders and politics.

García's treatment of the League of United Latin American Citizens (LULAC), an organization that has been characterized as accommodationist and assimilationist by the New Left, is telling of his analysis of the relationship between ethnicity and politics. According to García, LULAC embodies the identity and ideas of the Mexican American Generation. As he sees it, LULAC's strategy of pluralistic assimilation was responsible for helping to establish political hegemony in the Mexican American community (33).

That LULAC could be considered a hegemonic force within the Mexican American community is arguable. García fails, however, to examine how their strategy of asserting an "American" identity was based upon contradictory premises that would limit their effectiveness. By proclaiming their "whiteness," LULAC engaged in an early form of identity politics. The strategy of "becoming white" did not challenge racist ideology; its proponents did, however, recognize that to be white in racial terms had material benefits.[3] Efforts by groups who have been labeled "integrationist" or "accommodationist" to be classified as white can also be seen as an attempt to stretch the boundaries of racial categories. If all Mexicans could legally be classified as white, then the absurdity of racism as a construct would become even more apparent, because the category "Mexican" includes an extremely wide range of physical and biological traits, even those that could otherwise label one as "black." This is not to suggest that this assimilationist strategy was not without fault, nor is it meant to apply radical notions to an extremely conservative approach to change, nor to ignore the racism that exists among Mexicans. The attempt by Mexican Americans to forward their group interest based on their racial similarity to white Americans can be seen as another version of nationalism; yet, in this instance, the nation being privileged is the United States. Moreover, it leaves intact racist paradigms that are exclusive of entire classes of people. Ironically, as Ernesto Galarza once noted, because "Americans" were perceived as being exclusively white, racial prejudices had the effect of denationalizing Mexicans (qtd. in Muñoz 26).

García's and Gómez-Quiñones's conceptions of the relationship between ethnicity and identity differ. For García, identity is derived from one's consciousness, which in turn is influenced by one's class position. This does not seem significantly different from Gómez-Quiñones's analysis, except for the important fact that García privileges the "elite" middle class as being more capable of acting on injustice because they were, according to him, "more acculturated, bilingual, and as a result, more politically functional. Formally educated to a greater extent than ever before, they became better socialized to their rights as U.S. citizens" (*MA* 15). Summarily dismissing any premigration political consciousness of *mexicanos,* or any class consciousness among rank-and-file workers during the years 1930 to 1960, García parallels Mexican Americans' economic condition with their political one and suggests that ethnicity was something to be overcome if material and political empowerment were to be realized.

In a markedly different form of analysis, Gómez-Quiñones attaches only secondary significance to ethnicity. Instead, primary importance is given to one's economic class position as a determinant of one's identity. For Gómez-Quiñones, "within capitalism there are potentially or actively two class positions: workers and their allies versus the upper classes and their allies; and the ethnic impacts upon both" (*CP* 8). He classifies *mexicanos* as a people, not only because of their ethnicity, but also because they "are a separate economic sector, a community that receives disparate treatment, and they have been concentrated for generations in a particular geographic area . . . the Southwest" (1). Thus he focuses on relations of power between people as being generative of class. Gómez-Quiñones differs from García in defining the scope of political struggle even while he agrees in a limited way: "Political history may emphasize the behavior of the elites, but it is the mass context, impact, and consequence that are significant" (20). For Gómez-Quiñones, ethnicity is not negotiable; it is a fixed variable that is part of the equation determining one's social position.

Because of their role in shaping identity, socialization processes, both internal and external to the Chicana/o community, play an important role in Gómez-Quiñones's analysis. He also acknowledges that ethnicity and class relations function differently under different historical circumstances. "With annexation . . . the class relationships become both internal to the group and external to the larger society, and are mediated by pejorative distinctions between 'Anglo' and 'Mexican' which are social and economic" (8). The socialization process reinforced the dominant ideology and undermined competing ideologies. The majority of *mexicanos* have experienced subordination; this, in turn, has led to what Gómez-Quiñones classifies as "non-conforming consciousness": "Historically, the relation between the dominant political system, its fostered socialization and the economy translates for the dominated into non-conforming consciousness and the active conflict of insurgent politics, while for the dominant it means an adjustment to ensure their continued power" (29). García, on the other hand, views the embrace of the Americanization process by the middle class as a progression in group politics.

The different emphases placed on race, class, or ethnicity by political scientists and historians emerged from the real and sometimes contradictory political practices that Mexican Americans have engaged in over the years. This inconsistent approach to political problems has affected the ideological and theoretical approaches to social change practiced by Chicana/o intellectuals. It has also, as Gómez-Quiñones points out, led to an "ideological conundrum—reformism versus utopianism" (21).

Ideology

Since the nineteenth century, when Karl Marx and Friedrich Engels began referring to ideology as a form of "false consciousness," the term has evolved and been transformed in the hands of activists, academics, and political theoreticians. In all its theoretical uses—Marxist, poststructuralist, and so on—ideology has been construed as a particular conception of social relations, be they "real," ideal, or imaginary. In this section I examine the meaning of the word "ideology" for these two historians of Mexican American history as a way of understanding their representation of this period, the theoretical justification for their method, and the grounds on which the Mexican American Generation based their claims and aspirations for a reconfiguration of power relations. In this sense ideology will be more closely related to praxis or the premises underlying political strategies.

The varying ideological analyses of the means and ends of movements for social change are probably nowhere more apparent than in the tension between the two seemingly incompatible goals of reformism and utopianism. Although the language used to articulate the bases for change has evolved dramatically over the years, the politics of U.S. citizens of Mexican descent has almost always been reformist in nature. While the United States has not been immune to revolutionary uprisings involving violence and centered around issues of land, there have been no victorious, large-scale, or sustained attacks against the system of private property. Tactics to achieve reform measures have varied widely, and the rhetoric has become increasingly radical in tone. Carlos Muñoz and Juan Gómez-Quiñones have credited the anticolonial struggles of Third World peoples with being an influence on the populist rhetoric of the 1960s. Mario García's analysis of the limitations of the political strategies practiced by the Mexican American Generation is insightful. He concedes that the politics of status did little to alter the class-racial system of power relations that is an entrenched part of U.S. politics; indeed, this form of politics is still practiced today. García is blunt about the politics of Mexican American leftists when he states that the fundamental thrust of *mexicano,* Mexican American, and Chicano politics "during the 1930s and beyond [has] translated into militancy for reform rather than revolution" (*MA* 146). Within this reformist framework, however, there have been marked ideological differences. Although organizations like LULAC have been characterized as conservative and reformist, today one would have to acknowledge that a much more ideologically conservative sector exists among affluent Hispanics, who actively efface their Mexican identity as they advocate for their narrowly construed class interests. On the other end of the spectrum were leftists, usually associated with labor and proletarian interests, who belonged to groups like the Spanish Speaking Congress and who were progressive on social issues like immigration and equal rights for women. They stressed an internationalist perspective that ran counter to LULAC's position on the Mexican question.

LULAC stressed the importance of participating in the political process vis-à-vis the electoral process. But though they focused on removing barriers to participation (such as eliminating the poll tax), LULAC's strategy was to accept exclusivist structures and work around them rather than remove them (such as paying the poll tax, not eliminating it). In García's definition of LULAC's goals, the elitist and patronizing nature of both the organization and García come into clear focus: "LULAC's efforts at political socialization finally consisted of getting Mexican Americans to become interested and involved in state and national politics" (42). Here García denies the political consciousness of *mexicanos* by suggesting that to be political is to be American; to be apolitical, consequently, is to be Mexican. This view is reiterated by García in his analysis of trade-union activity: ". . . increased participation in unions symbolized the coming of age of Americans of Mexican descent, who, like their middle-class contemporaries, were now sufficiently acculturated to recognize and demand their rights as U.S. citizens. Rather than leading to conformity, Americanization or acculturation gave rise to protests in pursuit of American principles of democracy. . . . Mexican American workers interpreted the achievement of civil rights in economic terms" (176). As is apparent here, García's definition of leadership favors the educated middle class, whose objectives are more individual than mass-oriented, more quantitative than qualitative.

García assigns a millenarian dimension to this generation's politics by saying that its leaders were reacting to shared historical experiences and believed that their destiny or moment in history had arrived. Again, despite his awareness that generational units can differ politically and economically, García consistently speaks of *the* ideology of *the* Mexican American Generation, as opposed to *ideologies,* plural. Nevertheless, his desire to understand the Mexican American Generation on its own terms is significant because it signals a revision of revisionism. His research is invaluable for understanding the context in which Mexicans were striving for social change. In his examination of LULAC and its origins, García's intentions are clear. The formation of LULAC was accompanied by the adoption of organizing principles that led to its being tagged as "assimilationist" by later historians. By agreeing to restrict its membership to U.S. citizens of Latin extraction and by making English the official language of the organization, LULACers appeared to be willing to compromise their *mexicanidad* for the sake of political strategy and the social benefits that they hoped would follow.[4]

However accurate the assessment of LULAC as an assimilationist organization might be, its decision to assume that position must be viewed in the context of the political and social climate of the first quarter of the century, which in turn revolves around the meaning of national identity. From a social and economic point of view, Mexican immigrants were then as now utilized as scapegoats for a troubled U.S. economy. As the presence of the many contradictory impulses within LULAC's constitution indicates (the advancement of group goals simultaneous with the suppression of group identity), they were not so much trying to deny their heritage as attempting to foreground a legal basis for their political claims. This stress on citizenship, however, effectively divided *mexicanos* and Mexican Americans by supporting the "legal" and "illegal" distinctions used by nativists to relegate all "Mexicans" to a second-class status. By accepting the "illegal" status of undocumented immigrants, "Latin Americans" effectively placed "Mexicans" in a tertiary lass position. This tactic only served to give credence to anti-Mexican sentiment that was generated as a means of avoiding a close examination of the economic problems of the United States. This bifurcation with more recently arrived *mexicanos* did not occur as smoothly as García would lead us to believe. According to Cynthia Orozco, the political organizing that occurred at the 1927 Harlingen convention that preceded the formation of LULAC was extremely important because it involved behind-the-scenes maneuvering by a few individuals to assure the exclusion of *mexicanos*.[5]

In *Mexican Americans* García's organizing method is to present close examinations of individuals and particular organizations that are meant to exemplify the political spirit of the times. While Gómez-Quiñones uses the same methodological approach, his narrative and analysis are organized thematically as well. Gómez-Quiñones poses the political problem for Mexican Americans as one of continuing dependency: "Twentieth-century Mexicans in the United States do not have a state structure of their own; consequently, their politics exist in a dependent relation to a state whose principal instrument for dominating the Mexican community is this very power relationship" (*CP* 10). While not subscribing to the model of the internal colony, Gómez-Quiñones does claim a partial indigenous identity for Mexicans that informs his analysis. "Mexicans possess a historical homeland, which is one result of their Indian ancestry" (13). Furthermore, Gómez-Quiñones asserts that it is a legacy of negative experience that binds together the larger Mexican community, not political practice or a particular political identity. "Political cohesion is related to authority and rewards, yet often both have been weak. . . . For the most part, the few political rewards are controlled by outsiders. The unifying agents vis-à-vis domination have been discrimination, sentiments of nationality, generalized cultural practices, idealized familialism, and class membership—and all these are expressed in specific local settings" (15). Some of these cultural characteristics have also been used to maintain disunity by confounding the basis of shared experience. For instance, the emergent Mexican American middle class has historically disrupted, co-opted, or otherwise thwarted attempts at forging political unity. Class membership in the United States is a complex phenomenon that is not static, even, or progressive; the myth of equality and social mobility, no matter how limited, has been used consistently as an ideological weapon by all sectors.

Gómez-Quiñones is particularly critical of the way Mexican political unity in the United States has been perceived. His analysis is diametrically opposed to the liberal and conservative views that have failed to examine structural and institutional impediments to effective political practice. He critiques the naive assertion that Mexican representation in government would, in itself, guarantee political answers to the problems of Mexicans in the United States. According to this argument, "effective representation would ensure that the needs of Mexicans would be met at the local, state, and federal levels because 'government' is viewed as being not only able but 'willing' to take such action, even on behalf of disadvantaged groups. A pluralist myth lies at the heart of this liberal-conservative political assertion, and indeed liberal-conservative views dominate the analysis of Mexican political behavior" (18). Gómez-Quiñones makes an extended attack on liberalism's class and cultural bias that reveal it to be a conservative ideology in which "functions that maintain the system and keep it in balance are viewed positively, while success is defined as the maintenance of the status quo" (24). His analysis here strongly contrasts with García's. Within liberal pluralism there is a denial of structural inequities; only "social problems" are acknowledged and are subsequently designated as the fault of "deviant" individuals. Left unchecked, this "may promote an imbalance in social organization and the possibility of threatened social control" (*CP* 24). According to Gómez-Quiñones, both nationality and class mechanisms are used to maintain domination; this is especially true during times of economic crises. In order to take full advantage of employment opportunities, ethnicity has often been deemphasized: "Mexicans were asserted to be white, Latin, or Spanish American, and negative disassociation from Blacks was part of the package" (41). Here Gómez-Quiñones's analysis of working-class survival strategies returns full circle to the strategy of the middle-class-inclined LULAC.

One of the largest differences between the political ideologies of U.S. Mexicans in the twentieth century covered by these historians is the language through which the groups' demands have been articulated. The most "radical" change in ideology from the 1930s to the 1970s can be said to be an explicitly antiracist stance that opened up new organizing possibilities, but even in the '70s it did not effectively translate into cross-cultural unity among oppressed groups. Gómez-Quiñones's definition of politics as "the pursuit of group or individual material interests in the public arena by addressing government and using group mobilization to influence policy and other social aggregations" foregrounds the need to have effective and accountable leaders (3). If we accept his premise that "governance . . . is most often primarily an elite activity that is a negotiation between those who already have surplus and the authority to distribute it" (3), then the relationship between ideology and leadership is important to explore. How leadership is defined and determined involves a complex set of factors that are related to internal as well as external power relations.

Leadership

Beginning with Rodolfo Acuña's *Occupied America: A History of Chicanos* (1972), many Chicano historians have taken "great man" approaches to Chicano history. This is especially true of Chicano Movement historical literature, which tends to focus on the "Big Four": César Chávez, José Angel Gutiérrez, Rudolfo "Corky" González, and Reies López Tijerina. The problem is that few historians have been critical in their analysis of Chicana/o leadership. García, for example, identifies "exemplary" people and organizations that existed prior to *el movimiento* and must be seen as intellectual, political, and organizational predecessors of the 1960s. And though these individuals and organizations were important, García focuses intensely on a few at the expense of the many. Not enough comparative analysis of the styles, methods, and messages of the individuals and organizations is done to offer a synthesized, comprehensive perspective of Chicana/o politics of this era.

Particularly relevant here are García's conception of leadership and his generational analysis, premised on the notion that "political generations, by definition represent an elite or vanguard—as opposed to the masses" (*MA* 6). He uses the experiences of three successive decades—the 1930s, '40s, and '50s—and the cataclysmic historical moments that correspond with them—the Great Depression, World War II, and the Cold War—as an episodic framework to illustrate the first significant civil rights movement of Mexican Americans. He defines the Mexican American era as a political generation of U.S.-born and -raised Mexicans. According to García, "the convulsions of the Great Depression combined with new economic and political opportunities during World War II and with the historic discrimination in the Southwest against Mexicans and rising expectations among Mexican Americans to give birth to a new leadership, cognizant of its rights as U.S. citizens and determined to achieve them" (2).

García displays a tendency to focus on the elite, a tactic he acknowledges as being contrary to the counterhegemonic approach usually taken by ethnic historians who have tried to resist the "great man" approach to history. He seems to accept Higham's critique that there is "too little stress on leadership" in ethnic historiography. Yet García appears unsure whether "leaders emerge from the masses" or if ethnic groups are "the creation of their leaders," as Higham would suggest (12). His attempt to find a middle ground is explained in this way: "Evidence of the consciousness and actions or reactions of the masses is more difficult to obtain, especially if the focus is on the politics of community, and hence my study can only infer that due to the viability of certain *movements generated by the leadership* something resembling a larger social movement was occurring" (12, emphasis mine). In his conception of leadership, García differs with Manning Marable's assessment that "history creates humanity, as well as the conscious choices which are possible for any political leader to select" (Marable 77). Borrowing heavily from Higham (whose own study on ethnic leadership did not examine Latinos), García explains his willingness to define leadership in this way because of the "amorphousness of ethnic groups" who are undergoing a process of change in U.S. society as they move from being immigrants to

American ethnics. García's idealization of the role of individuals in history is limiting because it is nondialectical and reveals a weakness in his schema. Despite the significant contributions to political struggle by individuals, including Ignacio López and Carlos Castañeda, who were in strategically important institutional positions, García fails to see that it was the broader social arena of political activity and activists that gave them the credibility and substance upon which to act and articulate a political vision. Furthermore, by focusing on individuals, García's organizing schematic reveals an ideological bias that is representative of the middle class, who tend to utilize individual successes as a gauge of social acceptance for an entire group. Mass movements that posed a threat to the social order made it possible for elites to offer a safe alternative to the ruling class. To his credit, García does not focus on individual actors when discussing labor and the left. This, of course, reveals ideological differences about notions of leadership and politics that existed between the middle and lower classes during the period from 1930 to 1960. The heroization of leaders and the resulting tensions with the organizations they represented, as well as their legitimacy with the popular base that authorized them, continue to be a source of conflict in the politics of U.S. Mexicans.

In partial agreement with García, Gómez-Quiñones says that leadership changes "according to internal changes within classes, but generally it has been drawn from the three major classes and predominantly from the middle. . . . Autochthonous leadership was internal and organic to the local community; but under domination increasingly leaders were externally imposed, and frequently chosen because of their loyalty to the grantor. . . . [Thus] accountability is a continual problem" (Gómez-Quiñones, *CP* 10). By virtue of their status as acknowledged leaders, individuals find themselves struggling with competing concerns and discourses surrounding "their own interests, the interests of the community, and the demands of the dominant power" (10–11). This is the crux of the problem with leadership in an ethnic community. Its elitist nature has been perpetuated because leaders must be accepted by internal and external audiences. Furthermore, as Gómez-Quiñones points out, Mexican leadership and organizational development have been stifled by "two major institutions indifferent to Mexicans: the political parties and the universities; the first inhibited political space, the second human leadership material" (86).

In defiance of the generational paradigm so prevalent in Mexican American histories, Gómez-Quiñones's political history begins in the war period.

And though he acknowledges the specificity of this historical moment, he also realizes that Mexican political activity predated this moment. His analysis on political parties, socialization processes, and the role of the university begins where the first novel to be examined in this chapter ends; nevertheless, his observations will be relevant. The very title of Américo Paredes's novel *George Washington Gómez* foregrounds the ideologically conflicted notions of national identity and leadership we have been discussing thus far.

George Washington Gómez *and the Dialectics of Identity, Ideology, and Leadership*

In his reading of *With His Pistol in His Hand* as a sociological poem (*Mexican Ballads, Chicano Poems,* 1992), José Limón argues that Américo Paredes utilizes the structure of the *corrido* as a model for *Pistol.* Paredes's analysis assumes the structure of the object of his study. In a similar vein, Ramón Saldívar claims of Paredes's *George Washington Gómez* that "the guiding speech genre of the text" is the *corrido* (Saldívar, "Borderlands" 287).[6] Certainly the *corrido*'s form and socio-historical context do inform the text, but I will argue against Saldívar's assertion by claiming that *George Washington Gómez* actually challenges the validity of the *corrido* as a collective mode of expression, an insight that may signal the author's early awareness of the limitations of this expressive form as a political paradigm despite the formative role that *With His Pistol In His Hand* played in shaping Chicana/o critical discourse. The extensive and constitutive influence of Paredes's poetic rendering of the *corrido* as an articulation of resistance in the formation of a masculinist politics of analysis was referred to in this book's introduction. For the purposes of this chapter, it is less significant to demonstrate that Paredes blurred genres of writing in launching a critique of hegemonic discourse than to recognize that his work filled a role in legitimating Mexican American counterdiscourse (Limón, *MBCP* 74). *With His Pistol in His Hand* filled that need in two ways: it responded directly, critically, and intentionally to mainstream discourse about Mexicans, and it did so from within the academy by utilizing an organic cultural form. The organic and historic nature of this form was attractive to scholars who were wary of the mainstream critical frameworks that had been used to reproduce racist notions about the inherent inferiority of Mexicans.

The objective of this section of the chapter will be not merely to demonstrate the nascent yet enduring presence of the resistance narrative in Paredes's early work; the primary goal is to analyze Paredes's representation of what has come to be known as the Mexican American Generation. This analysis will focus on Paredes's conception of leadership, ideology, and identity as manifested in the novel's characters and structure. Besides sharing many plot and structural elements with the *corrido,* Paredes's fictionalized account of pre–World War II life in the lower Rio Grande Valley also closely parallels the plot structure of a *Bildungsroman;* the generic differences between these two in the production of meaning and negotiation of history is profoundly significant.

The novel, bearing the title of the central character, is the story of a young man coming of age in a hostile social climate. As he proceeds to find his place in U.S. society, he must come to terms with his individual identity and experiences in the context of the historically hostile relationship between Anglos and the majority of Mexicans in Texas, a relationship that has characterized Mexicans' collective experience and determined their social status as inferiors. Thus, national identity becomes a central issue of the novel and of the period. *GWG* also anticipates what is to become an enduring problem for Americans of Mexican descent: how to negotiate the tension between individual and collective identity, individual aspirations and group goals, allegiance to self-improvement versus group empowerment. Moreover, in this novel Paredes identifies and explores the ideological and political dilemma of the subaltern who seeks to function as an intellectual, a challenge he more decisively and paradigmatically articulates in *With His Pistol in His Hand.* Inasmuch as intellectuals function as representatives of their class, their allegiances are subject to interrogation.

The protagonist of the novel is born into a moment in which a dramatic historical shift is occurring that alters the economic relations between Mexicans and Anglos. As was noted in chapters 1 and 2, the shift in economic relations from 1848 through the turn of the century so altered social relations that Mexicans in South Texas were made to feel like foreigners in their native land. This shift in power represented an inversion of the historical relationship between South Texas Mexicans and Anglos: Anglos were no longer foreigners; Mexicans were. Politically, this meant that the U.S. government consolidated Anglo domination over Mexicans, whether they were American citizens or nonnationals. Taking the 1915 seditionist movement as its point of departure, the novel expresses the complex dimensions of the social relations among Mexicans and between Mexicans and Anglos. In denying the legitimacy of the state, the seditionists rejected their status as citizens. The harsh and often arbitrary repression of Mexicans that followed the uprising against Anglo elites resulted in further displacement of landholding Mexicans in South Texas. Ramón Saldívar points out that "Paredes's novel situates us in the midst of this historical scenario, taking its tone, however, not from the celebration of the tragic *corrido* hero, doomed to honorable but certain defeat with his pistol in his hand, but from the pathos of those innocents from whom was extracted the cost of defeat" ("Borderlands" 277).

Saldívar's invocation of the *corrido* hero's "honorable but certain defeat" describes a characteristic of the *corrido* that needs to be explored. First of all, resistance in *corridos* is defined as an individual male quest wherein a folk hero represents "the community's collective resistance to the new dominant Anglo power" (276). The continuing presence of the *corrido* as a residual cultural form is often presented as evidence of the entire culture's sanctioning of this socially symbolic act of resistance, despite the fact that it is predominantly a male genre and finds its primary performance space among an audience of men (Limón, *MBCP* 37). Described in these terms, the very nature of resistance excludes the possibility of female agency or participation. Moreover, the linking of honorable heroism to certain defeat suggests limited possibilities in the inverse equation of "dishonorable victory." In his narration of the process of subjective and collective identity construction, Paredes presents his readers with a protagonist who, in his ambivalent relation to his community of origin, oscillates between hero to antihero. If, as Saldívar suggests, the novel takes its tone from the "pathos of the innocents from whom was extracted the cost of defeat," then how are we to comprehend Paredes's depiction of the Mexican community? As tragic victims of history? As assimilationists? Are we left to interpret George's capitulation to the dominant ideology as a tragic consequence of defeat in the face of overwhelming odds? Or are other alternatives to resistance offered that are not inherently tragic?

The answers to such questions are embedded in the gendered structure of the novel and the discourses that inform it. In his reading of the novel as a *corrido*-inspired narrative, Saldívar notes that "in the traditional *corrido* . . . the fate of the individual and of the community are not separate. Rather, they are bound together in a unitary structure. . ." ("Borderlands" 282). But as an imagined representation of the real, the *corrido* posits a false unity that is predicated on the absence of women, a point Saldívar acknowledges. "As a socially symbolic act, the *corrido* both draws from and adds to the patriarchal constitution of Chicana/o culture. As gender-coded discourse, it identifies the Mexican-American community and represents it in monologically male terms" (288). In such a paradigm, women are assigned "only secondarily and by supplementarity [to] a grieving female space" (JoAnn Pavletich and Margot Backus, qtd. in "Borderlands" 288). In reading *GWG* as a narrative manifestation of the *corrido* and male-gendered discourse, Saldívar points out that the limitations of this paradigm are instantiated in the novel through the "failed utopian vision of the novel's end" ("Borderlands" 288), wherein the protagonist's subjectivity is fractured and he is unable to be at peace with his decision to suppress his Mexican identity in favor of being wholly American. Saldívar's reading is premised on the notion that, ideally, the hero of the text should triumph in his effort at self-realization, at becoming a productive member of his community. Even in his tragic fate the hero should be representative of the community's interests. The prominence of the question of identity in the context of hostile relations between Mexicans and Anglos in *GWG* raises the question, With which community will the hero align his interests? There is, however, an alternative, restive, and potentially powerful alternative vision inscribed in the novel—one that we will return to later. First, however, it is important to establish the novel's relationship to the *corrido* in order to fully appreciate its interrogation of it as a master paradigm for articulating resistance.

In addition to sharing the context and theme of the *corrido, GWG* also shares other similarities with it. Following but enhancing Paredes's work, Limón identifies characteristics of the *corrido;* these are features present in the novel that at first glance can be seen to support Saldívar's claim that the *corrido* is the primary speech genre of the novel. The essential characteristics of the *corrido* emphasized by Limón are a context of hostile relations between Anglos and Mexicans along the border; the *corridistas'* appeal to the audience's "understanding of the social relations and historical context for his story"; the establishment of a scenic structure, geographical locale, and opposing social forces; the swift motion of the story in which the hero is introduced; the *en media res* presentation of the story; the introduction of the hero in legendary proportions and his defiant stature; the presentation of Anglos as complex, multidimensional figures who contain positive as well as negative qualities; the abundance of deaths; the repressed and dominated presence of women in these patriarchal tales; and the ending in which the hero reaches a tragic end (*MBCP* 66–70). When juxtaposed against the plot structure of *GWG,* this condensed summary of the *corrido*'s features provides a basis for verifying its discursive influence.

The novel consists of five chapters, each one representing a decisive period in the protagonist's socio-cultural development. Part I, "'Los Sediciosos' / The Seditionists" clearly places the reader in the socio-political context of conflict from which most of the epic *corridos* of South Texas emerged and thus provides credence for the assertion of the significance of the *corrido* as a primary speech genre. With the exception of the hero's defiant stature, in Part I all the features of the *corrido* are fulfilled in the narration of events, including the presentation of the hero as a legendary figure. An important difference from the *corrido* is already present, however; the novel does not present us with a ready-made hero. According to Bakhtin, ready-made heroes are those that remain "unchanged and adequate to themselves"; ". . . the plot, composition, and entire internal structure postulate this unchanging nature, this solidity of the hero's image, this static nature of his unity. The hero is a constant in the novel's formula and all other qualities . . . can therefore be variables" (Bakhtin 20–21). The protagonist in *GWG* is yet to be born when the novel begins; in fact, it is in the scene where the newborn child is being named that an effort is made to construct him as a hero of legendary proportions. It is in this moment also that conflicting ideologies and notions of identity intersect and emerge as a continuing source of tension for the protagonist. A series of names are proposed and rejected. These names signify the ideological interests at stake in the formation of the child's subjectivity for the various family members present. In rapid succession, Crisósforo, José Angel, Venustiano, Anacleto, Gumersindo, and Hidalgo are all rejected as inappropriate by one or another of the family members. The names are rejected on the grounds that they are too grandiose or common, religious, radical, traditional (filial), or as having the wrong national orientation. Ultimately, it is Gumersindo Gómez, the father of the child, who responds to María's wish to give her son a "great man's name. Because he is going to grow up to be a great man who will help his people." Gumersindo names their son after "the great North American, he who was a general and fought the soldiers of the king" (*GWG* 16). In the final choice of the protagonist's name is a duplicity that anticipates the impossibility of his being the ideal hero. In an essay analyzing the construction of subjectivity in Chicana/o literature, Dana Maynard notes the duplicity and irony in Gumersindo's attempt "to inscribe his son in the hegemonic culture" by naming him after a great revolutionary: "Ironically, Gumersindo associates Washington's name with the fight for freedom and independence which is the very fight the Mexican *sediciosos* were organizing against Anglo oppression at that time. Thus even if Gumersindo makes a conscious allegiance with the Gringos as his son's 'people,' his unconscious values for anti-imperialism show through, and in the context of the uprising around him, undermine his professed allegiance" (Maynard 4). The duplicity and ambivalence surrounding the identity and ideology of the protagonist also signify the limited influence of the *corrido* as a primary speech genre of the novel. The naming scene ends with Feliciano, George's uncle, singing "The *Corrido* of Jacinto Treviño," thus signaling the hostilities of the current moment. This *corrido* appears once again in the novel, this time not as a dominant but a residual cultural form, when Antonio Prieto, George's classmate, sings it in the car after they have been denied entrance into the site of their high school graduation celebration because of racist segregation codes. Other than this brief reappearance, however, the *corrido* does not continue to shape the novel's structure or the author's ideological vision; other discourses intervene and interrupt the heroic construction of the protagonist.

In his political and cultural betrayal of Mexicans at the novel's end, however ambivalent and tentative this stance may be, George is not the tragic hero who has died in the defense of his people. The complexity of the issues of identity, leadership, and ideology in the Mexican American Generation as presented in the novel can best be understood by examining other primary speech genres that inform the text, and the specificity of the secondary speech genre the novel assumes. In "The Problem of Speech Genres," Bakhtin points out that "a one-sided orientation toward primary genres inevitably leads to a vulgarization of the entire problem. . . . The very interrelations between primary and secondary genres and the process of historical formation of the latter shed light on the nature of the utterance (and above all on the complex problem of the interrelations among language, ideology, and world-view)" (62). Depression-era anti-Mexicanism, in the context of an ongoing war of position between Mexicans and Anglos in South Texas, was made manifest by dual wage scales for whites and nonwhites, nativism, segregation, and deportation practices that often did not bother to distinguish Mexicans with U.S. citizenship from those without it. The discourses of anti-Mexicanism are themselves primary speech genres that, in turn, gave rise to assimilationist and racialist ideologies from within the Mexican community as strategies by which social tensions could be mitigated. But between the extremes of the *corrido* and assimilationism, there existed other assertive articulations of identity for Mexicans. As a secondary speech genre the novel captures a confluence of primary speech genres, including those that express repression and domination, sometimes in gendered form. Bakhtin notes that "In each epoch certain speech genres set the tone for the development of literary language" ("The Problem" 65). The national language is reproduced in the interplay between various speech genres and their manifestation in individual styles. However, the lack of a single national identity produces a duality of national languages within which Mexicans must negotiate. "The very problem of the national and the individual in language is basically the problem of the utterance (after all, only here, in the utterance, is the national language embodied in individual form)" (63).

Paredes depicts the Mexican community as a heterogeneous group whose experiences and interests as well as national identity differ according to class, social status, gender, and the degree to which they are perceived as racial others. According to Saldívar, the dialectical interplay between two cultures produces a product "of both American ideological and Mexican folkloric systems" ("Borderlands" 282); the formation of the subject is a result of formal socialization processes inculcated by the ideological state apparatus, the school, and the home culture, which is not ratified by the state. The specific nature of this citizen-product is indeterminate and is negotiated by the subject as an active causal agent. George's identity as a Mexican, however, is contained through a suppression of history in the educational system. But in the social geography of South Texas, there exists a multitude of counterdiscourses. The decisive moment in the formation of the subject—who henceforth has experienced life with a dual identity according to his assumption or rejection of race privilege—is his university experience, to which readers are not made privy. This period of his formation is conspicuous by its absence from the story and its apparent constitutive force on George's identity.[7]

Shortly after graduating from high school, George discovers his family's history of resistance to Anglo domination and that his father was murdered by Texas Rangers. Consequently, he decides to pursue higher education with the intention of fulfilling the family mandate that he become "a leader of his people." However, returning home after several years away from his community of origin, he is a changed person with different loyalties and values. Prior to going to college, George was a student who liked to "disagree with textbooks" and who was astutely aware that unequal political and social relations of power were created and maintained by a system that exploited people's perceptions of racial difference. The role of state apparatuses (ideological and repressive) in the formation of the protagonist is also foregrounded as the narrative depicts confrontations with various institutions—the educational system and the military in particular—and the ways these institutions are shaped by and perpetuate racism. Different members of the Gómez family and the South Texas community lose their fight against Anglo hegemony (territorial and ideological) and maintain or reject varying degrees of identification with Mexican historical and national identity. George is the biological and cultural offspring of a Mexican woman with a long history in South Texas and a Mexican father who is a *fuereño* (a Mexican national from the interior of the country).[8] But this protagonist, this emerging intellectual, is the ideological progeny of the nexus of cultural and social influences present in South Texas in the first half of the century.

The significance of this multitude of historical and cultural influences should not be underestimated. The novel's narrator provides a framework that urges a critical reading and makes the protagonist's reaction representative of other Mexicotexans:

> The Mexicotexan knows about the Alamo, he is reminded of it often enough. Texas history is a cross that he must bear. In the written tests, if he expects to pass the course, he must put down in writing what he violently misbelieves. And often certain passages in the history text book become subjects of discussion.
>
> "Isn't it horrible what the Mexicans did at the Alamo and Goliad? Why are they so treacherous and bloody? And cowards too."
>
> "That's a lie! that's a lie! Treacherous? That's you all over!"
>
> "It's in our textbook. Can't you read?"
>
> ". . . But the book, the book! It talks about us today! Today! It says we are all dirty and live under trees."
>
> The teacher cannot criticize a textbook on Texas history. She would be called a Communist and lose her job. (*GWG* 150)

After receiving undergraduate and law degrees from the University of Texas at Austin, George loses his critical attitude toward history in general and his own life in particular. He is unfazed by the knowledge that his father-in-law is a former Texas Ranger from the same town during the same time that his father was killed, for example. At the novel's end World War II is just beginning, and George, or "Guálinto," as his family calls him, has returned to his hometown on the South Texas border as a counterintelligence agent for the U.S. army. To the bitter disappointment of his family and friends, he has the suspect duty of patrolling the border region for possible insurgent activities. George admits to his uncle Feliciano, a former *sedicioso,* that he is less concerned about subversive activities generated from Mexican nationals than he is with the activities of Mexican Americans. George's ultimate dismissal of his former friends' efforts at political organizing as being nothing more than a "bunch of clowns playing at politics" who are "trying to organize yokels who don't know anything but getting drunk and yelling and fighting" is demonstrative of the dominant ideology he has internalized.

On Heroes, Individualism, and the Bildungsroman

It is through the institutions of education in general, and higher education in particular, that George's identity is interpolated. In these institutions his development is shaped. The importance of history and education in *GWG* identifies it as the most advanced form of the novel of emergence, or novel of education, in Bakhtin's delineation of the *Bildungsroman.* For Bakhtin, the decisive characteristic of this genre is the degree of assimilation of real historical time: "In it man's individual emergence is inseparably linked to historical emergence" ("Bildungsroman" 23). In this type of novel the protagonist is "on the border between two epochs, at the transition point from one to the other. . . . The organizing force held by the future is therefore extremely great here—and this is not, of course, the private biographical future, but the historical future. It is as though the very foundations of the world are changing, and man must change along with them" (23–24). The image of the emerging man is of vital importance. Because there is no ready-made hero in this genre, the hero becomes a variable and changes in him acquire plot significance. "Time is introduced into man, enters into his very image, changing in a fundamental way the significance of all aspects of his destiny and life" (21). This form of the novel can best capture the diverse ways that human beings can emerge as agents of history. In the type of novel we are concerned with here, "problems of reality and man's potential, problems of freedom and necessity, and the problem of creative initiative rise to their full height. The image of the emerging man begins to surmount its private nature . . . and enters into a completely new spatial sphere of historical existence" (24). Paredes's use of the *Bildungsroman* as a secondary speech genre is oriented, as with other forms of utterances, toward the active response of others. It is a generic artistic language form that is defined by its stability and normative features, to be sure; but it is also informed by the author's speech will or speech plan. According to Bakhtin, in our response to every utterance "we embrace, understand, and sense the speaker's speech plan or speech will. . . . We imagine to ourselves what the speaker wishes to say. . . . This plan determines both the choice of the subject itself (under certain conditions of speech communication, in necessary connection with preceding utterances), as well as its boundaries and its semantic exhaustiveness. It also determines, of course, the choice of a generic form in which the utterance will be constructed" (77).

The multiplicity of speech genres and discourses present in *GWG* make not just the protagonist but history itself the subject of the novel. Likewise, even the form of the novel is informed by the historical moment. The historical novel and the *Bildungsroman* are intimately intertwined during this period of the consolidation of capitalist hegemony. The discourse of individualism informing the politics of status and class conflict permeates the novel through the main character and influences our assessment of him as either exemplary or typical of his group. For instance, George is either a leader of or a traitor to his culture or his government; depending on whether one evaluates him as an individual or a representative subject, he is hero or antihero of his people. In many ways, *GWG* is a typical American novel of individual social success; as such George exemplifies the democratic principles of equality and social mobility. On the other hand, as an emerging intellectual from a subaltern class, his class and cultural allegiances assume larger significance. *GWG* is not just the story of an individual but one of class and cultural conflict at an important moment of social change. His intellectual status is thus emblematic of a political problem of the period.

Within the genre of the *Bildungsroman,* a certain story type informs *GWG.* Read as the story of an individual, *GWG* is an ironic tragedy with a protagonist whose fate is determined by a complexity of social and cultural forces. Raised under dual influences, George embodies the contradictions within an emerging social class. His capitulation to the dominant class is thus not surprising; put into historical perspective, it can be seen as a logical consequence of his life experiences. Ironically, it is his deceased father who most determines his fate and the limited and conflicting role that Feliciano can play as surrogate father. In this important moment of transformation in the political economy and culture of South Texas, and with all the patriarchal force that accompanies the wishes of the father, Gumersindo Gómez, the *fuereño* who has no ties to the land or tradition of resistance in South Texas, overrides his wife's expression that their son "be a great man who will help his people" by proclaiming instead that "He is going to be a great man among the Gringos" (*GWG* 16). Thus in this novel, as Limón has observed about *With His Pistol in His Hand,* Paredes implies that the *fuereños,* along with the gringos, "contribute to the social change coming to the area" (Limón, *DD* 80). Uncle Feliciano voices his concern about outsiders' views as being naive and ahistorical: "It was all very well for [the preacher], who came from up north to talk about love between all men and everybody being brothers. And it was very well for Gumersindo, who came from the interior of Mexico to be taken in by such talk. But a Border Mexican knew there was no brotherhood of men" (*GWG* 19). Feliciano's words express the importance of regional histories within national histories; border Mexicans experienced and witnessed the territorial displacement of Mexicans and their political and economic subjugation, a fact that was masked in legitimacy by unscrupulous officers of the law. Gumersindo's dictum that his son be "a great man among the Gringos," in conjunction with his death wish that Feliciano not tell Guálinto about his murder at the hands of Texas Rangers, haunts Guálinto and influences the course of his life:

> Gumersindo's aspirations for his son also force Feliciano to suppress his identity as a *sedicioso* and compromise his revolutionary ideology in order to help those goals be achieved.
>
> From cowhand to seditionist and raider, from there to bartender for Gringo soldiers he had been shooting at a few months earlier. Soon after, a ward heeler whose job was to herd his own people into voting booths for the benefit of Gringo political bosses. And now, party to a smuggling operation. Nothing to be proud of. But his nephew was getting close to school age, and Feliciano would need money, much money. (82)[9]

In his need to protect his family and provide the economic and social stability that will facilitate George's emergence as an intellectual and a leader, Feliciano secures the way by functioning as a power broker between Anglos and Mexicans and participating as an elite in the capitalist economy. Thus in the service of goals set by a *fuereño,* Feliciano exercises privilege and authority over other Mexicans; he becomes a functionary of the new economic and political order. As an entrepreneur he represents, according to Antonio Gramsci, "a higher level of social elaboration, already characterized by a certain directive and technical (i.e., intellectual) capacity. . . . He must be an organizer of masses of men; he must be an organizer of the 'confidence' of investors of his business, of the customers of his products, etc." (*PN* 5). Feliciano's privilege is further evident in his ability to reacquire land in the period that closely follows the deterritorialization of Mexicans from their land.

George's ultimate emergence as a traditional intellectual of the hegemonic order, despite his youthful rebellions against mainstream ideology, follows a pattern set for him by his uncle and is symptomatic of the problem of individualism and leadership that characterize this period of an emergent middle class in the Mexican-descent community. George's tragic flaw, his pursuit of knowledge from institutions of higher learning as a quest for social power and his subsequent development as an antihero of his community of origin, is not his individual failure but a result of a social system that failed to recognize the role of the university in reproducing stratified social relations. As a student in secondary schools in Jonesville-on-the-Grande, George's resistance was primarily limited to his capacity to articulate critiques, a skill that is seen repeatedly as evidence of his leadership capacity. As an adult, a degreed person, what he does with his oratorical skills is important. Gramsci contrasts the role of the traditional intellectual with the organic intellectual by pointing out that "the mode of being the new intellectual can no longer consist in eloquence, which is an exterior and momentary mover of feelings and passions, but in active participation in practical life, as constructor, organizer, 'permanent persuader' and not just a simple orator" (*PN* 10). The important distinction being made here between "speaking" and "speaking on behalf of others" as legal or political representative should not be lost. George's decision to be a lawyer is all the more ironic given the role of the courts in the "legal" deterritorialization of Mexicans from their land. Being a lawyer was an important position to occupy because legal strategies were being developed during this period to protect the legal and civil rights of *mexicanos* in the United States.[10] Santiago López-Anguera, a neighbor of the Gómezes, is presented as an ideal model for George. He wants to represent his people any way he can, and he comes to live in the barrio in order to be as accessible as possible. The notion that George is an exceptional figure who will bring salvation to his community is foregrounded throughout the novel and presented as a burden:

> In a way it was his family's fault that Guálinto had so much trouble with Miss Cornelia [his first grade teacher]. His mother, his uncle, and even Carmen had come to take it for granted that he would be a great man as his dead father had wished. A great man who would help his people to a better kind of life. . . . Sometimes they thought he would be a great lawyer who would get back the lands they had lost. At other times they were certain he would become a great orator who would convince even the greatest of their enemies of the rightness of his cause. (*GWG* 125)

The community's belief that formal education alone would make George a leader of his people is shortsighted, for they are unable to foresee the consequences of his development away from his community of origin. The significance of maintaining an organic link to the community is best illustrated by contrasting George and Elodia, another outspoken student in high school. When George returns from the university as a military intelligence officer, there is an organic political movement emerging in Jonesville, in which Elodia is an important figure. Thus, even as the projected hero fails, an alternative model emerges in Elodia and her comrades.

In choosing to end his narrative in what Saldívar calls a "moment of failed utopian vision," Paredes thwarts the expectations that have been invested in narrow notions of individual leadership and social mobility. Saldívar's search for a utopian vision reveals a modernist desire for a singular, unified subject who functions as the single representative of his group, in much the same way as the hero of the *corrido* operates. Such a model, however, depends upon the establishment of binary oppositions in the articulation of good and evil social forces. This critical approach hinges on the belief that a unified subject is always and everywhere possible and desirable. Applied to the politics of social groups, it lapses back on a paradigm of homogeneity wherein inherent loyalties and filial relations supposedly reside; rather than examining the dialectical interplay between ideology and agency, between individual desires and group aspirations, between privilege and disenfranchisement, and the discontinuities between group history and individual experience, hope is invested in a cult of leadership. Such an approach suggests that dialectical resolutions are determined and predictable. But the political economy of such analyses hinges on teleological visions that express desires, not certainties.

Paredes provides instead a constructive alternative at the end of the novel, one that moves the focus away from individual to collective leadership. It is a nascent political vision that offers an alternative to the paradigm of the male hero. If the utopian vision fails, it is because we are looking for a parallel counternarrative to official history, which constructs a cult of leadership. The desire for a savior-hero remains within the paradigm of individualism. This form of politics maintains the status quo because it reinforces the belief that "exceptional" individuals are the conduits of power and change. Moreover, in the context of social relations that privilege male authority, the politics of status reinforce unequal gender relations because women are less likely to have access to the higher education they would need to earn credentials for public life. The importance of education for the would-be male hero of the family is instantiated in *GWG* in several instances. "The little girls did not enter into [Feliciano's] plans. They would grow up and marry like all girls did. But for the little boy Feliciano worked and hoped. Guálinto would have to be a learned man in order to help his people" (49). This grooming of the male hero occurs at the expense of females. This is evinced most clearly in the decision that Carmen, Guálinto's sister, withdraw from school to assist her mother in the home, despite her being an exceptionally good student. The novel points to the limitations of the genre of the *Bildungsroman* as a paradigm for resistance and social change. Within the culturally specific context of Mexican patriarchy, this narration of male ascension reveals that individual success cannot be used as a gauge for the well-being of an entire group. It is possible, rather, for an individual representative to act in the service of a community of interests. The emerging, organic model represented by Elodia offers an alternative vision that has its analog in the labor movements of South Texas and their examples of collective action and female leadership.

In depicting intracultural strife and constructing the protagonist as antihero, Paredes eschews the modernist ideal of unity: its central and hierarchical systems of authority and its marginalization of cultural others in its claim of universality. In doing so he exposes modernism's alliance with power. Moreover, as if anticipating postmodern aesthetics, the ending of *GWG* is open-ended rather than closed; that is, no final solution for the narrative is reached, although several possibilities are suggested.[11] In its most common form, the *Bildungsroman* is a novel that affirms the values of the bourgeoisie; it serves as an affirmation of social structures. Hence many novels of realism are closed-ended. Paredes's challenge to this narrative is most clearly evinced in the protagonist's fragmented subjectivity as manifested in his recurring dream of childhood. The achievement of the American Dream of social mobility and education through the ideology of individualism leaves George with a "nightmare" of unresolved guilt about his betrayal of the Mexican community. Contained within George's dream are repressed individual memories and desires that figure as elements of an alternative personal and national historical narrative for the *mexicano* community.

Ramón Saldívar notes that a revision of history occurs in George's dream. In what figures as a utopian longing for simple solution, Guálinto's imagination invests itself in a historical moment preceding U.S. hegemony rather than simply returning to the insurrectionist battle into which he was born and inscribing himself as a victorious hero. Identifying a different historical origin allows him to skirt the complex issue of secession from the United States. Yet Guálinto's political unconscious recognizes the powerful potential of cross-cultural alliances invoked by the Plan de San Diego and thus imagines a successful alliance among *rancheros,* the Mexican state, Irishmen, and escaped American Negro slaves. With such a coalition of oppressed peoples formed, Guálinto's imagined army is able to defeat Sam Houston at San Jacinto, but only after they have witnessed the defeat of Santa Anna, who is immediately hanged for his role in the corruption and inefficiency of the central government along with the "traitor" Lorenzo de Zavala. In his dream, "Texas and the Southwest will remain forever Mexican" (*GWG* 281). Saldívar asserts that the dream is "Guálinto's political unconscious in the form of the collective memory instantiated by the sense of self modeled by his father's, his uncle's, and his mother' lives, [which] returns to offer an alternative ideology and self-formation" ("Borderlands" 285–86). Thus far, Saldívar's reading of the protagonist's political unconscious is convincing, but he suggests that the feeling of "emptiness, of futility" that Guálinto experiences after he has reclaimed all the Spanish lands, including Florida, with his multiethnic army, are a return of the "repressed to trouble the stability of his new-found bourgeois self" (286). He thus locates the source of Guálinto's anxiety in his class position. Although I agree that this reading has some valence, I think the dream also articulates, at multiple levels, an anxiety with his ethnic and gender identity. The nexus of George's class, gender, and ethnic identity, and the privilege he solicits from them in the service of domination are the source of his anxieties and his inability to understand or control the emergence of the repressed and its meaning.

George's utopian—and one should add, modernist—vision of unification among the oppressed is fraught with meaning. Initially, one might be tempted to apply Saldívar's observation about the seditionist movement being "an early enunciation of coalition politics among Third World groups in the U.S." to George's dream version of 1836. But like the nationalist movements of the 1960s that Saldívar invokes, and like the seditionist movement, the proposed coalition described by George is a call to arms, a declaration of war that is primarily addressing a need for a cross-cultural alliance among men, not women. There are important and telling differences, however, between the historical coalition being articulated and acted upon when George is born, that which he imagines as a boy, and those which haunt him as a man. In George's recurring dream, the coalition is broader, including the Irish; yet, interestingly, in his reformation and defense of Mexico (he would reject U.S. encroachment and react against the Mexican government's corruptness and inefficiency), he feels the need to exterminate the Comanches as a training exercise for a war of liberation against the United States. In George's unconscious reinscription of colonial power, Native Americans must remain an enemy force who need to be eradicated.

This genocidal imperative in George's "mother-loving dream" suggests an unreconciled ambivalence toward, if not open hostility against, his own *mestizaje.* This is corroborated by the gendered curse against his dream, which reveals his anxiety and hostility. If we trace George's conflicted relationship to his indigenous identity, we find that it is bound to a feminization of the indigenous heritage of his maternal side; consequently, his ethnic and gender identity are intertwined and become a cultural, social, and psychological battleground for his self-concept. As is the case with many Chicano historical narratives, the question of gender is not directly or fully addressed in this novel; yet, as was done with the missing record on Sara Estela Ramírez, we can access the significance of gender identity, ideology, and power by reading between the gaps and absences in text. With *GWG,* we can examine the meaning of the silence enforced on females and all things feminine in the novel.

Dana Maynard points out that Ramón Saldívar is correct to assert that *GWG* should be read as gendered discourse, but she also notes that he is not explicit enough in identifying "*how* Paredes's ontological project, his . . . imagined Chicano subjectivity, is closely tied to gender" (Maynard 2). Maynard observes that in the initial naming scene, a dialectical movement occurs between "ideal and real identity, between the aspiration of each name and the negative reality it ends up conveying" (3). Each proposed name, says Maynard, is a proposed effort at family-community unity that falters, "and each name, ultimately, and ironically, invokes its antithesis" (4). Moreover, and most significant for the point being made here, "the dialectic between proposed and rejected names is heavily gendered" and "the identity finally chosen . . . does not leave out the feminine vision so much as [it is] predicated upon it" (5). For example, it is María, the mother of the child, who articulates the need for a great man's name to suit the child's projected role as a leader of his people. But it is the father of the child who shifts the child's proposed cultural allegiances by prophesying that he will be "a great man among the Gringos" and who proposes the name of "the great North American, he who was a general and fought the soldiers of the king" (*GWG* 16). The grandmother follows this suggestion by identifying Hidalgo, one of the Mexican heroes who allied himself with indigenous interests. But her suggestion is dismissed in favor of the "American" hero, George Washington. Thus, the final decision is arrived at not only through a dismissal of the women's suggestions but through a rejection of an indigenous Mexican identity. Ironically, the repressed emerges in the Spanish approximate that the grandmother enunciates as "Guálinto." This irony is noted by Feliciano, who responds to the grandmother's comment that Guálinto is "a funny name" in comparison to Hidalgo. In a final moment of gendered irony, the protagonist's elder sisters are silenced as a disruptive presence by their father when they speak. Thus, the privilege that Guálinto is to receive over his sisters is already expressing itself in these early moments of his life.

Inheriting his father's light skin, Guálinto's Mexican identity is negotiable in ways that it is not for those with Indian features. Nevertheless, as a child Guálinto is educated in the folk history of Mexicans and is proud of his *mestizaje.* An inherent part of that identity is the historical animosity between Anglos and Mexicans; thus in his childhood games he fights the Texas Rangers. For Guálinto, power and cultural resistance are associated with masculinity. For instance, when he is being enrolled in school, he encounters a picture of his namesake, George Washington, and he is greatly disappointed: "He stared at the picture with disillusionment that was almost contempt. A face like an angry old woman" (109). He is happy, then, when his uncle tells his teacher that Guálinto is an Indian name. His teacher, who is condescending toward Mexicans and their customs even though she herself is Mexican, furthers this feminization of his cultural identity when she humiliates Guálinto for signing his name with his mother's surname at the end, the matronymical practice of Spain and Latin America. "When she got his paper Miss Cornelia called the class to attention and informed them that Guálinto had married a gentleman named García and that now he was Mrs. Guálinto G. García" (126). The feminized notion of language is reinforced by the fact that "he spoke Spanish, literally as his mother tongue: it was the only language his mother would allow him to use when he spoke to her" (147). Guálinto's counterhegemonic identity is destabilized, though, when he begins linking notions of power, sexuality, and social status to one another. This is most evident in his relationship to María Elena Osuna. As a member of an elite family, she is unattainable to him except through his services as a tutor. El Colorado points out to Guálinto that she was only interested in him because he was first in the class. In a racialized discourse that depicts Guálinto's middle-class status and social ambition, María Elena's beauty is contrasted to that of a working-class girl.

In pursuit of a boy who had insulted his sister's sexual honor, Guálinto finds himself in a part of the *barrio* he had never been in before. He encounters a *baile* and is intrigued by the beauty of a girl celebrating her *quinceañera*. "She wore her hair in a pompadour and she was pretty. Very dark but very pretty, in a way quite different from María Elena's white skinned beauty. . . . Pretty, but not for him, he thought" (243). Shortly afterward he encounters the boy he was looking for and they fight. The people from the party laud his fighting ability and he meets Mercedes, the girl he was admiring, in a highly erotic scene. Though he is very attracted to her, he resists spending time with her and makes an excuse to leave. His mind filled with erotic images and sexual desire, he promises to return. Experiencing a sense of triumph, he tells himself, "These were his people, the real people he belonged with. His place was among them, not the 'Spaniards' like the Osunas. He would marry Mercedes and live on the farm. He would go back" (247). He never does, though. This fear of the dark-skinned Mercedes's sexuality is also a fear of social stasis. He fears that choosing her closes his options for social advancement; in his mind it signifies the difference between staying on the farm and going to college. This rejection and devaluation of the feminine conflates cultural, class, and racial prejudices in a privileging of a combined sense of the masculine with social mobility. It also means that he becomes alienated from alternative modes of expressing dissent and cultural resistance that were both empowering and, like his fear of the sexual, made him fearful of females' power to hurt or disempower him. In *GWG* some of these alternative modes are presented in the gendered discourse of "women's" folktales.

The Legend of La Llorona: Repression and Insurgent Politics

Neighborhood of Zaragoza Park
where scary stories interspersed with
inherited superstitions were exchanged
waiting for midnight and the haunting
lament of La Llorona—the weeping lady
of our myths and folklore—who wept nightly
along the banks of Boggy Creek
for the children she'd lost or drowned
in some river (depending on the version).
i think i heard her once
and cried
out of sadness and fear
running all the way home nape hairs at attention
swallow a pinch of table salt and
make the sign of the cross
sure cure for frightened Mexican boys.

—Raúl Salinas

Oral folktales appear throughout the novel as another primary speech genre that binds Guálinto to Mexican culture. One scene in particular and one legend in general illustrates the force and function of folklore as a gendered discourse. In this scene Guálinto is eavesdropping on his uncle and two other men recounting stories based on personal or communal experiences blended with familiar folk legends. This all-male setting echoes the setting of *corridos,* but though violence is also central in these tales, a different type of tale emerges. Unlike in the *corrido,* where gender is addressed by exclusion, these legends speak more directly to the issue of gender in Mexican culture; moreover, these tales emerge from a different historical era, a factor that raises a question about the significance of historical and cultural origins and their relationship to analytical paradigms. The three stories that the young Guálinto hears address gender relations; they are about men abusing or ignoring women, and cultural allegiance. Thus, whether at the level of the real or the symbolic, intracultural violence is foregrounded.

Before moving to a discussion of the stories, it is important to note that this is not the first scene in the novel in which folklore is present as a formative force on Guálinto. It is linked in his subconscious to his fear of the dark, of nighttime, and the unknown:

> With darkness the banana grove and the trees beyond it became a haunted wood where lurked demons, skeletons and white-robed women with long long hair. The city's stormy politics had thrown up a vomit of murders and gun battles. Guálinto's immediate neighborhood, being at the edge of town, had seen more than its share of bloodshed. By that tree a man was killed by his best friend. Politics. Over there a woman was attacked and murdered. On a big hackberry tree beyond the backyard fence was a cross made of big nails driven into the trunk. Nobody knew exactly why the cross was there, but there were many stories explaining it. Here, there, everywhere were memories of the unhallowed dead. They haunted the night. They made the darkness terrible. (50)

In this litany of Guálinto's fears are references to popular folktales, such as La Llorona (the white-robed woman with long hair), and to local history (the acts of local violence). Bakhtin has noted the important role that folksongs and folktales play in literature as a means of "intensifying" the native soil. He states that "local folklore interprets and saturates space with time, and draws it into history" ("Bildungsroman" 52). In such a manner folklore functions to give past events meaning in the present; likewise, present events acquire significance as part of a larger historical pattern. History is thus not just static, something to be remembered, but a dialectical process of past and present events and social relations.

The first tale Guálinto hears the men tell is a "story of how God avenged a dead girl." Set in West Texas in a time before civil law, it is a story of the marriage and death of the village's "prettiest girl" at the hands of her husband, the town drunkard. One day in a drunken rage, having lost his money in a card game, the man beats his pregnant wife to death. Without a system of civil law through which to seek justice, and because she had no male relatives to avenge her, the village people are unsure "what to do with the husband of the dead girl they had just buried." When the husband returns from the funeral, he encounters the spirit of his dead wife and a beastlike incarnation of his unborn son. He is attacked and left to die by the beast. The husband is found by villagers before he dies, so he is able to tell his story. The only signs of his attackers are tracks left in the snow by a woman and a small child. After the tale is told, Feliciano tries to rationalize its mysterious elements by saying that the man may have been attacked by a bear. He is unable to explain the tracks in the snow, however.

This tale is followed with Feliciano's story about a time when he, his father, and a group of other cowboys were in cattle country and encountered a crazed, beastlike man howling at the full moon. After the screaming man passed on his way, a group of his family and friends arrived in search of him. They explain that the man was infected with rabies and "lost his nerve" before drinking the "poison" that would cure him. Don Pancho and Don José note that "in the old days . . . there were no injections, as they have now. Nothing except hot iron and garlic, which almost never worked" (*GWG* 91). Again, Feliciano is quick to point out that this was a natural phenomenon: a disease, not a ghost. This leads to Don Pancho's account of a localized version of the legend of La Llorona. In his version a milkman of Jonesville encounters La Llorona one night, but, rather than being frightened, he becomes angry and begins cursing her and almost hits her. He is unable to finish the story because Guálinto, who has been eavesdropping, becomes frightened and begins crying out of fear. He receives such a *susto* (fright) that he must be cured by a local *curandera*.

The legend of La Llorona is about a woman's search for her lost children who have drowned, in many cases at her hands, after one form or another of mistreatment by her husband; the tales discussed above are very similar and demonstrate the continued resonance this legend has as a communal history of the domination of women.[12] It also speaks to race and class domination as well as betrayal. The second tale conveys a lesson about folk medicine and modern medicine, but it also highlights the crazed man's refusal to trust in a *curandera's* "poison" as a source of healing. Each of these tales speaks to the importance of the family and community as a source of both pain and support. These stories bear closer examination because Guálinto is exposed to them before he enters school, when his primary socialization is occurring at home, and because they are told by men, Guálinto's primary role models. These stories are significant since they play an important role in the formation of his ethnics and his class and gender identity. Guálinto's reaction, his fear of these tales of vengeful, defensive, and pain-stricken women, is a problem that must be investigated. First, let us establish an understanding of La Llorona as a powerful cultural symbol.

In his important essay on La Llorona as a cultural symbol of Greater Mexico, José Limón asserts that the legendary female figure needs to be understood on two levels: "first, as a positive, contestative symbol for the women of Greater Mexico and second as a critical symbolic reproduction of a socially unfilled utopian longing within the Mexican folk masses who tell her story. She speaks to the social and psychological needs left unmet by the hegemonic, hierarchical, masculinized, and increasingly capitalistic social order imposed on the Mexican folk masses since their beginning" ("La Llorona" 60). As an articulation of the domination of women and the folk masses that is popular in both Mexico and the U.S. Southwest (69), it is important to note that this legend has its origins in the colonial period of the sixteenth century and is often seen as a lamentation for the loss of cultural identity. This understanding of the legend is based on an allegorical reading that positions the maternal figure as metaphor for the indigenous people, who cries in pain for her "lost" children in the period of racial, cultural, and political domination of colonialism. In versions of the tale in which men are traumatized and in some cases killed by their encounter with La Llorona, such as the one told by Don Pancho, we see much more than the representation of a grieving mother whose cries represent a general condition of domination; rather, in this version, in which La Llorona has supernatural qualities to harm men, her function is to protect and speak on behalf of the interests of women against male domination (77). In other feminine symbols of Greater Mexico, such as the Virgen de Guadalupe or La Malinche, there is an "identification of the socially weak with the maternal feminine." Given the correlation between patriarchy and political/class power that Victor Turner has noted, we should, according to Limón, comprehend the "motif of sexual betrayal as a masculinized/feminized symbolic reproduction of class and power distinctions extant since the colonial period" (84). It takes a nuanced reading of this tale, though, to avoid reading it as a victim's tale of grief or as a moral about the "evilness" of women. Unlike the stories of the Virgen de Guadalupe or La Malinche, La Llorona is a legend that has remained predominantly in the hands of women (77); this testifies to its endurance as a powerful and enabling articulation of resistance.

Limón points out that if we are to truly understand the full potency and potential of this story then we must realize that "it is not enough to grieve . . . a subversive symbolic strategy must hold out some possibility for recovery" (87). In Limón's reading, the children's death by water is ambiguous, for water also represents rebirth; thus the reunion of the mother with her children is possible, as is the social rebirth of Mexico (87). The infanticide contained within the tale is the symbolic destruction of the basis for patriarchy, the promise of a "restoration of maternal bonds" and a restored world of love in which men as abusers of power are absent (76). The significance of this tale as a cultural symbol, as an expression of resistance and utopian possibility, is even more salient if contrasted with what Saldívar calls the failed utopian vision of the novel's end: just as a return of the repressed that haunts George, La Llorona haunts and inhabits the political conscious of the people of Greater Mexico.

The utopian vision I refer to here has two instantiations in the last chapter of the novel, ironically titled "Leader of His People." The first is the recurring childhood dream referred to above, in which George organizes a coalition of forces and fends off Anglo encroachment in Mexico and recovers Spanish territory. The second unfulfilled vision is that George will return to his hometown and live up to the expectations held by his childhood friends and family that he become a leader against Anglo hegemony. I would argue that these utopian visions are inherently flawed, for they depend on a debilitating notion of individual leadership—an investment in a singular male hero. Moreover, George's politics of exclusion further blemish his repressed dream. This troubling political vision mirrors his rejection of his *mestizaje;* rather than leaving him with a sense of wholeness, he is left feeling incomplete. Unable to imagine forging peace with Indians in his dream, he wages war and defeats those who, in his mind, have become feminized as a result of colonial conquest. And despite operating on behalf of Mexico, his dream is a fantasy that seeks to fulfill a European imperial agenda in its recovery of all the lands lost by Spain; thus, Mexico and its cultural practices and values, as well as its indigenous population, is also rejected as a legitimate, autonomous model of nationhood.

Why does George so strongly reject what he perceives as feminized? Surely one source of this rejection is the internalized inferiority he experiences as a rejected suitor of the upper-class, light-skinned María Elena Osuna, and certainly the patriarchal discourse of Mexican society that makes him feel shame for his sister's betrayal by an Anglo lover contributes to this association of the feminine with the weak and the disinherited. Moreover—and this observation should reiterate the point that patriarchal discourse from within Mexican culture works against the creation of communal heroes—the construction of George as a hero was, from the outset, built at the expense of the women in his family. George cannot both fully embrace the privilege he has received and acknowledge his complicity in female suppression. Thus weakness becomes a "natural" condition of the Mexican/indigenous feminine and all that he wishes to distance himself from in his pursuit of power. George's marriage to Ellen Dell, an Anglo graduate student of sociology, can be seen as a consolidation of his disdain and fear of his culture. Ellen's intelligence, "plain" looks, seriousness, and kindness are contrasted with María Elena's beauty and lack of "brains." Furthermore, George knows they are "meant for each other" when he learns that she is studying Mexican migrant labor in central Texas (*GWG* 283). Not only is Ellen all that Mexican women are not in George's estimation, her status as a scholar of Mexican migrants provides George with social and ideological incentives to find her appealing. In *Anglos and Mexicans in the Making of Texas,* David Montejano remarks on the relationship between sociology and history; although his comments refer to a more recent period, he makes an observation that is relevant here. He notes that the process of integration is often "heralded" by the "discovery" of social groups as objects of study in institutions of higher education. Thus in the early sociological studies on Mexicans, "even the indigenous Spanish Americans were a `relatively recent immigrant group when *social* rather than legal status' was considered" (Montejano, *AM* 260–61). Moreover, Montejano observes a "striking but common paradox" in this field, "where the historical legends of the Alamo, cowboys, and Longhorns co-exist innocently alongside sociological studies of Mexican Americans as immigrants. Immigrant approaches . . . serve to shift the emphasis away from war and annexation, denying the memory of these origins for contemporary Mexican-Anglo relations. Rather than a people living under the shadow of the Alamo and San Jacinto, Mexican Americans are now seen as another group marching through the stages of assimilation" (261). Ellen's intelligence, including the academic discipline with which she is allied, which ignores the legal status of Mexicans as well as their history of conflict with Anglos, accommodates all George's aspirations erases all he wants to distance from himself.

Like the crazed, rabid man who lost faith in the folk medicine and ran from his family and friends, George runs from his own folk. Forgetting the curative powers of the community and the antidote that quells the fears created by the legend of La Llorona (described in the excerpt from Raúl Salinas's poem), George does not run home for a sure cure but instead runs away. He does not, as Juan Gómez-Quiñones has said, see culture as a "safe house" but as a source of danger.

There is, however, a utopian vision inscribed at the novel's end. It is a vision that speaks to the power of the weak, the dominated, the feminine. The utopian vision at the end of the novel is not, as Saldívar argues, simply an imaginary revision of a past battle, nor Guálinto's reidentification with his community as the hero-savior, but a utopian vision that looks forward to a reconstruction of social relations—a historical process that strives to end all inequalities in the process of its own fulfillment. "Power as patriarchy must be destroyed if a new social order is to re-emerge and survive in Greater Mexico, one that . . . speaks not only of women but through the power of women for *all* the socially weak" notes Limón ("La Llorona" 88). Recall that the hint of this possibility is inscribed in the novel through Elodia, the strong, assertive and sole woman of the emerging Mexican political movement in Jonesville, who, through her tears, calls George a "Vendido sanavabiche!" for his betrayal to his community. Through her anger and her tears we are reminded of La Llorona and the politics of betrayal. Through her active pursuit of change in political and social relations we are reminded of that which Paredes does not name but we know to be nonetheless true: that in this era there were many women who were organizing and speaking on behalf of other women and for all the residents of Greater Mexico.[13]

According to Bakhtin, "the first and foremost criterion for the finalization of the utterance is the possibility of responding to it . . . of assuming a responsive attitude toward it . . ." ("The Problem" 76). The ending of *GWG* evokes a response by suggesting a tentative direction in which to look for answers—in the articulation of political visions by groups that retain or establish organic ties to the communities of the oppressed. One such person who worked alongside those struggling for change was Emma Tenayuca, who in 1938, at about the same time Paredes was finishing *GWG*, was an eloquent and forceful spokesperson for the women who launched a successful strike against the pecan-shelling industry in San Antonio, a politically consummated Elodia in the reality of history.

"About Emma Tenayuca and the Pecan Shellers"

What is a pecan sheller's life worth?
Emma Tenayuca asked herself / she looked
at the woman across the desk
who knew . . .

she was looking to Emma for an answer
that would come up pure: something clear
sounding like something
right . . .
Emma said
something had to be done—
i'll go with you
together / alongside
10,000 plus out of 12,000 pecan shellers
very expectedly walking out
even though the newspapers said
that the workers had
unexpectedly gone on strike

the woman thinks back on it now: sometimes
justice comes to those who wait on
the promised day / the goodwill of others
then shakes her head
and figures that it usually comes
only to people tired of shelling pecans for
$2.73 a week / $251 a year
who knows what a pecan sheller's life is worth

and enter their fight
sideways / backways
not always sure which direction is next
—yet enter their fight—

—Teresa Acosta

Thus far a close analysis of *George Washington Gómez* has allowed us to investigate the kinds of complex negotiations of power that occur at a local level, away from institutional sites of power. Feminists have long recognized the importance and validity of documenting the local and the personal as manifestations of political discourse. In "About Emma Tenayuca and the Pecan Shellers" (see appendix 2 for the complete poem), from which the above lines are extracted, Teresa Acosta poetically reconstructs the dynamic between a laborer and a spokesperson/leader who is being solicited to work in the pecan shellers' behalf. Acosta does not privilege the voice of

Emma Tenayuca but instead writes her poem as a dialogue between her and the laborer. The poet makes clear that Tenayuca is not an all-knowing leader but someone with whom the laborers want to work in eliminating exploitative work conditions. Acosta portrays Tenayuca as an engaged listener who respects the workers' analyses of their experience and their motivations. And though the woman is "looking to Emma for an answer / that would come up pure: something clear / sounding like something / right," Tenayuca is portrayed only as a willing recruit to the cause whose role as spokesperson is to be representative of the interests of the workers. Because she was an eloquent spokesperson for the pecan shellers during their strike, Tenayuca's words occupy a central position, figuratively and literally, in stanza seven of the thirteen-stanza poem. The planning and organizing of a walkout break public expectations and the stereotype of the passive Mexican woman. Tenayuca's contribution is shown to be her solidarity and respect for the workers as well as her commitment to action. In a characteristic that is a trademark of Acosta's poetic style, she identifies the source of her inspiration in a footnote. In this case, the line "something had to be done" is taken from an interview. This method lends integrity and historical accuracy to Acosta's poetic rendering of this historical event. With Tenayuca's words as the centerpiece of the poem, Acosta utilizes the voice of the worker to provide a context for the events that precede and follow the strike.

Once again, Acosta's poetry, as it does throughout this study, assists in the construction of a contrapuntal narrative of women's history that defies the vision constructed by historical narratives and, in many cases, literary narratives as well. The political work of Emma Tenayuca as a member of the Communist Party, U.S.A., and her allegiance to working-class Mexicans provides a stark contrast to the intellectual work of Paredes's Guálinto. This contrast is marked not only by the difference in class alliances between organic and traditional intellectuals but also by these two figures' relationships to their cultural heritage, community history, and different perceptions of the boundaries of nationhood. In contrast to George W. Gómez's conflicted relationship with his indigenous identity, in a 1984 acceptance speech for an award given her by the National Association of Chicano Studies (NACS),[14] Tenayuca emphasized the positive significance of her Indian heritage and the inspiration she drew from it: "On my father's side, we never claimed anything but Indian blood. . . . And I was very, very conscious of that. It was this historical background and my grandparents' attitude which formed my ideas and actually gave me the courage later to undertake the type of work I did in San Antonio. . . . I think it was the combination of being a Texan, being a Mexican, and being more Indian than Spanish that propelled me to take action. I don't think I ever thought in terms of fear" (Calderón and Zamora, "Manuela" 275–77). In 1937, Tenayuca was the general secretary of ten chapters of the Workers Alliance of America (272). After becoming chair of the Texas Communist Party in 1939, "Emma's effectiveness and popularity as a Mexican labor leader often made her the focal point of anti-union and anti-Mexican hysteria, which eventually forced her to leave Texas to ensure her personal safety" (274).[15] It was in this capacity that she coauthored with her Anglo husband, Homer Brooks, a well-known essay on the Mexican working class and the relationship between Mexican American nationals and nonnationals. "The Mexican Question in the Southwest" articulates her affinity with the working class and is born of her firsthand experiences of injustice.

In her NACS acceptance speech, Tenayuca recounts an episode that occurred when she was seventeen, just before she became involved in union organizing. A family of migrant workers had been chased off of the land they had harvested without pay and had to seek recourse from the Mexican consulate for action even though they were *Tejanos* (277). This event inspired her to take action and to recognize the precarious, vulnerable status of migrant workers. Tenayuca and Brooks ask, "Should the conclusion . . . be drawn that the Mexican people in the Southwest constitute a nation—or that they form a segment of the Mexican nation?" They answer no. They view the geographic, economic, and political life of Mexicans and Anglos as being inextricably intertwined. They do, however, see discrimination by the upper class and the state as the major obstacle preventing "the national unification of the American people" (Tenayuca and Brooks 262). Moreover, in critiquing what they see as "sterile paths" to political action, they examine the politics of LULAC, noting that it should not be seen as a static organization but one that could potentially play a positive role in promoting social change

> In the past, [LULAC's] viewpoint was colored by the outlook of petty-bourgeois native born, who seek escape from the general oppression that has been the lot of the Mexican people as a whole. It meant an attempt to achieve Americanization, while barring the still naturalized foreign-born from membership.

> It resulted in the glorification of the English language and Anglo-American culture to the extent of prohibiting Spanish within the local societies. And, finally, it ignored the need for labor organization among the masses of super-exploited workers. This program of the LULAC resulted almost from the beginning in its isolation from the Mexican masses, who felt that it would lead them nowhere except to a possible split between the native born and the foreign born.
>
> Recently, this splitting policy of the LULAC has undergone significant changes. An amendment to its constitution recognizes Mexico as the cultural motherland. In several cities . . . LULAC has entered into cooperative relationship with other Mexican groups, including labor organizations. (265–66)

Tenayuca and Brooks's essay, like the cross-cultural collaboration of Eimer and González, is further evidence of the complex alliances and political strategies that compose Mexican Americans' political and literary history. If it is true that political counterhistories often do not take cultural histories into account, as has been implied throughout this study, then in the repressed politics of Paredes's *George Washington Gómez,* it is also true that literary narratives often elide oppositional politics, such as those of Tenayuca.[16]

World War II was a convulsive historical moment that exacerbated many of the concerns surrounding class, ethnicity, ideology, and political strategy that we have been addressing thus far in this chapter. We turn now to a text that was written in the midst of an emerging political movement in the 1960s but is situated around the lives of farmworkers in the post–World War II period.

Tomás Rivera and the Construction of Community in the Post–World War II Period

> *Bartolo passed through town every December when he knew that most of the people had returned from work up north. He always came by selling his poems. By the end of the first day, they were almost sold out because the names of the people of the town appeared in the poems. And when he read them aloud it was something emotional and serious. I recall that one time he told the people to read the poems out loud because the spoken word was the seed of love in the darkness.*
>
> —Tomás Rivera, *. . . y no se lo tragó la tierra*

> *We had to present two public presentations a year, or poetry declamations. The first poem I declaimed was "El Minero." . . . You had to dress your part. What the teacher wanted to teach us was the idea of work. . . . She was teaching us the idea of work, in a sense the idea of community, that all these people are important in your lives. That's why everyone portrayed a job. We had to recite in front of the class and then in the Ideal Theater, where all the neighborhoods would gather to hear the children orators. . . . Our teacher was very oriented toward work, the ideal of work, the dignity of work. It was also implicit in their etiquette, too, the idea that it was the way you taught respect for people. Everyone in society, no matter what he does, if he works, has dignity within the structure.*
>
> —Tomás Rivera

As I noted in the beginning of this chapter, the post–World War II period of Mexican American history is often characterized by Chicana/o historians as leading to the Chicana/o civil rights movement. Having risked their lives in a "war for democracy," Mexican American veterans, and indeed the entire extended community, "believed the national promise that when they returned home, the American Dream of social mobility and middle-class status would be theirs. . . . But the benefits, the dreams, and the cash were not equitably distributed. Blacks, Mexicans, and persons of Asian ancestry, all legitimately Americans, had been left out" (Gutíerrez, "Community" 44). In general this period is seen as a watershed for increased political consciousness and activism stimulated by the "noble" goals the war was said to represent. It is during this period as well that the term "Mexican American" was popularized, supplanting "Latin" and "Spanish American" (Gómez-Quiñones, *CP* 34). Juan Gómez-Quiñones believes that because of individual and collective contributions to the war effort by the Mexican community, equities were expected in return: "Their political legitimacy was viewed as fortified. Wartime promises of equality led to a new optimism in the Mexican communities of the U.S. regarding the postwar period" (*CP* 33). Mario García points out that "the war to save democracy and the struggle for the Four Freedoms . . . provided progressive unions . . . with additional ideological support and inspiration for achieving union representation and equal justice for racial minorities" (*MA* 186). Both historians acknowledge that this "consciousness" and activism was not without precedent in the Mexican community, especially amongst the labor sector.

Most of the labor organizing that occurred, however, either in conjunction with or independent from mainstream labor organizations, was concentrated among industrial workers or trade unions. Although agribusiness was becoming increasingly industrialized, it still relied on manual labor as the most efficient and least expensive means of harvesting crops. The organizing activity that occurred among industrial workers and trade unionists has received much attention by Chicana/o historians, but scant attention has been paid to agricultural laborers in both labor and political histories of this period. It is as if a labor force is deemed worthy of notice only after it commands attention through protest activity.[17] Extant documentation of farmworker experience of this period is primarily centered around the problems with the *bracero* program. This highlights an ideological dilemma that has characterized the approach to the farmworker "problem" as it has historically been addressed by Mexican American leaders and community political organizations.

In general, the social status and work conditions of farmworkers prior to the 1960s have been vexed by a perceived tension between their status as workers and their "illegal" status as noncitizens.[18] While many leaders and organizations in the Mexican American community acknowledged the exploitative work conditions faced by migrant farmworkers, these same organizations often capitulated to nativism and anti-Mexican hysteria and thus supported the eradication of the *bracero* program, stricter enforcement of immigration by the border patrol, and massive deportations (García, *MA* 51–53, 95–98).[19] The arguments for these campaigns against Mexicans rested, then as now, on the idea that undocumented workers drained social services, displaced "American" farmworkers of Mexican descent because they could be paid less, and were a criminal threat. The ideological dilemma of nationality manifested in the immigrant question works in favor of agribusiness's interests because it thwarts organizing against the maltreatment of workers. In contrast to the ambivalent, marginalized status that Mexican nationals and farmworkers occupy in Gómez-Quiñones's and García's histories, their presence is central in Tomás Rivera's *. . . y no se lo tragó la tierra / . . .and the earth did not devour him*. In portraying the shared humanity between the documented and the undocumented, and the conditions of their daily existence under exploitation, inequality, and liminal social status, this novel documents the lived experiences of farmworkers and demonstrates the relative insignificance of citizenship as a political problem.

The postwar period was a crucial juncture in the history of Mexicans in the United States. Aided by the GI Bill, many veterans acquired an education and laid the groundwork for the emergence of a critical mass of Mexican Americans in universities, a process that was to culminate in the 1960s and '70s with the development of Chicano-studies programs. But lest I too quickly proclaim this as universal progress for Mexicans in the United States, it is also important to note that this access to institutions of higher education also quickly became a class marker as well as one that distinguished citizens from noncitizens—a fact that exacerbates the ideological problem of the relationship between identity and nationhood. It would take the insurgent activism of the United Farm Workers and their predecessor organizations in the early '60s to address fully the plight of the farmworkers as a labor and human-rights issue. In the context of an ongoing political movement by Chicanos, Tomás Rivera, an ex-farmworker turned professor, published his novel about the lives of migrant farm workers in the post–World War II period.

There is an abundance of scholarship on *. . . y no se lo tragó la tierra.*[20] Early scholarship primarily focuses on his themes of exploitation, his documentation of the economic and material conditions of farmworkers and the psychosocial consequences of those conditions, the construction of individual and collective subjectivity, as well as the innovative structure of the novel as a *Bildungsroman* and its relationship to the process of remembering. More-recent studies by Ramón Saldívar, Hector Calderón, and José Limón attest to the enduring significance of *Tierra,* Rivera's only published novel. These studies utilize contemporary critical approaches, cultural-studies and postcolonial theory in particular, to explore issues of identity, folklore, and narrative strategy. In this section, while I will draw on select criticism, I am less concerned with performing a material or structural analysis of Rivera's novel or with offering a definitive statement on the total work than I am with reading the protagonist as an ideal subject, a representative figure of a utopian vision that many critics find articulated in the novel's end. This focus continues the investigation being conducted into the construction and articulation of leadership, ideology, and identity in this chapter.

In taking such an approach, I do not mean to suggest that these conceptual categories are separate areas of analysis. Rather, they form a triad that has served as a foundation for the writing of political histories, and since the objective of this study is to read the literature against the grain of the histories, such an approach, especially with a relatively short, albeit dense, text, will facilitate this comparison of the literary and the historical. I begin with the last of this trilogy of analytical concepts because the community of migrants (documented and undocumented, "legal" and "illegal") depicted in the novel has been historically marginalized within the Mexican community of the United States. Such an observation is not meant to suggest that this amorphous community is either homogenous unto itself or essentially or fundamentally different than the rest of the Mexican American population. Instead, what must be attended to here is the specificity of their status as migrants, for it is this structural position in the regional, national, and international system of capital that defines their particular geopolitical status even while it connects them to a binational Mexican community and other migratory border crossers throughout the world.

Situated in the 1950s, the decade preceding the sustained social movement for justice that came to be known as *el movimiento,* this text examines the people who move geographically, seasonally, and continuously in search of work to meet their basic human needs. Migrant farmworkers are, by definition, a displaced and deterritorialized people who are nevertheless tied to the land by their labor. The imperative to move in search of basic human needs has other concrete effects on the social and political status of migrants. The lack of a permanent home signifies a condition of economic and political instability. Consequently, their uprootedness prohibits effective political participation because their context shifts in accordance with the seasons and the sites of harvest. Though their status in the social structure impedes political participation and representation, they are concretely affected by the state's educational, legal, and military institutions. Because they are structurally disempowered by their status as migrants, they are both physically and psychically removed from the rest of the population—they are marginalized within the social, intellectual, and political landscape. Their movement in time and space as a mode of survival is far different than the concern for social mobility that preoccupied the middle class. The "brown faces in high places" attitude that characterizes the politics of status and the politics of the antisegregation movement, which strove to gain access to public space, sharply contrasts with migrants' concerns for shelter, transportation, food, health care, and fair wages.

In an interview with Juan Bruce-Novoa, Rivera links the notion of movement with life and justice as well as with consciousness: "Within those migrants I saw that strength [for intellectual emancipation]. They may be economically deprived, politically deprived, socially deprived, but they kept moving, never staying in one place to suffer or be subdued, but always searching for work. . . . If they stayed where there was no work they would die, and they didn't die" ("Interview" 151). Migrancy is thus seen as a sign of strength and endurance. This theme of movement is closely linked to ideology and political practice, a more nuanced and metaphorical meaning of movement as a search for justice, stability, and political empowerment. This is instantiated in the novel as a search for consciousness and is made literal in the move of the protagonist from under the house to the top of the tree in the last vignette. Thus, ideology is mapped out spatially. The novel is a story of an emerging, not an insurgent, consciousness; consequently, political action remains at the abstract level and moves from a precritical to a metacritical consciousness. Hector Calderón has said that "the book parallels the Chicano Movement of the late '60s and early '70s through its reassessment of traditional culture, its historical self-consciousness, and, especially, through its developing sense of group solidarity" (Calderón 102). I would argue, however, that while the book may anticipate the Movement in that very generalized way, it clearly predates it in its lack of specific strategies for collective action and an agenda for social change.

In "The Lost Year," the opening story of Rivera's novel, the child protagonist's loss of words symbolizes his removal from himself, his fellow humans, and reality—his removal from history. He drifts between a dream world and a state of mental confusion in which he knows not how to differentiate between consciousness and unconsciousness: "It almost always began with a dream in which he would suddenly awaken and then realize that he was really asleep" (*Tierra* 85). The protagonist is rendered powerless and static by his inability to identify the cause of his confusion: ". . . he turned his head to see who was calling, he would make a complete turn, and there he would turn up—in the same place" (85). Marx refers to the alienation of an individual as that condition in which "man's own deed becomes an alien power opposed to him, which enslaves him, instead of being controlled by him" (Marx 160). The protagonist's realization that he is also a source of his own confusion signifies a need for introspection. It is precisely at the point of remembering that the novel begins.

The twelve vignettes recount a year on the migrant trail—different places and people's experiences are recollected with the unnamed central figure acting as protagonist or witness. The anonymous collective voice resists the identification of a specific individual subject, but because it is clear that the voice in the framing stories, "The Lost Year" and "Under the House," are the same, and because this central figure "assumes knowledge of and responsibility for each of the scenes narrated," we can assume his presence in each of the stories (Sommers 102). It is through his representation of events that we are given an interpretive framework to understand how they effect him as an individual and as a member of a larger community. The stories that follow are a damning indictment of agribusiness and capitalism as the workers are exploited, abused, and struggle to subsist as "un pueblo olvidado" at the margins of political and social life. Central to this struggle are attempts to better their condition through formal education and the acquisition of knowledge that will offer insight into their abject poverty. But the implied critique is not directed entirely outward; contained also is a critical look inward at the cultural values and beliefs that promote social and intellectual stasis. Thus intracultural social relations become the object of critique simultaneous with the indictment of an oppressive economic system.

One vignette in particular, "The Night Before Christmas," graphically illustrates the simultaneity of critiques directed both inward and outward. The process of consuming is as alienating as the process of labor for the characters in this novel. Marx said that people take for granted the fact that we acquire things with money; because money in and of itself is valueless, it attains value because we allow it to represent labor and effort in abstract form. Under a market economy, goods are too often acquired simply for the sake of owning them. More often than not, the utility value is left unconsidered since consumers are taught that there is a pleasure in the possession of goods instead of in their use. It is often the case that people acquire objects as a means of obtaining the status they can confer. Thus commodities are fetishized to the extent that they are imbued with nonintrinsic value (Marx 227–30, 319–20). This aspect of the alienation of the consumer is illustrated in "The Night Before Christmas" when a mother ventures to town to purchase toys for her children.

The commercialization of this holy day is highlighted by the "barrage of commercials, music and Christmas cheer over the radio" (*Tierra* 134). Despite the fact that Doña María cannot afford to buy gifts for her children, she is compelled by the outside forces of advertising and cultural conformity to do just that. Her children are no longer appeased by gifts of oranges and nuts, nor do they have the ability to make their own toys like Don Chon did when he was young. Don Chon's reference to his childhood provides a sharp contrast between the nature of the society he is currently living in and that of his past. The act of making his own toys constitutes an act of unalienated labor, something he did strictly for himself, a nonreified act.

His wife recognizes that it is unfair to compare two societies so inherently different: "... but it's different here. They [the children] see so many things" (135). Similarly, just as the nature of labor has been distorted, so has the significance of the holiday. There is no mention of the religious origins and function of Christmas; instead, it has become strictly a commercialized activity in the United States.

In the minds of the children, whether or not they receive gifts depends on whether or not they are deserving. They have been conditioned by the barrage of commercials to consider self-worth something that is measured against material goods. The children seem to know that they should not expect much from their parents, yet they have been allowed to believe in a mythical figure who will reward them on Christmas Day—*if* they are deserving.

Doña María is unable to function outside the familiar confines of her home. Her agoraphobia is characterized as a fear of public places that precipitates anxiety attacks, dizziness, and shortness of breath, among other symptoms. Agoraphobics feel a need to avoid crowded conditions and thus flee whenever an attack occurs (Chambless and Goldstein 2). Thus, as Doña María goes to the store, she is struggling against two forces—her compulsion to buy and her fear of crowds. Although her desire to buy gifts for her children is unselfish, it is an act that bears harmful consequences for her. Once in the store, the interplay between her phobia of crowds and her compulsion to buy overwhelms her. The store becomes an amorphous blob; there is no distinction between people and merchandise: "Only stacks and stacks of merchandise and people crowded against one another. She even started hearing voices coming from the merchandise" (*Tierra* 138). She is pushed to the brink of insanity by the struggle going on within her, one that is a manifestation of social forces. In this ultra-alienated state of anxiety she becomes an automaton, operating without thinking, driven only by her irrepressible desire to get the gifts she is seeking, until she eventually loses consciousness of reality and finds "herself drifting in a sea of people" (139).

"The Night Before Christmas" demonstrates the alienation of someone whose acts are standing over and against her, instead of being ruled by her, as the central character herself seeks to satisfy an artificial desire. Implicit in this story is a condemnation of this reality and an approval of the traditional, more aesthetic way of celebrating this holy day. A return to the original significance of Christmas would relieve the emphasis placed on the exchanging of gifts among individuals. The more life-giving and natural gifts of food contrasts sharply with the store-bought gifts the children desire. Doña María is driven by a desire to conform to the socially contrived definition of a good mother. Her aborted shopping excursion is a futile effort. Although her attempt to break through the routinized, restrictive environment of home is a rebellious act, it is doomed to fail because she is driven by the wrong motivations. At one level her children are depicted as the motivation for her actions. More significantly, though, she seems compelled by the consumerism generated by the media.

This vignette also condemns patriarchy as a facet of Mexican American cultural reality that has contributed to the alienation of Doña María. Although Doña María's phobia is psychologically explicable, it is a condition that is not biological in nature but sociological. Many psychologists feel that agoraphobia is the result of sex-role stereotyping that leads women to view themselves as helpless and dependent, and thus more vulnerable than men.[21] Furthermore, this learned act of perceiving oneself in a stereotypical female way is only reinforced by media stereotyping and males who are influenced by an extremely macho sex-role stereotype (Chambless and Goldstein 79). Whether as a cause or a consequence of her psychological condition, Doña María is dependent on her husband for all her needs outside the home. Her house is her world. She is unfamiliar with downtown despite living only a few blocks away. Her husband is all too willing to reinforce the traditional belief that a woman need only depend on a man and everything will be fine. Rather than seeking outside help for his wife, Don Chon reinforces her condition by willingly assuming the role of protector and sole provider.[22]

Having identified some of the areas of critical inquiry and the multidirectional critical impulse of Rivera's narrative, I would like now to return to two issues raised earlier, the role of education as a path to social liberation and the protagonist as individual and collective subject, with a particular focus on the interrelationship between the notion of leadership and the ideological vision posited by this novel. Earlier I suggested that in the absence of a particular name the protagonist becomes a figure universally representative of all migrant workers; this view, however, becomes problematized when we chart the trajectory of his development. Each of the three critics I named earlier as more-recent examples of Rivera scholars also have in common an examination of the ideological vision of the novel as a utopian narrative. We will turn to their work by way of an earlier, harshly critical essay that addresses the ideological vision of *Tierra.*

The essay I refer to is Juan Rodríguez's 1978 "The Problematic in Tomás Rivera's . . . *and the earth did not part,*" first published in *Revista Chicano-Riqueña* and reproduced in *Contemporary Chicano Fiction* (1986). What Rodríguez finds problematic is a "false non-progressive interpretation of Chicanos and Chicano reality" (J. Rodríguez 132). The false reality is evinced for Rodríguez in the presentation of "simplistic" characters who lack critical attitudes, political consciousness, and independence, and who consequently are passive about their oppressed condition. More important for our discussion here, he sees the problem as an ideological one that emerges from the structure and genre of the novel, and, more specifically, the manifestation of these formal elements as they effect the development of the central character. According to Rodríguez, the child protagonist "becomes a center of consciousness that controls and colors—structures—the action to serve his particular needs . . . to find his identity" (132–33). Consequently, he feels that there is an inherent tension in this novel of education between the aspects of its exteriority (the migrant workers' world of physical struggle against oppression) and its interiority (the child's world of critical reflection) (133).

Ultimately, Rodríguez claims that since this is a novel of education, the child's search for identity subsumes the concrete material struggle of the collective because the genre necessitates the separation of the individual from his group. In the pursuit of education and intellectual development, the protagonist needs solitude to reflect. For Rodríguez, this is manifested in "Under the House" when the child is separated from others; unable to bring everyone together literally, he has to *imagine* his community in order to speak to them again as he continues the process of remembering. A hostile relationship is produced between the protagonist and the rest of the community, says Rodríguez, one that he characterizes as stemming from the child's withholding of knowledge. Thus, the child is presented as dynamic, the community as static. Moreover, he asserts that because education, or the lack of it, plays such a central role in the novel, Rivera is naively proposing that this is the primary social problem facing the migrant community. No intellectual hero who is pure thought and no action can save the farmworkers from the harsh realities of the world, especially if that hero lives isolated from the community. He extends his argument to the author's life, and to Chicano academicians in general, to indict traditional intellectuals who identify with the institutions for whom they work against their own community.

Rodríguez's essay, while not entirely convincing, nevertheless raises important issues regarding the ideology that informs imagined utopias and leadership vis-à-vis intellectuals. I will address two of his claims and then discuss the issues he raises in light of other criticism. In his reading of "Under the House," Rodríguez posits a hostile relationship between the community and the protagonist based in general on his isolation from the community and in particular on the children's throwing rocks at him as he hides in the dark. One response to this incident counters the criticism Rodríguez raises about the "simplicity" of the characters. The intracultural critique occurring throughout the novel in stories like "Hand in His Pocket" demonstrates the protagonist's awareness that members of the community are not incapable of harming one another. The children's and their mother's defensive response to his presence under the house is predicated on their not knowing who he is. Once he emerges, they do not continue to attack him; instead they feel sympathy for him because he is "losing track of the years" (*Tierra* 152). This quote, coupled with the children's observation that "there is a man under the house," strongly urges a reading of the protagonist as an adult who, in his mentally confused state of alienation resulting from social infantilization by the dominant culture, has reverted to a childlike state—hence the many years he has to recover. Thus his isolation from the community and his inability to speak to them are not born of luxury but of social incapacitation. The protagonist's actions, his inability to speak and interact with others, are manifestations of an alienation that results from his economic condition. Rodríguez does not provide sufficient evidence to support his thesis that the protagonist is acting from a position of privilege, selfishness, or hostility.

The same is true of the second major claim Rodríguez makes to support his assertion about the protagonist's contradictory relationship to his community, which is that the emerging intellectual figure is selfish with his knowledge because he is unwilling to "communicate his vision of the world" (J. Rodríguez 135). To support this claim Rodríguez points to two instances when the protagonist fails to share insight he has acquired into the "falsity" of folk beliefs and an "oppressive fear of God." Alternative interpretations for his motivations should be considered when the boy decides not to tell his mother that he drinks the water she places under his bed to protect him from evil spirits, and when he decides to withhold his discovery that there is no God who controls their lives. Both folklore and religion function as epistemological structures that provide meaning and stability to the lives of the people. The protagonist's realization of the limits of these beliefs portrays a sensitivity to their stabilizing force and a respect for their function in people's lives. It also demonstrates a cultural respect for elders and their values. Moreover, his awareness of the limits of these epistemological models is not accompanied by a simultaneous discovery of an alternative interpretive framework for understanding the world; rather, it is a nascent critique of ideologies. There is not, as Rodríguez would have us believe, an absolute withholding of knowledge in either case. In the first instance, he intends to tell his mother "when he was grown up," presumably a time when he would not be challenging her position of authority in the family and her role as his protector. In the second case, he makes a partial revelation to his mother when he tells her after he has cursed God that "the earth did not devour anyone, nor did the sun." What he keeps secret from her is his transgression against a revered cultural and religious belief system, which would have been seen as a lack of respect for the mother's wishes and values. He does, in fact, share the knowledge he has gained. These problems aside, however, Rodríguez's critiques of the development and class alliances of intellectuals and the privileged role of education as a strategy for liberation bear further examination.

Ramón Saldívar has said that *Tierra* is "imbued with a sense of political urgency" (*CN* 77) in which the protagonist's "dawning class consciousness must occur by degrees and first as a personal act of understanding the causes of his people's victimization and oppression by a common enemy" (80). For Saldívar, the utopian vision of the novel is essentially about discovering possibilities for an alternative reality: "Having attained [the] necessary protopolitical level of Feuerbachian dialectical insight through the reduction of his illusions, the child's full attainment of a political understanding of his place in a system of class oppression, of seeing the world as a product of socially interactive labor, of recognizing the need for collective action . . . cannot be far off" (84). Hence the utopian hope for a better future is "the possible unity of a collectivity" (88) and the articulation of the power of self-determination. For Saldívar, the narrator (the writer) plays a crucial role in recovering history and expressing a working-class consciousness by constructing a form that will give voice to the collective (88). This notion of an imagined collectivity and working-class consciousness as the expression of utopia in the novel also characterizes other criticism.

Calderón, for instance, agrees with Saldívar that the utopian vision of the novel is instantiated in its form: the reader is "challenged by Rivera's oppositional strategies to project alternative social possibilities" (Calderón 107).

The utopian vision is constructed on the basis of an ideological critique "in the sense that Chicano readers are made aware of the structural and cultural limits of their own class and cultural situation" (107). While Calderón concurs with Rodríguez's assessment that there is a tension between individual and collective aspirations, he concludes that as it is articulated in the novel, the "utopian vision of the future is due as much to the expression of collective hope as to the decentering of individualism. . . . [The] thematization of individualism . . . is structurally counterbalanced by the tales and fragments with their many nameless characters and the ending frame" (112). Moreover, Calderón sees the absence of a patronymic for the protagonist as evidence of Rivera's critical perspective on male egocentrism and *machismo* and a dismissal of the notion of the preordained hero. Calderón concludes by suggesting that Chicano literature in general, *Tierra* in particular, is in the process of constructing a new master narrative, a necessary task in understanding the emergence of a Chicano consciousness whose salient features are "the rejection of the metaphysical and the acceptance of the social, the decentering of the autonomous subject and the reconciliation of individual desire with a wider social movement" (113). Like Saldívar, Calderón links utopia with the development of a critical ideology that will expose the machinations of social relations, cultural practices, and world history. Consequently, they both see the protagonist at an important liminal stage between being prepolitical and an exemplary individual whose role it is to facilitate the realization of a utopian future for the collective.

In contrast, José Limón, like Rodríguez, expresses discomfort with the "paradoxical achievement" of the protagonist's "collective utopian emancipation based on 'understanding,' and on his desire to think" (*DD* 196). Limón is concerned with the cultural costs involved in the valorization of the protagonist's utopian achievement. Limón evaluates the status of *curanderas* in Mexican culture and the implicit devaluation of cultural practices that occurs when old and new, traditional and modern forms of knowledge are juxtaposed with one another. To facilitate his analysis he examines the first anecdote in which the boy demystifies the folk practice of putting water under the bed to ward off evil spirits. In his analysis of the costs associated with the protagonist's emancipation in *Tierra,* Limón acknowledges the struggle that many literary critics engage in to privilege the acquisition of knowledge by the young boy, whom they see as a precursory figure of the Chicano Movement. According to Limón, these critics almost always implicitly or explicitly accept or rationalize the way the protagonist uses his new-found knowledge as a critical weapon to diminish the value of traditional forms of knowledge. Limón does not perform an extended analysis of *Tierra* and its protagonist, but based on these comments about the juxtaposition of different forms of knowledge, a possible strategy for evaluating the dilemma created between the exemplary individual and the greater community can be extracted. This model is not some new paradigm of leadership or political analysis. Its solution is neither more nor less clear than that posited by Saldívar and Calderón—to view the protagonist as a bridge between two stages of dialectical historicism. Rather, it is based on the acknowledgment that there is no singular model of rationalistic, objectivist discourse, or leadership for that matter, that will offer a clear path to a utopian future. Out of the tension between the old and the new, between the traditional and the modern, a sometimes productive way of sustaining tensions and paradoxes has emerged in postmodernism.

This mode of representation is already embedded in the book, which exhibits a postmodern form in its fragmented stories and a postmodern theme in the fragmented consciousness of the protagonist. Yet it is also true, as Limón points out, that the continued political warfare of people of Mexican descent is "fundamentally *modernist* in character" (*DD* 202). There is a genuine desire for "progress" in the Mexican community—for concrete improvement in economic, political, and social terms that can be measured quantitatively and qualitatively in everyday living conditions. Rodríguez makes much of the fact that the protagonist has to imagine an intellectual peer at the end of the novel. But, however limiting this may be, is not this imagined character more powerful than the disembodied voice of the protagonist at the beginning of the novel? Migrant farmworkers, especially, live and know fragmented states of being. The fact that others of their class are spread out all over the fields of the United States only suggests more powerfully the need to imagine community and the need for spokespersons to articulate their demands for social justice. With their contributions to the development and modernization of society pushed to the side by official histories, the farmworkers, documented or undocumented, have to access the channels of power that exist.

With the evocation of nationalism suggested by the "need to imagine community," an alternative interpretation of *Tierra* is implied, one that merits further examination in another context; here I will only suggest the possibilities it holds. In *Nations and Nationalism,* Eric Hobsbawm reminds us that the word *"tierra"* is also linked to *"patria"* (15). Given the binational status (and, in some instances, one might say *condition*) of the migrant-farmworker community, it is difficult to reference them to a single nation-state. However, as a deterritorialized and disenfranchised people it could be asserted that they have a hostile relationship to both nation-states—Mexico and the United States. Applied to the novel, and to the title story in particular, this observation may offer a more political, rather than philosophical and/or metaphysical, framework by which to assess the protagonist's antagonistic relationship to the earth—especially as it is expressed at the end of the title story: "He looked down at the earth and kicked it hard and said, 'Not yet, you can't swallow me up yet. Someday, yes. But I'll never know it'" (112). An explanation of this story that foregrounds farmworkers' geopolitical economic condition would also facilitate the deromanticization of Mexicans' relationship to the land that is common in both historical and literary narratives. This interpretation allows us to circumvent the limitations of the usual readings of this story as a sign of the protagonist's rejection of oppressive religious beliefs in favor of secular humanism. Instead, what this reading offers is a critique of farmworkers' living and working conditions that complements the standard critique of ideology.

Marx made the point that members of the working class will often have a passive and receptive attitude toward an ideological structure (even if it creates the conditions of their oppression) because "they are in reality the active members of this class and have less time to make up illusions and ideas about themselves" (Marx 173). In contrast to alienated workers, nonalienated humans produce to survive, not vice-versa. Marx used the term "free conscious producer" because these people are free to themselves, free to pursue interests that are pleasurable, free to cultivate their intellectual and creative capacities to their fullest potential. Moreover, in this "free" state, there is no conflict between man and nature or man and man. "An individual free from alienation is one who can be any and all those things which he desires as an individual or species being" (95–105). One of the most powerful visions instantiated in *Tierra* is the legacy of Rivera's work: his simultaneous presentation of utopia and dystopia.

Conclusion

Embedded in *George Washington Gómez* and *. . . y no se lo tragó la tierra* is a modernist utopian vision of possibility, yet the authors also invoke a postmodern dystopia, facilitating an examination of the way things *are*. The protagonist of *Tierra,* like George W. Gómez, does not discover himself through book knowledge despite all his privileged education. Both protagonists are haunted by memories of the past; but *Tierra*'s finds resolution in communal memory while *GWG*'s remains haunted by historical impossibilities. Rosaura Sánchez has said that "Set against the alienated modernist subject of world history, the postmodern subject is fragmented, decentered, and schizoid" ("Postmodernism" 5). Her description would seem to fit both novels' protagonists; this is corroborated by her statement that "it is the decentered or schizophrenic subject, free from all metaphysical traps, free to simply desire, which best describes postmodernist subjectivity" (5). But how, then, do we account for *Tierra*'s unrealized desire for wholeness and George Gómez's unresolved anxiety about his past? This question manifests itself in the enduring problem of unclear visions about political goals and strategies that have characterized the political practice of people of Mexican descent in the United States. It is, at the political level, the ideological conundrum between reformism and utopianism described by Gómez-Quiñones.

How does this manifest itself in political and social histories? What observations can be made about the different or similar constructions of the Mexican American Generation based on a reading of these literary and historical narratives? The literature discussed in this chapter is better able to capture both the modernist desire and the postmodern subalternity that characterize the vast majority of Mexican Americans' lives. The fictional narratives document the intracultural strife that is so often elided in social and political histories; moreover, in the refusal of the historical narratives to acknowledge the lived experience of marginalized sectors of the community, an inverted utopianism emerges that fails to interrogate the heterogeneity of the Mexican population. This ability to sustain and document intracultural tensions as well as larger hostile social and economic forces provide literature with an ability to give us a fuller sense of the experience and lived histories of people, whether they are in the midst of political struggle or not. The next chapter will explore the "private" and "public" works of a writer who was an integral part of the political activity that came to be known as the Chicano Movement.

CHAPTER 4

Identity, Memory, and Self-Representation in el Movimiento

I feel that given the time and the money I could write my message to the world. . . . Why else should a man write? If not to tell somebody something.

I read the crap in the books and the newspapers and the magazines and even the sports page, and I feel, god damn it, it needs to be said better. Somebody needs to tell Faulkner and Williams and Salinger and all the rest that tho they write beautifully, better than I shall ever write, still they are not saying anything . . . they're "commenting on our social behavior." Shit! We don't need comments, we need direction.

—Oscar Zeta Acosta, Letter to Betty Daves Acosta, April 12, 1961

Though certainly not monolithic in their forms of activism or their ideology, participants in the Chicano Movement, a period of intensified political activity loosely situated between the years 1965 and 1978, shared many objectives.[1] What informed the activists of this era was a shared awareness of social injustice faced by people of Mexican descent in the United States. In their analysis of the social subordination and labor exploitation faced by Mexican Americans, these activists sought to mobilize their community to end discrimination around issues as diverse as housing, military recruitment, labor, education, and immigration (R. Gutiérrez 45; Muñoz 14–15).

Furthermore, not only did they seek social and political equality through the eradication of racism, they also demanded cultural autonomy and "national" self-determination.

The period of intense Chicana/o civil rights activities, popularly known as *el movimiento,* is often demarcated by certain momentous events, such as the 1963 "electoral revolt" in Crystal City, Texas; the 1965 Plan de Delano proclamation issued by the National Farm Workers Association; the founding of the Crusade for Justice in 1965; the 1967 Tierra Amarilla shoot-out between law enforcement agencies and the Alianza Federal de Mercedes; the establishment of the Mexican American Youth Organization (MAYO) and the United Mexican American Students (UMAS) organizations on campuses; and the 1968 school walkouts in Los Angeles. From a global perspective, the Chicano Movement should be seen as part of the larger pattern of Third World resistance to imperialism and the emergence of new nationalisms occurring throughout the world at this time in Africa, Latin America, Asia, the Caribbean, and the Middle East. On the level of politics, tactics, and theory (especially focused on cultural forms of resistance), Chicanas/os were influenced and affected by events in the Third World.[2] What separated this era of intense activism from previous civil rights work by Chicanas/os was the militancy and rhetoric that characterized their claims for social justice and equality, as well as the newly adopted concept of self-determination.

The cultural renaissance associated with the Chicano Movement saw the proliferation of Chicana/o works, both literary and historical. The cultural nationalist orientation of the movement's participants is evinced in many of these writings, across genres and disciplines. However, much of the poetry of this era was affected by residual forms of Mexican cultural expression, and certainly much of it was influenced by dominant forms of "American" poetry.[3] Compared to poetry, a surprisingly small number of literary narratives about the Movement were produced.[4] In the social sciences, textual production was directly related to institutional access. In the academy in unprecedented numbers, Chicana/o historians and social scientists began researching and writing a significant body of historical narratives about their people.[5]

The negotiation of power simultaneous with the construction of a Chicana/o identity during the Movement era can be mapped across several discursive fields. Large-scale mobilization of people provoked a response by local and national security forces, which is also part of the dialectic that forms Chicana/o identity during this time. Oscar Zeta Acosta's semiautobiographical novel, *The Revolt of the Cockroach People* (1973), and Carlos Muñoz's history *Youth,*

Identity, and Power: The Chicano Movement (1989) are two of the most significant book-length narratives about this period written by people who were active participants. Teresa Acosta is a poet whose historical as well as political consciousness was shaped by the turbulent events of the 1960s and '70s, as was noted in chapter 1. Though these authors' political involvement authorizes them to write from a particular vantage point, it also highlights the issue of self-representation. While continuing to examine generational constructions and self-representation in historical and literary texts, in this chapter I will also focus on how Chicana/o identity was constructed within the Movement and exploited by oppositional forces outside of it.

Teresa Acosta's Rejection of Resistance-Only Narratives

Before examining in detail the different ways that Oscar Acosta and Carlos Muñoz have presented the theoretical and active components of the Movement, I will further examine Teresa Acosta's historiographical poetics. In the preceding chapters Acosta's poetry has been examined primarily for the purpose of demonstrating the historical and political continuity she feels with her important but relatively unknown precursors. Acosta's poetry links her present-day reality to the past, and in so doing helps document the history of women of Mexican descent. Her poetry is informed by what is lacking in written histories. Below is an exemplary poem that challenges textbook history; it is dedicated to her father and is from her first book, *Passing Time* (1984):

For Maximo Palomo

the official history that
traces in pictures and words,
endlessly depicts
in minute detail
the stealing of your honor
the selling of your manly labor,
the pain you endured
as sons and daughters
drifted from you,
met their death in the
hour of thorns and swords
will fail you

just as will history texts
written with the cutting pen of
palefaced brown/stone men who recall 1848
and
forget to tell about
the man who cradled children to sleep,
soothed their damp hair,
told them stories,
played la golondrina on his violin,
and laughed
aloud
at dusk.

Note: The United States and Mexico signed the Treaty of Guadalupe-Hidalgo in 1848, thus ending the Mexican American War.

In this poem, the "failure" of both official history and Chicano history is located in the unspoken stories of men who were not disabled by betrayal, defeat, or nostalgia. "For Maximo Palomo" works against one of the primary forms of the written history of Mexican people in the Southwest—the resistance narrative. For Acosta, this history is not inaccurate but inadequate and incomplete. There are other narratives, other modes of survival that she wants to document. She is particularly interested in recreating and foregrounding women's voices, which are often absent in historical texts. As a field of inquiry that has until relatively recently been dominated by male historians, she identifies the failings of Chicano history in its disproportionate focus on male resistance against agents and agencies of domination. This is the implicit message of her poetry about women. In "For Maximo Palomo," however, she points to the way resistance narratives have contributed to limited notions of manhood. The tender and loving father who "cradled children to sleep, / soothed their damp hair, / told them stories," played music, and laughed is another absent figure that falls victim to the "great man" approach to Chicano history.

Acosta has no lack of appreciation for important historical moments. Like this one, many of her poems include footnotes that state historical facts, but for her, historical dates need to be kept in check and not allowed to become the only lens through which we understand the past. Her criticism of Chicano historians in this poem is biting. They are the "palefaced brown/stone men who recall 1848 / and / forget." In these lines she points to the privileged social status of historians, who are perhaps palefaced from working indoors and who make a living writing a past that grants them privilege in the present. The image of the palefaced men here contrasts sharply with the "mestiza-cafecita" faces of Chicanas who identify with their indigenous ancestors in other poems, such as "Preguntas y frases para una abuela española." This attention to skin color signifies the racialized nature of the ideological and structural assimilation confronted by those who seek a place in dominant institutions. The divided but connected words "brown/stone" have a double meaning. On the one hand, a brownstone is a class marker that points to a domestic dwelling usually associated with the middle class; on the other hand, in considering important only those historical events that mark resistance with feats of physical strength and bravery, these brown (Chicano) men are not animated by intimate emotions; they are hard, unfeeling, and ossified. In their inability or unwillingness to find historical value in models of manhood that do not fit the resistance paradigm, many Chicano historians have posited limited notions about the relationship between culture and resistance.

The gendered violence performed by historians upon our understanding of all Chicana/os that Acosta documents is but one sign of a repressed history rife with contradiction. In its narrative form, history as ideology becomes the problem. As such, these ideologically informed notions about what constitutes history become a strategy of containment, "a way of achieving coherence by shutting out the truth about History" (Dowling 77). The writing of an officially sanctioned Chicano history that inherits "blind spots" from dominant paradigms is similar to the structural limitations Marx pointed to in *The Eighteenth Brumaire of Louis Bonaparte* and Jameson reiterates in the *Political Unconscious:* "What makes [petty-bourgeois intellectuals] the representatives of the petty-bourgeoisie is the fact that in their minds they do not get beyond the limits which the latter do not get beyond in life, that they are consequently driven theoretically, to the same problems and solutions to which material interest and social position drive the latter politically. This is, in general, the relationship between the political and the literary representatives of a class and the class they represent" (Jameson 52). In a Jamesonian framework of metacommentary, Acosta's poetry articulates the real conditions of existence for Chicanas/os who must reconcile the everyday aspect of their lives with their history as presented in books. The deconstruction of male resistance narratives that pervades Acosta's poetry provides a critical lens through which we may examine "factual" and "imagined" narratives of the Chicano Movement in relation to one another, as well as in relation to her own poetics of representation. The remaining sections of this chapter will examine the kinds of valuation that Carlos Muñoz and Oscar Zeta Acosta have embedded in their historical narratives and the ways in which these strategies perpetuate or reveal containment.

The Problem of Identity and the Chicano Movement

There is a brief but interesting intersection between Oscar Zeta Acosta's novel of the Chicano Movement in Los Angeles and Carlos Muñoz's history of that period. *Revolt of the Cockroach People* begins with Acosta's protagonist, Buffalo Zeta Brown, searching for "THE STORY" so he can write "THE BOOK." His quest leads to an invitation from the Chicana/o Militants to attend a boycott of high schools they have helped organize, one of a series of walkouts that later came to be known as the Los Angeles Blowouts. The subsequent arrest (three months after the event) of thirteen of the organizers on charges of conspiracy to disrupt the school system puts Brown, a lawyer, in the uncomfortable position of having to decide whether or not to defend them from a possible forty-five-year sentence. As he discusses his doubts with the defendants in jail, many of the men want Brown, a "righteous Mexican," to defend them, rather than a "*gabacho* lawyer." Carlos Muñoz was a member of the actual group arrested, and Acosta portrays him in an unflattering manner. Acosta presents him and other students as being timid in comparison to the militant community activists. Expressing his doubts about Brown's abilities, Muñoz engages in the following exchange with Gilbert:

> "I have a friend who's a lawyer . . . he works for the ACLU," Muñoz says. He is a student.
>
> "Fuck the ACLU!" Gilbert cries out. "I don't want no fucking white-ass liberal to talk for me. . . . You do it Buffalo. Just don't cop out on nothing cause I ain't copping shit!" (Acosta, *Revolt* 53)

After it is agreed that he will represent them, Brown proposes holding a demonstration outside Parker Center police headquarters; again, tension exists between the university student and the others. "'Well . . . I doubt that the college students will join in this,' Muñoz says. 'Fuck the college sell-outs!' Gilbert roars" (55). When Brown returns to the organizing office it turns out that Muñoz was right: "the college students and their advisers are against the idea."

> "We shouldn't even be talking about it," a well-dressed kid says.
> "Yeah, man, you want us to get busted for conspiracy, too?"
> "And how do we know someone here isn't a spy?"
> Everyone looks at one another. There is an edge of tenseness.
> "There's no law that says we can't have a picket line," I say.
> "Then why are those guys in jail?" a law student asks. (56)

By including references to the ACLU and the quality of one of the student's clothes, Acosta depicts class difference, or at least its perception, as the source of tension. These references to race and class in the above passages raise questions regarding the differing nature and basis of legal and political representation and about the relationship between the university and the community.

Muñoz's own, later description of the East Los Angeles Thirteen in *Youth, Identity, and Power* is quite different. In fact, he identifies most of them as students: "None of the 'LA Thirteen' were in fact communists or members of 'subversive organizations.' They included Sal Castro; Eliezer Risco, editor of a new community newspaper named *La Raza;* and Patricia Sanchez, a member of MAPA. The remaining ten were all student activists and key leaders of their respective organizations. . . . At that time president of UMAS at California State College, Los Angeles, I was also a member of the 'LA Thirteen'" (Muñoz 68). That the majority of the defendants in this case were, in reality, students, is hard to deny. Muñoz identifies all of them by name. They also all appear to have been involved in community-based projects as well. It is this latter identity as community activists that Acosta utilizes. In a similar manner to the way that Muñoz's focus on students authorizes him as a spokesperson with insider information in his analysis of the Movement, Acosta seeks to legitimate himself as an "authentic" spokesperson of the community. In defining the scope of their narratives according to particular sites of struggle, Acosta and Muñoz authorize themselves. The basis for their interpretive authority is thus determined by whose interests they align themselves with, and the distinction—predicated on the supposedly different relationship to "truth"—between fiction and history. As a political scientist, Muñoz is confronted by the academy's expectation that he rely on verifiable "facts" to tell an "objective" history. In academic discourse, the historian as creative writer with a personal history and subjective point of view should disappear. Against this conception of the author as "neutral" is the opposing notion of the artist as a free-floating, creative individual. Underlying this conception of the artist is the acceptance of art as a product of individual imagination and artistic vision. As lawyer and writer, Acosta has the liberty to tell his stories creatively.

The barrio, the university, and the courtroom are all specialized locations that point to a particular social status, and the tension between the students and community activists depicted by Acosta in the above scene dramatizes a power differential created by these varied social sites and the status associated with them. For community activists, the everyday conditions of their existence, such as the quality of housing in their community, police brutality, and missing or neglected city services, produce a hostile relationship with city authority that signifies their second-class citizenship. On the other hand, as a specialized site for the production of knowledge, the university produces professionals for the managerial class, and entrance into it often signifies an ascent in class status. A shared recognition of the discriminatory aspects of the public school system brings the university students and the community activists together, but it is not a relationship free of tensions and contradictions. Political mobilization around anti-Mexican racism contributed to the formation of an identity-specific organizing strategy. However, the differences in their primary organizing bases, the university and the community, often make it necessary for the different actors involved to negotiate power among themselves.

Until Muñoz published *Youth, Identity, and Power: The Chicano Movement,* book-length studies of this significant time in Chicana/o history were almost nonexistent, with the exception of Acosta's fictionalized version in *Revolt.* Furthermore, as Muñoz points out in his introduction, in the literature about the 1960s "nonwhite student radicalism and protest . . . is generally missing. . . . The history of that decade has been largely presented as a history of white middle-class youth radicalism and protest" (Muñoz 2). Books that do acknowledge the presence of people of color in the antiwar, civil rights, and women's movements usually limit their analysis to the inclusion of African Americans, as represented by the militant Black Panthers or a well-known figure like Malcolm X, or they emphasize the nonviolent protests and organizing strategies of groups like the Student Nonviolent Coordinating Committee (SNCC) and the Southern Christian Leadership Conference (SCLC). Thus with few exceptions, in books that do include a representation of activism by people of color, Mexican Americans are almost always *not* represented, except when those books are focused exclusively on the Chicano Movement. The inclusion of African Americans by some mainstream historians may be a result of the way in which analyses of racial difference have been polarized and presented in this country as a problem between blacks and whites, resulting in ahistorical and unanalytical perceptions of ethnic differences. The legacy of slavery in this country and the enormous amount of cultural guilt it evokes is perhaps one factor that has contributed to the emergence of a dialogue on racism that always includes African Americans but rarely other groups affected by racist ideologies.[6] Muñoz's stated intention in *Youth, Identity, and Power* was to fill a gap by providing a substantial and critical history of the participation of people of Mexican descent in the antiwar and civil rights movements.

Muñoz foregrounds identity as the terrain for understanding Chicano Movement politics. He suggests that the "Chicano Movement needs to be placed in the context of . . . the politics of identity or the identity problematic" (8). For Muñoz, identity goes beyond reflecting "consciousness," it reflects ideology. It is the Chicano, as opposed to Mexican or Mexican American, identity that represents a cultural nationalist identity during the Chicano Movement (7). Furthermore, understanding this identity is key to understanding the political and cultural expressions of *el movimiento.*

The problem of identity surpasses the search for an appropriate identifier, though nomenclatures become significant because a new identifier is assigned idiosyncratically with each succeeding generation. For people of Mexican descent living in the United States, the question of identity involves coming to terms with ethnicity in a society that increasingly attempts to solidify its hegemony by ghettoizing cultural diversity and propagating the myth of an homogeneous national culture. The meaning of identity in political and social terms depends upon one's "national" and ethnic identity. For Chicanas/os, as with other ethnic groups, tension exists between their ethnic and national identity. Nationality is a signifier that serves multiple functions; it can be a marker of one's citizenship status, one's national origin, and it may reflect one's political ideology or consciousness.[7] Ethnicity, on the other hand, is usually a marker of one's social position. According to Manning Marable, ethnic identity is derived from a population's cultural synthesis of the heritage received from its land of origin and its experiences in the United States. Ethnic consciousness is a "matrix comprised [*sic*] of the music, art, language, folklore, belief systems, and other cultural manifestations and social institutions" of a people (Marable 188). In social and political terms, ethnicity refers to the manner in which dominant institutions relate to and manipulate certain groups for political and material benefit. Often, ethnicity is not distinguished from ideas about race and is enmeshed in racist or racialist ideologies. Categories of race are manipulated and formed based on ethnic differences and function to express, either implicitly or explicitly, power relations. According to Marable, the insidious conflation of racial and ethnic categories is revealed by examining "white" America; "[To] be 'white' in contemporary American society says nothing directly about an individual's cultural heritage, ethnicity or genetic background. To be 'white' in racial terms essentially means that one's life chances improve dramatically over those of nonwhites, especially in terms of access to credit, capital, quality housing, health care, political influence, and equitable treatment in the criminal justice system" (189). A trialectical relationship exists between one's ethnicity, national identity, and politics.

The uneven nature of integration and the different regional cultural contexts of Mexicans in the United States have also contributed to an uneven development of political consciousness amongst them, and thus we see the different emphases on identity politics in California and Texas (Muñoz 10).[8] Mexicans living throughout the Southwest and Midwest have a varied historical relationship with Mexico. Tejanos, for instance, have a unique relationship to their Mexican heritage—varying from strong identification to ambivalence to outright rejection. This is due not only to the proximity and length of the border shared by Texas and Mexico, but also because the long, intensely hostile relationship between Anglos and Mexicans in Texas has made social integration more difficult and less attractive for many Mexican-Texans. This dynamic is played out in various ways for people of Mexican descent in other states and regions.

What Muñoz says about the relationship between consciousness and the organizing process concurs with García's and Gómez-Quiñones's ideas about Mexican American politics and situates his own project, since he has said that the Chicano Movement was composed of working-class youth: "Identity has . . . been a central problem in political organizing. . . . The leaders of middle-class organizations have generally promoted a white ethnic identity for Mexican Americans in the shaping of tactics and strategies for a politics of assimilation, integration and accommodation. The leaders of working-class organizations, on the other hand, have largely forsaken the question of ethnic identity and promoted the class interests of workers in the organization of strikes and unions" (10). In Muñoz's analysis, the historical conjunction of social and political forces in the 1960s created a unique set of circumstances whereby a critical mass of working-class Chicano youth were in a middle-class context as students in higher education. Given the fact that many of the youth involved in the Movement on university campuses were working-class, first-generation college students, Muñoz argues that they represent a new generation because of their significantly different life experiences within a social institution on a collective level. The significance of this relationship with institutions of higher education is that the very purpose of the institution is to train and "legitimize" the managerial class. Because they were members of a subordinated class, the decisions of these students regarding class and ethnic identity would assume political significance.

In "Towards a Concept of Culture," Gómez-Quiñones has pointed out that culturally identified Mexicans in the United States have a transitional group culture and identity whose relation to the dominant culture is fluid. The cultural poles are U.S. Mexican and Anglo (Gómez-Quiñones 62). Thus, working-class youth within dominant institutions are important because, depending upon their political consciousness, they can ally themselves with either the dominant or the subordinate class. In an effort to place his analysis at a distance from "mainstream academic approaches" that have tended to characterize the student movement as a psychohistorical phenomenon or a revolt of the advantaged who rejected materialism in favor of humanism, Muñoz sought a paradigm that took the specificity of their disadvantageous social and class status into account. In his analysis, student movements and youth radicalism are "manifestations of *both* class and generational conflict" (Muñoz 15, emphasis mine). Muñoz's analysis falls short, however, because in his isolated focus on the students, he fails to examine critically their relationship with the greater Mexican community and the Movement's ideological shortcomings, especially many male activists' refusal to challenge patriarchal authority and male privilege.

Muñoz is silent about a fundamental contradiction of Chicana/o activism on campuses in the 1960s. Though many of them spoke of the need to "return to the humanistic values of the Mexican working class," they did little to challenge sexism and economic exploitation (15). In fact, by their very status as students within institutions they spoke from a privileged position and were, through education and the entitlement often granted to degree holders, in the process of removing themselves from the working class—in social and economic terms. Their status as emerging intellectuals of their class makes the issue of representation crucial. It is this important question that renders Muñoz's "Chicano youth as a class" a problematic bifurcation of the community.

While García views the Mexican American Generation's embrace of the Americanization process as a progression of group politics, Muñoz suggests that this same process impedes group unity. According to Muñoz, the development of identity has been hindered by generational conflicts and adaptation to U.S. citizenship, as well as by the Americanization process inculcated in U.S. schools. Mexicans learned the "values, beliefs, and ideas of the dominant culture at the same time that they suffered from anti-Mexican racism" (20). From Muñoz's perspective, all prior movements had been launched either on the basis of a working-class identity or an assimilated American identity. It is the linking together of these two identities, which had historically been at odds with one another, that makes the "Chicano Movement . . . an historic first attempt to shape a politics of unification on the basis of a non-white identity and on the interests of the Mexican working class" (12). This claim is debatable; throughout the twentieth century there have been many *mutualista* and *obrero* societies in Arizona, California, and Texas that have defended the class and cultural interests of Mexican workers.[9]

The perceived need to solidify their bicultural experience moved Chicana/o students of the 1960s to foreground both their ethnic and class status. They decided to tackle the socialization process directly as a means of creating a new identity. "To a large degree, the movement was a quest for identity, an effort to recapture what had been lost through the socialization process imposed by U.S. schools, churches, and other institutions" (Muñoz 61). By asserting cultural identity in a racist society, the Movement was perceived as being much broader in scope than previous attempts to promote social change. Shaping a "politics of unification on the basis of a nonwhite identity and culture on the interests of the Mexican working class" required that ingroup class and ideological differences be minimized for the appearance of unity (12). However, as José Limón has pointed out in "The Folk Performance of 'Chicano' and the Cultural Limits of Political Ideology," a new identity—in this case, *chicanismo*—cannot be imposed upon a group against its will, not even in the name of *la causa*. As Limón observes, no matter how well-intentioned one may be, identity formation is an ingroup process, and if ingroup terms are taken out of a certain context, they will not function in the same manner.

In giving primary importance to the role of youth in forging the Chicano Movement, Muñoz's work contains ideological contradictions that tend to universalize the experience and significance of this era. Gómez-Quiñones has said that students were "central to the political vortex" in the years 1966 to 1970, but he limits the impact youth had on the overall political and economic landscape. Gómez-Quiñones insists that student activism be understood in the context of ongoing labor and immigration struggles and an expansion of activism that included older as well as younger people. Muñoz, however, justifies his emphasis on youth because he says they represented the overwhelming proportion of Chicanos who were Movement-identified. He places the "development of youth radicalism as a whole in the context of a framework that acknowledged racial, class, and gender inequality as significant factors in the shaping of student movements" (Muñoz 15). Muñoz argues that student activism was not "irrational or antidemocratic in nature, but rather [it was composed of] political forces aiming to make society more just and more democratic" (15).

Persistent throughout Muñoz's analysis is a desire to present the Movement as "radical"; he defines it as "counterhegemonic" and "oppositional." He saw the Movement as representing a "new and radical departure from the politics of past generations of Mexican American activists. It called for new political institutions to make possible Chicano self-determination" (16). Yet Muñoz does not present any evidence to support his claim that new political institutions were being formed. Certainly the Movement's rhetoric, strategies, and practices were different in form, but its goals did not differ significantly from the goals of its predecessors. Moreover, he assigns the Movement qualities it did not have despite the fact that there are other places in *Youth, Identity, and Power* where he admits that the absence of such features was, in part, a reason for its failure. He says that the Movement "opposed racial, political and patriarchal domination and economic exploitation" (16). This was certainly not the case with regard to an antipatriarchal critique, especially in light of the many contemporary feminist critiques of the *chingón* politics practiced by male leaders in *el movimiento*.[10] Furthermore, Muñoz consistently maintains that the Chicano Movement was nationalist, not—in its particular manifestation in the 1960s and '70s—a position that is easily reconcilable with the antipatriarchal or feminist character he wants to assign it. The critique of sexism and homophobia within the Movement is based on the male-dominant leadership within organizations; the privileging of a traditional conception of gender roles within *la familia,* which included a gendered division of labor and rhetoric that was informed by the politics of emasculation.[11]

García, Gómez-Quiñones, and Muñoz all acknowledge that the conservative political climate that preceded the 1960s was steeped in cold war ideology. Thus Mexican American politics was affected by the anticommunist climate of the 1940s and '50s, as many organizations participated in the postwar antifascist patriotism by continuing to promote a white ethnic identity that suppressed cultural difference (Muñoz 48–49). Gómez-Quiñones assigns partial blame to the community leadership for capitulating to anticommunist hysteria. "The strategy and tactics of Mexican American organizations during the War emphasized working in cooperation with authorities and institutions because of the dedication to the allied war effort expressed by Mexican American community spokespersons" (*CP* 40). However, by the time the Plan de Delano was written in 1965, there had been a backlash against conservatism and the "revolutionary" rhetoric had escalated to the point that activists were able to call the farmworkers' strike a "nonviolent revolution" and the election of Mexican Americans into political office in Crystal City an "electoral revolt" (Muñoz 54–56).[12] Referring to the ideology of the emerging student organizations in the 1960s, Muñoz says that "most of these new student organizations had objectives similar to those of the Mexican Youth Conference of the 1930s and the Mexican-American Movement of the 1940s. They emphasized the theme of 'progress through education' and concentrated on activities related to recruitment of Mexican American students and helping them stay in college" (58–59). Muñoz thus acknowledges, without conceding the point, that the politics of the 1960s were reformist in nature. The willingness to face bodily harm did not represent a significant ideological departure with the past but merely a different strategy. The "violence" associated with protest politics is more descriptive of government repression and media representation than the politics of the activists. The overreaction of the institutions made the activists of the '60s appear more radical than they truly were, to others as well as to themselves.[13]

Youth, Identity, and Power argues for the Movement's uniqueness. Muñoz objects to the notion that all political activity, regardless of ideological orientation, fits into a paradigm of resistance. Like García, he believes that prior to the '60s *mexicanos* in the United States were politically immature, but he sees this as a direct consequence of domination: "The subjugated status of Mexican Americans has had a profound impact on their intellectual and political development" (19). The antiracist nature of Movement ideology did represent a significant departure from the previous generation's politics: group culture was asserted rather than denied. But traditional, not revolutionary, cultural practices were foregrounded; thus the importance of *la familia,* with all of its patriarchal force left intact, could be reasserted as an expression of cultural pride. Cultural nationalism was touted as the basis for unity. This strategy assumed that all Mexican Americans harbored cultural pride despite class differences and that culture could thus be a unifying agent. Ideas such as the need for an independent political party (within the same electoral framework), people's cooperatives, community control, and bilingual education were all aspects of nationalist self-determination that Muñoz offers as proof of its radicalness, but they were really reformist in nature. Each of these challenges attempted to modify the existing system, but they did nothing to challenge fundamentally the violent nature of a society based on a system of private property, limited participation in democracy, and patriarchal relations of power. Gómez-Quiñones has been particularly critical of the way Mexican political unity has been perceived. His analysis is diametrically opposed to the liberal and conservative views that have failed to examine structural and institutional impediments to effective political practice. He critiques the naive assertion that Mexican representation in government would in itself guarantee political answers to the problems of Mexicans. According to this argument, "effective representation would ensure that the needs of Mexicans would be met at the local, state, and federal levels because 'government' is viewed as being not only able but 'willing' to take such action, even in behalf of disadvantaged groups. A pluralist myth lies at the heart of this liberal-conservative political assertion, and indeed liberal-conservative views dominate the analysis of Mexican political behavior" (*CP* 18). Muñoz leaves unexamined precisely how the objectives or strategies identified above were supposed to represent a "radical" politics. One apparent departure from the past that he identifies was the use of "internal" (diplomatic) *and* "external" (protest) strategies, as stated by the United Mexican American Students (UMAS).[14] "We feel it is necessary that we work within the existing framework to the degree that it not impede our effectiveness. It is historically evident that working within the existing framework is not sufficient;

therefore, our external approach will consist of exerting outside pressure on those institutions that directly affect the Mexican American community" (67). This strategy did represent a change from the purely internal approach of the Mexican American Generation. For many, direct action was perceived as being more militant, but protests for integration within the existing social order hardly represented a threat to the power structure. The relationship established between the students and their community of origin, assuming they were working class, was significant. The *Plan de Santa Barbara,* written in 1965, was the seed of a master plan for the development of Chicano studies. It called for promoting a view of colleges and universities as "strategic agencies in [the] process of community development" (Muñoz 81). Any successful assertion of power on a college or university campus depended upon community support.

One of the most significant changes in the political practice of U.S. Mexicans in the twentieth century was the development of a militant language through which to articulate their demands. The most radical change in ideology from the 1930s to the 1970s was the formulation of an explicitly antiracist stance that opened up new organizing possibilities, but this position was not effectively translated into cross-cultural unity among oppressed groups.[15]

Muñoz's project in *Youth, Identity, and Power* is to follow the development and growth of the Movement Generation. This generational focus makes his project similar to García's. Though ostensibly *Youth, Identity, and Power* is about youth as a class, focus on this idea is not sustained. Muñoz is actually writing about the Movement as a generational phenomenon. He follows *his* generation's move through school, as well as into the La Raza Unida Party and the development of the National Association of Chicano Studies. Like many of the activists of that generation, he is uncritically nostalgic for the politics of yesteryear and conflates the Chicano student movement with *el movimiento* in general. The sustained focus on youth on campuses is fundamentally a focus on elites because they represent such a small proportion of the overall Chicana/o population. This analysis privileges the campus as the site of struggle, when in fact it should be seen as one of many contested sites.

Movement lawyer and self-proclaimed "flower vato" Oscar Zeta Acosta offers his readers an alternative perspective of Chicano counterculture and the rebellious politics that occurred in the streets and in the courts, one that provides a broader view of the Movement, even as the author's perspective was shaped by questions surrounding his individual identity.

Oscar Zeta Acosta and the Quest for a Collective Identity

> *I feel that given the time and the money I could write my message to the world. . . . Why else should a man write? If not to tell somebody something. . . . I want to leave something. And it's not going to be in law. If I leave anything, it's going to be thru what I say or what I write.*
>
> —Oscar Zeta Acosta, Letter to Betty Daves Acosta, April 12, 1961

> *The book offer has made me enemies. That I would think to make money off the struggle for freedom of the Cockroaches has made some people whisper traitor, vendido, tio taco, uncle tom, and a capitalist pig to boot. . . . I have explained it to them a thousand times . . . now there is no Zanzibar to tell our story, no way for us to use the media to get us back our land. I shouted it to the roof tops: we* need *writers, just like we need lawyers. Why not me? I* want *to write.*
>
> —Oscar Zeta Acosta, *Revolt of the Cockroach People*

A period of ten years separates Acosta's writing of the first quote above from the second one. And though separated by a decade, these lines suggest a continuous concern by their author for the significance of writing. There are several important differences in the writing context between Acosta's letter to his wife and the lines that appear in his second novel, *The Revolt of the Cockroach People.* It is important to examine the different circumstances from which these lines emerge. Taken from the Acosta papers in the Chicano-studies collection at UC Santa Barbara, the first quote is from private correspondence and reflects Acosta's desire for posterity.[16] Furthermore, in a manner similar to the way he presents Buffalo Zeta Brown in *Revolt,* in this letter to his wife, Acosta, a law student, is a man concerned with his role and place in society. Yet unlike the protagonist of *Revolt,* at the moment Acosta writes to his wife he is not actively engaged in political struggle. In 1968, however, he did become an activist and a legal representative for Chicanos involved in *el movimiento* in Los Angeles. The juxtaposition of these lines calls into question the relationship between Acosta's private and public selves as represented by his novel. Moreover, examining these lines should provoke readers of his fictional works to interrogate the relationship between his fiction and his history. This imperative requires that critics go beyond using insight gained from his personal papers merely to "flush out" our understanding of

Acosta as author; instead what is demanded is a criticism that takes into account the different genres, contexts, and theoretical and historical relationships that connect his writings.

In a 1973 letter to a newly acquired literary agent identified only as "Helen," Acosta defines himself and his work:

> What I sell is myself. I am an adventurer. I engage in violence and madness. But with style. I am not a kook. I am a scoundrel and an outlaw. And I am dead serious.
>
> I have been a farm laborer, a jazz musician, a mathematician, a Baptist missionary, a lawyer, a leader of the Chicano Movement, and a writer. I am known as Brown Buffalo, Zeta and Dr. Gonzo: Buffalo is gentle, Zeta is violent and Gonzo is mad.[17]

Acosta follows this introduction of himself with an overview of his writings, including plans for a third book to be called *The Rise and Fall of General Zeta.* After declaring his confidence as a writer, Acosta describes one more identity he has to cope with: "I don't need anyone to cry on, I need a person who will fight for me, and you can't do it unless you're aware of the discrimination that exists against niggers like myself."

These self-identified subjects Acosta ascribes to himself are based upon a combination of real-life occupations and fictional personae that appear in his books. In identifying himself as an object of racism in the epithet "nigger," Acosta also calls attention to the obverse side of identity formation: that identity assigned to a subject, in Althusserian terms, by ideological and repressive state apparatuses as a subject of a particular society and nation. As an "interpolated subject" of a racist, sexist, and homophobic society, then, Acosta interacts with, is formed by, and is in some measure aware of these various ideologies. The challenge mounted against the hegemony of the state makes the ISAs (Ideological State Apparatuses) "not only the *stake,* but also the *site* of class struggle, and often of bitter forms of class struggle" (Althusser 147). Acosta's identity, then, is not his alone to (re)create. As "leader" of the Chicano Movement, Acosta became the object of surveillance by the FBI, who described him as a "revolutionary activist" in internal memos. Because "the 'Law' belongs both to the (Repressive) State Apparatus and to the system of ISAs" (Althusser 143, footnote 9), Acosta's status as lawyer makes him a crucial link between the streets, the courts, and the historical record of these events, even as he fictionalizes it.

Unlike Muñoz's history of the Movement, *Revolt* is not structured around the university but around the legal system, be it in the courtroom, the jail, the county coroner's office, or in street confrontations with police. Given the prominence of Chicana/o university students in the discourse about the Movement, they are conspicuously decentered in Acosta's account as the source of strategy and the primary actors. Yet they are present in the characters of Black Eagle and Mangas, two of the Chicano Militants with whom Brown socializes. With the assistance of Brown and community members of Catolicos por La Raza, students mount the criticism and protest of the church for its lack of support for Chicanas/os in higher education. That they appear decentered from the source of the action is perhaps more a reflection of contemporary discourse on the Chicano Movement (Muñoz's book is a prime example) than it is of their actual involvement. Acosta depicts them as one of many subgroups within the community that need assistance and provide impetus and strategy to Movement activities.

Acosta and Muñoz do share the common view that identity is a crucial question for the youth of this period; indeed, identity is a crucial question for youth of every generation. But in Acosta's narrative, their struggle for identity is not sufficient to give them more prominence in the Movement than members of the greater Mexican community—whose support was always crucial for the various forms of activism, wherever it took place.

Both of Acosta's books, *The Autobiography of a Brown Buffalo* (1972) and *The Revolt of the Cockroach People* (1973), have received an abundance of critical attention, much of which acknowledges the protagonist's search for identity but interprets it as a strictly personal quest. The recent availability of Acosta's unpublished writings at the UCSB Special Collections Library and Ilan Stavans's compilation and publication of selected works will likely reshape our knowledge and opinion about Acosta by giving us access to his private thoughts, including his self-awareness and anxiety regarding his own ethnic identity. Despite his self-proclaimed egotism, apparent in the books and in his personal papers is the fact that Acosta is, in many ways, a product of his times.

Though Stavans in his brief introduction to the *Uncollected Works* calls Acosta's letters to his wife "repetitive and obnoxiously unpolished" (Stavans xii), I would argue that the repetition of certain themes and concerns in a brutally honest fashion is precisely their value, for it is from these unedited works that we can gain psychological insight into an enormously complex individual. The lack of distinction between fact and fiction, between his life, history, and storytelling, serves as one of the distinctive markers of Acosta's novels. Reading Acosta's unpublished writings reinforces for the reader the deeply entrenched nature of his anxieties and frustrations in a way that perhaps we can only appreciate with the distance of time. Acosta's preoccupations with his identity, sexuality, disempowerment, and legitimacy become even more painfully evident in his private writings. *The Uncollected Works* is an excellent addition to Acosta's oeuvre, for these writings illustrate that Acosta's struggles with his identity and his search for community were a lifelong process, not mere literary hype. In examining this work, Acosta's life is further authenticated by its complexity (a point that is, unfortunately, effaced in Stavans's representation of Acosta in *Bandido: Oscar "Zeta" Acosta and the Chicano Experience*).[18]

The Autobiography and *Revolt* are about the narrator's quest for self-understanding. His identity is of central importance in these literary works. But it is significant only to the extent that it represents a collective quest for social justice. The plot of *Revolt* is generated by the protagonist's search for story material. Buffalo Zeta Brown seeks out the Chicano Militants with this interest in mind, but he is solicited into Movement activities as a legal and political representative, and his commitment to *la causa* intensifies as he grapples with police, politicians, judges, and priests. The plot develops around the various legal cases and street actions that Brown and his fellow militants engage in. Besides serving as documentation of the various political and legal activities of Chicanas/os in Los Angeles during this era, these momentous occasions also serve to illustrate the development of the protagonist's understanding of himself and the formation of his political consciousness. Identity thus functions as a social marker and, in some instances, as a register of political affiliation. In the case of the East L.A. Thirteen, the establishment of a legally recognized ethnic identity is of paramount importance for demonstrating discrimination on the part of the justice system. Identity becomes a basis for action, not just an existential question.[19] My analysis of Acosta's novel on the Chicano Movement in Los Angeles scrutinizes how Acosta's identity is inscribed by himself and others, with the intent of gauging his ability, as an "engaged political activist and writer," to represent the struggles and goals of the Movement.

Imagining the Self: Fact, Fiction, and History

In the draft of an unpublished autobiographical essay titled "From Whence I Came," Acosta reveals the source and strategy of his narrative technique:

"Sometimes I wish I knew more about my origin, about my ancestors. I've never really tried to learn. The things I think I know are part history and part story. I have written and thought so much about it that I can no longer, if I ever could, distinguish fact from fiction. The little old lady who taught me used to tell us stories about herself usually late at night before bedtime. They were also part fact and part story" (Stavans, *UW* 22). The lack of distinction between fact and fiction, between his life, history, and storytelling, serves as one of the distinctive markers of *Revolt*. Concerns that Acosta had in his own life inform the book. The tensions within *Revolt*'s main character, Buffalo Zeta Brown, are multiple. Two of his primary internal conflicts are his desire to be a writer rather than a lawyer and his insecurity about his ethnic identity. These concerns preoccupied Acosta and are revealed in his private writings.

Acosta's letters to his wife reveal a man who was extremely insecure, bothered by doubts about his lack of clarity toward life, full of anxieties, regrets, and fears, including a fear of being mentally ill. Acosta's personal papers contain approximately seventy letters to his first wife, Betty Daves. One letter, dated June 16, 1957, includes a proposal for marriage. Subsequent letters are signed "Your Husband." In a letter dated October 24, 1957, in a not uncommon routine of asking for Betty's forgiveness, Acosta says, "Please forgive me for being a sick bastard. Maybe I'll go to a neurotic psychiatrist. Maybe???"[20] These letters further document marital troubles and frequent relocations by both Acosta and Daves.

In many of his letters Acosta refers to uncertainties pertaining to his cultural identity. For instance, he appears to locate his source of confusion about his ethnicity in this excerpt from a letter from Los Angeles to Betty dated December 9, 11:10 P.M.: "Teach me, damn it, to appreciate your love. Don't be hurt that I haven't at times, I'm only a 22 year old kid who has been and is in the midst of a great battle with God and man. Understand my position. I'm a first generation American-Mexican. The *indio* is still inside; don't resent it, channel it to mix with your Anglo Saxon blood." In yet another letter to Betty, Acosta articulates a more specific desire for cultural and national wholeness:

> Last Saturday I treated myself to a box seat at the opera house and saw this Spanish flamenco group. Betty, I have never in all my life been so close to beauty and art. I felt thruout the show that I had at long last found myself. I felt pangs of identification; pride and passion boiled

> within my soul as I saw the modern and the old blended into one act. . . . altho I am not really a full blooded Latin my one great wish is to become one. I think that has been one of my great troubles. Not to over do it, but I believe that because I have not had a country or a people with which I can fully identify myself I have been so lost. (Stavans, *UW* 72)

At this point in his life, Acosta appears to be self-absorbed, alienated from his community of origin, and unable to feel a part of anything larger than himself. Yet we see a nascent nationalism in his desire for "a country or a people." Based on his letters, his period of separation from his wife appears to be an attempt on his part to come to grips with his identity. "I have tried to tell you in my past letters that I know now that I can be a man if I have something to live for, something to work for, some hope, some goal, some person" (1959, Tuesday, P.M.). It becomes clear that his need for something or someone to give his life meaning is a desire to be depended upon, something Betty is unwilling to do. "Lovely wife, you have not receive my full love, ever. The closest was when you were sick and lost our baby. Because at that time, during your entire sickness, you showed a need for me and dropped all forms of independence, intelligent behavior and hostility towards men in general, and because you were a woman, a woman needing and wanting her man, my love was released" (December 16, 1957). We can discern Daves's independence from this letter and Acosta's problem with it. Acosta's ability to love depends upon her dependence on him, a problem they are unable to resolve, as his need to be needed is not fulfilled within this personal relationship. Oscar and Betty Acosta were divorced in 1963. After that, there are only occasional letters to his son Marco and intermittent correspondence to his parents, friends, and publishers. It was a combination of his individual search for importance, his desire to find something meaningful to write about, and his lawyering skills that led him to Los Angeles in 1968.

From a letter to his parents and the experiences he writes about in *The Autobiography*, we know that he left his position as a lawyer for an Oakland legal-aid clinic in 1967 because he was unhappy: "As you well know I have been at war with myself and the universe, with mankind and God, with the whole of society and all it has to offer, I have been in this conflict so many years I can't even remember when was the last time I felt at peace. I had thought that once I got out of school and started working I'd be content. But that year of being a lawyer was one of the most horribly stultifying of my life" (letter to parents, July, 1967). Acosta's sentiments regarding the legal profession are also touched upon in two type-written pages that are not addressed to anyone in particular and end in midsentence just as he is about to offer an analysis of his clients' condition. These thoughts are written immediately after he leaves Oakland on "A search for the definition of values in my life." "I have put [this trip] off for ten years now. After one year in college, in 1956, I knew then that I didn't want what college and degrees and carrere [*sic*] and money and fame, fortune, glory, etc., . . . It isn't me. Forget what me is, I don't know. But I do know what it is not. It is not a suede shoe lawyer listening to other's problems as if he could actually do something about them. The problem is their condition, not a . . ." (Acosta papers, June 23, 1967). We can see here Acosta's frustration with traditional forms of lawyering and writing, for he is yet unable to fully articulate his critique. Acosta's lawyering activities on behalf of Chicanas/os in Los Angeles a year later are remarkably different, for they most certainly extend beyond just "listening." He depicts a radically different type of lawyer in his novel.

Acosta's involvement in the Movement led him to discover his cultural identity, an event that enabled him to write to a friend,

> And after a nine year layoff, I started writing again. . . . As you'll recall, if your head is on straight, I did not write for those years because I could not find "my voice." After some time in therapy and more particularly, some time in the mountains and about a hundred acid trips, I realized it had nothing to do with a voice—but with an identity. And when that came, Shazam! I work at it, the words, the revolution, and the law about twelve hours a day.
>
> In the process, I married a flamenco dancer who digs my style and became, as they say, a leader of my people. (Stavans, *UW* 119)

Strangely enough, in search of writing material that would motivate him, ex-lawyer Acosta goes to Los Angeles at the same time that many white, progressive lawyers were going to offer their assistance as so-called legal-aid and civil rights attorneys.[21] Just as they were cultural and regional outsiders, so was Acosta in many ways. However, his anomaly as a Chicano lawyer, his cultural heritage, earned him insider status that the progressives were unable to achieve.

Rebellious Storytelling

Revolt, while not a strict historical or biographical account, is grounded in real historical events and people and thus is commonly regarded as semiautobiographical.[22] Acosta represents Buffalo Zeta Brown as an unconventional character whose moods alternately swing from arrogance to insecurity. The narrative structure of the book is built around his search for understanding his place in society, but the action of the novel is primarily located in the courtroom and in the streets, important contested sites from which to launch collective claims for justice.

Revolt was one of the most popular and controversial novels to emerge from the Chicano Movement. Written by a significant participant in Movement politics in Los Angeles *Revolt* is a fast-paced narrative about the years 1968 to 1971. The book employs GonzoJournalism, a style known for its brashness that Acosta, along with Hunter Thompson, helped popularize. GonzoJournalism was considered both innovative and controversial because it rejected any attempt at "objective" reporting of events—writers were participant observers.[23]

The controversy surrounding *Revolt* involves a combination of factors. On the one hand, it is not presented as anything but a fictional novel. Yet many of the events and people Acosta writes about are historical. In character with his authorial boldness and unpredictability, some of the characters' and organizations' names are changed, some are only thinly veiled. He thus calls into question the relationship between history and fiction. The disclaimer at the beginning of the book reads: "All the events and the names (with the exception of public officials) in this book are entirely fictitious and any resemblance to actual events and names of living persons is wholly coincidental." But even this boundary becomes blurred in the book. In the novel, the Brown Berets become the Chicano Militants, Ruben Salazar becomes Roland Zanzibar, Hunter Thompson is Stonewall, and the newspaper *La Raza* becomes *La Voz.* Yet Los Angeles's mayor, Sam Yorty, several of the activists, Corky Gonzáles, César Chávez, Anthony Quinn, Angela Davis, police informant Fernando Sumaya, and many others, including the Chicano Liberation Front, retain their real identities. Acosta's purpose for concealing some names is not apparent; it does not appear to be about protecting or condemning particular players. His inconsistency in masking reality or the "true" identity of people unsettles any reader who would like to read this as an autobiography by obliging them to think imaginatively about these historical events. Though many of the events in the novel seem so absurd as to be unreal, when juxtaposed against the historical record in the form of newspaper reports, Acosta's letters, journal entries, and FBI reports contained in the UCSB archives (only a portion of them appear in the Stavans collection), we discover that the absurdity of his engagements with law enforcement agencies, politicians, and the activists lies in the proximity to, not the distance from, historical accuracy. Thus these primary documents help us better comprehend the personal, social, and political context of Acosta's actions and outlook. On the other hand, *Revolt* is controversial because the explicit language of the narrative, the depiction of drug use within the Movement, and the uncritical representation of sexism and homophobia all posed a potential threat to the integrity of the Movement—a perceived threat based upon the notion that it is dangerous and self-defeating to reveal ingroup dynamics, weaknesses, or contradictions.

As a historical novel of this era, though, *Revolt* offers insight into the relationship of the political activists to one another and the apparent contradictions that led to a decline in political efficacy, with special regard to the masculinist and chauvinistic character of cultural nationalism. Acosta's dramatization of the interplay between individuals and ideologies is illuminating in its honesty, for it documents recognizable social dynamics that mark political and ideological differences as they are played out among individual subjects and subjectivities, a dynamic that traditionally constructed "objective" histories are rarely able to document. The book is full of epithets, racial slurs, and sexist and homophobic remarks that invite critique; yet they, too, are applied inconsistently, to friend and foe alike. The only epithet he uses persistently is "cockroach." But this becomes an umbrella term for the dispossessed, oppressed, and colonized people of the Third World, which exists both outside of and within the First World. It also refers to those who would resist domination, including white allies of Chicanas/os.

In his capacity as a lawyer, Acosta speaks for his clients in the courtroom quite successfully. How accurately he is able to represent the activists and the context of their lives and work in his novel is open to interpretation. For the purpose of this study, it becomes *the* standard of measurement. By comparing his narrative to historical evidence, such as newspaper accounts and state documents, we can gain insight into the constructed and subjective nature of representation. These different sources inform us as much about Acosta the individual as they do about the workings of hegemonic institutions and the perceptions of the Movement held by hegemony's representatives, the media, law enforcement agencies, the church, and politicians.

In writing a history of the Movement as it occurred at one particular place, Acosta makes no attempt to be comprehensive. He is faced with questions similar to those that Muñoz and other politically engaged writers must face: what to tell, what not to tell, how much to tell, and whose version of events to tell. Unlike Muñoz, however, Acosta did not wait twenty years to produce his narrative. What does his rendition of those events include and exclude? What does it tell us about him? About historical memory? About strategies for storytelling, organizing, and lawyering?

In a manner similar to Muñoz's, Acosta foregrounds identity as a central concern of the novel; however, he is less concerned with "proving" this through historical documents proclaiming the need for a new and unified identity that could be used as a mobilizing force than he is with showing why it was a necessity.[24] His novels show more concern for an understanding or interpretation of events than they do for reconstructing them as an end in itself. The genre of fiction becomes a way of freeing the author from the preoccupation with details that the discipline of history requires. Furthermore, though his novel falls outside the boundaries of the traditional biographical genre, Acosta takes full advantage of the close relationship between fiction and history in his story. Georges Gusdorf has said that the autobiographical conscience emphasizes the interpretive function of autobiography, an act that is inherently at odds with any notion of objective reality:

> The prerogative of autobiography consists in this: that it shows us not the objective stages of a career—to discern these is the task of the historian—but that it reveals instead the effort of a creator to give the meaning of his own mythic tale. Everyman is the first witness of himself; yet the testimony that he produces constitutes no ultimate, conclusive authority—not only because objective scrutiny will always discover inaccuracies but much more because there is never an end to this dialogue of a life with itself in search of its own absolute. (Gusdorf, qtd. in Kowalczyk 206)

As Kimberly Kowalczyk has noted, autobiographical fiction is not new, as the writings of James Joyce and D. H. Lawrence demonstrate. What is innovative about Acosta, she says, is the manner in which he "depersonalizes himself to such an extent that he becomes a fictionalized character much further removed than the protagonist of an autobiography tends to be" (Kowalczyk 198). The deemphasis on his personal story in *Revolt* might not be readily apparent because there are so many similarities between Buffalo Zeta Brown and Oscar Zeta Acosta. The continuity between *The Autobiography* and *Revolt* has been well established. But the protagonist's search for identity is not an end in itself. *Revolt* is not just about Brown's or Acosta's search for identity, although it is that; it is also about Chicanas/os' collective search for historical and political consciousness that will aid in the struggle for justice.

As presented in his books, identity is not about constructing a monolithic community or a fixed individual. Acosta seeks to demonstrate that all identities are suspect and time-bound. In his two books he narrates the journey of an individual from existential angst to collective identity and empowerment. His move away from self-absorption begins at the end of *The Autobiography* when he decides to seek out the Brown Berets in East Los Angeles:

> My single mistake has been to seek an identity with any one person or nation or with any part of history. . . . What I see now, on this rainy day in January, 1968, what is clear to me after this sojourn is that I am neither a Mexican nor an American. I am neither a Catholic nor a Protestant. I am a Chicano by ancestry and a Brown Buffalo by choice. Is that so hard for you to understand? Or is it that you choose not to understand for fear that I'll get even with you? Do you fear the herds that were slaughtered, butchered and cut up to make life a bit more pleasant for you? (*Revolt* 199)

And though many aspects of *Revolt* are concerned with his individual quest for identity, especially as revealed in episodes of stream of consciousness that illustrate his self-doubt in his renaming of himself, he begins to move toward a collective consciousness. Brown's relationship with the activists in Los Angeles becomes an educational experience in Chicano culture. He, on the other hand, is representative of hippie counterculture: "I told . . . [Lady Feathers and Black Eagle] about acid and they told me about Chicano culture. . . . I had been away from my people for so long that I had forgotten many of our tribal rites and customs. But over the months they have not ceased to instruct me" (67). Brown is fired from the public defender's office because of his new name, Buffalo Zeta Brown. Zeta, he explains to us, was the hero of an old movie, *La Cucaracha.* "A combination of Zapata and Villa with María Felix as the femme fatale. . . . And Brown Buffalo for the fat brown shaggy snorting American animal, slaughtered almost to extinction" (37). In assuming the name of a fictional character associated with the Mexican Revolution, he begins to assert a counterhegemonic identity.

In an early review of *Revolt,* Arthur Ramírez noted that Acosta tells his life story episodically, not chronologically. The episodes that structure the novel are primarily legal cases precipitated by charges resulting from demonstrations and protests against various forms of discrimination, and the protests and demonstrations that the activists engage in to generate publicity and education around the cases. Brown is a defense lawyer, which means that a great deal of time and money are spent keeping his clients out of jail. He is unorthodox and creative in his approach to lawyering; the very nature and degree of seriousness of the charges place the burden of proof on the defense. The three most significant cases that he must argue before the court are the defense of the L.A. Thirteen, the defense of the St. Basil Twenty-one, and the defense of the Tooner Flats Seven. Brown is successful in each of these trials, as was Acosta. Conspicuously absent in the novel is his defense of the Biltmore Ten, who were accused of setting fire to the Biltmore Hotel during a speech by Governor Ronald Reagan in 1969. The only time Brown loses a case is when he is unable to prove that Robert Fernandez, a youth arrested for a misdemeanor, was killed "at the hands of another" while he was in jail.

The latter two cases are important for different reasons. The case of the Biltmore Ten was being retried in 1971, with Acosta as the attorney for the defense. It was during the course of this trial that Acosta gave up his law practice. According to a newspaper report from the *Los Angeles Times,* dated November 16, 1971, which is contained in his FBI file, the first trial ended in a hung jury. The news clipping also mentions that in the first trial Acosta was twice cited for contempt of court and jailed for seven days. Furthermore, while the case was in court, Acosta was arrested for possession of "dangerous" drugs. The following segment of the news report is enlightening:

> [Acosta] mentioned his arrest as well as his own court behavior and radical political beliefs as reasons why it would prejudice the cases of Ramírez and Eichwald-Cebada if he continued to defend them. In revealing his intention to quit law, Acosta said of his court problems with judges and Alarcon in particular: "I don't know if I ever was a lawyer or whether I acted like one during the trial." "I have to agree

with you that you never acted like a lawyer in this court," Alarcon told Acosta, who once ran unsuccessfully for sheriff of Los Angeles County.[25]

The exclusion of this case from the chronicle of events detailed in *Revolt* suggests a desire to end the book on a note of success, with the Tooner Flats Seven being found innocent of all felony charges. We know from Acosta's letter to his literary agent, Helen, however, that the case of the Biltmore Ten was to figure prominently in his third book, although he intended to represent it as a victorious case. In *Revolt,* and in Acosta's own life, the Fernandez case and the trial of the Biltmore Ten demonstrate the limitations lawyers must confront. Despite the overwhelming evidence that Fernandez did not commit suicide, Brown is unable to break the conspiracy of silence that surrounds the jailhouse. He responds by bombing a Safeway grocery store and deciding to run for sheriff on the platform that he will abolish the sheriff's department. In the case of the Biltmore Ten, he realizes that he has lost all credibility with the judge and the jury because of his arrest on drug charges. Whether or not he is guilty of these charges is beside the point; as the object of a police scandal, his status as lawyer is compromised.

The Dialectics of Identity and Power in The Revolt of the Cockroach People

The three major trials and the events from which they emerged are significant milestones in the formation of the protagonist's identity. The Chicano activists are arrested as a result of participating in protests wherein they were advancing claims for equality and against discrimination. The issue of Brown's individual and the Chicanos' collective identity plays a crucial role in the scenes that unfold, both in the street and in the courts. Furthermore, each case vividly demonstrates the development and refinement of the activists' understanding of the nature of the battle they are waging. They become enmeshed in a dialectical struggle with civil authorities over their social and political status and rights.

When the L.A. Thirteen are charged with conspiracy to disrupt the schools, Brown is solicited into service on behalf of the activists. He agrees to represent them reluctantly. When he arrived in Los Angeles his intentions were to write and to remain uninvolved in politics. He is a product of the era's myth of American individualism. "Politically I believe in absolutely nothing. I wouldn't lift a finger to fight anyone. In a way I agree with Manuel: the best way to accomplish what you want is simply to work for it, on an individual level" (*Revolt* 28). He first introduces himself to the Chicano Militants as a writer, not as a lawyer. They, however, are more interested in his lawyering abilities. After he is invited to attend the Blowouts, he tells himself, "I know I am on track of a story at last" (36). When he is marching down the street with the students boycotting school, he is preoccupied about possible literary themes and titles at the same time that he is enthralled with the barrio. His wonder at the everyday availability of *menudo* marks him as an outsider to the community at this time: "'MENUDO EVERYDAY,' the signs say. And then I remember that menudo is the stew made only on holidays, at Christmas time, for a wedding, a baptism and on those days that the fathers have tripe, corn and lime for the morning-after hangovers. But here they make it *everyday.* It would make a good title for a short story. Not just on Saturday and Sunday but *everyday"* (41). But his own memories of a racist educational system provoke him to identify with and support the community and student activists who are fighting for equity in education. Initially confused about what direction to take and unsure about his role, Brown pays a visit to César Chávez, who urges him to "take care of business" (46). But while visiting Chávez, Brown encounters another sign that is to have an impact on him. It reads:

> LA VIDA NO ES LA QUE VIVIMOS.
> LA VIDA ES EL HONOR Y EL RECUERDO
> POR ESO MAS VALE MORIR
> CON EL PUEBLO VIVO.
> Y NO VIVIR
> CON EL PUEBLO MUERTO.
>
> *[Life is not as it seems,*
> *Life is Pride and Personal History.*
> *Thus it is better that one die*
> *and that the people should live,*
> *rather than one live*
> *and the people die.]*
>
> —Lopitos
> Acapulco, Guerrero, *1960* (*47*)

Deeply moved but not yet ready to make the kind of full commitment to *la causa* that Chávez demonstrates, Brown decides to help in a limited manner.[26]

However, the indictment of the East L.A. Thirteen forces him to make a deeper commitment because the stakes are so high: the defendants face a possible forty-five-year sentence.[27] Acosta's depiction of Brown's defense strategy differs from the historical record. In the novel, Brown wins the case on the grounds that the "indictment was constitutionally defective" because it violated the defendants' right to "march and verbally protest, and evidence that minor acts of violence had occurred at the site was not evidence of a criminal conspiracy" (71). The victory sets a "new precedent in the prosecution of conspiracies in a political case" (181). However, in the actual case of the L.A. Thirteen (*Salvador Castro v. Superior Court,* 1969), Acosta's legal strategy was to challenge the jurisdictional power of the grand jury that indicted the activists on the grounds that the composition of grand juries in Los Angeles County revealed a history of discrimination (*El Grito* 16–17). Acosta the writer chose to depict this challenge to the composition of the grand jury in *Revolt* as a minor and ultimately ineffective strategy in the case of the Tooner Flats Seven.

How are we to interpret this difference between the historical record and *Revolt?* By presenting the defensive strategy in the case of the L.A. Thirteen as one of First Amendment rights, Acosta is able to demonstrate more vividly the criminalization of political practices by the civil authorities. This sets the groundwork for the portrayal of increased repression by the police and the courts. By taking liberties with the sequence of historical events, Acosta can provide a sharp contrast in police tactics' disrupting the Movement at different times. In one of the few scenes in which Brown is using the past tense to offer hindsight to the meaning of events, he notes the difficulty of proving conspiracy charges: "Unless, of course, the Grand Jury had been told that the Chicano Militants had also *planned* to set off fire alarms, burn trash in the toilets and throw eggs at the police cars. In those early days, however, the cops didn't have undercover agents" (*Revolt* 71).

The role of undercover agents as organizational infiltrators assumes great significance in the case of the Tooner Flats Seven, who were charged with arson, firebombing, inciting to riot, and conspiracy during the August 29, 1970, Chicano Moratorium. Police infiltrated ethnic organizations by recruiting members of that ethnic group and requiring them to pose as committed activists.[28] The field reports and testimony given by these agents become yet another form of "official" history that Chicana/os have had to contest. In the novel's version of the Tooner Flats Seven case, the most damaging testimony comes from Fernando Sumaya, who testifies that the Chicano Militants had planned to initiate a riot. Brown is unable to discredit Sumaya completely, but he does demonstrate that as an undercover agent for the police, Sumaya was also an accomplice to any illegal actions because he took no preventive action against "criminal" acts. Furthermore, in discrediting Sumaya, Brown takes the age of his audience, the jury, into consideration, because "young people usually vote for the underdog" (235). He believes that all he has to do is cast reasonable doubt on the integrity of the witness. He achieves this by asking questions that compromise Sumaya's testimony regardless of how he responds. If he answers truthfully he will implicate himself directly. If he is unable to answer, his selective memory makes him an uncredible witness for the prosecution. The following exchange centers around Sumaya's role in the killing of Roland Zanzibar, the Chicano journalist for the *Los Angeles Times* and news director of KMEX, L.A.'s most popular Spanish-language television station, who wrote several scathing editorials against the L.A.P.D.'s abuse of power in the barrios:

> "Now, during the time you were in the bar . . . did you see anyone with a gun or weapon of any kind?"
> "No."
> "And you are certain that you did not report a person with a gun? You didn't call the police or Sheriff to report an incident at the bar prior to your exiting?"
> "Not that I remember."
> "In other words, you might have done it?"
> "I don't know. I just don't remember."
> "But you do remember throwing bombs with Waterbuffalo and Bullwinkle?"
> "Yes, sir."
> . . . "And did you make any attempt to stop them?"
> "I was told not to break my cover." (238–39)

Brown calls him a "lying spy," and witnesses for the defense depict Sumaya as an agent provocateur who urged them to commit illegal acts.[29] Brown sees the courtroom situation as a struggle for interpretive authority in which each side strives to present the more persuasive version of events: *"All of them . . . every single witness, both prosecution and defense . . . is lying.* Or not telling the whole truth. The bastards know exactly what we have done and what we have not done. . . . But they have all told their own version of things as they would like them to be" (251). Acosta's depiction of the attempts by the two lawyers and the witnesses on both sides to shape a coherent story for the sake of the jury is insightful for understanding his notion of the way people construct history and of the role and value of storytelling in legal practice.

In "From Whence I Came," Acosta mentions the relationship between memory, facts, and emotion that may shed light on why he is not comfortable with altering events: "It just doesn't make sense to me that men who write journals of their journeys either into or out of hell, and that is what all fiction is about, it just doesn't make sense to me that men should spoil it with facts. It is the feeling, the memory that matters. What's all this *business* about getting the account right?" (Stavans, *UW* 19). Not only does this "story" of his speak to his understanding of the false distinction between fact and fiction, but it also provides us with a way to understand how "truth" is constructed in a courtroom, as in the above example. Further on in this early attempt at writing his life story, Acosta admits, "We could get into a longwinded discussion about the philosophical differences between fact and fiction. But when all is said I suspect it's a difference without a distinction. I've read too many cases where different people testify to the same event in such different terms that one can only suspect that either numerous things happened all at once or else that each person has his own bird's eye view of things and tells it as he sees it" (6). Acosta's reflections on the nature of perspective finds its way into *Revolt* in the case of the Tooner Flats Seven. Brown takes advantage of the storytelling nature of the court, complete with a captive audience, to manipulate the outcome by representing the defense as victims of a corrupt and dishonest police force. He also knows the limits of his own credibility, which has been damaged by the testimony of police representatives, and so he forgoes closing remarks. This prevents the prosecutor from offering a summary as well. The jury finds the Tooner Flats Seven not guilty of all felonies.

The case of the St. Basil Twenty-One is won in a similar manner, but with a much more elaborate storytelling performance from Brown. In his closing arguments for this case, Brown depicts the defendants as underdogs subject to a conspiracy on the part of the police and the church. Moreover, the preponderance of Brown's objections to the proceedings of the court and the numerous contempt-of-court charges he is given bring a carnival-like atmosphere to the courtroom: "The trial of the St. Basil Twenty-One lasted one month. [Judge] Nebron held me in contempt of court ten times. After the fifth time, the headlines simply said, "Brown in Jail Again." . . . The crowds packed the courtroom and waited in the hallways for empty chairs. It was the best show in town. Standing room only" (*Revolt* 156). The issue of identity becomes a crucial component of the trial. In his closing arguments the prosecutor tries to depict the defendants, including their attorney, as political deviants who have been manipulated by "outside influences" and who themselves are "revolutionaries," and "radicals." He poses this question to the jury: "Are they simply citizens exercising their civil liberties . . . or are they mad dogs who would pervert all this country stands for?" (157).

Brown's closing argument in this trial is a history lesson that provides a larger contextual framework than the courtroom to understand the cultural and political identity of the defendants. He situates the defense's case within the larger historical narrative of the Americas in general, and within the framework of the mythical homeland of Aztlán in particular:[30]

> "A group of law students came to me one day last fall and asked me to help them arrange a meeting with Cardinal McIntyre. . . . But that's not *really* where the story begins. . . . Let me take you back to a place and time of sorrow. Permit me, if you will, this short digression.
>
> "It is 1509 A.D. . . ." (158)

Thus Brown begins to recount the conquest of the Aztecs by the Spaniards and the takeover of the Southwest by white Americans. It is these historical grievances, based on a belief in the prior possession of the land by Mexicans, that Brown wants the jury to understand. But he knows that ultimately the jury has to make its own decision about how to interpret the different versions of events, both of the immediate and the distant past. After bringing the audience and himself to tears, Brown ends his emotional appeal by saying: "Thank you for listening to my nonsense. . . . I hope you can put it together better than I" (162). In effect, he uses a counterhistory to make the most persuasive argument he can, but he leaves it to the jury's subjective interpretation to give it meaning. Brown's unconventional tactics works. The majority of the defendants are acquitted. In effect, Brown's method empowers and motivates the jurists to act.

As with the other cases presented in *Revolt,* Acosta diverges from the historical record. In the novel, the trial is depicted as one in which all twenty-one of the accused are being tried at once. In fact, two separate trials occurred, with eleven and ten defendants each. Throughout these trials, Chicana/os in Los Angeles found it necessary and important to produce independent newspapers to complement or counter the mainstream press's version of events about the Movement. Many of these alternative newspapers were also used as organizing tools. One weekly's report on the case of the St. Basil Twenty-One offers a critique of lawyers that is relevant for this analysis of the relationship between representation and legal practice. "Church vs. Catolicos" in *La Raza* corroborates many of the instances of police and church abuse that Acosta depicts in *Revolt.* Moreover, the article provides details of the case excluded by Acosta that provide insight into the emergence of a politics of identity. Written at the end of the first trial, the article mentions that Acosta was selected as the group's attorney and that he had assistance from "two other Anglo lawyers who stated their desire to enter the case" ("Church vs. Catolicos" 20), a fact not mentioned in the novel. In chronicling the events of the trial, the article notes that during the first week the Anglo lawyers "'expressed' their desire to leave the case because of the estimated length of the trial." Its author's comments on this are worth citing at length:

> It is interesting to note that this is the general example that is followed by non-movement lawyers who initially give hope to defendants and then leave them holding the bag.
>
> The case of Catolicos Por La Raza illustrates the sincerity and insincerity of lawyers. The CPLR trial was clearly a political case in which the Roman Catholic Church, through Monsignor Hawkes and three other priests, filed the complaint against the defendants. Most lawyers will not get involved in political cases because of the ramifications that are involved. The Roman Catholic Church is a powerful institution that many fear. A lawyer's clientele can desert him if they disagree with his political motives, and thus his bread and butter are gone. It is only movement oriented lawyers that try political case after case because they believe in what the defendants are fighting for. The desertion of the defendants by the other two lawyers gives more credence to what our people are not only stating, but feeling. "Dentro de mi raza todo, fuera de mi Raza, nada!" [Within my people everything, outside of my people, nothing!] (20)

This analysis suggests that one factor crucial to the emergence of identity politics was the foundation of shared group experiences and risks that bound people together.

These risks extended beyond the confines of the courtroom and the realm of legal practice. As a Movement lawyer, Acosta was also rebelling against traditional notions about the role of lawyers and intellectuals. This practice is evident in his courtroom strategies, in his relationships with his clients, and in his writing. In this way, Buffalo Zeta Brown mirrors Acosta in his personal and political practices. As the above excerpt suggests, Acosta was not motivated by financial or personal gain. Though he often appeared "unprofessional," he practiced what Gerald López would call "lay" or "rebellious" lawyering. This practice is characterized by the insider status the lawyers earn that allows them to be more authentic spokespersons. Perhaps the most important defining characteristic of insiders is the day-to-day experiences and interactions they share with one another. Traditional lawyering is often paternalistic because the lawyer is perceived as being the primary source of knowledge and power. López describes how power can be negotiated in legal and social settings without there being an imbalance of power, especially if there is appreciation for different forms of knowledge:

> Along with the many informal strategies we daily use, law provides more formal strategies to understand and shape our relationships. Contrary to popular belief, law is not a set of rules but a set of stories and storytelling practices that describe and prescribe social reality and a set of conventions for defining and resolving disputes. Law is not a collection of definitions and mandates to be memorized and applied but a culture composed of storytellers, audiences, remedial ceremonies, a set of standard stories and arguments, and a variety of conventions about storywriting, storytelling, argument-making, and the structure and content of legal stories. . . . Like the practice of everyday living, "law" delineates something we learn how to do. (*Rebellious Lawyering* 43)[31]

Acosta used this understanding of the narrative nature of legal practice to develop defensive strategies within and outside the courtroom. He also used this awareness to inform the narrative strategy of *Revolt.* As Brown's political awareness grew, he began to see that though he was a manipulator of words and stories in the courtroom, as in the cases outlined above, outside the courtroom his clients and their allies found alternative ways to empower themselves. As an insider who lives and works *with* his clients, not just on behalf of them, Brown learns the importance of a decentralized leadership and multiple strategies. He is aware, however, that the legal system's notion of leadership in the Chicana/o community is patronizing and that the system is unable to comprehend fully the power and intelligence of the lumpen elements of the community, despite their infiltration of some sectors of the Movement. Brown uses these limits in perspective to his advantage in the courtroom when he has an exchange with police Chief Davis:

> "They say that ever since [the inquest into the death of Roland Zanzibar], you have been directing the activities of the Chicano Liberation Front."
>
> I laugh. Deep down in my gut I laugh. I can hear Gilbert laughing with me. I can hear the dudes who presently live in my own pad on Sixth Street. . . . Right now the bastards are probably brewing up some molotov for tonight's action and here I am being called the *mastermind.* . . . Those guys wouldn't do what I told them to if their lives depended on it. They are *vatos locos.* . . . It is they who have converted me and driven me to this brink of madness. . . . *I* am the sheep. *I* am the one being used. But, why not take the title on my way out? Sure, I'm the mastermind. Why not? (*Revolt* 248)

Although these thoughts might be read as a sign of self-aggrandizement, Brown uses the prosecution's assessment of his role to undermine his witness's testimony:

> "Isn't it a fact that Wilson killed Zanzibar because you felt he knew too much?" The jury is leaning forward.
>
> Judd Davis is looking me straight in the eye. "That's no more true than the allegation that you're personally ordering the bombings of our government buildings. . . . You're getting paranoid, Brown."
>
> "I have good reason for it, Chief." (249)

Because Brown allows the court to believe that he is the mastermind, Davis's analogy backfires on him. If the jury is willing to believe that Brown is the mastermind, then it is quite possible that the police did order the assassination of Zanzibar.

In response to challenges of the status quo, civil and legal authorities constructed a "radical" identity for any politicized member of an ethnic group. The abuse of power by civil and legal authorities directed toward ethnic communities is intensified whenever insurgent political practices emerge. This radicalization and criminalization of political groups occurred even if the threat was symbolic and within legally permissible parameters. Political mobilization on behalf of ethnic communities was considered anti-American; thus on the very basis of their identity, ethnic groups in the United States are often viewed as enemies of the state. José Angel Gutiérrez has documented some of the history of official, extralegal repression of Mexicans in the United States. This history extends back to the nineteenth century and, according to Gutiérrez, includes surveillance of Mexicans in unions, universities, political parties, and community organizations. One of the lessons Gutiérrez draws from his research is that "Chicano organizations, regardless of ideological or philosophical leanings, have been made the target for government surveillance. . . . This blanket approach for protecting the 'national security' of the United States suggests that Chicanos are suspect because of their 'Mexicanness'" ("Chicanos and Mexicans" 49). Moreover, not a single individual or organization that has been the object of surveillance has ever been convicted of any crime against the state (49). The xenophobic assumptions underlying these actions by the government lead Gutiérrez to conclude that any "Challenges to the existing order will continue to be perceived as manifestations of potential subversion and not as collective desires of a people to improve the domestic social system" (53–54). In the dialectical struggle for empowerment and identity, political and cultural awareness becomes criminalized.[32]

Oscar Zeta Acosta became the subject of FBI surveillance on March 3, 1970. The documents released by the FBI to his brother Marco Acosta in 1990, which are included in the Acosta papers housed at the University of California, Santa Barbara, offer us some insight into how the FBI, the Secret Service, and the L.A.P.D. conspired to ascribe certain identities to political figures. Included in these documents are Acosta's police record, dating back to a "resisting public officer" charge in 1952; a copy of a press release announcing his declaration of candidacy for the office of sheriff (taken from a bulletin board at the UCLA campus the same day it was posted); newspaper articles referring to his defense of the Biltmore Ten and his arrest on drug charges; and internal memoranda within the FBI.

The memos are intriguing for a number of reasons. They document an intense campaign of surveillance that classifies Acosta in a number of different ways. His name and aliases are listed as Oscar Zeta Acosta, Oscar Acosta, and Oscar Z. Acosta. One of Acosta's aliases, however, is consistently blacked out by the FBI. The Explanation of Exemption form justifies this deletion by saying that it "could reasonably be expected to disclose the identity of a confidential source." We know from news reports that many Chicana/o organizations were infiltrated by undercover police. The erasure of one of his aliases due to confidentiality suggests that this name may have been Acosta's ingroup name, perhaps Brown Buffalo. Acosta did sign at least one letter with that name. This 1972 letter indicates that he used this name when writing information that might implicate him in illegal acts.[33]

Acosta's racial identity is also variously categorized by the FBI, alternating from "Spanish American" to "White" to "Caucasian" to "Mexican American." In a more detailed 1972 description, he is ". . . a practicing attorney in Los Angeles, California and is well known for his fiery defense of militant Mexican-Americans and his courtroom verbal battles with the judges. ACOSTA has been active as a speaker in rallies and demonstrations organized by militant Mexican-American organizations and the Peace Action Council." None of the militant organizations is identified. A copy of a U.S. Secret Service memo notes that Acosta's activities fall within their domain because he made "Threatening or abusive statement[s] about U.S. or foreign official," and that he participated in "civil disturbance, anti-U.S. demonstrations or hostile incidents against foreign diplomatic establishments." In a memo dated November 19, 1971, Acosta is connected with the Chicano Liberation Front. Although much information is deleted, what is legible is interesting. The CLF is said to operate as an urban guerrilla organization that "espouses" violence and has a "demonstrated propensity for violence." A note on the cover page reads: "ACOSTA was not recommended for interview at this time because it is believed he may cause embarrassment to the Bureau." He is also categorized as a "security flash threat" by the FBI. Their reluctance to interview Acosta indicates that they were aware of the limits of the intimidation tactics they practiced. An interview with him would have been an admission of their surveillance, and they probably feared it would have negative repercussions, since Acosta may have used this as further evidence of police harassment. The response to police abuse of authority was not always predictable to the policing agency; oftentimes it backfired and provided impetus for the organizers. After 1972, the surveillance reports on Acosta wane until one dated March 5, 1973, that states, "informants and source have not reported any activity," and "Inasmuch as subject has been canceled from the ADEX and there are no outstanding leads remaining, it is recommended this case be closed." Apparently the recommendation was not taken, for there is a report on October 19, 1973, from San Francisco, in which all information beyond his name and the city is deleted. The last record on Acosta contained in his FBI file reads, "There is no information available to indicate that the subject is presently involved in revolutionary activities . . . and no outstanding leads in this matter, it is recommended that captioned matter be closed." No note was made in his file when he disappeared off the coast of Mexico in June of 1974. Obviously, one does not have access to the complete story of a person's life when reading FBI records, especially when those records are the subject of official censorship. Furthermore, the FBI lexicon and the narrative structure of their reports are notoriously vague, misleading, and deceptive. The fact that his file is never officially closed and that no mention is made of Acosta's disappearance and presumed death looms large when we consider the aggressive nature of FBI activities in the Counter-Intelligence Program (COINTELPRO), including their role in assassinations of highly visible leaders in the American Indian Movement and the Black Panther Party.

Acosta documents police repression of activists throughout *Revolt.* He also demonstrates how the entire community was criminalized by the intense political climate. For instance, in the case of Robert Fernandez, the *"vato loco"* who was killed while in police custody, we discover from his sister that "It all began . . . just because he shouted 'Chicano Power!' and raised his fist" at a passing police car (*Revolt* 91). This criminalization of Chicano identity was part of a larger systematic campaign of intimidation.

According to Edward J. Escobar, the campaign to destroy the Chicano Movement in Los Angeles conducted by the Los Angeles Police Department with assistance from the FBI consisted of three primary strategies:

> First, police used their legal monopoly of the use of coercive force to harass, to intimidate, and, if possible, to arrest and prosecute individual Chicano activists and to suppress Chicano protest demonstrations with violence. Second, the LAPD infiltrated Chicano organizations, such as the Brown Berets and the National Chicano Moratorium Committee (NCMC), to gain information about their activities and to disrupt and destroy those organizations from within. Finally, the LAPD engaged in red-baiting, labeling Chicano organizations and individual activists subversives and dupes of the Communist party in order to discredit

them with the public and, in particular, the Mexican-American community. ("Dialectics" 1485)

In an astute analysis, Escobar suggests that while the L.A.P.D. was partially effective in achieving its goals, its very tactics became issues that the activists used as further evidence of discrimination; in turn, this increased grassroots participation in Movement activity. Furthermore, police violence spurred violence by some elements of the Chicana/o community, the Chicano Liberation Front being the most prominent. No one who claimed affiliation with this organization was ever indicted. The conflict between authorities and activists thus helped politicize the Mexican American community by intensifying their awareness of their ethnic identity.

The overreaction of the police to external—that is, nondiplomatic—forms of protest created a hysteria that was out of proportion with the claims being made by the Movement. Escobar identifies four main goals of the movement, each of which was essentially reformist in nature. The first was to maintain pride in their ethnic identity; the second was to foster a political understanding that Mexican Americans were an oppressed minority group; the third was to forge a political movement through which to empower themselves; and the fourth was to end discriminatory practices against Chicanos. And, as Escobar notes, "Although Chicanos often used provocative rhetoric and engaged in confrontational politics, the basic goal of the Chicano Movement—gaining equality for Chicanos within American society—was essentially reformist, not revolutionary" (1492).

Chicano identity served different motivational roles for the government and the Chicana/o community. Worried about any challenge to the existing political and economic order, the government mobilized to construct the Chicana/o community into a threat to national security. Chicanas/os, on the other hand, used their nonwhite identity as a way to gauge their political and economic condition and as a basis for mobilization to promote change within the existing political, social, and economic framework. The effort to mobilize large numbers of people included an attempt to create a unified identity for all *mexicanos* in the United States.

By the end of *Revolt,* Brown's individual quest for identity is deemphasized for the sake of a collective one:[34]

For me, personally, this is a kind of an end. And a beginning. But who cares about that? I was just one of a bunch of Cockroaches that

> helped start a revolution to burn down a stinking world. And no matter what kind of end this is, I'll still play with matches.
>
> It's in the blood now. And not only my blood. Somebody still has to answer for Robert Fernandez and Roland Zanzibar. Somebody still has to answer for all the smothered lives of all the fighters who have been forced to carry on, chained to a war for Freedom just like a slave is chained to his master. Somebody still has to pay for the fact that I've got to leave friends to stay whole and human, to survive intact, to carry on the species and my own Buffalo run as long as I can. (*Revolt* 257–58)

In the end, the legacy he leaves behind is not his own, but that of Chicanas/os who will carry on the struggle for social justice. Brown has changed from being self-absorbed to seeing himself as part of a collective. Whereas he once took flight from the legal-aid clinic in Oakland where he felt overwhelmed and driven to the limits of his sanity by a steady flow of poor blacks and Chicanos seeking "whatever meager justice is afforded to impoverished minority men and women attempting to allay the domestic tragedies of mid-century American life" (Saldívar *CN* 91), he now has turned the law on its head. Rather than helping people merely cope with survival, he found a way to use his lawyering and his writing not only to make substantial changes in the legal system, but also to influence the social discourse about, and the political conscious of, Chicanas/os.

In "The East L.A. 13 vs. The L.A. Superior Court," Acosta explains the legal nuances of the case and its potentially far-reaching consequences for all underrepresented groups who are excluded on the basis of race discrimination. Acosta also comments on the legal profession. His remarks may offer some insight into why he felt the need to leave the profession: "Why this defense has not been previously raised, either by Mexicans or any other excluded class, unfortunately reflects upon the legal profession. That it requires imagination and hard work is understandably a contributing factor; but perhaps the most compelling reason for their failure to raise the issue is that ultimately what the lawyer says in such a motion is an indictment of the profession which he professes and a castigation of the society to which he belongs" ("East L.A." 18). It was later that same year that Acosta left Los Angeles and the legal profession to write "THE BOOK" that tells "THE STORY" of his involvement in the Chicano Movement. He concludes the above article with a statement on the current circumstances of the Movement and Chicano nationalism:

> But what of the Chicano radicals-becoming-revolutionaries? It is much too early to say what direction their nationalism will travel; too soon to even suggest that their actions will be governed by the society's response to their claims for equality.
>
> . . . [T]he Mexican Americans ultimately rest their claims on the right of prior possession and ancestry. And whether we speak of historical or Einsteinian time, it was but a few moons ago that this Southwest was inhabited exclusively by Indians. (18)

We see in Acosta's reference to Chicano nationalism here that it is not a well-defined political concept or strategy; although, to the extent that people of Mexican descent could use prior possession of the land and subsequent broken treaties as a basis for making legal claims, it did have practical value in the courts.

In *Revolt* Acosta critiques the irresponsibility of Movement leaders in espousing an ill-defined nationalism. In the aftermath of the Chicano Moratorium, Brown recalls a speech he gave at a demonstration at Laguna Park two years earlier in which he called government-sponsored social-reform programs a continuation of a "policy of pacification." This leads him to conclude:

> [T]here is only one issue: LAND. We need to get our own land. We need our own government. We must have our own flag and our own country. Nothing less will save the existence of Chicanos.
>
> And I let it go at that.
>
> I did not tell them how to implement the deal.
>
> I did not, nor did any other speaker, tell them to take up arms prior to August 29, 1970. (*Revolt* 201)

The issue of territory and Chicano nationalism is a vexing one.[35] Although there was much talk among Chicana/o activists about regaining the Southwest during this time, no clear strategy or goals for achieving this were ever articulated. With the exception of a few land-rights activists, the Chicano nationalism espoused by many Movement leaders was mostly an attempt to forge a unified identity.[36] Chicano nationalism was, for the most part, limited to the realm of culture and spirituality. It was believed that the pride and sense of unity based on ethnicity this might inspire could then be utilized as a basis for political action. Much as police repression inspired unity and awareness of their oppression within the Chicana/o community, Chicano nationalism should also be seen as part of an ideological dialectic in response to American racism and nativism.

Conclusion: Chingón Politics and Movement in el Movimiento

> *Our leaders regroup in one corner. . . . Are we men? Do we want freedom? Will we get laid tonight if we cop out now? And what would our children say?*
>
> —Oscar Zeta Acosta, *The Revolt of the Cockroach People*

> *There are other ways to survive politically and spiritually. What we must abandon is a manhood that rests on demeaning womanhood, a sense of identity for one that requires imposing nonentity on the other. Some of us said those words in the '60s; the [1989 Raza Unida] San Antonio reunion suggested how much they needed to be said again. . . . The men can go on being* chingón *dinosaurs if they must—but let us hope you* carnales *find new ways to be strong.*
>
> —Elizabeth Martínez, "Chingón Politics Die Hard"

In a 1972 letter, Acosta wrote: "I pulled a number and within hours the FBI was on my tail. I left L.A. with my wallet and my typewriter. Soccoro and I drove a '62 Fleetwood across the desert and over the boundry [*sic*]. . . . I'm definitely in exile. But I'm not sure from what. I think I'm running from my friends as much as my enemies. Both had become unbearable. If not indistinguishable." His works speak to the costs associated with political involvement for social change. If we juxtapose the course of Acosta's life with that of Muñoz we see two very different trajectories in the relationship between intellectual and political leadership. Both authors were to narrate their involvement in the Chicano Movement; Acosta documents the particulars of life in Los Angeles and Muñoz provides a national/historical scope, although his major emphasis is on political activity in California. Acosta and Muñoz are both from El Paso; thus their lives are marked by a literal removal from their community of origin. Muñoz seeks an education in L.A.; Acosta's parents relocate to California in search of work. There is in Acosta's personal writings a clear relationship between travel and political movement, one that is psychological and intellectual at one level but that, under other circumstances, is highly political in nature. Acosta used movement/travel to clear his mind, to search for his destiny, to organize his thoughts; he also used it to remove himself from the social movement he was engaged in. In each case the costs were exorbitant. When he went to Mexico in 1970, he returned to find that he had lost his credibility; when he went in 1974, he was simply lost. Acosta's exile, whether self-imposed or resulting from official harassment, would eventually lead to his complete disappearance under circumstances that are still unclear and open to multiple interpretations. Both Muñoz and Acosta became involved in the Chicano Movement through affiliations that took them across many boundaries and that, for Acosta at least, led to many transgressions—legal, social, and otherwise.

Neither Acosta nor Muñoz problematizes the gendered articulation of power and its relationship to Chicano nationalism and Mexican culture in their representations of the Chicano Movement. They both present it as an element of the culture and the politics of the Movement, but, for the most part, it is presented descriptively rather than analytically and is thereby reduced to a matter of little consequence.

Acosta presents sexuality as another component of Brown's cultural identity with which he is trying to come to terms through his involvement in Chicano politics. Early in the novel, the male contingent that has tried to gain access to St. Basil's Church find their "manhood" challenged, and they are faced with a decision about the consequences involved in not forcing their way in: "Are we men? Do we want freedom? Will we get laid tonight if we cop out now? And what would our children say?" (*Revolt* 13). In the fight that ensues, Brown's gaze is revealing: "I see another woman running at full boat. It is Gloria Chavez, the fiery black-haired Chicano Militant. She charges down the aisle in a black satin dress that shows her beautiful knockers and she carries a golf club in her pretty hands" (18). Throughout the early part of the novel Acosta uses sexual intimacy as a measure of Brown's acceptance by the Chicana/o community; it is depicted as a reward of political involvement, as the following passage demonstrates: "For two years now I've sniffed around the courthouse, I've stood around *La Voz* waiting for one of these sun children to come down on me, to open up to my huge arms and big teeth. And yet I've not scored once. How many times have my pants been hard? . . . How many times have I shouted `Viva La Raza!' waiting for a score?" (86). No challenge to this sexualization of politics is given voice in the text. Zeta momentarily displays an awareness of the liberating potential of politics for women in the struggle for social change. When Gilbert wants to exclude the young women from participating in a bombing, Brown says, "Why not?

Isn't revolution for all the people?" (120). This lone comment suggests the potential for change in gender relations, albeit in muted form.

Muñoz obviates the significance of gender and sexism in the Chicano Movement in a different way. The emergence and proliferation of Chicana critical discourse since the early 1970s might have influenced Muñoz's analysis of relations of power within the Movement. He does identify a gendered division of labor within Movement politics by acknowledging that women "played an active role" within student politics (Muñoz 88) and were "an important component of most [La Raza Unida] Party chapters" (116). Yet his account of the role of women is limited to identifying names of people, with no analysis of the particular problems, issues, or power dynamics they confronted. Furthermore, there are only four indexed references to "women," each of which constitutes no more than a couple of paragraphs. In his two references to sexism in the Movement (in MEChA and in La Raza Unida), Muñoz limits his comments to describing, in the most matter-of-fact manner, women's efforts to create either independent feminist organizations or women's groups, such as La Federación de Mujeres de Partido Raza Unida. He makes no extended critique of patriarchy, sexism, gender relations, or the masculinist nature of Chicano nationalism and political practice. Nor does he provide a context for comprehending the significance and effect of the decision by women to seek social justice independent of male-dominated organizations. A primary reason for the formation of MALCS in 1982 was the sexism and lack of analysis on gender issues in the National Association of Chicano Studies.[37]

Notwithstanding their shared lack of critical analysis on gender, Acosta and Muñoz write about the Movement from different perspectives. They write about and for two different communities. Acosta's vision of the Movement is that it was broad-based and had some degree of support from the larger Mexican community, that it utilized multiple strategies for drawing attention and support to its cause, and that its efforts were focused on critiquing various social institutions of repression, including the church, the legal system, and the educational system. Muñoz's vision of the Movement as articulated in *Youth, Identity, and Power* is that it was much more narrow in scope and mostly confined to the college campus. Acosta's is a populist perspective while Muñoz's is a focus on a newly emerging educational elite within the community. Although Muñoz does not present his paradigm as a generational approach per se, the very parameters he sets for the Movement reveal it as being just that. His narrative does offer some insight into

Chicana/o intellectual history, but it is of a privileged sector, and as such continues the limited analysis of political activity by the Mexican-descent community that is engendered by the generational paradigm. Acosta's narrative is less concerned with presenting analysis than it is with reproducing the psychological and affective aspects of life as a *movimientista.* Neither, however, probes the gender contradictions contained (literally and literarily) within the *movimiento,* contradictions gleaned in the poetry of Teresa Acosta, a woman of the *movimiento*—contradictions fully exploded in the post-Movement era.

The post-Movement, postmodern writers that will be examined in the next chapter challenge the boundaries of Chicana/o identity established by the Chicano Generation.

CHAPTER 5

Redefining Political and National Borders

The Construction of Identity in the Post-Movement, Postmodern Period

A strong community means a national culture which provides for satisfaction, progress and critical awareness, group solidarity, values of self-sacrifice for the common good, and a world view. Art is central to this process.

The forms and ethos of one art must be broken—the art of domination; another art must be rescued and fashioned—the art of resistance. . . . This art emerges from the experience of struggle. It glimpses a different way of life, of organizing society. . . . It is art that is not afraid to love or play due to its sense of history and future.

—Juan Gómez-Quiñones, "On Culture"

Identity Politics in the Hispanic Era

In this analysis of the relationship between generational historical narratives and fiction, the issues of identity and nationality have been central to comprehending the web of ideologies that inform real political practice and representations of those practices. In the important but often overlooked essay from which the first epigraph above was extracted, Gómez-Quiñones notes that "it is the twentieth century in which ethnic names do a dance" ("On

Culture" 11). In a section of the essay subtitled "History and Culture," Gómez-Quiñones says that "from the past to the present, generally, Mexicans refer to themselves as Mexicanos when speaking in Spanish." It is, however, in English

> and in regard to North American racist society [that] group labels become a problem and are tenuous and mystifying. To the Anglo, "Mexican" has pejorative connotations, and the Mexican of upper and middle class aspirations is sensitive to these. "Spanish" becomes a polite conversational euphemism used by the Anglo to distinguish between "good" and "bad" Mexicans. In the Southwest, "Latin" also came into use as a euphemism for Mexican during the 1920s. The fuller phrases "Spanish American" and "Latin American" are for more formal occasions and so are "Hispano" and "Hispano American." In the fifties and sixties more assertive public names succeeded one after the other; "Mexican American" and "Chicano." Obviously past labels avoided "the word." But conditions, times, and consciousness opened the question of "lo mexicano." (11)

From the perspective of the present moment, the omission of any reference to "Hispanic" dates this essay. This identifier has become the latest step in the ethnic name dance by those of Mexican descent who wish to identify with a cultural heritage that is socially and politically oriented toward the United States. Ethnic identifiers emerge from within communities and thus reflect the heterogeneity of people's beliefs; identifiers also are codified by political institutions. Victor Valle and Rudy Torres note that the Census Bureau has changed its classification of Latinos over the years:

> In 1940, Latinos were classified as "black" or a "racial" non-white group. In the '50 and '60 Census, the category of "white persons of Spanish surname" was used. In '70, the classification was changed to "white person of Spanish surname and Spanish mother tongue." Then, in '80, the expansive "non-white Hispanic." Latinos were back to square one. Because the census uses a "white" and "black" paradigm to classify residents, it has shuttled Latinos back and forth between the two extremes. In each case, the principle behind the label is the perceived presence or absence of color. (Valle and Torres 20–21)

Elizabeth Martínez points out that while "Latino/a" is problematic, it "is less eurocentric and inaccurate than 'Hispanic.'" For Martínez, "Latino" or "La Raza" is best able to describe the people who have "experienced colonialism, direct and indirect, by Spain and Portugal and by the U.S." ("Beyond Black and White" 23). Cultural identification and political orientation are interrelated, but they are not determinant of one another. It is less significant that "Hispanic" is a term generated by the government bureaucracy than it is to consider the reasons for its relatively wide usage and acceptance.

Given the fact that there is a recurring pattern of identifying historical generations with a particular ethnic label (Mexican American, Chicano), coupled with the popularization of the term "Hispanic" by the government bureaucracy and the mainstream press, it may be conjectured that the "post-Movement" generation will be labeled and identified as the "Hispanic Generation."[1] Although it is clear based on the historical literature that the specific kinds of political activity that characterized the Chicano Movement have ended, it is not clear precisely when this happened. The Movement's so-called end is evinced by historians' willingness to proclaim and even identify its end, yet there is no clear consensus on the date and often no reason provided for choosing a particular date. Carlos Muñoz suggests that the Movement had declined by 1971 (*YIP* 75–86); Gómez-Quiñones gives the outside parameter of the Movement as 1978 (*CP* 101); Eduardo Escobar uses activism in Los Angeles as the measure of the longevity of the Movement in the years 1968–1971; Ramón Gutiérrez is the exception when he speaks of the Chicano Movement as a period extending from "1965 to the present" (R. Gutiérrez 44), but he says that the "heyday of the movement was 1965–1969" (47); David Montejano says that "by 1975 the civil rights movement in Texas and the Southwest had largely been exhausted. Many of its aims had become institutionalized and its more activist elements accommodated. Exhaustion . . . came from internal friction about leadership and tactics, and from external pressure applied by state authorities" (*AM* 289).

Significantly, it has been mostly male Chicanos who have written about the Movement and the Chicano Generation as a generation per se, as a finite period that had a beginning and an end. Moreover, the majority of these sociologists and historians are themselves products of that intellectual and political generation, many of whom were participants as students, faculty, or both. This is not to say that Chicanas have not written about the Movement period; indeed many have written critical analyses of the Movement, with much work focusing on sexism and homophobia as a source of internal friction. Their analyses have not been, however, efforts to document its origins, decline, or particular events; that much is assumed. The lack of Movement history written by women that focuses on particular events or leaders within a specific temporal framework, coupled with the consistent critique of sexist leadership structures and organizational practices, suggests that the generational model is itself inadequate for examining the primary concerns and interests that Chicanas identify as important for understanding this period—or other periods, for that matter. An underlying premise of this study should by now be clear: the use of the generational paradigm as an analytical and narrative framework to examine political practice has prohibited analyses of power relations that are not centered around male-oriented social and political institutions. Consequently, the genealogy of political practice that is produced in generational histories is biased toward male economic and/or political elites and leaders.

As with the sampling of Teresa Acosta's poetry we have surveyed, many Chicana writers that either participated in, followed, or were excluded from the Chicano Movement have contributed to an ongoing critique of Chicano historians and the Movement in their literature. In the process they have produced a body of work that defies traditional generic constraints. Moreover, in the popularization of multigeneric, multi-author anthologies advanced by women of color, they have also placed their writing at the service of a practical political agenda. The cross-cultural, crossgeneric texts I refer to here are collections of essays, short stories, poetry, visual art, journal entries, and interviews, such as *This Bridge Called My Back: Writings By Radical Women of Color* (1981), *Cuentos: Stories by Latinas* (1983), *Compañeras: Latina Lesbians* (1987), *Making Face, Making Soul / Hacienda Caras: Creative and Critical Perspectives by Women of Color* (1990), and *Chicana Lesbians: The Girls Our Mothers Warned Us About* (1991). Following the initial production of the early anthologies, several Latina writers published autobiographical collections that assumed the same multigeneric form. Chief among these are Cherríe Moraga's *Loving in the War Years: lo que nunca pasó por us labios* (1983) and Gloria Anzaldúa's *Borderlands/La frontera* (1987). Although the writing of these types of collections is now most popular among Latina feminists, the multi-author, multigeneric anthology as a politicized literary form has a longer history whose development can be paralleled with Chicano Movement publications such as *Festival Flor y Canto: An Anthology of Chicano Literature* (1974), *Canto Al Pueblo* (1978), and *Flor y Canto II* (1979).[2]

Although these early anthologies were primarily publications of select highlights from literary festivals, we must recall the sociopolitical context of those festivals in the early 1970s and their intimate relationship to political activists, activities, and organizations. We should also recall from chapter 2 that "creative" literature has an even longer historical relationship to other prose forms vis-à-vis its publication in Spanish-language newspapers. The utilization and revision of older forms to address current exigencies is one of the prominent characteristics of contemporary Chicana/o literature. Chief among these reinvigorated forms is the essay. With the exception of the continued examination of Teresa Acosta's poetry, this chapter will focus on recent essays by Latina/os.[3]

Chicana/o cultural production is best understood in the conflictual context of the sociopolitical conditions from which it has emerged. Indeed, a single text can offer us insight into the forces that have helped shape and constrain literary production by people of Mexican descent living in the United States. In the foreword to the second edition of *This Bridge Called My Back,* Cherríe Moraga says that she and coeditor Gloria Anzaldúa consciously set out to create a "book which concentrated on relations between women" (Moraga and Anzaldúa 11). This stated purpose argues that this collection of essays, poetry, and interviews was compiled to fill what the editors considered a gap in Latina/o literature. Other books, it is suggested, have concentrated on relations between men or possibly between men and women and have thus failed to address the full range and power of women's cultural expression. But as Moraga makes clear, a book's focus is subject to change according to the exigencies of the political moment. Consequently, "once a movement has provided some basic consciousness," a closer analysis of both the local and the global situation can be undertaken. Operating from a "position of power rather than compromise," Moraga believes it is now possible to publish another book that will address relationships of power that have continued to be imbalanced or exploitative. By suggesting a relationship between the production of a book and the production of political consciousness, Moraga asserts that books themselves can function as a means of altering, interrupting, or challenging social discourses. Furthermore, as the lines from Moraga's "The Welder" suggest, conflict can be a constructive agent of change.

In "The Welder" Moraga is "interested in the blend / of common elements to make / a common thing." The fusing together of like metals "*is* possible" according to the poet, "but only if things get hot enough . . . ."

The poem thus calls for an embracing of heat, of fire; it is a metaphorical call for debate that is grounded in the specificity of shared experiences and an acknowledgment of differences as well:

> *For too long a time*
> *the heat of my heavy hands*
> *has been smoldering*
> *in the pockets of other*
> *people's business—*
> *they need oxygen to make fire*
>
> *. . . I am the welder.*
> *I understand the capacity of heat*
> *to change the shape of things.*
> (*This Bridge Called My Back* 218–19)

As a builder of meaning, Moraga indicates that she is aware that strong, protective structures result only from carefully crafted plans and difficult labor "within the realm of sparks / out of control."

My analysis of Chicana/o-Latina/o literature in this chapter proceeds under two premises. First, although the forms of political practice and literary production have in some cases changed to meet new exigencies, a vital and wide-ranging array of politics is being practiced by youth, former *movimientistas,* and sectors of the community across class and gender lines that were not formerly active; and second, many post-Movement writers are expanding the boundaries of Chicana/o identity established by the Chicano Generation. The literature that will be central to this chapter will counter Alex Saragoza's dismal appraisal of the current moment as well as the grounds for "celebrating progress" that David Montejano offers; these historians' assessments of the current historical moment will be examined in detail. This chapter will contrast their perspectives with the reconfiguration of historical and geographical boundaries by Cherríe Moraga, Guillermo Gómez-Peña, Rubén Martínez, and Teresa Acosta. By confronting more directly the nature of ingroup differences and the construction of identity and political practice based on gender, sexuality, and nationality, Cherríe Moraga, Guillermo Gómez-Peña, and Rubén Martínez help expand and complicate our contemporary notions of Latina/os in the United States.

The above authors combine concerns about movements (political and geographical), conflict, and intellectual leadership in their writings. Moraga's *The Last Generation,* Gómez-Peña's *Warrior for the Gringostroika,* Martínez's *The Other Side: Fault Lines, Guerrilla Saints, and The True Heart of Rock 'n' Roll,* and the poetry of Teresa Acosta challenge narrow notions about ethnicity, community, and ideology in this "Era of the Hispanic" by positing a pan-Latino identity. In this period, a feminist-informed critique has shifted some of the focus away from public institutions toward other sites of power—the family, the body, and real and metaphorical boundaries that shape identity—while maintaining a material analysis of Chicana/os' lived reality.

Before embarking on a discussion of the literary and historical representations of the post-Movement Generation, I would like to consider for a moment this book's title. The subtitle, "The Literary Making of Chicana and Chicano History," in large part reflects issues that I think are imperative for Mexican-origin people residing in the United States to address. Despite the grounding of these concepts in acadamese, I hope that my analysis and writing provide insight that makes this study more than just an intellectual exercise in reading, writing, research, organization, and style—that is, I hope that as an interpretive project it will have relevance beyond the relatively small audience of people who read academic books. Such aspirations on my part are not articulated as an individual desire but rather in recognition that the postcolonial concerns—history, identity, politics, and creative discursive practices—are intimately tied to social and political practices at the local and global level and thus become another terrain on which power, broadly defined, can be interrogated and negotiated. The precolon part of my title, "Historia," is meant to suggest the indeterminacy of history and fiction as ongoing processes of negotiation between the past and the present. My motivation for choosing to explain the title at this point is to call attention to my own authorship and the reconstruction of stories and histories that have been integral to this study.

It seems to me that the central question of the current chapter—one that confronts me, the author; the historians whose work has been central to this study; and the writers of literature—is how to evaluate and discern the patterns of the present moment without the benefit of hindsight and without knowing outcomes. Phrased another way: What is the relationship between writing and making history? How do we create our own history and what is at stake in such a project? How, for that matter, is the question to be understood? Such questions can be misread so as to create a false division between the various forms of writing, a distinction that could, depending on one's interests, privilege one form of writing over another. Instead, I would argue that neither form of writing, imaginative or historical, is a politically disinterested form. It would not do to pretend that we can totally blur genres, although that is indeed an argument that I have advanced to some degree. In this context, the word "making" is able to capture the ambiguous and tenuous nature of both literature and history. "Making" implies imagination and the literary, as in "making verses." It also implies the construction or manufacturing of something, the ability for something to be transformed.

Literature has historically been at the service of the study of history. That is, history accounts for literature as one form of "evidence." Consequently, the Declaration of Independence, *The Communist Manifesto,* or "Queer Aztlán: The Re-formation of Chicano Tribe" by Cherríe Moraga are important historical documents signifying a desire for a change in social relations. The authors of these texts are recognized historical figures who are judged in accordance with their actions as well as their ability to articulate a vision and to provoke others to act by engaging their imaginations with alternative possibilities for the future. In this sense, successful authorship may be judged by an author's ability to influence others to take action and assert agency over the course of history. But the central elements of rhetoric, of persuasion—logic, ethos, and pathos—are not the exclusive purview of explicitly political texts. We should also consider the way readers respond to and are challenged by texts like *Caballero, George Washington Gómez, The Revolt of the Cockroach People,* as well as the poetry of Sara Estela Ramírez and Teresa Acosta. Considered this way, history and literature have a more intimate relationship with one another, especially if the historian and the creative writer are "committed writers" in the Sartrean sense—if they are writers whose purpose is to motivate people to assert agency in the making of history.

The writers examined in this last chapter can undoubtedly be considered committed writers. My focus is to illustrate how they negotiate their relationship to writing and the making of history. Their work sharply contrasts with historical literature about the present period. Indeed, by definition history refers to the past, not the present. This is a crucial difference between history and literature: literature is not constrained by the past, the present, or, for that matter, the future, for its setting. Almost any observation of the current moment by a historian as historian would be seen as incomplete and lacking in "objectivity." If "presentism," the interpretation of the past as framed in the light of current exigencies, is a concern for historians, then it would seem that objectivity about the present moment would be even more difficult to achieve. This concern with presentism is really a question about the integrity of analytical frameworks in an institutional setting that values objectivity and distance from one's subject matter. For historians, to have a political agenda is to be susceptible to charges of bias. But this distinction between objectivity and subjectivity in historiography seems to rest on the belief that there is a single historical "Truth," the tenet against which subaltern history is predicated. Chicana/o historians have not allowed this charge to affect their writing of a history of their people. But another underlying premise of this study is that presentism *has* affected the writing of Chicana/o history. Because the vast majority of Chicana/o history has been written by scholars who emerged from the Chicano Movement, the cultural nationalism of the period has in many instances overdetermined its significance. Thus the Chicano Movement serves as the standard by which past political practices are measured.[4] A tension exists between historians' political commitments, their need for perceived objectivity, and their historical perspective.

In the Introduction to *Nations and Nationalism Since 1780: Programme, Myth, Reality,* Eric Hobsbawm discusses the politics of the historian. According to Hobsbawm, "no serious historian of nations and nationalism can be a committed political nationalist. . . . Nationalism requires too much belief in what is patently not so. . . . Historians are professionally obliged not to get it wrong, or at least to make an effort not to" (Hobsbawm 12–13). A "serious history" of a people, says Hobsbawm, cannot be written "unless the historian leaves his or her convictions behind when entering the library or the study" (13). His warning that the historian's politics be checked at the door is ominous. Although Hobsbawm is here referring to nationalism as a potential source of bias, one wonders if he believes that historians cannot be uncompromised if they write about issues in which they have a vested interest. For whom, then, does the historian write and why, if not for a belief that the written interpretation of history is informed by and informs various notions of peoplehood? In this study about literary and historical practices, I have juxtaposed historical narratives against fiction and poetry because these forms of writing constitute and identify other sources and sites of power that facilitate a move away from social hierarchies based on class, gender, and racial ideologies. Moreover, the generational paradigm privileges formal leadership structures as well as the economically, socially, and institutionally powerful. In shifting the focus to negotiations of power and narrative strategies that occur outside officially sanctioned circuits of power,

I have relied on the heterogeneity of experiences and relations to illustrate the serious limitations of generational constructs. In each chapter we have seen that generational identities are invested with certain ideological interests to the historian. An against-the-grain reading has revealed the existence of competing ideologies and narrative strategies—in other words, the simultaneity of multiple political generations coexisting within the same community.

Having raised these questions about the "making" of history, ideological investment, and political commitment, I turn now to representations of the post-Movement era by two Chicano historians—David Montejano and Alex Saragoza. The last section of David Montejano's *Anglos and Mexicans in the Making of Texas, 1836–1986* is called "Integration, 1940–1986." Applying a combination of a world-systems approach and a "provincial" point of view to economic change and sociological history, Montejano does not utilize a generational approach to interpret history. In this framework of sociological history, "basic existential categories of social life—notions of class, race, religion, status, gender, and so on," are given prominence (*AM* 319). Montejano describes his methodology as follows:

> One way of describing the nature of sociological history is through an analogy to drama. In comparison to most social history, sociological history is sparse on details concerning character development, background setting, and dramatic movement. The dramatis personae are subsumed by social categories, the background limited to a few symbolic props, the movement of the story condensed and truncated by case studies. Symbolic and didactic in character, the effect of the sociological-historical narrative is rather like the allegory. Its effectiveness depends to a large degree on whether the chosen symbols or concepts can convey the theme or argument without subverting the human character of the story. (319)

The author's reliance on the literary language to describe his narrative and interpretive style only serves further to underscore my thesis about the interrelationship of history and literature. Moreover, it highlights the centrality of interpretation and emplotment in his work. For Montejano, integration "refers primarily to the granting of effective citizenship" to Texas Mexicans as signified by the decline of structures of segregation in the political, economic, and civil arenas (260).

In chapter 3, I made use of Montejano's observation about sociologists who examine all Mexicans under the same rubric as "new" immigrant groups. I now return to an expanded version of that quote and include with it the last sentence of the introduction to "Integration" as a way to begin examining the literary elements of his "story" about Mexicans and Anglos. Having drawn our attention to sociology's double standards in examining different social groups, Montejano says that he is willing to "overlook" such problematic details in certain works, such as Leo Grebler, Joan Moore, and Ralph Guzmán's *The Mexican American People,* "in light of their positive assessment for the future of the Mexican American." "What cannot be ignored," he writes, "is the striking but common paradox where the historical legends of the Alamo, cowboys, and longhorns co-exist innocently alongside sociological studies of Mexican Americans as immigrants" (261). Pointing to the limitations of an ahistorical sociological framework, Montejano observes, "Immigrant approaches, such as that of Grebler, Moore, and Guzmán, serve to shift the emphasis away from war and annexation, denying the memory of these origins for contemporary Mexican-Anglo relations. Rather than a people living under the shadow of the Alamo and San Jacinto, Mexican Americans are now seen as another immigrant group marching through the stages of assimilation. *For the possibility of gaining full citizenship, such historical revisionism may be a small price to pay"* (261, emphasis mine). Despite acknowledging the subjective selection of criteria and the analytical framework being deployed, Montejano's willingness to "pay the price" of historical revisionism underscores the politics of interpretation at play in his own work.

"Integration, 1940–1986" is composed of two chapters, "The Demise of 'Jim Crow'" and "A Time of Inclusion." What I am most interested in examining here is the final chapter, in order to identify the plot structure of this historical narrative. Montejano brings his history to a close in 1986, the year of the sesquicentennial "celebration" marking Texas's independence from Mexico. While noting that the "Texas Mexican community lags far behind on all mainstream indicators in the areas of education, health, income, and political influence," Montejano stresses the "assimilative opportunities" that the civil rights movement won for Mexican Americans. "The most important sign in this regard consists of the contemporary public role of Mexican Americans as political actors in Texas" (288). This emphasis on electoral politics, coupled with his focus on San Antonio as the "showcase" for the success of the Voting Rights Act, signals a shift away from a critique of uneven economic development and the subsequent unequal distribution of power; it implies a desire to end his narrative on a high note in order to offer a "positive assessment for the future" of Texas Mexicans, much like Grebler, Moore, and Guzmán do.

After providing an analysis of the crucial role played by Texas's Raza Unida Party in demonstrating the potential of a Mexican American voting bloc, Montejano proceeds to "illustrate" political gains by pointing to local and state elections in which the Mexican American vote affected the outcome—in many instances placing Mexican Americans in office. "An ironic consequence of the ethnic nationalism of the 1970s was the securing of a measure of political integration for the Mexican American Community" (292). He thus gauges successful political representation quantitatively by comparing past and present numbers of Mexican American elected officials. In a subsection titled "The Elaboration of Urban Classes," Montejano uses data to illustrate a dramatic shift in occupations for Mexican Americans—from unskilled laborers to skilled and professional workers—as evidence of economic integration. He does not, however, reconcile these shifts in occupational categories with the continued economic disenfranchisement of Mexicans that he conceded earlier.

Montejano concludes his narrative with a note on Mexican American politics and social status by situating himself in his hometown of San Antonio, where Henry Cisneros, the former secretary of Housing and Urban Development in the Clinton Administration, was the mayor in 1986. He notes that in public addresses marking the sesquicentennial in front of the Alamo, "it is not surprising to hear Cisneros emphasize the American identity of Texas Mexicans, for Cisneros himself represents the reconciliation that has taken place between Anglo and Mexican in Texas. . . . The politics of negotiation and compromise have replaced the politics of conflict and control" (306). Montejano's bias toward San Antonio as an exemplary city is evident throughout this conclusion. San Antonio *is* unique, and for that reason we should be cautious when it is put forward as the standard with which to measure the conditions of Mexican Americans' lives. With its heavy reliance on military bases and its status as one of the only U.S. urban centers with a majority Mexican-origin population, as well as a "sizable middle class and skilled working class," it is, in fact, *not* representative of the living and working conditions for the majority of Mexicans in Texas. Montejano recognizes that there are still many social issues that are sources of tension between Anglos and Mexicans, but he ends his narrative with a positive projection for the future: "In the 1980s, the struggle between exclusion and inclusion continues. What is different from previous battles, however, is that Mexican Americans have become an important factor in the political chemistry of the Southwest. It seems unlikely that such momentum can be stopped" (307). Invoking the Alamo, Henry Cisneros, and the city of San Antonio as symbols of progress to make a final comment about the politics of race, class, and ethnicity, Montejano's allegorical drama reveals itself as yet another romance about social reconciliation that does not take into account the more common experience of disenfranchisement and hostility that the greater Mexican community, especially the recently arrived, continue to face daily in rural towns and in urban centers like Houston and Dallas, where social stratification and de facto forms of segregation persist. In an effort to project future reconciliation, Montejano's analysis fails to offer constructive insight that could be used to further consolidate the momentum he claims is underway.

In contrast to Montejano's positive assessment of the current moment is the perspective put forth by Alex Saragoza in "The Significance of Recent Chicano-related Historical Writings: An Appraisal." Saragoza's major purpose in this essay is to provide an overview of the development of Chicano historiography, which he does by reviewing the methodology and focus of recent publications in the field. He, too, has an opinion about the current historical moment. One of the primary problems faced by Mexican-origin people in the United States, according to Saragoza, is a dismal economic condition that prohibits economic advancement and social mobility. He sees intracultural fragmentation as a result of ideological differences that stem from class interests and mass culture.

The tone of Saragoza's assessment borders on despair, as is evident in passages like the following:

> The wider society has sustained ideals and views of self-worth that have made the poor painfully aware of their difference. Chicanos, especially youth, have had relatively fewer resources to acquire the trappings of prestige and status defined by a consumer culture that they cannot ignore or escape. The blame, it seems, has been often internalized and expressed through attempts to find self-validation and esteem that are at hand, controllable. Frustration and disillusion usually have not been far behind. The studies of Joan Moore, Ruth Horowitz, and

> Martín Sánchez-Jankowski suggest the saddening outcomes of a historical process for significant segments of the Mexican-origin population. (Saragoza 43–44)

An overriding concern with intracultural fragmentation pervades Saragoza's essay, so much so that he sees the Chicano community as being overwhelmed by economic, ideological, and cultural forces beyond its control that are "further fracturing the Chicano community into increasingly distinct segments" (45). In critiquing the nationalist illusion of a unified community, Saragoza points to past scholarship that sought commonalties in an effort to "interpret the past as a group experience." In his effort to acknowledge the heterogeneity of Mexican-origin people and their diversity of experience, he appears unable to find any grounds for collectivity. He is, however, critical of those who "lament the allegedly singular disunity among Chicanos, assuming, mistakenly, an exceptional semblance of solidarity among other social movements. Such complaints ignore the historical origins of the rifts within the Chicano community and they fail to appreciate the forces that have undermined the possibilities of a political project embracing the diversity among Chicanos" (46).

At times it is difficult to discern whether Saragoza's discouragement results from the conditions faced by the community or the state of historical scholarship. Clearly, he believes that historians are important to the community: "Historians will continue . . . to carry the burden of providing the primary research for understanding the evolution of the Chicano community" (49). But such a perspective suggests an approach to history that privileges historians by positioning them as mere witnesses of the past, not as active agents of change and contributors to a future trajectory. As if anticipating such a critique, Saragoza offers these thoughts: "For those who seek political lessons from the past, Chicano history offers caution, but not despair. . . . The commonalties in the Chicano experience have waned; historians cannot refashion the past to vindicate political purpose or need. For activists, the diversity among Chicanos—history argues—must be the linchpin of any political strategy or project. The fracturing of the Chicano Movement stands as testimony to the absence of a stable, trenchant common ground among people of Mexican descent" (50). Thus Montejano and Saragoza offer us two very different perspectives on the post-Movement period. The former celebrates the possibilities for the future by using electoral politics as the measure of success; the latter sees the Chicano Movement as an illusory utopian moment that has become fractured and ineffective under the burden of intracultural class and ideological differences.

Neither historian accounts for the ongoing political activity that occurs away from the ballot box—the continuing work of a wide array of older organizations like the United Farm Workers and the Southwest Organizing Project, as well as LULAC and the GI Forum. Also left unconsidered is the work of newer labor organizations, such as the women of Fuerza Unida of San Antonio, who have framed their struggle for just compensation against Levi-Strauss, Inc., as an international effort to hold multinational corporations accountable to workers on a global level. Also to be considered are projects like The Border Campaign and the Coalition for Justice in the Maquiladoras, binational social-justice organizations operating out of the Lower Rio Grande Valley of Texas, which have called for investigations by both the Mexican and U.S. governments of working and health conditions confronted by *maquiladora* workers residing in the *colonias* situated next to industrial parks. Presumably unnoticed by the historians are the numerous grassroots cross-cultural environmental organizations that have been holding corporations, the U.S. government, and mainstream environmental organizations accountable for their negligence regarding the particular ways communities of color are effected by urban and rural development policies.[5] Students on university and college campuses across the nation have continued to confront old problems with institutional racism, as evinced by ongoing efforts to create a more meaningful curriculum and to increase the recruitment and retention of students and faculty of color. Again, these efforts are not addressed in the essay; nor is the new dilemma of students of color having to seek political accountability from minority faculty, administrators, and ethnic-studies centers. Contrary to proclamations by scholars like Carlos Muñoz that student activism is virtually nonexistent and ineffective, El Movimiento Estudiantil Chicana/o de Aztlán (MEChA), an organization founded in 1969, is still alive, active, and militant; its annual national conferences have grown and chapters in the Midwest have recently formed. There is also active participation in international solidarity work by Chicanas/os, especially with Latin American countries, as well as immigrant-rights networks such as the American Friends Service Committee's Immigration Law Enforcement Monitoring Project.[6] I list the work of these organizations to suggest that the Chicana/o community is, as it always has, responding in a variety of ways to the exigencies of the current moment. This list is by no means comprehensive; it is meant only to be suggestive of the range of social, political, economic, and cultural issues that are being addressed. To many people, the post-Movement period is measured against the Chicano Movement rather than being understood on its own terms. Many historians, sociologists, and writers have identified the "fracturing" of the Chicano Movement as a result of internal tensions. This may indeed be accurate, but that does not mean that political work ended with the decline of particular leaders or particular organizations. To lament the end of the Movement—its decline or fragmentation—is to wax nostalgic. Activism today has changed form to accommodate sophisticated and complex strategies by corporations and a public that demands evidence and accountability. The strategic use of writing, research, and technology are central to the success of the work of these organizations, as are older militant forms of public protest.[7]

It is tempting to follow this discussion of the politics of the current moment with texts by authors who are affiliated with political organizations and who write documents that contribute directly to a particular political project. This type of writing would include journalism, press releases, pamphlets, articles, and analyses of public policy that activists use as counter-narratives to texts produced by corporations, the government, and the mainstream press. A strict focus on this resistance literature, while sorely needed, would be premised on the dissolution of the traditional boundaries of literature. In my opinion it is a worthwhile and necessary project to undertake, but in the context of this study it might serve only to recenter resistance narratives, political leaders, and political organizations. Those counter-narratives by Chicana/os do exist and demand examination to assess the emergence of new narrative and analytical strategies. But new forms of writing have emerged from within older forms as well, and it is these more subtle forms of political engagement that will be assessed here. The writers we turn to next present an array of issues that address the complexity of Chicana/o politics and identity in this post-Movement, postmodern age. Unlike the texts that emerge from a specific political situation and affiliation, which often have a limited circulation, are often published by the organizations themselves, and/or are categorized in bookstores (when they are carried at all) as "political science," these collections of poetry and informal essays are recognized as literature; they allow me to advance the against-the-grain reading of historians' perspectives in a manner consistent with the previous chapters.

Writing Wrongs in the Nation, on the Border, and in the Barrio

> *History is "advancing" at an unprecedented speed. A writer-friend tells me, "Everything we write nowadays is outdated before we've finished." I have to agree. Still, history is always stumbling, always limping a few steps behind prophecy. And it is prophecy that drives this writing—not my personal prophecy, but the prophecy of a people.*
>
> —Cherríe Moraga, *The Last Generation*

> *Our generation belongs to the world's biggest floating population; the weary travelers, the dislocated, those of us who left because we didn't fit anymore, those of us who still haven't arrived because we don't know where to arrive at, or because we can't go back anymore.*
>
> —Guillermo Gómez-Peña, *Warrior for Gringostroika*

Cartographic metaphors have become common parlance in literary and cultural studies to refer to movement, growth, and development: we speak of the boundaries and borderlands of culture, mapping and remapping characters, narratives, events, and historical contexts. It has become almost a territorial imperative, a disciplinary obligation, in cultural and postcolonial studies to know how to read and deploy this language to comprehend the nuances of geopolitical relationships and cultural dynamism and exchange. Implicit in this usage is an awareness that the arrangement or order of things (people, geographies, boundaries, borders) are not arbitrary but salient signifiers of power relations. The oft-used metaphor of the border (to refer to a site of cultural negotiation and exchange) is symptomatic of the capacity of this language both to offer insight and to obscure, for when it is used to speak solely of social and cultural relations, we too often forget that the border is a site of juridical control where people are policed, detained, and turned away—often violently—where people's legitimacy, their very humanity, is determined by their citizenship status. I point to this phenomenon of cartographic and cartological management and its human/cultural consequences as an entry point for discussing the relationship between transnationalism and Latinos because I see it as an opportune moment to rethink—remap, if you will—human relations. In fact, I will argue that this is something that is already being practiced by the cultural critics whose work I discuss below. Each of them, through the use of the informal essay, a genre that is particularly enabling for cognitively reorienting the reader, understands how the border functions as part of the ideological and repressive state apparatus that hinges on notions of citizenship; but rather than dismiss it, to borrow a phrase from Cornell West, they see it is as an opportunity for a structural restraint to be turned into a conjunctural opportunity.

The trio of authors I will discuss explore the problematics of national borders, nationalism, and identity in a changing world. Though they might be most easily assimilated into the rubric of Chicana/o literature, their work resists such easy classification. Since its establishment as a legitimate field of study in the late 1960s and early 1970s, and because of its uneasy location in two language departments (Spanish and English), the teaching of Chicana/o literature and the writing of its corresponding body of criticism have required negotiating two national histories. The continuing appeal of such phrases as "Greater Northern Mexico" to refer to the sociopolitical and cultural territories occupied by people of Mexican descent in the United States speaks to the challenge of not reducing the history of this settler-and-immigrant, colonizer-and-colonized group to one historical narrative.[8] More recently, however, responding to changing demographics and continuing demands from students, as well as an increase in the production of a diasporic literature by Latinos from many national settings (Cuba, the Dominican Republic, Puerto Rico, Nicaragua, Guatemala, El Salvador), a U.S. Latino literary rubric is being constructed. In considering the coalescence of such a paradigm it is imperative to untangle and keep discrete the historical narratives of each national group. Cherríe Moraga, Rúben Martínez, and Guillermo Goméz-Peña each advocate some form of pan-Latino identity that I believe offers a political vision of what might enable this field to cohere.

Before discussing the literature I would like to situate it in relationship to the emerging discourse on transnationalism. Recently there have been debates about the relationship between ethnic studies and postcolonial studies. Although I will not offer a review of these discussions, I will say that I have always found the insights from so-called Third World theorists particularly insightful for thinking about Chicana/o cultural production in a global context—even as I have had to understand the need to qualify and adapt said insights to the particulars of a U.S. situation. But this has not always been so far a stretch theoretically as it might at first seem, for as Masao Miyoshi has noted: "Colonial history since 1945 converges with U.S. history." In "A Borderless World?: From Colonialism to Transnationalism and the Decline of the Nation-State," Miyoshi argues that "colonialism is even more active now in the form of transnational corporatism" ("Borderless World?" 728). The applicability of the critique of colonialism and its insight into relations of power within the so-called First World are even more salient in the contemporary period, when "National culture is increasingly irrelevant; multiculturalism holds the day now as a tradeable commodity" (Miyoshi, "Sites of Resistance" 69).

As Latinos in the United States receive both renewed and new attention in different forms—as exploitable labor in service and manufacturing industries (from high-tech to garment work, one finds the same piecemeal labor); as migrants who transgress the borders of the nation-state; and as producers of marketable commodities in the form of artifacts, literature, food, music, and so on—we need to assess the academy's role in the circuit of control: Is it one of domination, exploitation, or empowerment? In this era of so-called free trade, how do we reconcile the teaching of Latino literatures with the simultaneous rampant xenophobia and anti-immigrant discourse? Is this to be understood as part of the struggle to reconstruct the national identity of the United States? What is the status of these debates in interdisciplinary fields such as American studies? It has become increasingly necessary to call for analytical frameworks that cross borders just as capital does—to trace the effects of transnationalism on global cultures. Eva Cherniavsky has pointed out that ". . . with the emergence of postcolonial literatures and theory as a legitimated disciplinary category within American institutions, the discourse of American exceptionalism that has reigned in the field of American studies . . . has suddenly and startlingly begun to yield to the recognition of U.S. participation in the world-making histories of imperialism and colonial domination" (Cherniavsky 88). Such a recognition has two important implications, as noted by Miyoshi: one is that "the 'global' economy is, in fact, nothing but a strategy for maximum exclusion" ("Sites of Resistance" 71) and the other is that it was only "under pressure from feminism, identity politics, and multiculturalism [that] conventional disciplines [were] forced to loosen their boundaries and transnationalize their expertise" (71). Because ". . . workers in search of jobs all over the world are changing global demography in the third industrial revolution through legal or illegal migration to every industrial center in industrialized or developing nations" ("Borderless World?" 748–49), we can expect both new cultural forms and products from them as they bring their traditions and renew, influence, and adapt to already existing cultural communities in the United States. Because these migrants, especially those from Latin American nations, tend to seek out already existing Latino communities and rarely have access to cultural circuits of power, it is those artists from pre-existing U.S. Latino communities who serve as their cultural and political allies. And while the term "postcolonial" has been rightfully critiqued by theorists like Miyoshi, who argues that "ours . . . is not an age of *post*colonialism but of intensified colonialism" ("Borderless World?" 750) I would like to agree with Cherniavsky that ". . . a *post*colonial approach to U.S. history and culture would speak to the contradictions of a naturalized/nationalized colonial domination," one that is too easily elided when all cultures are measured in relation to some reified "American culture" (Cherniavsky 88). I will now turn to a brief reading of essays by Moraga, Martínez, and Gómez-Peña. In what follows I will pay particular attention to their engagement with the discourses of history, nationalism, and cultural identity.

All of these artists have published books that are multigeneric in form, including poetry, essays, journal entries, and, in the case of Gómez-Peña, performance-art texts. The question of identity is central to these multigeneric texts, not as an end in itself, but as a basis for comprehending the present historical moment and as a compass for future direction. The work of Moraga, Gómez-Peña, and Martínez is at once intensely personal and profoundly political. And, as the above epigraphs indicate, all are preoccupied with the current geopolitical status of their generation of the Chicana/o-Latina/o community. The essays in these collections, in particular, are an attempt to articulate their relationship to their home communities in terms of the changing nature of identity and place and what this reveals about the sociopolitical status of Latina/os in the United States. Moreover, each of these authors writes about experiencing social, psychological, and political fragmentation. Their writing represents an effort to share their angst and anger, as well as to provide tentative direction for empathetic readers. Thus they each assume an engaged, if limited, audience.

In this overview of their work, I will not attempt to analyze the totality of their collections; I am less interested in assessing structures or what their work says about them as individuals than I am in arguing for the value of the informal essay as an interventionary and imaginative narrative in which to address contemporary exigencies. Because of the fragmentary nature of their work, my own exposition will be essayistic in form.

The essay is a particularly powerful genre for expressing the tenuous nature of these authors' assessments of the present moment as well as their concerns for an identity in flux. Historically, the informal essay has been utilized to try out new ideas; thus it is reflexive, personal, and based on experience. In this regard, little attempt is made to be scientific, objective, or conclusive; it is a form that invites open-endedness and possibilities for change. Moreover, the essay often employs personal anecdotes in the service of analysis; authors often write of themselves as representative figures of their generation or community. These essays seek to offer insight for the present or a vision of the future. Most of the essays included in the collections of these authors have had prior public exposure as articles or conference papers. In each case the context and occasion of that original exposure tell us something about their purpose.

Each of the authors presents identity as a central issue of the post-Movement period and notes the inadequacy of a strictly Chicana/o identity. Although each author identifies as either Chicana/o or Latina/o, each one's personal identity complicates our understanding of the Chicana/o community, and together they present a more complex picture of social and historical patterns of change. Cherríe Moraga uses the term "half-breed" to describe her biological, bicultural identity resulting from the union of her mother, a woman of Mexican descent, and her French and British Canadian father; Guillermo Gómez-Peña is a middle-class *chilango* (a Mexico City native) who emigrated to the United States and became "Chicanoized"; Rubén Martínez is the son of a first-generation Mexican father, and his mother is an immigrant from an elite family in El Salvador. Each author recognizes that, as a result of changing patterns of immigration, Mexican culture in the United States is being "Latinoized"; increasingly there is a mixture of non-Mexican Latinos, especially Central Americans, who are changing the cultural composition of urban communities and who share a common social and political condition. This is especially true in the urban areas of California, from which each author writes. In part, their essays address the changing nature of the Chicana/o community and its effect on efforts at collective action.

Because these writers are concerned with notions of identity and community, each finds it important to address the question of nationalism as a conceptual and organizational framework for political action. Moraga believes that it is imperative to address questions of identity and nation in order to respond effectively to the political crises confronting Chicana/os. Her work is motivated by a "sense of urgency that Chicanos are a disappearing tribe" (*LG* 2). She believes that the process of acculturation is resulting in the slow death of Mexican culture in the United States. In the introduction to *The Last Generation* she explains why she writes essays: "After a long period of silence, I had imagined I had given up the essay, until the political urgency of the times—the Gulf War, the collapse of the Soviet Union, indigenous peoples' international campaigns for sovereignty, the hundreds of thousands of deaths of gay people, women, and people of color from AIDS and breast cancer, the Los Angeles Rebellion, and the blatant refusal by the United States to commit to environmental protection at the Earth Summit in Brazil—called me to respond" (3). She thus views the essay as a particularly appropriate interventionary form. To ground her writing in history she also perceives the reflexivity of the essay as a way to move through time: "The journey of this writing is as much a journey into the past as it is into the future, a resurrection of the ancient in order to construct the modern. . . . I see my task as that of the ancient Mesoamerican scribes: to speak to these cataclysmic times, to expose the 'dream world' of individualism, profit, and consumerism" (4).

Moraga's fear of the loss of culture, that this is the "last generation" of Mexicans in the United States who will know their heritage, stems from multiple sources. At the most personal level, it stems from observations about her family and her sexual orientation—her "tío's children have not taught their own children to be Mexicans," and a continuing process of *mestizaje,* or miscegenation, has resulted in her family's looking more European than indigenous; moreover, as a lesbian, she is "the only one [in her family] not contributing to the population. My line of family stops with me" she says (9). At a social level she observes that the Chicano/Latino population in the States is being deculturalized by a process of "Hispanicization." Moraga's intervention in this process through her writing assumes two strategies—to expose the process of deculturalization as a violent hegemonic process and to call for reclamation of a Pan-American, panindigenous identity and movement.

Moraga's strongest and most elaborate interventions occur in her two longest essays in the collection, "Art in América con Acento" and "Queer Aztlán: the Re-Formation of Chicano Tribe." In "Art in América con Acento" Moraga embraces a pan-Latino identity and eschews the historically and culturally inaccurate euphemism "Hispanic," which "proffers to the Spanish surnamed the illusion of blending into the 'melting pot' like any other white immigrant group" (57). Written a week after the 1990 Nicaraguan election, in which the Sandinistas were voted out of office, she decries imperialism and is ashamed of being a U.S. citizen, longstanding sentiments that she expressed in another context as "Los Estados Unidos es mi país, pero no es mi patría" (54). She looks to her identity and her occupation to question her relationship and hold herself accountable for the U.S. government's actions against the sovereignty of Latin Americans: *"I am Latina, born and raised in the United States. I am a writer. What is my responsibility in this?"* (53). The remainder of the essay is her response to this question.

Moraga combines analysis and observation to provide a basis for cross-cultural alliances with other Latinos throughout the Americas. She examines the ironic effect of a Latino diaspora resulting from the Anglo military and capital invasion of Latin America: ". . . the United States' gradual consumption of Latin America and the Caribbean is bringing the people of the Americas together. What was once largely a chicano/mexicano population in California is now guatemalteco, salvadoreño, nicaraugüense. What was largely a Puerto Rican and Dominican 'Spanish Harlem' of New York is now populated with Mexicans . . ." (55). Moraga sees her role as a writer as one of providing clarity and persuading others to understand the political and cultural significance of the choice between assuming a Latino versus a Hispanic identity. "As a Latina artist I can choose to contribute to the development of a docile generation of would-be Republican 'Hispanics' loyal to the United States, or to the creation of a force of 'disloyal' americanos who subscribe to a multicultural, multilingual, radical re-structuring of América. Revolution is not won by numbers, but by visionaries . . ." (56).

Moraga does not harbor romantic illusions about a homogenous Chicano/Latino community; she understands that class, race, and gender ideology influence people's affiliations. This is a problem confronted in the art world as well, where attention from the mainstream culture secured legitimacy for some writers and literary critics who then moved away from producing politically engaged work. She offers alternative possibilities for an identity that at once erases the significance of national borders and embraces a world community composed of people with shared languages and cultural practices—"identities that dissolve borders" (62). The specifics of how to achieve a community that embraces difference are articulated more clearly in "Queer Aztlán."

In this essay Moraga assesses the viability of an indigenous nationalism as a political organizing ideology. In contrast to Guillermo Gómez-Peña's critique of nationalism as being passé, Moraga sees it as a necessary and practical strategy for building alliances. This is a seemingly odd move considering the by-now longstanding critique of sexism and homophobia in ethnic nationalism in the United States; however, Moraga initiates her reformation of nationalism by situating herself outside the Chicano Movement, as a member of a sector of the population that was excluded. She does not see the problems with exclusionary nationalism as being inherent, however. Her experience has taught her that the inconsistencies and contradictions that excluded her from the Chicano Movement exist in many forms in other political organizations as well: "I experienced," she wrote, "the racism of the Women's Movement, the elitism of the Gay and Lesbian Movement, the homophobia and sexism of the Chicano Movement, and the benign cultural imperialism of the Latin America Solidarity Movement" (146). Countering these experiences are other, more identity-specific movements that formed in response to or in spite of the more broad-based ones; these include a national Chicana feminist consciousness, a lesbian-of-color movement, the founding of an independent national Latino/a lesbian and gay men's organization, and indigenous people's international campaigns for human and land rights. The "Queer Aztlán" she proposes takes elements from all these movements and proposes a synthesis into one political movement. Such a proposal to reshape and reform the Chicano Movement is one that will be contested; however, no longer seeing herself outside of the Movement as a result of her alliances with groups that challenged the limitations of a narrow nationalism, she strives to refashion it from within.

Just as her initial process of politicization occurred through her recognition of her lesbianism, Moraga's desire to articulate the need for a positive nationalism, a "Chicano homeland that could embrace all its people, including its jotería," stems from her experience with anglocentricity in "Queer Nation," an urban direct-action gay, lesbian, and bisexual organization. Moraga's recollection of experiences in different movements shapes her reconstruction of identity. At the core of her identity is the collective experience and living memory of colonialism; this is the central experience that enables her to use an anticolonial identity as the foundation for "Queer Aztlán." Moraga's recovery of memory begins with a recollection of the Chicano Movement, including the negative and positive aspects of it and other "progressive nationalisms." Mourning the dissolution of an active Chicano Movement, she nevertheless believes it still exists in a state of reprieve. She says, "For me, 'El Movimiento' has never been a thing of the past, it has retreated into subterranean uncontaminated soils awaiting resurrection in a 'queerer,' more feminist generation" (148). In such a state, the Movement can not only be recalled, but reenacted—with crucial differences, however. The positive elements she wants to salvage from the older Movement and Chicano nationalism, which she appears to conflate, are its commitment to preserving the integrity of the Chicano people, its righteous radicalism, its unabashed antiassimilationism and it *rebeldía*. The negative elements she rejects are its institutionalized heterosexism, its inbred machismo, its lack of a coherent national strategy, and its tendency towards separatism, which can "run dangerously close to biological determinism and a kind of fascism" (149). An anticolonialist stance, however, can accommodate a strategy for decolonizing the female body, whereas an antiheterosexist position does not address the racism confronted by people of color, including men. Any movement, she says, must be "culturally and sexually specific" (149). Using the language of Third World liberation movements allows her to call for a nationalism that "decolonizes the brown and female body as it decolonizes the brown and female earth" (150). Holding onto the concept of nation is an imperative for her, "because without the specific naming of the nation, the nation will be lost."

The nation Moraga imagines is one that has open borders, not closed ones, and can therefore accommodate new immigrants. But it is not one that uses a selective memory to construct internal borders, leadership positions, gender roles, and sexual hierarchies. In Queer Aztlán, those who were former outcasts of the Chicano Movement—lesbians, heterosexual women, and gay men—would be looked to for their insight into "those areas within our cultural family that need to change" (160). Central to successful change must be a willingness to give up gender-, class-, sex-, and race-based privilege. One way Moraga invokes imagination to avoid a repetition of past mistakes is to locate her re-imagined nation not as Mexico but as a "tribe," a social structure that does not depend on the notion of a nation-state; rather, it proposes an alternative socioeconomic structure.

Moraga adopts a more specific anticolonial position, an indigenist one. Her historical reference, then, is not nation-specific but rests on a geopolitical alliance with all indigenous peoples. Such a position requires the avid defense of native people's political and territorial sovereignty and the sovereignty to inhabit wholly one's own body and soul. Her proposal for a Queer Aztlán is an activation of past memory and a projection of the future. "A new Chicano nationalism calls for the integration of both the traditional and the revolutionary, the ancient and the contemporary. It requires a serious reckoning with the weaknesses in our mestizo culture, and a reaffirmation of what has preserved and sustained us as a people" (174). Moraga's vision for the future is not taken for granted but is presented as an imperative for a political vision, even if it is unattainable. "Without the dream of a free world, a free world will never be realized" she declares (164).

The urgency with which Moraga writes against time, her return to the ancient wisdoms for insight into the construction of community, her insistence that there is truth in metaphor, and her desire to resurrect and reform a nationalist movement that is both territorially defined and metaphysical, all suggest an effort on her part to find a way to articulate a modernist vision in a postmodern world. The contentious relationship between modernism and postmodernism that is central to Moraga's work is also addressed by Gómez-Peña and Martínez as a struggle between conflicting ideologies of representation whose contestation occurs during a significant period in ethnic and Third World history. These "ways of looking at the world" deserve to be more fully explored for their enabling and disabling potential. This is a concern that will be taken up in the last section of this chapter, but for now, we move to the writings of a border artist whose present and future visions both complement and contradict Moraga's.

On both the aesthetic and philosophical levels, Moraga's modernist feminist project seems to contrast sharply with Guillermo Gómez-Peña's *Warrior for Gringostroika*. Gómez-Peña's collection is a compilation of previously published materials that appeared mostly in art magazines and journals. Like Moraga and Martínez, Gómez-Peña is concerned with the condition of his generation, and this concern becomes a theme in his writing. Gómez-Peña and Martínez both include "generation" poems in their collections, which reflect their perceptions about the present moment. Gómez-Peña's poem "My Generation" exudes despair and pessimism, as the following lines illustrate:

> *My generation generates chaos*
> *witnesses chaos*
> *multiplies chaos . . .*
> *My generation generates incomplete wisdom*
> *produces broken art/fragmented poetry,*
> *anachronistic children . . .*
> *My generation is unable to finish the*
> *performance.* (*WG* 148)

In addition to poetry, *Gringostroika* contains a "performance chronology" of photographs of the author's collaborative performance pieces at different public sites. Also included are selected "performance texts" and "critical texts." The critical essays in this collection address issues of identity, social policies, and politics affecting Latinos; the status of Latino art; the border as a site of violence; and cultural and economic negotiation and as a metaphor for geopolitical relations. Gómez-Peña's use of the border as a metaphor in his writing and performance pieces is central to his aesthetic, but he maintains an ambivalence to the border as a signifier and metaphor of relations of power:

> The border as metaphor has become hollow. Border aesthetics have been gentrified and border culture as a utopian model for dialog is temporarily bankrupt. But the border as a region of political injustice and great human suffering still exists. The border remains an infected wound on the body of the continent, its contradictions more painful than ever; its supremacist groups still hunting migrant workers as sport; its vigilantes pointing their car lights south; its helicopters and police dogs terrorizing Mexican and Central American peasants who come to feed this country. Sadly, the border remains unchanged. . . . ("Death on the Border" 9)

Metaphors abound in literature about the U.S.-Mexico border. It has been called a desert, a scar, a scab, a wasteland, a laboratory of the human condition, a war zone, a tortilla curtain, and a geopolitical wound, among other things. These metaphors reflect the range of attitudes about this international boundary line as a place of pain; a site of violence, neglect, and waste; an uncontrolled "free" zone of capitalist activity, poverty, and vice; or as a gateway for human traffic into the "land of opportunity." In popular discourse on the border, its residents and migrants are often reduced to stereotypes born from a media-generated hysteria.

It is difficult not to use metaphors when talking about the U.S.-Mexico border. Plain, descriptive, everyday terms seem inadequate and inappropriate for articulating the lived material, the cultural and social realities that have emerged around and across this international boundary. Despite the difficulty of "translating" border experience, in the last decade a vast border discourse has emerged whose primary vehicle is language, although many multimedia presentations, particularly those of visual and performance artists like Gómez-Peña, also use imagery to deliver a message about the border.

Gómez-Peña's innovative work as an artist-activist member of the San Diego–Tijuana Border Arts Workshop, which is dedicated to forming transnational relations, questions the social and cultural relations between the United States and Mexico by exposing the contradictions that result from a refusal to acknowledge the interdependence between the two countries. *Warrior for Gringostroika* brings together Gómez-Peña's various artistic genres to make an indictment against fixed notions of identity, nationality, and language, which fail to consider the ways these concepts are altered, changed, or challenged along the U.S.-Mexico border on a daily basis. Gómez-Peña has a love-hate relationship with postmodernism and multiculturalism, two concepts he sees as being abused, overused, and misunderstood; but these concepts are central to his writing. He believes in the power of art to transcend historically based prejudices and myths and to heal the fractured reality of the present.

Gómez-Peña's essays are multilingual and promote collaboration among races, sexes, and generations, but they speak against the co-optation or vampirism of the cultures of the "other." He warns against the appropriation of cultural others and sees this possibility as a dangerous component of the multicultural craze in the artistic and academic worlds. To Gómez-Peña, the streets are the best stage and truest test for whether one's art is relevant and meaningful. He has used border bridges, the river, and federal courthouses as stages for his productions. In doing so Gómez-Peña uses his art to make links between spatial politics, material forces, and issues of representation. Furthermore, his cross-cultural, transborder performances and theory maintain a consistent focus on migration as a multinational phenomenon that must continually be historicized and understood dialectically.

As the title *Warrior for Gringostroika* suggests, as does these essays' having originally appeared in art magazines, the author's audience is the educated elite; the book is an effort to reconstruct gringo culture in light of the reconstruction of societies that is occurring simultaneously with the realignment of global powers. What follows is an assessment of the concepts and strategies that Gómez-Peña articulates in one of the critical essays in this collection, "From Art-Mageddon to Gringostroika." Like Moraga's work, Gómez-Peña's essays are interventionary. Central to his concerns is the ongoing national debate on the value of multiculturalism and art. Though he speaks as a Latino, in opposition to Moraga's positive evaluation and use of ethnic identity as an organizing principle, Gómez-Peña finds that postmodern culture has made it "increasingly difficult to sustain separatist or essentialist positions" (*WG* 56). While territory is important to his arguments, he refers less to land redistribution and more to institutional space and funding for cultural and economic development projects. Because he writes against any form of nationalism, he, like Moraga, posits a Pan-American identity; yet, in writing against a narrowly defined "American" national identity, Gómez-Peña is calling for reform of the American nation, not its dissolution. Using the quincentenary and the end of the millennium as historic signposts, he comments, "The impulse behind the clumsy multicultural debate is the collective realization of the need to readjust our anachronistic national institutions and policies to the new social, cultural, linguistic, and demographic realities of this country. What we are all clumsily trying to say is that we want to be part of a 'multi'-participatory society that truly embraces us all. . . . This is not radical politics but elemental humanism" (58). The "new realities" that Gómez-Peña speaks of result from the ongoing diaspora from the South and the East and the subsequent cultural impact of the people "who paradoxically come from countries previously destabilized by the United States itself" (61). He elaborates on this observation in "The Multicultural Paradigm": "The current Latino and Asian immigration to the U.S. is the direct result of international conflicts between the so-called First and Third Worlds. The colonized cultures are sliding into the space of the colonizer, and in doing so, they are redefining its borders and its culture. . . . The First and Third Worlds have mutually penetrated one another. The two Americas are totally intertwined" (45–46). Because his audience of art-magazine readers is highly educated, Gómez-Peña utilizes the metaphor of the border and the reality of the diaspora to speak of a moving cartography of cultures and identity that can embrace contradictions, a theoretical move that ultimately depends upon and reveals the privileges of the socially mobile occupants of elite culture, a move that would have little effect on the social interactions of the mass of working-class immigrants. Statements like the following evince his focus on a discrete audience: "As artists, we now understand that we can speak two or more languages, have two or more identities and/or nationalities, perform different roles in multiple contexts, and not necessarily be in conflict with ourselves and others" (56).

Steeped as his ideas are in a pluralistic humanism, Gómez-Peña sees art and artists' roles in the reformation of society as mediative. Consequently, censorship as a form of cultural and ideological intolerance must be challenged, and a dialogue must be established. Gómez-Peña's ideas on dialogue are expressed more fully in "The Multicultural Paradigm," wherein he notes that dialogues among people(s) assumes many forms. He defines dialogue as the "opposite of national security, neighborhood watch, racial paranoia, aesthetic protectionism, national sentimentalism, ethnocentrism, and monolinguality" (48). He suggests that it is only through an ongoing public dialogue in the form of publications, conferences, and collaborative intercultural art and media projects that the wounds caused by physical and cultural borders can begin to heal.

Gómez-Peña's concept of community, though different than Moraga's, is also linked to his understanding of the role of the artist as visionary: "As responsible artists of this end-of-the-century society, we must challenge the anachronistic notion that says we are only meant to work within our particular ethnic, political, or sexual communities, strictly art contexts, or marginal leftists milieus. . . . any socially responsible person . . . who truly believes in and practices cultural democracy and racial and sexual equity must be considered a member of 'our' community" (62). Left unspoken in his renegotiation of cultural space, however, is how to include the economically disenfranchised. Exercising his political imagination at the end of the *Gringostroika,* his privileging of a government run by artists culminates in the final dissolution of ethnic identity, because "there will be so many artists and intellectuals of color working in our cultural, educational, and media institutions that there will no longer be need to label us . . ." (63).

In contrast to Gómez-Peña's specialized audience, Rubén Martínez's collection of essays, poetry, and journal entries, *The Other Side: Fault Lines, Guerrilla Saints and the True Heart of Rock 'n' Roll* signals the reemergence of journalism as a new force in Chicana/o Literature. Many of Martínez's essays in this collection originally appeared in the *L.A. Weekly,* where he maintained a regular column for several years. Martínez's essays combine political commentary with social satire, cynicism with idealism. His frank appraisal of the current moment bespeaks a new breed of leftist intellectuals who are keenly aware of both the pitfalls and the pragmatism that fuel identity politics. He also has a sharp eye for the ways in which lumpen culture rebels at not only the mores of mainstream society, but also those of its own community. Power is disbursed, be it at the hands of the graffiti artists of East Los Angeles or the *rockeros* of Mexico City. His observations of the current moment bespeak, too, the political angst and uncertainty of a middle-class, anxiety-ridden, self-aware postmodernist whose fragmented self is nostalgic for a time when it was acceptable at least to believe in the idea of unity. "I must hold on to some hope: that the many selves can find some kind of form together without annihilating one another" (*OS* 2).

The Other Side contains photographs of the Martínez family and street life in Los Angeles, San Salvador, and Tijuana. Martínez's essays are the musings of a traveler who crosses borders and who has come to discover that traveling alone cannot heal the wounds of history, capitalism, technological and political difference—especially during times of war and natural disaster. He is both witness and active participant in the local and national power struggles he documents; yet, unlike many of the people of whom he writes, he stands in a position of privilege, able to fly into or out of dangerous situations. This privilege, granted to him by money, professional status, and his U.S. citizenship, is a source of inner tension with which he grapples. The tensions between the reactionary and the revolutionary paradise reside within his own family; his is a world wherein "the other" is an invalid concept, for both intra- and intercultural dynamics are utilized to maintain unequal social relations among people. The literal and figural borders that Martínez negotiates in these essays point to the material and ideological processes by which the past and future are fashioned in the present.

Martínez expresses the same sentiment of destabilization and crisis confronting the Latino community that characterizes Gómez-Peña's and Moraga's work. In his poem "Generation," he depicts the violent reality of everyday life and death, the fear of apocalypse at the century's end, and the tenuous comfort offered by making alliances with others:

> *If I dare*
> *to say "we,"*
> *would it salve*
> *the fault?*
> *These nights fear my arrival.*
> *So do I.*
> *We, I mean.*
> *. . . Has my generation*
> *died yet?*
> *Is it millennium's*
> *end,*
> *so dance! . . .* (141)

Of all the writers addressed in this book, Martínez is the only one whose politicization occurred in the "post-Movement" period; a product of a binational heritage and U.S. socialization, Martínez situates himself in the middle of historical change—between the Revolutionary period of Third World liberation movements and the U.S. civil rights movement on the one hand and the end of the cold war and the global realignment of power on the other. A crumbling of old orders has resulted in instability, and out of this he sees the necessary task at hand as one of reparation and reconstruction, "but within the mending there is still war, and the echoes of repression are loud and clear" (2). Just as Gómez-Peña writes about the collision and coexistence of cultures, so does Martínez; these ideas are instantiated within him and in the city he observes as his idealism is curbed by "the awareness of its impossibility":

> I told myself that by the time I was thirty, I would be a world traveler, healing the wounds between cultures, between ideologies, between selves and others, and sign treaties with my various selves—Mexican, Salvadoran, middle-class Angeleno, *barrio* dweller, poet, journalist, etcetera. . . . I give thanks, however, that I was born at a time when I could live so many realities at once: that I could sit in a San Salvador café and argue about a new language with poets who survived the death squads. . . . And that I could be in San Salvador in Los Angeles by hanging out in Little Central America, and in Los Angeles in Mexico City by dancing to the rhythms of its underground rock 'n' roll. (2)

Because of the context in which his essays appear and the genre of journalism, Martínez's essays are not extended treatments of a subject designed to motivate a specialized audience; he addresses a much more general audience, who may or may not have an investment in Latina/o politics. This collection does include a "Manifesto" in the form of a poem, however; this poem merits examination for its expression of his perspective on the absurdity of the postmodern condition of Latinos' lives. Below are fragments from the poem that illustrate the mixing of cultures and the ongoing war being waged within and outside the barrios of Los Angeles by the state and internecine struggle:

> *Can anyone tell me what time it is?*
> *¿O es que nadie lo sabe?*
> *. . . What time is it in downtown L.A.*
> *when the L.A.P.D. raid the sanctuary at La Placita?*
> *And in the city that bans santería sacrifices,*

a thousand Pollo Loco stands notwithstanding? . . .
Can you feel the earth shudder?
This generation's shaky, bro' . . .
This is not 1969 and Marx
has a bad rap on the international scene,
but there's the FMLN in downtown San Salvador,
(and the death squads are in L.A.) . . .

This is war, and the battle
will be block to block wherever
the Wes and Theys face off.
Third World in the First:
that's what time it is.

History is on fast forward
it's the age of synthesis . . .
All kinds of battles are yet to come
(race and class rage bullets and blood);
choose your weapons . . .
just know that everyone is everywhere now
so careful who you shoot. (133–36)

In contrast to Gómez-Peña's positive assessment of the potential of multiculturalism and cultural synthesis as an agent of peace and reconciliation, Martínez depicts it as a source and target of violence as it gets negotiated on the streets. Moreover, he is mindful that race and class ideologies underscore urban violence and disruption. Written in 1989, twenty years after the "heyday" of the Chicano Movement in Los Angeles, there is little concrete evidence of social and economic gains; moreover, as Moraga and Gómez-Peña note, U.S. imperialism continues to have a devastating effect on the geopolitical landscape as populations and power shift north and south.

The range of concerns expressed in "Manifesto" are evinced in the last essay of the collection as well, "LA Journal IX." In this brief two-and-a-quarter-page journal entry, Martínez collapses a collage of images, experiences, and reflections. Whereas in many of his other essays he is witness-documentor of other people's artistic, political, and everyday actions and words, the journal entries allow for more self-reflexivity and provide readers insight into his life as one more person representative of the crisis of the current moment.

Having just heard gunshots, he has to remind himself that ". . . this is Los Angeles, not San Salvador, this is 1991, not 1979, this is gang strife, not civil war. I don't believe myself. Images past and present: It is 1979 and 1991 and San Salvador and Los Angeles and gang strife and civil war all at once" (165). Central to this piece is his altar, which comprises various valuables of his past and present life and contains images and people who have appeared in his writing. The altar is an art form traditionally practiced by Latinas; Martínez's use of it signifies his need for a home space. According to Amalia Mesa-Bains, "the home altar presents family history and cultural belief systems. . . . Characterized by accumulation, display, and abundance, altars allow history, faith, and personal objects to commingle" (Mesa-Bains 131). The montage of images on Martínez's altar includes a photo of his ex-lover, a photo of Mexico City musicians, a photo of a graffiti artist who suffered a gunshot wound (a picture included in the collection), a Palm Sunday leaf, an invitation to a reception in Cuba, a postcard of the U.S.-Mexico border, and newspaper clippings, among other things. This mixture of people and places represents for him the fractured and mobile nature of life near the end of the twentieth century that leads him to call Los Angeles an antihome. But the symbols of people and places gathered here also represent the positive possibilities for the future in a blend of culture, creation, and politics. Because L.A. is his home base, his work expresses the changing nature of life for Latina/os in the United States. The tenuous nature of existence in this time and place of poverty, disease, and systemic violence keeps him and others searching for a way to blend the many forces that compose his identity before the forces and the people annihilate one another.

Central to my argument throughout this book is a call for a revision in the way we comprehend the history and culture of Mexicans and other Latinos in the United States, one that enables a future that is not predicated on past injustices and is not enmeshed in the monologic of a singular national history. In offering an order to the past—be it one based on events or individuals—historical narratives reconstruct and interpret social relations of power. The question is whether or not this reconstruction ratifies those relations or seeks to expose the ideologies, practices, privileges, and the material basis that sustain them. The essays examined above provide insight into other sites and circuits of power that expose the "imaginative" aspects of historical narratives and official nationalisms, as well as the visionary elements of ethnonationalisms. What I have tried to illustrate are the ways in which history and identity are evoked by U.S Latinos—as a corrective to

Euro-American master narratives and as a basis for claiming full citizenship in the economic and political life of this country. For an assessment of Chicana/o life from a different cultural milieu, we turn once again to the work of *tejana* poet Teresa Palomo Acosta.

Teresa Acosta's International Proletarian Poetry

> *"who will live to tell of what happened to us grandmother?" a young mexica asked.*
> *la anciana responds: "among the survivors there will be poets,*
> *they will relate that which happened to us."*
>
> —Raúl Salinas, "About Invasion and Conquest"

> *If my history of paper-made flowers*
> *Were to be told, you would not believe it.*
> *For it lies too far beneath the surface*
> *Of the more proper stories, attired in the pain*
> *That is my due suffering. Meanwhile I have ascended*
> *To partake of the other side: survival of the beautiful.*
>
> *Don't you dare think I have tossed out*
> *The roll book I keep to account*
> *For agony-filled cries.*
> *I turn to it almost every day . . .*
>
> —Teresa Acosta, "Myths and Legends Tell No Lies"

Thus far in this analysis of Chicana/o literary and historical narratives, Teresa Acosta's poetry has served as a contrapuntal voice to the master narratives of both elite histories and Chicano histories. In each chapter, one of her poems has been examined as a way to complicate our understanding of the history of Mexicans in the United States. In chapter 1, "Chipita" facilitated an against-the-grain reading of the understanding of nineteenth-century history we inherited from Américo Paredes, and it allowed us to comprehend better the limitations of González and Eimer's reconstruction of that era in *Caballero*. In chapter 2, Acosta's essay "Tejana History as a Poem: Sara Estela Ramírez and Me" and her poem "Apparition (ca. 1896)" helped us to see the significance of Chicana literary precursors for this poet, as well as to imagine what we know to be obvious fact but what rarely gets addressed in histories: the impact of land dispossession and the imposition of a hostile civil system on disenfranchised *mexicanas.* "Emma Tenayuca and the Pecan Shellers," in chapter 3, situated women as workers and leaders during the Great Depression and illustrated their resistance to exploitative work conditions. Written in the midst of the Chicano Movement, Acosta's "For Maximo Palomo" served as a sharply nuanced critique of the limitations of resistance narratives and complicated our understanding of masculinity and its historical representation in chapter 4. In this chapter, which reads against historians' anticipated construction of a "Hispanic" Generation, I will examine some poetry by Acosta that demonstrates her shared concerns with the writers that were addressed in the previous section. She, too, writes about inner-city strife and the ravages of development; she is concerned with borders and border crossings as well as the violence of multinational exploitation that affects women in particular; and she also returns to the past as a way to build a future and understand her identity.

Published by independently owned Red Salmon Press in Austin, Texas, *Nile and Other Poems* is Acosta's latest collection of poetry since *Passing Time* was published by another independent press in 1984. The circumstances shaping the publication of her work contrast sharply with the resources available to produce more "marketable" work like that of Moraga, Gómez-Peña, and Martínez, whose collections were published by South End, Greywolf, and Verso, respectively. This is a revised and expanded edition of an earlier collection, *Nile Notebooks, 1994,* a self-published collection of sixty poems originally reproduced on a photocopier and bound at a local copy store in Austin, Texas. The path to publication of this collection serves as testimony to the inadequacies of and limited access to the publishing industry for Chicanas. It is the limited distribution and circulation of her work that has mandated that her poetry be included in the appendixes of this study.

The poems in *Nile* address a wide array of themes. Like Sara Estela Ramírez's work, many of Acosta's poems are about nature, while others are dedications to relatives. She also inscribes poems to other writers (June Jordan and Tomás Rivera, for example) and to people she has read about in history books or newspapers, particularly those who were the subject of state violence, such as Chipita Rodríguez and Anna Mae Aquash, or violence by anti-unionists, such as farmworker Juan de la Cruz. The majority of the poems in *Nile* portray the everyday details, decisions, and contradictions of being a Chicana. These latter poems assume primarily two forms: they are either depictions of "ordinary" experiences such as of grocery shopping, looking out windows, cooking, and trying to comprehend the fast pace of urban life; or they are portrayals of the lives of relatives and unnamed women, often elders, who live in dignity despite their age, hard work, and poverty.

Acosta's bilingual style displays the duality of her bicultural existence as a *tejana* whose family has lived, participated in, and witnessed the negotiation of culture and power in Texas. Her poetry documents the lived history of everyday people within and outside the home as workers and economically and politically disenfranchised people who were obliged to adapt and respond to the exigencies of their time. Acosta's response to living in this historical moment is guided by an imperative to come to terms with that past and to expose the absurdities, ironies, and cruelties of life in a world sustained by inequalities. In the sampling and cursory readings of her poems that follow, we will see concerns that she shares with Moraga, Gómez-Peña, and Martínez, particularly in her depiction of history as a process and the way she avoids pronouncements of despair or celebration but instead documents the resistance and negotiation of everyday life.

Like Rubén Martínez, who tells of graffiti artists' writing (the artists identify themselves as writers) in the language of war as the artists do (they "bomb" and "terrorize" public property with their art) in order to claim and create community, Acosta understands the alienation that motivates those writers. "World Map II: inscripciónes en las paredes" is a countercriticism, an alternative interpretation, to that of state and civil authorities, as the first and third stanzas clearly illustrate:

> *Graffiti is a map of sorts.*
> *Y el mapa de graffiti en mi ciudad*
> *No tiene fronteras.*
> *Never mind what the newspapers and los jefes say.*
> . . .
>
> *El graffiti*
> *Maps territories*
> *Escarpments,*
> *The DMZ.*
> *In my city,*
> *Which pretends to have thick walls*
> *Between los haves y los otros.* (*Nile* 73)

The reclaiming of falsely partitioned territory that demarcates class and racial boundaries through outlawed "writing" constructs an alternative cartography of the city that delegitimates segregationist urban planning. A similar concern with the violence and terror of official borders is evident in "Crossing 'a Piece of Earth.'"

In this poem, the officials who monitor and maintain the integrity of the world map along the U.S.-Mexico border are armed border-patrol guards. Acosta undermines the "brand newest official government map" by acknowledging its inaccuracy in the everyday practice of "illegal" crossings and the falsity of the constructed mythology that naturalizes and attempts to make noble the existence of the border. Her "unofficial" narrative remapping of the border relies on the history of dispossession and violence upon which the construction of the border was predicated, as is evident in the following excerpt:

> *At the border*
> *where the gatekeepers eye me*
> *I dream up a way to set my own eyes . . .*
> *As a means to know the land*
> *And our history as a fluid movement in time*
> *Underground. . . .*
> *It makes its own lay of the land*
> *And tells me that I know the time has come*
> *To stop waiting for a ruling*
> *promoting the just use of land/rights*
> *On either side of the border I cross. . . .*
>
> *The gatekeepers want so to stop*
> *The flow of history slipping from them*
> *As it undulates underground.*
> *They collar us into migra vans*
> *For the trip back*
> *And we*
> *Plan another crossing to*
> *Another piece*
> *Of the simple earth*
> *In union with our version*
> *Of the Mexico/US map.* (*Nile* 97–98)

Acosta's revised map is similar to the vision of the reclaiming of lost lands that the earthquake represents for El Eco in *The Brick People;* the "underground" migrations of workers from *el otro lado* is seen by Acosta as a corrective to history, one that is a logical consequence of U.S. imperial policy, as Moraga and Gómez-Peña also note. The "flow of history" that these northward migrations represent destabilizes official national narratives of origin and posits an alternative "manifest destiny." Acosta's vision of a world without borders is one that relies on a deconstruction of the global economy and an alliance with other deterritorialized peoples, especially women, on whom that economy depends. In "When Women Sew for a Living, They Rarely Earn Their Keep" Acosta addresses the global exploitation of women's labor. The opening lines show that though national borders exist, the global economy connects nation-states and their people:

> *In Colombia*
> *Y Malaysia*
> *Hungary*
> *South Korea*
> *Indonesia*
> *y los estados unidos, too:*
> *When women sew for a living, they rarely earn their keep.*
> (*Nile* 95)

The similarity of harsh working conditions and underpay are the key to reading this map of the economy:

> *Yes, their hands are in constant motion all day:*
> *For twenty cents an hour in Indonesia,*
> *For a $1.20 an hour in Colombia,*
> *For a $1.57 an hour in South Korea,*
> *For a $1.70 an hour in Hungary.*
> *For $6.25 an hour in America.*
>
> *Only in Norway—home of the $17.10 an hour seamstresses—*
> *Do women who sew for a living earn their keep.* (96)

The two-line verse following this litany of low wages speaks to the real possibility of, and sets a precedent for, change in a system that underpays and devalues women's work. This global class and occupational alliance with working women is only one form of cultural and class negotiation that Acosta addresses. In other poems she explores her political and historical relationship to her indigenous and Spanish heritages.

"Desaparecida" is similar to "Chipita," "Emma Tenayuca and the Pecan Shellers," and "For Maximo Palomo" in its self-declaration as a poem based on a historical event and person. Acosta places either an author's note or a preface before a poem, or a note at its end, that provides dates and/or biographical information on her poem's subject. The author's note to "Desaparecida" explains the circumstances of the murder of Anna Mae Pictou Aquash on the Pine Ridge Reservation in 1976. The poem narrates Acosta's process of remembering Aquash and the process of Aquash's disappearance from official records and the mainstream public's memory, with the exception of the tribeswomen who give her a proper burial and place in their history. The last stanza of the poem documents a mutual history and cultural heritage:

> *Your tribeswomen bring back your memory to me in full sight*
> *of*
> *Our history as indígenas and as far as their story can take me*
> *in*
> *My chain link to you, I began to coax the discarded pieces of*
> *Evidence into an answer to the desperate calling out for your*
> *People. I form them into*
> *One*
> *Solid*
> *Piece*
> *Of evidence of love to envelop me and you—forever.*
> *With all your memory found and kept in sight each day,*
> *Lastingly sacred like the*
> *Picture of my mother you remind me of, Annie Mae.* (*Nile*
> *Notebooks, 1994* 43)

Acosta's poem is testimony to the tentative and empowering alliance between Mexicans and indigenous peoples and to the difficulty of discovering and documenting a mutual history of repression and shared cultural practices.

Documenting shared experience among women appears to be a central goal of Acosta's poetry. In the introduction to this book I noted that in poems like "Preguntas y frases para una abuela española," Acosta strives to find this common ground even when it is painful territory, in order to "set some crooked things en nuestra historia / At least at a slant, / if not straight." Providing a counterhistory is central to Acosta's aesthetic. Her poetry of reconciliation is not dependent on replacing one perspective with another, but it explores possibilities of the past and the future that have been left unexamined. In this manner, her work is exemplary and offers a powerful revision of the past and present from which we can learn to seize control of our imaginary and historical destinies.

Conclusion

On Paradigms, Movements, and Borders

> *Each generation must out of relative obscurity discover its mission, fulfill it, or betray it. . . . the preceding generations have both resisted the work of erosion carried by colonialism and also helped on the maturing of the struggles of today. We must rid ourselves of the habit . . . of minimizing the action of our fathers or of feigning incomprehension when considering their silence and passivity. They fought as well as they could, with the arms that they possessed then; and if the echoes of their struggle have not resounded in the international arena, we must realize that the reason for this silence lies less in their lack of heroism than in the fundamentally different international situation of our time.*
>
> —Frantz Fanon, *The Wretched of the Earth*

Central to my thesis in *Historia: The Literary Making of Chicana and Chicano History* is a call for the continual revision of the *historia* of Mexicans in the United States, one with a widened scope that includes intracultural processes and negotiations, one that enables a vision of a future that is not predicated on past injustices, and one that is forward-looking even as it struggles against forgetting. This critique has been primarily centered on identifying the limitations of the generational paradigm; however, implicit throughout this study there has also been a critique of other paradigms, such as the resistance narrative, that have produced or perpetuated "blind spots" in our understanding of history. Moreover, literature and its relationship to cultural practices has been offered as a complementary and sometimes corrective narrative to historical accounts that seek to universalize the experience of Mexicans in the United States by imposing a generational perspective or narrow definitions of political struggle on their subject. Generational histories tend to be totalizing narratives (despite disclaimers to the contrary), because they ask us to ignore rather than account for the existence of simultaneous histories. Therefore, what is left outside of these periods once we accept a narrow definition of identity and ideology is systematically effaced or deligitimated. In most cases these exclusions are ideological in nature—be they based on class, social construction, or political affiliation. The manner in which these exclusions are legitimated, however, is epistemological in nature and shapes the paradigm of analysis and reconstruction of history.

In offering an order to the past—based on events or individuals—historical narratives reconstruct and interpret social relations of power. The question is whether or not this reconstruction ratifies those relations of power or seeks to identify and explain the ideologies, practices, privileges, and the material basis that structures those relations. The ordering of things, as well as assigning meanings to them, is an epistemological project that determines the parameters and objects of study, the valuation of evidence, and the creation of meaning. As Nancy Jay points out, these principles of order—the principle of identity, of contradiction, and of the excluded middle—are not representative of the empirical world, in which almost everything is in a process of transition (Hartsock 24). It is from a desire to order the world in a particular way that generational histories emerge; it is a paradigm based on exclusion, built on the illusion that the experience of one sector of the community is somehow more legitimate than others. Predicated upon exclusions, this construction at times values the experiences of the elite; at other times it privileges certain forms of resistance over others; and often it places more weight on certain forms of evidence than others. The result is a limited understanding of the experiences of Mexicans in the United States. In the implicit evaluation of experience and the creation of community that results, those who are left unaccounted for are constructed as "other."[1]

The literary narratives and poetry that were examined in this study provide insight into other sites and circuits of power, which expose the imaginative aspects of history and illustrate the historical dimensions of myth. Related to the central concern of this investigation of the relationship between history and creative literature is an important and as yet unarticulated question: How does a community retain its collective history and memory?

Does, in fact, such a thing as collective historical memory exist? In "Between Memory and History," Pierre Nora claims that "memory has never known more than two forms of legitimacy: historical and literary. These have run parallel to each other but until now always separately. At present the boundary between the two is blurring . . ." (Nora 24). Another answer to this question might be found by considering the relationship between the social function of history and what that function tells us about its construction and the paradigms used to fulfill that function. This exploration should account for less official forms of retaining history, such as individual and communal memories: myth, legend, folklore, and song. Memory, though embedded in both the historical and the literary, has a contestatory relationship to history. Historians are suspicious of memory's accuracy and subjectivity.

Chicano/a literature and history were not legitimated as fields of study until a social movement emerged that claimed space within and access to the social institutions that define and reproduce social relations. The memory evoked by ethnic literature and history in the United States was recalled as a corrective history to Euro-American master narratives and as a basis for claiming full citizenship in the economic and political life of this country. In the international context of decolonization in the mid–twentieth century and the resulting crisis of representation that destabilized the authority and hegemony of Western European culture and its institutions, the master narratives or supreme fictions of monoculturalism were delegitimated. Many critics use this same era to frame the emergence of postmodernism, which is said to represent a cultural crisis of identity for people who once had the luxury of thinking ethnocentrically. The shared origins of legitimacy for Chicana/o literature and history during the time of the realignment of cultural, political, and economic power places them in a contradictory relationship to modernism and postmodernism. Politically, the desire to construct or imagine community or nationhood is predicated upon a belief that people who share a cultural heritage also have a common base of experience whose past can be narrated and whose future can be charted. On the one hand, in these aspirations for social and political empowerment, Chicana/o critical discourse participates in a culturally specific project that is fundamentally modernist in character; on the other hand, with the ongoing critique of the limitations of nationalism for fully addressing issues of gender, sexuality, and the disavowal of the existence of a unified subject and the concomitant realization of the multiplicity of histories, a postmodern aesthetics and methodology has been embraced.

Nancy Hartsock claims that social and national liberation movements have "two fundamental intellectual/theoretical tasks—one of critique and one of construction. We who have not been allowed to be subjects of history are beginning to reclaim our pasts and remake our futures on our own terms" (Hartsock 25). A primary task in this project, Hartsock proposes, is the construction of "subjectivities which will be both multiple and specific." The validity of this claim is borne out in the development of Chicana/o historiography and literary history, which has moved from articulating a critique and a call for cultural unity that was initially race-, ethnic-, and class-specific to addressing intracultural constructions of gender and sexual orientation, concerns that have made unity elusive and illusory. The analytical and chronological frameworks used for recalling the past shape the domain of relations that are analyzed.

Following the trail of literary and historical writings by Chicanas, Ramón Gutiérrez notes that in 1977 a new chronology for Chicana history was proposed, one that begins in 1519, not 1848 (R. Gutiérrez 51). Such a decision was strategic and imperative for writing a history of intra- and intercultural gender relations, especially in light of the centrality of Malintzin Tenepal (aka "La Malinche"), the indigenous translator and mistress of Hernán Cortes. This shift in historical paradigms provided Chicanas with a paradigmatic figure through which to comprehend imaginatively and historically the process by which the female body had been colonized by both colonialists and nationalists. For Chicanas, then, a redefinition of historical origins has led to a redefinition of community.

Recall that in the first paragraph of the introduction to this book I made note of Norma Alarcón's observations regarding how representations of Malintzin Tenepal have functioned as a mobilizing ideological force. In the process of revising history, Chicanas have turned to other historical figures who, because of social constraints, are no less enigmatic. Sor Juana Inez de la Cruz, a seventeenth-century Mexican nun, is a good example. Sor Juana is a particularly appealing figure because she can be seen as a "speaking" subject through her writings. However, because of her relationship to the colonial state and the church, she is an ambivalent figure of representation. Nevertheless, she has appeared as heroine in numerous poems and plays. One play in particular, "Sor Juana" (1983) by Estela Portillo Trambley, is interesting in its alteration of the historical record in order to create an admirable intellectual figure, one who ironically is declared a heroine through her renunciation of writing. Because it addresses the role of intellectuals in institutions, the play merits a brief examination in this closing section on paradigms, movements, and borders.

As a female intellectual, Sor Juana was an anomaly in seventeenth-century New Spain. She defied the clergy's feminization of ignorance and invaded their discursive space. In *Plotting Women,* Jean Franco points out that both religious and secular authorities exploited her celebrity status. Even today her uniqueness is singled out. According to Franco, "contemporary stories have tended to represent Sor Juana as a heroine pitted against a villainous church, depicting her as a woman fighting a male institution, an artist conformed by official ideology, a woman whose talents were held in check by sexual repression" (Franco 25). Franco sees a problem with these narratives, which are based on the imposition of a false unity on a corpus of writing, a form of expression that Sor Juana did not have complete ownership of, much less the ability to determine or influence its publication.

Franco points out that both religious and secular authorities took advantage of Sor Juana's celebrity status. Religious authorities targeted her as a "New World" saint, sometimes before but mostly after, her death. In the eyes of the church, the fact that she renounced writing several years before her death made her "conversion" to traditional church ideology all the more complete. Secular *patrones,* however, used her writing as an example of the spiritual wealth to be found in the New World. In seventeenth-century New Spain, a *criolla* had only two choices. She could choose to marry or to enter a religious order—both choices involved relinquishing control over one's mobility and being subservient to male authority. Clearly Sor Juana's choice between marriage and the convent meant sacrifice—the elimination of possibilities—and clearly she chose the path that gave her freedom to develop and express her intellect, albeit in a limited fashion.

Trambley included in her play an abundance of details of Sor Juana's life and the many people who affected her life. This play foregrounds the contradictions that existed in Sor Juana's life as a result of her choice to live in the convent rather than in the court—and the almost absolute separation of these spheres from the outside world and from the indigenous and enslaved inhabitants of the colony. Two things can be deduced from Trambley's decision to foreground Sor Juana's life in this way: she wanted to illustrate collaboration between the church and state in the colonization of the New World, and she wanted to demonstrate that Sor Juana was part of this privileged class, even while her status as a *criolla* (birthright and gender) placed painful limitations on her individual choices. There is no lack of appreciation for

Sor Juana's intellect by Trambley. But by imaginatively rendering a more complete picture of her life, including her amicable childhood relationship with her family's indigenous slaves, and by including private, unwritten thoughts and conversations of Sor Juana, a different figure emerges.

The cooperation between church and state led Sor Juana to justify colonialism and to respect the state's power to determine social relations. Despite this characteristic of her writing, she is still often seen as a prototype feminist because she was a woman who wrote independent and bold intellectual statements during a period when women had little or no access to education or a public audience. In Trambley's revision of Sor Juana as a subaltern heroine (rather than an exceptional writer), she interprets her renunciation of writing as a desire to end the frustrating and limited engagement with the world of the intellect, which had made her lose touch with the world around her, beyond the walls of the court. Trambley's play is thus highly critical of Sor Juana's intellectualism. Consequently, her renunciation of writing is a "return to the world of the living."

Trambley's version of Sor Juana's life in a larger context of Indian resistance to colonial powers makes available a radical reading of her renunciation. By rejecting her role as intellectual she dissociates herself from the official ideology of church and state. On the surface, her devotion to charity (feeding the poor) might seem like the church's typical approach to a problem, which offers no real solution, but in the context of rebellion, Sor Juana is subverting her role within the church because she is feeding those who are participating in the rebellion and aligning herself with them. Hence, her conversion can be seen as a move from the role of the traditional intellectual to one who is aligned with the oppressed.

To emphasize further the meaning of her ideological shift, Trambley revises Sor Juana's contestatory relationship with her confessor, Father Antonio Nuñez de Miranda. The historical records show that Nuñez de Miranda was vehemently against allowing women to write or speak on church matters. To make the relationship meaningful it is necessary that Father Antonio's character be developed in a particular way. In the play he spends his time working with the poor in the remote northern regions of the colony. Away from the city and the church, he begins to identify with the Indians. For this reason he can be critical of the process of colonization and the exploitation of the people and resources that the Spanish are conducting. He chastises Sor Juana for "lov[ing] the rich Spaniards so!" and for living a life of luxury in comparison to that of the indigenous people. His identification with them is complete. The crucial exchange below demonstrates several different strands of critical thinking in Trambley's dramatic reinterpretation of their relationship and its ideological implications:

> FATHER: How little you understand. North of Coahuila—immolation—anger against the God we gave them. Their most insane pagan god is better than the God given to them by the Conquistadores.
> SOR JUANA: They have lost the Way . . .
> FATHER: I'm not so sure. I have been one of them too long not to understand their anger and their fear.
> SOR JUANA: All that I care about is that you're safe and that you're here and that I shall see you often.
> FATHER: How blind you are my daughter. The palace, the convent, that is not the world—nor those books that consume your life.
> SOR JUANA: I know these are rebellious times.
> FATHER: How well you mouth the words of your masters.
> SOR JUANA: My masters!
> FATHER: For almost two decades you have spent your life writing, singing the praises of the masters. *Villancios* for a long parade of viceroys, vicerines—loas and sonnets about the Spanish great. Your praises have been bountiful for those who have conquered your people, exploited them.
> SOR JUANA: They are my friends. They are the only world I know . . .
> FATHER: Have you forgotten your beginnings? You are mejicana! . . .
> SOR JUANA: You don't love me! You take such pleasure in trying to destroy what I believe. . . .
> FATHER: What you believe! It's what you *are* that's important. Look to your own people.
> SOR JUANA: What would you have me be?
> FATHER: In Fresnillo, where I was born, there is a dry little shrub that clings ferociously to life. Its roots dig into the sand, the hostile sun violates. . . . The shrub shrivels up against the violence all around. That is the Mexican today—the Indian—the zambo slave. My spirit is like that shrub, my soul, my passions. I am a Mexican, so I fight! I beg money off the rich, I hide the fugitive, I scramble around for food and medicine, because their hunger, their pain, their enslavement, their deaths wound me, consume me . . .
> SOR JUANA: I feel with you, but you must understand—I fight the

same struggle. My voice carries all over, my words of love, compassion, brotherhood, peace . . .
FATHER: I'm speaking of human beings—not words!
SOR JUANA: You refuse to understand!
FATHER: And you refuse to see! (Trambley 177–78)

The above exchange contains both a criticism of intellectualism that is disconnected from the material world and an assertion of an anticolonialist national consciousness. Interestingly, Father Antonio's reference to the land north of Coahuila indicates present-day Texas, a significant point considering that Trambley is an El Paso native.

Trambley's play consistently criticizes Sor Juana's complicity with the colonial powers while retaining an appreciation of the constraints under which she operated as a result of being a woman intellectual who defied her role in society. The implied yet unfulfilled romance between Sor Juana and Father Antonio serves to emphasize her realm of limited choice and her consequent decision to do that which would give her the most freedom. The criticisms are crucial to Trambley's plot because they give Sor Juana's renunciation of writing a different interpretation, one that resonates with political implications. Franco interprets Sor Juana's renunciation as "tragic," a "capitulation to the clergy, [the] sacrifice of her books and musical instruments, her renunciation of learning in favor of good works—all of which can be seen as a defeat—and one that was a defeat for all colonial women" (Franco xv). But Trambley's reconstruction of Sor Juana's life seeks a different end for her, one that is defiant, not defeated, in her alliance with the subaltern peoples. Sor Juana becomes a figure who symbolically rejects her role in colonialism and begins working, like Father Antonio, for *los mejicanos*. Her transformation occurs after she unsuccessfully hides a fugitive insurgent, a former slave of her family whom she loved. She remembers the impact it had upon her: "I saw you dangling from the hanging tree. My eyes cannot erase it. My mind cannot erase it. A sovereign fact, this death of yours, which was . . . a death of me. Oh, the raw concreteness of the world! The mind is not enough, is it?" (Trambley 188).

Does Trambley's creative revision prevent Sor Juana from being a feminist prototype? The intellectual work in her writing is deemphasized and devalued because of its complicity with colonial power. In contemporary critical discourse, there is an increased awareness of the strategic role of intellectuals in supporting or working against the ruling classes. Given the relations of power in Spanish colonial society, between men and women and between the church and civil society, it is almost impossible to find a place of resistance for intellectuals, especially women. Trambley's play suggests that Sor Juana's life can be seen as a life of resistance in a very limited way; it is also a life that culminates in the most significant act: the denial of individual privilege in favor of an alliance with subaltern peoples. It is an act that is not to be interpreted against intellectualism but to be understood in the context of a site and time where there was no avenue of expression for a woman intellectual that did not promote the interests of the ruling class.

I recognize that it may seem an odd move at this point to discuss a text that is so clearly an imagined revision of the past rather than one that is more historically accurate. I think, however, that it is useful to vex the categories of "real" and "imagined" social relations because so often in attempting to project a better future, we are called to articulate the "not real" in the same way as alternative histories have had to write against the real and imagined histories of elites who presented their narratives as if they were comprehensive and indisputable. Moreover, this discussion of intellectuals and institutions reminds me that in the process of making ourselves both subjects and objects of history, minority intellectuals must not lose sight or become disengaged from the ongoing war "out there."

Identifying alternative sites of power and strategies for negotiation and resistance has been important to this study. The history of social relations and power needs to be further addressed to fully learn from the past. The literature and history of other sites of containment have yet to be written. Movement literature, be it that of social movements, migrant literature, or travels to other countries under the auspices of, or against, the U.S. military, needs to be fully explored. Deserving of attention as well is the emerging body of border literature that is assuming a different form than that which documents turn-of-the-century border conflict. Alternative writing, such as graffiti, can offer insight into resistance literature that defies social institutions and assumes control over public and private space. In this regard, Chicana/o prison literature has received scant attention and merits further exploration. I make no pretense of offering a panacea for restructuring present and future social relations. If, however, this study contributes to a better understanding of the present through a reassessment of the complex relationship between historical and literary texts that will assist in the realization of an imagined but possible future, then *haciendo y leyendo nuestras historias,* making and reading our histories/stories, in this way will have value.

APPENDIX I

Teresa Palomo Acosta

CHIPITA[1]

(Author's note: Chipita Rodríguez's life is clouded in mystery, as is her death in 1863, when she was hanged by the state of Texas. On June 13, 1985, over a century later, Gov. Mark White signed Senate Concurrent Resolution Fourteen, absolving her of murder.)

(First a preface: to prove to myself that you are dead, I sift through someone else's footnotes. They weigh like lead. I find I cannot carry them or you—alone.)

So, ok,
Only now someone asks
About you
Wants to know the truth
And insists on loving you—
Myth, legend, lie. All.

Yes, all of us hating the slayers.
Wishing them dead also
—Piled in a heap of trash under Corpus Christi's sun
In agosto.

But all the truth
Is buried deeper still
—within your dust.
Maybe only the wind carries it
As notes for the music
Of robins
And measly sparrows
Flying above us.
They pass along the street
You walked one day on the way to Doña Chona's

For a last plática before the weekend.
But we cannot hear the language you speak
Anymore.

Only the robins can, alighting on that tree,
with their measly cousin sparrows, the jays,
The mockingbirds.
Only they have nestled amid the twigs
Of that tree which is otherwise
Crooked—naming the day you died
Amid its branches.

Aquí near the end of the twentieth century, we try to go on as
Before:
Tease the day,
Wear high heels, lipstick, le dernier cri,
Sell life insurance,

Teach bilingual mathematics to niñitos
Flip burgers,
Try a lawsuit. We think we have outlived the past.
Chipita—
The last time I thought of you, I was alone and tired.
I was in a library
Comparing my poetic sensibility
To other poets
—Skimming through their books,
Wasting time.

Your face appeared
—just like that—
In the middle of my mid-morning self-pity.
There you were
Dressed in sea blue,
In a cape. You turned and stared at me. Then
Your face softened into a smile—its warmth was brazenly
Bare in the middle of the library where students

Coyishly turned
Pages
And napped and
Regretted they were there.

I stopped what I was doing
Immediately.
I wrote down your first name
As if we were on friendly, intimate terms.

You wanted to talk to me
About yourself
Describe who you are,
—Who you were alive.

You said,
"I ate pears, manzanas.
I often enjoyed coffee."
"I loved my son,"
You emphasize this last part
And pause.

You do not want me to forget:
"I loved my son. Some of the legends say I died
Because of him. Ah, what they'll say
To put you into history."

"But I didn't really die for him.
—Though for some brutish reason,
I died in a certain way because of someone's power."

—Eran bolillos,
Los que me mandaron a matar—
"They knew which levers to pull,
Were in the circles where you can order
Someone to die.
—Oh, maybe sometimes
They have their reasons,

I know. But me?"

"Think about it, 'mija,
As you walk
The air-conditioned corridors in your three-piece suit
Coordinated with everything.
Think about it
Because you want to believe all of your education
Will keep you warm in your icy cell
When they take you away,
Insist you pay for me.

Forever."

APPENDIX 2

Teresa Palomo Acosta

ABOUT EMMA TENAYUCA AND THE PECAN SHELLERS' STRIKE

What is a pecan sheller's life worth?
Emma Tenayuca asked herself / she looked
at the woman across the desk
who knew
and who was saying:

we sit at these long tables
shelling pecans
harmless things
that I myself love to eat
and put in our capironga during lent

well, anyway,
we sit some 15 hours a day hunched over
75 hours a week hunched over
for 5¢, say, 6¢ a pound
at $2.73 a week
at $251 a year

she was looking to Emma for an answer
that would come up pure: something clear
sounding like something
right

she went on:
Seligmann thinks about his ledgers
and
we,
we want enough to be human

she looked at Emma side/ways
and sighed
and cleared her throat

and Emma said
something had to be done

the woman went on:
we mean to survive/
have some reason
to go back and hunch over the miles of pecans
we pick through—y con tanto cuidado

Emma said
something had to be done—
i'll go with you
together / alongside
10,000 plus out of 12,000 pecan shellers
very expectedly walking out
even though the newspapers said
that the workers had
unexpectedly gone on strike

the woman thinks back on it now: sometimes
justice comes to those who wait on
the promised day / the goodwill of others
then shakes her head
and figures that it usually comes
only to people tired of shelling pecans for
$2.73 a week / $251 a year
who knows what a pecan sheller's life is worth

and enter their fight
sideways / backways
not always sure which direction is next
—yet enter their fight—
knowing that there is a

cleanness
in a workroom empty
of Seligmann's
BIGGEST LITTLE Texas industry

a cleanness
that is empty of his profits in our hunched backs
backs
which have to be stretched
up and right
upright
all
the
time

The line "something had to be done" is from an interview with Emma Tenayuca, which appeared in The Texas Observer *in 1983.*

APPENDIX 3

Teresa Palomo Acosta[1]

WORLD MAP II: INSCRIPCIÓNES EN LAS PAREDES

Graffiti is a map of sorts.
y el mapa de graffiti en mi ciudad
No tiene fronteras.
Never mind what the newspapers and los jefes say.

It bellows, screams, and taunts.
Makes declarations,
Speeches,
Spills out el güiri, güiri
Between amigas y enemigas.

El graffiti
Maps territories
Escarpments,
The DMZ.
In my city,
Which pretends to have thick walls
Between los haves y los otros.

It carves a permanent heart
In nails
Everywhere.
Climbs
Embankments
Ditches
And carefully constructed miles of moats.

It refuses
To believe
That the grass
Blooms

Here
Or on that fabled greener side.

It writes backwards
And talks directly,
Mainlining mamás y papás y los authorities.
Saying:
No nos miren hací—
Como si fueramos animales.

Never mind what the newspapers
Y los jefes say.

PREGUNTAS Y FRASES PARA UNA ABUELA ESPAÑOLA

Sabe, bisabuela, I just barely thought about you tonight.
For the first time considered I might be related to you.
Because we mestiza cafecitas con high cheekbones believe
We're almost ninety-nine percent Indian
And we may be ninety-nine percent right.
Still, como me llamo Teresa Palomo Acosta
And have wavy-ish hair—cuando me crece—
I fantasize that a bisabuela
Who spoke totally proper Spanish
Is mine and I hers.

And so, bisabuela, I need to know—just between us two—
Did you wear mantillas de encaje,
A chongo, a trenza, or a shawl?
Were you a gitana, a castanet-flaying flamenco bailante?
Were you the pre-fandango mujer,
The precursor to us
Who've grown fond of el tacuachito
In our mezcla de tambora de rancho y acordeón,
Un bajo sexto: los beginnings de otra onda.

Y quiseiera preguntarte:
Are all these estereotipos I should deny?
Although, a mí, como mi gustan las mantillas
—Y todo los demás.

There's more, bis, bisabuela.
Were you haughty and arrogant?
Ready to do in la india
Clutched by el soldado español
As he crossed your path?
Or did you also hide from him
In a corner of your hacienda?

Oye, mi bisabuela
These days I have to face the música,
Figure out how our lives intertwine
Even though we get colored in so many tints:
This high cafe
This cafe con crema
This crema con strong black tea
And this crema solita.

Ah, sí,
You should know también,
That we pochas know the difference between
Pues y pos.

And cannot apologize for our brand of El Castellano
Aquí close to the end of the twentieth century
Mezclando más y más
What we are.
Negotiating every step.
Mira, bisabuela del siglo diez y siete,
La Leona y las jefas del rincón de los cinco:
La Becky (sí, Rebeca)
Y la Sophie (sí, Sofía)
Te mandan saludos y abrazos.
Y yo también.

But I'm still worried about all that responsibilidad
We both carry:
To set some crooked things en nuestra historia
At least at a slant,
If not straight,
Between us.

DESAPARECIDA

(Author's Note: The body of a woman was found on February 24, 1976, some fifty yards from a highway which ran through the Pine Ridge Indian Reservation. A coroner's report concluded that she had died from natural exposure and a burial was order[ed] for "Jane Doe" by the Pine Ridge police. Later it was discovered that the woman was Anna (Annie) Mae Pictou Aquash, a young Micman woman from Shubencadie, Nova Scotia. She was a member of the American Indian Movement. At the request of her family another autopsy was performed. This time the coroner concluded that death had occurred from a gunshot wound fired into the back of her head with a .38-caliber gun.)

I think of you after reading a poem which asks in desperation,
Where
Have
We
Hidden
The
Indians?
I sit and ask myself what to do with all my memory of you, Annie
Mae Pictou Aquash? How do I keep my memory of you
Sacred
When you have disappeared from the whole country's memory
Been frozen out/left dead on the road? What were you made of
Before you were made to be discarded
Canvas shoe
Jacket

Severed hands?
Particles
Unaccounted for pieces
Of evidence
Of fragments
Of the wounds
Someone shot into your body, them, too, unaccounted for/not
Known to have existed/not in the original record/
For now you are only
A canvas shoe, jacket, fingertips from severed hands, now only
Wasted evidence for the FBI claiming the need to cut your hands
From your body for identification in
Washington: its
Rows of steel cabinets/
Cutting through your life's work again and again without coming
Up with a single truth about your worth
Mere discards
Their reports note/
Still your memory from the news stories arises and arises again
And again, Annie Mae Pictou Aquash/
And the FBI figures prominently in the lead. So I look for you in
Books and magazines and newspapers where you take up a few
Column inches for a few weeks of our memory
Then
Disappear
I look and read and look and
Read and finally learn from their own words that other Indian
Women could not leave you as so many particles discarded on the
Road. They come to take up your body and your story where the
FBI records are closed. And I read and learn and read and learn
That the Indian women come to give you burial.
Each
With her own grief and strength comes to scatter sage and cedar,

Comes to lay you on boughs and hang streamers to wave in the
Four directions, to fly over you through
Winter/spring/summer/fall.
Your tribeswomen
Come here,
Annie
Mae
Pictou
Aquash
Come to a place on the road
Where we have made you disappear from us. They weave your soul back together in the Indian way
From
The
Fragments
Of our hearts left alongside you
And on all the other roads
Where other Indian people
have been left to disappear
In full sight of history.
Annie Mae
Pictou Aquash.
Your tribeswomen bring back your memory to me in full sight of
Our history as indigenas and as far as their story can take me in
My chainlink to you, I begin to coax the discarded pieces of
Evidence into an answer to the desperate calling out for your
People. I form them into
One
Solid
Piece
Of evidence of love to envelop me and you—forever.
With all your memory found and kept in sight each day,
Lastingly sacred like the
Picture of my mother you remind me of, Annie Mae.

WHEN WOMEN SEW FOR A LIVING, THEY RARELY EARN THEIR KEEP

In Colombia
Y Malaysia
Hungary
South Korea
Indonesia
Y los estados unidos, too:
When women sew for a living, they rarely earn their keep.

For hours, months, years, a lifetime,
They wear out their thumbs and index fingers tying threads into
Knots of handstitched finery.
Then their hindsight goes and
Their backs give out.
Their necks grow weary
And never seem to straighten without pain.
Yet no one even brings them a glass of water to drink
Or offers to rub their fingers with perfumed oils.

For twenty cents,
    A $1.20
    A $1.57
    A $1.70
An hour
They ply their trade.
They make tucks and hems and gathered sleeves.
They cut and shape hats, suits, ruffled curtains.
Things needed and the many luxuries: adding pearl after pearl
After pearl to an evening gown.

They do this on their kneels
Staring down or up for hours
For the food money to take home: sometimes only a meager
Pan seco de cada día.
Nothing else.

Yes, their hands are in constant motion all day:
For twenty cents an hour in Indonesia,
For a $1.20 an hour in Colombia
For a $1.57 an hour in South Korea
For a $1.70 an hour in Hungary.
For $6.25 an hour in America.

Only in Norway—home of the $17.10 an hour seamstresses—
Do women who sew for a living earn their keep.

Elsewhere it's plain and clear
As a solid, white, cotton, knit,
Precisely ankle-length, exactly-contoured skirt,
When women sew for a living, they rarely earn their keep.
But how we admire their fine stitches, taut and sure and small.
Masterfully obscure in the rich brocades.

CROSSING "A PIECE OF EARTH"

At the border the gatekeepers sit with loaded guns.
Just this side of it I look at the brand newest official government map
For directions to a US/Mexico round trip.
Though I know that the map cannot measure precisely
The lay of the land.
Now changed by the brand newest migra laws.
They have altered our conscious excursions to each side
And our ownership or land/rights.

At the border
Where the guards with guns are stationed
I begin to reconsider
The rules I have relied upon
To cross the borders
That divide earth from earth
On the same terrain.
How can I re-define one slice of the land

Turned into a flat treadmill
Of personal causes that stretch over its bridges:
Day labor, drug dealers, simple family outings/
Trading one form of persecution for another?

At the border
Where the gatekeepers eye me
I dream up a way to set my own eyes
On other markings in the desert nearby
—The sagüaros—
As a means to know the land
And our history as a fluid movement in time
Underground.
One that curves into the spaces
Left over in the sagüaro's squarish corners.
It leaps through aqueducts and under the bridges
And into paradise.
It makes its own lay of the land
And tells me that I know the time has come
To stop waiting for a ruling
Promoting the just use of land/rights
On either side of the border I cross.

For the men who keep the rules
Re-order the time and space and lay of the land.
They make our part
Their natural inheritance
And insured that we are soaked inward,
Made invisible and inaudible

Still, I know that at the border
The places for me to discard my map and wade into the water
And assuredly swim across
Stretch farther
Than either
We
Or laws
Have eyes to see.

Since, well, the truth
About borders is desperate enough
To force upon us many versions
Of the facts
With guns for re-enforcement
If facts alone will not do.

The gatekeepers want so to stop
The flow of history slipping from them
As it undulates underground.
They collar us into migra vans
For the trip back
And we
Plan another crossing to
Another piece
Of the simple earth
In union with our version
Of the Mexico/US map.

This cycle becomes permanently fixed.

NOTES

Prologue

1. A note on terminology and the politics of identifiers is necessary here. Though I will have occasion within the book to elaborate on the many identifiers used to reference the Mexican-descent population living in the United States, it is important to clarify what guides my choices throughout the text. I have been trained by Chicana- and Chicano-studies scholars. Without exception, "Chicana" or "Chicano" has been their term of preference for themselves, their community, and for the subject matter they teach. This is the academic field in which my interdisciplinary training was forged. This referent signals my scholarly as well as my ideological orientation. The use of the term "Chicana/o" signals my interest in being gender-inclusive. When I utilize "Chicano," I consciously intend to signal the masculinist, or all-male, nature of the subject matter under discussion. When referring to the Chicano Movement, I have chosen to maintain the traditional terms of reference to this era as a proper noun. Though we know that this era was by no means male-exclusive, the lack of gender inclusiveness is an issue that is still salient and thus still signified by this term. Other identifiers—"Mexicano," "Mexican American," "Latin American," "Latino," and "Hispanic"—are used in keeping with the historical periods in which these terms were used and/or created by the population at large or the scholars who write about them.

Introduction

1. For an excellent extended reading of this poem, see Sheila Contreras's essay "Re-Reading 'the Historical Facts of Descent': Teresa Palomo Acosta's Questions to a Spanish Grandmother." *Reflexiones*. Austin: University of Texas CMAS, 1998.

2. Evidence of this in the field of Chicana/o studies can be seen in several essays published in the last few years by several social historians who have explored these connections. For instance, see Ramón Gutiérrez, "Community, Patriarchy and Individualism: The Politics of Chicano History and the Dream of Equality," and Mario García, "History, Literature, and the Chicano Working Class Novel: A Critical Review of Alejandro Morales's *The Brick People.*" This turn to literature as a source of evidence in making claims about the social and political history of Mexicans in the United States demonstrates the close interrelationship between history and literature. See also Rosaura Sánchez's "The History of Chicanas: Proposal for a Materialist Perspective" for an essay by a linguist/literary critic on the state of Chicana history. This is not to say that the blurring of the disciplines is accepted by all or never met with resistance. Some historians and anthropologists, Eric Wolf for one, resist the notion that literature is a reliable source of historical information or consciousness. Wolf contends that literature has limited value to historians and can be used only to corroborate other forms of evidence.

3. These include Mexican, Mexican American, Latino, Chicano, Latin American,

Hispano, Nuevo Mexicano, Tejano, Californio, and Mexico-Texan. See Montejano for a discussion on how "Mexican" became a "flexible" racial category that signified the social and class position of people of Mexican descent in Texas after 1848 in "Is Texas Bigger than The World System?: A Critique from a Provincial Point of View."

4. These historians are not necessarily the originators of these labels. Armando Navarro and Rodolfo Alvarez, among others, also use similar generational identifiers.

5. Some of these periods, such as that of the Mexican American Generation, are neatly defined by historians with specific years denoting beginnings and ends. In general, however, there is a lack of consensus on specific dates. So there are years that remain unaccounted for in the effort to construct a sequential timeline of generations. This points to a weakness in the paradigm that uses key historical moments to mark beginnings and ends: it results in gaps.

6. Concomitant with the recovery of archival writings from New Mexico, Colorado, and Arizona, there has been a reassessment of the relationship between literature and these regions' histories. An excellent example of this revisionist work is evident in the first two chapters of Tey Diana Rebolledo's 1995 study of Chicana literature, *Women Singing in the Snow: A Cultural Analysis of Chicana Literature.*

Chapter 1. Refashioning Resistance

1. See Ramón Saldívar, chapter 2 (*CN*), "The Folk Base of Chicano Narrative: Américo Paredes's *With His Pistol in His Hand* and the *Corrido* Tradition," for a prime example of this; I use the word "seminal" ironically in order to draw attention to a decidedly masculinist framework and point of origin.

2. See Limón, chapter 3 (*MBCP*), "With His Pistol in His Hand: The Essay as Strong Sociological Poem" for a reading of Paredes's poetics.

3. See the foreword to *Recovering the U.S. Hispanic Literary Heritage* for an outline of the scope of this formalized project. Of course, recovery assumes many "informal" forms in the ongoing research of scholars. Historian Antonia Castañeda ends her essay on *mestiza* women in the above volume by stating that "we . . . must begin to rethink our concept of history and literature so that, in recovering *[mestiza]* voices, we reclaim our literary heritage in its fullness, complexity, and power" (275).

4. See Herrera-Sobek, *The Mexican Corrido: A Feminist Analysis* (1990); Limón, *Mexican Ballads, Chicano Poems* (1992); Rosaldo, *Culture and Truth* (1988).

5. After an extended search, Limón was able to verify her ethnicity, but few details of her life are known.

6. According to Garza-Falcón, the resurgence of interest in González's work was initiated by Teresa Acosta and Cynthia Orozco at the Texas State Historical Association's 1991 conference on Mexican Americans in Texas history (74).

7. Two examples are Jim Sagel's *Túnomas Honey* (1983) and Daniel St. James's *Famous All Over Town* (1983). Interestingly, questions of authenticity are rarely pursued when discussing authors who have a bicultural heritage—John Rechy, Cherríe Moraga, and Dagoberto Gilb to name three. Rechy's initial exclusion as a Chicano writer was based more on a resistance to his focus on homosexual culture than his racial authenticity.

8. This biographical information is extracted from a speech given by Teresa Palomo Acosta on the occasion of a special tribute to González and Américo Paredes at the Mexican Americans in Texas History Conference in 1991.

9. Possible alternate titles listed on the typescript title page included: *The Hacienda, Eyes to See, Heritage, "Mea Culpa," Dew on the Thorn, This is My House,* and *Mine, Mine!*

10. In "Memory, Language, and Voice of Mestiza Women on the Northern Frontier: Historical Documents as Literary Text," Antonia Castañeda reminds us that much Spanish colonial literature equated women with land and nation; "women and land are conquered, tamed, husbanded or seeded" (266).

11. It is testimony to the salience of the Texas Rangers as a signifier of domination that the authors of *Caballero* and *George Washington Gómez* utilize intermarriage with one to signify a perceived betrayal by one of the main characters.

12. The authors' glossary defines *"marica"* as "Milksop. An effeminate man." But in common parlance, and in Spanish-language dictionaries, a *marica* or *maricón* is a gay man, a homosexual. Its contemporary English approximate as a derogatory term would be "fag" or "queer."

13. Jovita González was friends with Carlos Castañeda, who received his Ph.D. in history from the University of Texas in 1932. An early revisionist historian, Castañeda was concerned that the Spanish-Mexican foundation of Texas history be recognized (see his book *Mexican Americans* 231–251). By the mid-1930s he had published *The Mexican Side of the Texas Revolution* and two of the seven volumes of *Our Catholic Heritage of Texas, 1519–1950*. See Felix Almaraz's biography of Castañeda, *Knight Without Armor: Carlos Eduardo Castañeda, 1896–1958,* for a comprehensive overview of Castañeda's groundbreaking work.

14. In this regard, Jovita González's fieldwork on intermarriage between elite Mexican women and Anglo officers may be seen as a possible historical source for the novel's plot. The relationship between González's research and this novel awaits further exploration.

15. Personal correspondence with Teresa Acosta, October 24, 1994.

16. Karla Faye Tucker was executed on February 3, 1998. She was the second woman to be officially executed in Texas.

17. This notion of poetics is borrowed from Barbara Harlow; see *Barred: Women, Writing, and Political Detention* (256).

18. On the relationship between capital punishment and race, as well as the parallels between lynching and capital punishment, see *Unequal Justice: A Question of Color* by Coramae Richey Mann (200–208).

19. Personal correspondence with Teresa Acosta, October 24, 1994.

20. Personal correspondence with Teresa Acosta, January 17, 1995.

Chapter 2. Migration Literature as a Foundation for a National(ist) Literature

1. Romo, 13; see Oscar Martínez for the evolution of foreign dependency that results from these economic and military push-pull factors (111–19).

2. Alvarez makes a point of noting that Mexicans were largely unaware of this caste status until after World War II, when economic opportunities were more readily available

but racial attitudes prohibited group advancement. Social stratification was thus more rigid than class for people of color in the United States.

3. Cynthia Orozco's forthcoming study of 1920s and 1930s civil rights activism in Texas is an important contribution in this area.

4. See Luis Arroyo's "Notes on Past, Present, and Future Directions of Chicano Labor Studies" in *Aztlán* 6.2 (1975) for a discussion of the various approaches to Chicano labor history.

5. "The First Steps: Chicano Labor Conflict and Organizing, 1900–1920," (13–45). *Aztlán*. 3.1 (1973).

6. See *Between Borders: Essays on Mexicana/Chicana History,* Adelaida R. Del Castillo, ed.; *Women's Work and Chicano Families,* Patricia Zavella; *La Chicana: The Mexican-American Woman,* Alfredo Mirandé and Evangelina Enríquez; *Cannery Women, Cannery Lives,* Vicki Ruiz; *The Decolonial Imaginary: Writing Chicanas Into History,* Emma Pérez; and *Refusing the Favor: Spanish-Mexican Women of Santa Fe, 1820–1880,* Deena González.

7. See Ricardo Romo's *East Los Angeles* (31–59) and Mario García's *Desert Immigrants* (6–8).

8. DeLeón's *They Called Them Greasers: Anglo Attitudes Towards Mexicans in Texas, 1821–1900* and Mario García's *Desert Immigrants* both write against this problem and perpetuate it. For instance, DeLeón notes how early Anglo histories of Texas referred to Tejanas only as objects of Anglo men's fancies (9–10). However, both he and García limit their discussion of women to their role in familial and cultural practices. In contrast, Chicana history foregrounds agency by women in the public and private spheres.

9. Pérez's book is an interesting exception because it covers a recent immigrant's experiences of crossing and trying to survive in the late twentieth century. Rather than accept an inferior status in the United States, at the end of the novel he rejects the U.S. lifestyle and returns to Mexico.

10. 1988 edition, Arte Público Press.

11. García's vulgarization of Morales's aesthetic reveals his investment in social realism. For further discussion of the role of magical realism in the novel and its common misreading in the United States, see Gutiérrez-Jones (84–85).

12. Gutiérrez-Jones argues that this initial episode, based on an actual memoir dating back to the colonial period, writes the manipulation of dependency by colonizers and the supernatural responses to it by the subjugated group. In this way he suggests that we may read "the 'otherworldly' forces in Morales's text as analogues for demographic changes, especially in the Southwest," and the attendant struggles and negotiations for power.

13. The extent to which a house represents bourgeois notions of happiness and the "American Dream" has been an issue of debate about other Chicano texts. In "Sandra Cisneros' *The House on Mango Street* and the Poetics of Space," Julián Olivares disagrees with Juan Rodríguez's assessment that Esperanza's desire for a house represents Anglicization, individualism, and escapism (168). Olivares says that such a condemnation "ignores the ideology of a social class's liberation." Instead, he agrees with Erlinda Gonzales and Tey Diana Rebolledo "that the house is symbolic of consciousness and collective memory, and is a nourishing structure" (168). In relation to Cisneros's work, this debate assumes an understanding of the way gender is configured in relation to space and

power. In *The Brick People* both Octavio and his wife, Nana, want a house, but here the determinate factor in power relations is a racialized spatial order. García ignores the fact that there are no other housing options available to the Revueltas family, except for living with extended family in crowded conditions.

14. Though *The Brick People* was written before the 1991 "riots" in Los Angeles, the historical basis of the economic and social tensions between Anglos, Asians, African Americans, and Latinos figures prominently in the narrative. The novel thus reconstructs a fictional history that offers insight into contemporary social antagonisms.

15. Morales's use of "cockroach" as a label with a double meaning follows a tradition of whose origins I am not certain but which was popularized by Oscar Zeta Acosta in his novel *The Revolt of the Cockroach People.* Raúl Salinas also uses it as a self-reference in his poetry, calling himself a "cockroach poet."

16. This subtitle is taken from the title of an essay on Ramírez by Emilio Zamora, Jr.

17. Personal correspondence with Teresa Acosta, January 17, 1995. See appendix I for complete poem and citation.

18. My work here is grounded in research supported by a 1995 Recovery Project Grant in which I sought to expand the scope of Ramírez's recovered works. An abbreviated version appears in *Recovering the U.S. Hispanic Literary Heritage, Volume III* (Arte Público Press).

19. At the turn of the century, material and cultural forces combined to make Laredo a place of intense political activity. Industrialization was rapidly progressing, as was labor organizing in response to it. Removed from the interior of Texas, where racial conflict was most severe, Laredo was an important site for binational politics and union organizing. In 1904, it became the temporary headquarters of the PLM; in 1911, it hosted El Congreso Mexicanista; and in 1918, Laredo was chosen as the site for the Pan American Federation of Labor conference. The 1911 meeting of El Congreso was significant for a number of reasons, but most important for this chapter is the participation of women. In fact, out of this meeting emerged a women's organization called La Liga Femenil Mexicanista. See José Limón, "El Primer Congreso Mexicanista de 1911: A Precursor to Contemporary Chicanismo." According to Zamora, Clemente Idar organized "about ten craft unions composed of carpenters, bricklayers, clerks, painters, cooks, waiters, and other workers," ("Chicano Socialist" 226).

20. Letter from Ramírez to Magón, May 20, 1901. Ramírez wrote in Spanish. All translations are by Inés Hernández-Ávila and taken from her unpublished dissertation, "Sara Estela Ramírez: The Early Twentieth Century Texas-Mexican Poet," the most extensive work to date on this author. As part of her dissertation Hernández-Ávila translates all the known surviving work of Ramírez. (Her study is currently being revised for publication.) Vast quantities remain unaccounted for. Hernández-Ávila's dissertation is based on the available writings of Ramírez—which are eight of her letters to Magón, twenty poems and essays, and one published speech that she gave on the twenty-fourth anniversary of the Society of Workers. These poems and the speech were all published in either *La Crónica* or *El Demócrata Fronterizo.* Ellipses in parentheses indicate places where the original manuscript was either damaged or otherwise illegible. The "club" referred to was one of a network around which the PLM was organized. These smaller affiliate liberal clubs responded to local concerns and performed educational and organizational work in preparation for a coordinated move against the Díaz regime.

21. The wife of a local magistrate, Doña Josefa aided Hidalgo in moving people to rebel against the Spanish elite. "Sara Estela Ramírez: Sembradora" (Tovar 17).

22. Cockcroft uses Ramírez's last known letter to Magón, dated March 9, 1904, as evidence of the personal nature of antagonism within the PLM leadership, most notably that between Ricardo Flores Magón and Camilo Arriaga. In this letter Ramírez informs Magón that she has decided to work with Arriaga. Expressing her disillusionment at the internal friction in the Party, she calls her decision "spontaneous" and says that she believes "with groups working in this way, separately and in distinct places, we will be in harmony and we will get along better."

23. Besides Ricardo Flores Magón's well-known "A La Mujer" essay, Enrique Flores Magón and Práxedis Guerrero published several pieces on women's equality.

24. The *Plan de San Diego* called for a rebellion and the establishment of an independent republic of the Southwest. Victory was to be achieved by an army composed of Mexicans, blacks, Japanese, and Indians. The rebellion did not occur in the form in which it was originally devised. Approximately one month prior to the scheduled date of insurrection, an organizer was captured with a copy of the *Plan*. Even though there was no officially proclaimed beginning to this uprising, there were numerous small uprisings and raids against the Anglo elite conducted by Mexicans in South Texas. These activities were followed by a period of intense repression from the Texas Rangers and the U.S. cavalry. Hundreds of Mexicans were killed, many of whom were not at all associated with the armed insurrection by Texas Mexicans. After the *Plan* was originally discovered by Anglo law officials, it was not taken seriously until the attacks began occurring with alarming frequency. Whatever different influences may have come into play as variables in the implementation of the *Plan,* it had its roots and human resources in the Texas-Mexican community. In the years 1915 to 1917 it is estimated that anywhere from five hundred to five thousand Mexicans were killed in South Texas (Montejano, *AM* 125).

25. The large geographic expanse of its membership, differences in local situations, and a decentralized leadership produced ingroup tensions. There were ideological crosscurrents within the PLM: Chicano reformism versus Mexican Revolutionarism and Chicano irredentist aspirations versus Mexico-oriented reformers (Gómez-Quiñones, *Sembradores* 3). The PLM contributed to the struggle of Chicano industrial and agricultural unionism, but according to Gómez-Quiñones, perhaps the major failure of the PLM was that "it did not seize the Chicano labor-community framework, the natural base for its successful organizing, structure it, and expand it and orient it to the problems of the southwestern communities" (3). The *Plan de 1906* (July 1) was the single most important and seminal statement made by the Magonista PLM. In large part it became the working platform for the Mexican revolution. One clause in the *Plan* referred directly to the right of *mexicanos* outside of Mexico to receive land in Mexico (26). Verbally and in writing, the PLM linked the issues of working-class oppression in Mexico and the United States. In 1908 the PLM committed itself to anarchism. One of the party's papers carried selections from Peter Kropotkin's work. "During 1908 the PLM's Austin, Texas, newspaper, *Reforma, Libertad, y Justicia,* urged workers and peasants to undertake a violent revolution against capitalism" (6). For strategic reasons, the PLM did not make public its adoption of anarchism.

26. See chapter 3 of Pérez's *The Decolonial Imaginary: Writing Chicanas Into History*

for an expansion and even more detailed analysis of the gender limitations of PLM rhetoric.

27. A point made by Zamora (*CSA* 235).

28. Elizabeth Salas's book *Soldaderas* traces a genealogy of Amerindian women and Mexicana warriors to contemporary Chicana feminists.

29. Benito Juárez was the indigenous populist president of Mexico in 1861 and again from 1867 to 1872. He was instrumental in leading the fight against French occupation. His tenure marked the beginning of the liberal reform movement, which was to end with the ascension of Díaz to power. In 1899, on the anniversary of Juárez's death, students in San Luis Potosí marked the date by staging an anti-Díaz demonstration (Cockcroft, *IP* 73). Thus there was a recent precedent for using the anniversary of his death to protest political and social conditions.

30. These poems, "A Juárez" by Nina Ernestina Flores, "Remitido: En Defensa 'A Juárez' y Homenaje al Igniniero Bulnes" by Pedro Leal Cortes, and Constancio Peña Idiaquez's "A Juárez," deserve closer readings as individual poems than I can give here. They also signal the extent to which Ramírez's poetry was indicative of the social and political times as well as the aesthetic sensibility they gave rise to. This is even more evident when a broader examination of the poetry published in these papers is taken into account. The range of subject matter is evident in a selection of titles to the poems: "La Creación: Poema Indio," "Horas Tristes: A Mi Esposa," "El Cometa del Halley," "Raza Impura," and "Triptico" are but a few examples. Many of these poets' names appear only once, but there are some important exceptions, names that appear numerous times. Of these, Ernesto Siliceo Martínez appears as a prolific poet who consistently published his work in the papers.

Chapter 3. Shifting Identities, Harsh Realities

1. Arnoldo DeLeón's book on Mexican Americans in Houston is a good example of the uncritical adoption of generational labels. Part II of De Leon's book, "The Mexican American Generation, 1930–1960" uses the same period structure as García. Rodolfo Alvarez says that the label "Mexican American" was not popularized until the 1940s. Prior to that, most folks, as evidenced by the League of United Latin American Citizens (LULAC), identified themselves as Latin, Spanish, Mexican, etcetera. The hyphen (Mexican-American) appears in a period when claims based on citizenship and a proven loyalty, vis-à-vis military duty, were at their height.

2. The synthesis García proposes is more akin to an Hegelian dialectic than a Marxist one. He seems to suggest that as immigrants strive to become ideal "Americans" the process of assimilation is inevitable and welcomed. But ethnicity and assimilation are not static phenomena; they result from two very different social processes. One could productively propose to understand Chicana/o identity dialectically by examining the relationship between "American" identity and culture and "Mexican" identity and culture. Posing assimilation as one of the elements of the dialectic seems to me to be begging the question.

3. Manning Marable has pointed out that because of the construction of racial categories, being white in the United States "essentially means that one's life chances improve

dramatically over those of nonwhites, in terms of access to credit, capital, quality housing, health care, political influence, and equitable treatment in the criminal justice system" (189).

4. The identifier "LULACers" reflects the self-designated term adopted by LULAC. Such a move, not limited to LULACers, reflects a desire to distance themselves from the term "Mexican," which, as the narrator of Paredes's *GWG* states, "had for so long been a symbol of hatred and loathing that to most Anglotexans it had become a hateful and loathsome word" (118). From the perspective of the 1990s, the references to "Latin Americans" and "citizens of Latin extraction" might appear to be an appeal to a pan-Latino identity. It was not; rather, it was a concerted effort to emphasize their "American" (U.S.) political orientation. Mexican-origin people were the overwhelming majority, if not exclusive, Spanish-speaking population in the Southwest at this time. LULAC's and other middle-class organizations' and individuals' identification as Latin American was an embracing of their U.S. identity. Ironically, since the 1960s, when an internationalist ideology was formed and alliances sought with Third World groups, the term "Latino" or "Latin American" has come to signify a leftist, often antinational, pan-Latino perspective. This broadening of identity, especially as it applies to the literature of people of Mexican origin, will be examined in chapter 5.

5. In her unpublished dissertation, *The Origins of the League of United Latin American Citizens (LULAC) and the Mexican American civil rights movement in Texas with an Analysis of Women's Political Participation in a Gendered Context, 1910–1929,* Cynthia Orozco notes that noncitizen *mexicanos* composed a majority of the voting members of the three organizations at this time. However, the climate against including noncitizens generated by the organizers and facilitators of the conference was so hostile that a walk-out was staged by *mexicanos* prior to the vote, which effectively conceded the question to those in favor of exclusion. See especially chapter 4 of the dissertation, "The Harlingen Convention of 1927: The 'Mexican' Problem and the Exclusion of Mexican Citizens." See also Benjamin Márquez's *LULAC: The Evolution of a Mexican American Political Organization* (1993).

6. Bakhtin makes a distinction between primary and secondary speech genres. "The difference between primary and secondary (ideological) genres is very great and very fundamental. . . . Secondary (complex) speech genres . . . arise in more complex and comparatively highly developed and organized cultural communication (primarily written) that is artistic, scientific, socio-political, and so on. During the process of their formation, they absorb and digest various primary (simple) genres that have taken form in unmediated speech communion. These primary genres are altered and assume a special character when they enter into complex ones. They lose their immediate relation to actual reality and to the real utterance of others" (62).

7. In a February 24, 1994, conversation with Paredes in his office at the University of Texas at Austin, Paredes said that one of the reasons for this narrative gap was that he "had no [experiential] basis from which to write about the college experience." All he knew, he said, "was that people went to college and came back thinking they were better than others."

8. In *Pistol,* Paredes juxtaposes *"fuereños,"* meaning outsiders, against "gringos," which he translates as "foreigners" (13). Both terms emerge from the border and are meant to call attention to people's status as nonnatives to the border.

9. According to Orozco, "Bosses developed political machines to manipulate La Raza's vote. In the late nineteenth century, Democrats developed a color scheme to facilitate voting by the illiterate and/or the Spanish speaker. Bosses merely instructed voters to place an "x" for either the Red or Blue candidate" ("The Origins" 68). Feliciano's job as a ward heeler for a Judge Norris, the political boss of the "blue" party, is based on an actual practice.

10. In this regard, see "Roused from Our Slumbers," chapter 3 of Guadalupe San Miguel's study *"Let All of Them Take Heed": Mexican Americans and the Campaign for Educational Equality in Texas, 1910–1981.*

11. In a February 24, 1994, conversation with Paredes, the author indicated yet another possibility for the narrative, its continuation in the form of a sequel. He said that if he would have written this second novel, George W. Gómez would have been only a peripheral character and that the plot would have focused on the organizing work of Elodia and Antonio Prieto. He also said that in this novel, George Gómez would have had a "change of heart" toward his community.

12. These two stories have many more elements of the legend, including the nocturnal setting, the drunken husband, the familiar white robe and flowing white dress she wears, the notion of women's vengeance—sometimes with divine intervention, sexual betrayal, and elements of the supernatural.

13. See Victor B. Nelson Cisneros, "La clase trabajadora en Tejas, 1920–1940," for an overview of workers' conditions and unionism during this period.

14. As a result of a vote by members who believed Chicana studies was effaced by the masculine identifier, the association formally changed its name to the National Association for Chicana and Chicano Studies in 1995.

15. She eventually returned to San Antonio where she worked as a teacher until 1982. She died on July 23, 1999.

16. For an interesting, although very short, essay that praises her achievements but also includes critical perspectives from Tenayuca's peers on her leadership and interpersonal communication skills, see "Emma Tenayuca: La Pasionaria" by Carlos Larralde.

17. In noting the emphasis on urban history, Alex Saragoza points to the irony of the "relatively little work done recently on rural areas, despite the significance of the farm labor issue to the Chicano movement" (footnote 25, p. 52).

18. The relationship between Mexican American politics and the farmworkers changed in the 1960s, when the plight of farmworkers was brought to the forefront and "popularized" by labor organizers such as César Chávez. Though this occurred during a time simultaneous with the Chicano Movement, and though Chávez was hailed as a leader, it is important to note that Chávez eschewed identification as a Chicano leader; he preferred to be seen as a labor organizer.

19. Gómez-Quiñones and García quote different numbers, 1 and 3 million respectively, for the number of Mexicans who were deported during "Operation Wetback" in the years 1951 to 1953.

20. Rivera died in 1984 at the age of forty-nine. He was Chancellor of the University of California at Riverside at the time. The amount of scholarship on his creative work continues to expand. A 1988 bibliography, included in a special *homenaje* to him composed of

critical essays and his own prose and poetry, lists over 125 entries, most of them on . . . *y no se lo tragó la tierra.*

21. Several convincing essays on this view are presented in Diane L. Chambless and Alan J. Goldstein's book *Agoraphobia: Multiple Perspectives on Theory and Treatment.*

22. For feminist criticism on *Tierra,* see Patricia de la Fuente's "Invisible Women in the Narrative of Tomás Rivera" and Sylvia Lizárraga's essay "The Patriarchal Ideology of 'La noche que se apagaron las luces,'" both in *International Studies in Honor of Tomás Rivera.*

Chapter 4. Identity, Memory, and Self-Representation in el Movimiento

1. Muñoz suggests that the movement emerged and declined between 1968 and 1971 (75–86); Gómez-Quiñones gives the parameters of the movement as being between 1967 and 1978 (*CP* 101); Escobar uses activism in Los Angeles as the measure of the longevity of the movement in the years 1968 to 1971; R. Gutiérrez is the exception when he speaks of the Chicano Movement as a period extending from "1965 to the present" (44), but he says that the "heyday of the movement was 1965 to 1969" (47).

2. For examples of writings that refer to the influence and relevance of Third World theorists such as Fanon, Guevara, and Cabral, see Gómez-Quiñones's "On Culture" and *Mexican Students Por La Raza;* and Acuña's preface to *Occupied America,* 2d ed.

3. For the former, see the examples identified by José Limón in *Mexican Ballads, Chicano Poems;* for the latter, the poetry of Raúl Salinas is exemplary. Salinas candidly acknowledges that his poetry is influenced by Walt Whitman, William Carlos Williams, and the Beat poets. He is always careful to note, however, distinctions or departures in subject matter, style, and linguistics.

4. For extended analyses of Movement poetry, see Marta Sánchez's *Contemporary Chicana Poetry* and Rafael Pérez-Torres's *Movements in Chicano Poetry.* Several Chicano Movement activists and scholars were also poets and storytellers even as they made history through their involvement in Movement politics. Chief among these are Rosaura Sánchez and Juan Gómez-Quiñones. In a study focusing on the relationship between literature and history, it might seem particularly appropriate to conduct an extended examination of Gómez-Quiñones's poetry. In his analysis of Gómez-Quiñones's poetic production, José Limón has noted that his "poetry is deeply influenced by the poet's professional and lived sense of history" (*MBCP* 132). Such work is a worthy future project and promises to be insightful, but here, with the exception of Teresa Acosta's poetry, I am privileging a reading of narrative forms that take history as their central subject matter.

5. *El Grito: A Journal of Contemporary Mexican American Thought* was initiated in 1967; *Aztlán: Chicano Journal of the Social Science and the Arts* was founded in 1970; Rodolfo Acuña's *Occupied America* was published in 1972.

6. This phenomenon has its parallel in the cultural marketplace. Several Chicano writers, critics, and publishers (J. Saldívar, 109; N. Kanellos, lecture, fall 1987) have made references to a "brown curtain" in the publishing industry that constitutes a form of cultural censorship. They have noted that resistance to viewing Chicano literature as "American" literature by the mainstream academy and general public may be because many of the

experiences narrated by Chicanos (and other ethnic groups within the United States) are about conflict with U.S. systems of power, especially those based on ethnic and cultural difference.

7. See Gómez-Quiñones on "identity as consciousness" in *Chicano Politics* (6–9) for how this is played out and negotiated at the group level.

8. The politics and economics of race have also influenced Mexicans in the United States to support racial categories and resist being labeled "colored." This was a contradictory position since it left intact racist notions that supported antiblack sentiments. Actions like this by the Mexican community were more likely to occur in Texas, which had a longer history of hostility and sharper economic distinctions as well more strictly enforced Jim Crow laws separating whites from nonwhites. See Mario García's "Mexican Americans and the Politics of Citizenship: The Case of El Paso, 1936."

9. See Emilio Zamora, Jr., "Chicano Socialist Labor Activity in Texas, 1900–1920" and Juan Gómez-Quiñones, "The First Steps: Chicano Labor Conflict and Organizing, 1900–1920."

10. See Elizabeth Martínez, "Chingón Politics Die Hard."

11. One example that depicts the defense of *la cultura* in these terms is from Oscar Z. Acosta. In speaking of the indictment of the East L.A. Thirteen, he says there are "several defendants who are militantly nationalistic Mexican Americans (Chicanos) accused of conspiring to organize and participate in the disruption of segregated Mexican American high schools—a felony—in protest of an emasculating acculturation . . .". "The East L.A. 13 vs. The L.A. Superior Court" (12). For extended documentation and analysis of sexism in the Movement and in literature see "Proceedings from the Houston Conference Mujeres Por La Raza of 1971"; Anna Nieto Gómez, "Sexism in the Movimiento," *La Gente,* February 1975; Adelaida del Castillo, "Mexican Women in Organization," *Mexican Women in the United States;* and Cynthia Orozco, "Sexism in Chicano Studies and the Community."

12. The *Plan de Delano,* developed when the National Farm Workers Association decided to go on strike with Filipino farmworkers, was written by Luis Valdez. The *Plan* proclaimed the beginning of a nonviolent revolution for social justice by the "Sons of the Mexican Revolution."

13. See Edward J. Escobar's essay "The Dialectics of Repression: The Los Angeles Police Department and the Chicano Movement, 1968–1971" for an analysis of the dynamic relationship between protest and repression.

14. The dilemma between diplomacy and militancy often occurs in Third World contexts as a choice between armed struggle versus negotiations. In this regard, decisions on strategy represent a crucial crossroads, each with particular problems. Historically, the choices are not necessarily mutually exclusive; rather, the threat or actual deployment of violent actions or public protest can often function as a point of leverage in the call for negotiations, as it has in El Salvador, South Africa, Northern Ireland, and Palestine.

15. Alliances and coalitions between people of color on university campuses in the U.S. are often characterized by agreements that are crisis-driven, often single-issue-oriented, and ad hoc in nature.

16. My research was based on the UCSB archives, but many of the private and unpublished works of Acosta are now available in print (*Oscar "Zeta" Acosta: The Uncollected*

Works. Ilan Stavans, ed.). For the sake of accessibility, I will reference the published collection when appropriate.

17. Undated correspondence from Oscar Zeta Acosta Collection. I am able to identify the year because of a reference he makes to a letter he wrote on November 12, 1972, and another shortly before Christmas of 1972, which came before the letter to Helen. I have not been able to determine Helen's last name or the name of the publisher she represented.

18. Elsewhere I have conducted a more extended review of *The Uncollected Works* and what I consider to be Stavans's sensationalist representation of Acosta in *Bandido.*

19. In an article in which he details the specifics of the L.A. Thirteen case, Acosta explains that the defense "retained expert witnesses and collected cardboard boxes filled with documentary and statistical evidence in order to legally establish their identity as a people separate and distinct from the majority, thereby meeting the constitutional requirement of 'classification' which is a pre-condition to a demand for consideration and representation for their group on the Grand Jury." (*El Grito* 14)

20. Many of Acosta's letters to his wife are undated, but one is able to discern their approximate dates based on frequency, return addresses, references to his age, and content.

21. See Gerald López's introduction to *Rebellious Lawyering* (1992) for his recollection of this period in Los Angeles history. He points out that these lawyers were "relatively few in number; they were overworked; they never directly touched most peoples' lives. In other ways, however, they were quite conspicuous. They all seemed to be outsiders—white and male. And they all appeared . . . to dress, speak, and act not at all like us" (1).

22. See Kimberly Kowalczyk's "Oscar Zeta Acosta: The Brown Buffalo and His Search for Identity" and Arthur Ramírez's "Review Essay: *The Autobiography of a Brown Buffalo* and *The Revolt of the Cockroach People.*"

23. In an undated letter to The Playboy Forum, Acosta takes issue with an article that had identified Thompson as the creator of GonzoJournalism. His claim for developing this style is also reiterated in the letter to Helen, his agent referred to above. He identifies other features of this style: "In point of fact Doctor Duke and I—the world-famous Doctor Gonzo—together we both hand in hand sought out the teachings and curative powers of the world-famous Savage Henry the scagbaron of Las Vegas and in point of fact the term and methodology of reporting crucial events under fire and drugs which are of course essential in this age of confusion—all this I say came from the mouth of our teacher who is also known by the name of Owl" (Stavans, *UW* 109).

24. The *Plan de Delano* (1965), the *Plan Espiritual de Aztlán* (1969), and *El Plan de Santa Barbara* (1969) are good examples of attempts to forge a unified identity.

25. FBI file # LA 10-75361. The article is written by *Times* reporter Ron Einstoss.

26. Acosta apparently did visit Chávez in 1968. A March, 1968, letter to Marco Acosta reads: "My night job is working with the Mexicans. Down here we call Mexicans Chicanos. That is what I am. I am a Chicano. You are a Chicano too if you want to be. But you have to learn how to speak Spanish. . . . This weekend I went to Delano and talked with a man who is a friend of Robert Kennedy. Robert Kennedy is President Kennedy's brother. He was there to tell everybody what a great man César is. César is a Chicano. He is not afraid of any body. He wants me to help him put the cops in jail because the cops are bad, stupid pigs."

27. In "The East L.A. 13 vs. The L.A. Superior Court," Acosta explains how the indictment of the "leaders" was a political power play on the part of the Republican administration, who was promoting a "law and order" campaign for the national primaries. The indictment also escalated the stakes because "the issue was no longer discriminatory education. Now it was abusive and excessive prosecutorial power by an unrepresentative government" (14). He thus calls the democratic nature and legitimacy of the justice system into question.

28. See Josie Carrillo, "Infiltration into the Chicano Movement"; José Angel Gutiérrez, "Chicanos and Mexicans Under Surveillance: 1940–1980"; "Freddie and the L.A.P.D. Conspiracy," *La Raza;* and Edward J. Escobar, "The Dialectics of Repression: The Los Angeles Police Department and the Chicano Movement, 1968–1971" for specific examples and a partial history of infiltration into organizations of people of Mexican descent.

29. At the inquest into the death of Rubén Salazar, many witnesses testified that Salazar suspected he was being followed and had received threats from police officials. See *Occupied America* (369–437) and *La Raza* Vol. 3 (1970) for eyewitness accounts and details of the inquest. In a September 4, 1970, news report in the *Los Angeles Times,* Acosta called Salazar's death a "political murder, plain and simple" (qtd. in Escobar, "Dialectics" 1503).

30. See Alurista's essay "Myth, Identity and Struggle in Three Chicano Novels: Aztlán . . . Anaya, Méndez and Acosta." He claims that *Revolt* was the first novel to be published that made reference to Aztlán.

31. Gerald López also blurs the boundaries between fact and fiction in describing his narrative strategy for his book. "I don't name real people or depict actual struggles: Everything I describe is fictional. But I do draw on my observations of and my work with a wide range of people, groups, and institutions. Yet I don't limit myself only to what I have seen and heard. Instead, by using imagined characters and storylines I try to expand the boundaries of, nearly as much as I report, all that I so much admire" (8).

32. In 1972, *La Raza* (1.7) published a series of articles on police repression of activists that demonstrate the extent to which the L.A.P.D. was willing to go to harass, discredit, and otherwise immobilize activists through intimidation, arrest, or violence.

33. Written to "David" from Morelia, Michoacan, Mexico, this letter begins: "I pulled a number and within hours the FBI was on my tail. I left L.A. with my wallet and my typewriter. Socorro and I drove a '62 Fleetwood across the desert and over the boundry. In Mazatlan I bought a kilo of weed and we finally got married in a church that Villa slept in."

34. His notion of leadership had altered dramatically as well. In an April 12, 1961, letter to Daves, we catch a glimpse of his early individualized and patriarchal notions of leadership:

> You said since you've known me it's always been, What is Oscar going to do? To save my soul I can't think of how else it could be. This to me was the whole basis for your coming back and my terminating my therapy. Where he leads, I will follow, is the way the hymn goes. I would merit no respect if I were not the leader. The important thing for you to realize is that without followers there would be no leaders. The leader only exists because there is a follower. He leads not himself, but he leads, not in spite of, but because of, the followers.

35. An FBI report dated June 1, 1970, recounts a protest on the steps of the Los Angeles city hall. The report provides a summary of the different speeches, which includes one by Acosta. Besides denouncing the deportation policies of the INS, Acosta also "called for unity among minority races, but stated that the blacks would have to accede to the territorial demands of the Mexican Americans" (FBI file # 100-75361-7, Acosta papers).

36. Probably the most high-profile case among these would be that of Reies López Tijerina and the Alianza de Pueblos Libres in New Mexico. Carlos Muñoz makes the point, though, that Tijerina never advocated Chicano nationalism. The Alianza struggle for land was one based on the legitimacy of their land grants, not a quest for national self-determination (Muñoz 7).

37. An excerpt from the 1983 MALCS declaration reads, "The scarcity of Chicanas in institutions of higher education requires that we join together to identify our common problems to support each other and to define collective solutions. Our purpose is to fight the race, class and gender oppression we have experienced in the universities." The MALCS statement from the 1992 Summer Institute reads, in part:

> The MALCS Institute is one of the few places Chicanas can come together without the influences of male and /or Anglo consciousness or opinion. For most Chicanas, this is the only place to come together. While some charge that this is separatist, the MALCS reply is not one of apology. This is our space. The dynamics of this Chicana space are worth guarding, even in the face of criticism from those we respect and work with in our home institutions.
>
> It is our sincere hope that the critics outside MALCS will understand the above position and respect the reasons this space has been created.

Chapter 5. Redefining Political and National Borders

1. Indeed, this is already occurring. See José Angel Gutiérrez, *The Making of a Chicano Militant* (11), and Carlos Muñoz, *Youth, Identity, and Power* (10–11)

2. Crucial to the publication of women-of-color collections was the founding of feminist presses that were committed to publishing their work. These include Third Woman, Kitchen Table, and Spinsters/Aunt Lute. There is a surprising lack of anthologies by Latino/Chicano men. This, perhaps, reflects sexism within Latino presses, which may be more willing to publish entire collections by men than women, a resistance to collaboration by men, and the lack of need for publishing "new" voices and perspectives. This latter view is sustained by the recent publication of anthologies by men participating in the emerging debate on Latino male sexuality.

3. Here I utilize the term Latina/o because, as will become evident in the extended discussion of these authors' works, it is an identifier that they invoke to express their internationalist outlook.

4. This is a point that Cynthia Orozco makes about past interpretations of LULAC (*Origins of LULAC* 3). Mario García makes a similar argument regarding the Mexican American generation (*MA* 18).

5. Robert Bullard's work has been exceptionally important for bringing legitimacy to this political work. See *Dumping in Dixie: Race, Class, and Environmental Quality* (1990), *Toxic Struggles: The Theory and Practice of Environmental Justice* (1993), *Unequal Protection: Environmental Justice and Communities of Color* (1994). Numerous state and regional networks have been formed to share strategies and research as well as political alliances around this work. For instance, in Texas, the Texas Network for Environmental and Economic Justice is a statewide coalition of organizations; this organization has representatives in the Southwest Network for Environmental and Economic Justice as well. Both of these networks comprise grassroots Latino and African American organizations. They also participate in networks that were initially composed of progressive whites, such as the Southern Organizing Committee for Economic and Social Justice. For a history of coalition building in the environmental movement, see Antonio Díaz's essay "New Developments in Building Regional Networks for Environmental Justice."

6. In an unpublished 1990 essay, "The FMLN and Revolutionary Change," Antonio Díaz and I investigated the complex relationship between the Central American solidarity movement and the U.S. Latino community. We discovered that many Chicanos and other Latinos chose to organize on this issue separately because they found it important to link local issues with international ones, whereas the "mainstream" solidarity movement focused on oppression resulting from U.S. imperialism abroad.

7. See, for example, the 1992 America's Watch Report, *Brutality Unchecked: Human Rights Abuses Along the U.S. Border with Mexico*. This document combines journalism, history, and personal testimony to analyze the abusive practices of *la migra.*

8. See Tomás Almaguer's "Ideological Distortions in Recent Chicano Historiography."

Conclusion

1. The ideas that inform this analysis are derived from Nancy Hartsock's article "Rethinking Modernism: Minority vs. Majority Theories."

Appendix 1

1. Published in *Nile and Other Poems.*

Appendix 3

1. These poems are from *Nile and Other Poems*. "Desparecida" appears in *Nile Notebooks.*

BIBLIOGRAPHY

Acosta, Oscar Zeta. *The Autobiography of a Brown Buffalo.* 1972. Reprint, New York: Vintage, 1989.

———. "The East L.A. 13 vs. The L.A. Superior Court." *El Grito* 3, no. 2 (winter, 1970): 12–18.

———. The Oscar Zeta Acosta Collection ms. The Chicano Studies Collection of the University of California, Santa Barbara. CEMA 1 [California Ethnic and Multicultural Archives]. 1936–90.

———. *Oscar "Zeta" Acosta: The Uncollected Works.* Edited by Ilan Stavans. Houston: Arte Público Press, 1996.

———. *The Revolt of the Cockroach People.* 1973. New York: Vintage, 1989.

Acosta, Teresa Palomo. "Jovita González de Mireles: An Appreciation." Proc. of a Conference of Mexican Americans in Texas History. May 3, 1991. San Antonio: University of Texas Institute of Texan Cultures, 1991.

———. *Nile and Other Poems.* Austin: Red Salmon Press, 1999.

———. *Nile and Other Poems: A 1985–1994 Notebook.* Austin: N.p., 1994.

———. *Passing Time.* Austin: N.p., 1985.

———. "Tejana History as a Poem: Sara Estela Ramírez and Me." Tr. Barker Collection, University of Texas, Austin.

Acuña, Rodolfo. *Occupied America: A History of Chicanos.* 2d edition. New York: Harper & Row, 1981.

Alarcón, Norma. "Traddutora, Traditora: A Paradigmatic Figure of Chicana Feminism." *Cutlural Critique* (fall, 1990): 57–87.

Almaguer, Tomás. "Ideological Distortions in Recent Chicano Historiography: The Internal Model and Chicano Historical Interpretation." *Aztlán* 18, no. 1 (1987): 7–28.

Almaraz, Felix D., Jr. *Knight Without Armor: Carlos Eduardo Castañeda, 1896–1958.* College Station: Texas A&M University Press, 1999.

Althusser, Louis. "Ideology and Ideological State Apparatuses (Notes Towards an Investigation)." *Lenin and Philosophy and Other Essays.* Translated by Ben Brewster, 127–86. New York: Monthly Review, 1971.

Alurista. "Acosta's *The Revolt of the Cockroach People:* The Case, the Novel, and History." *Contemporary Chicano Fiction: A Critical Survey.* Edited by Vernon E. Lattin, 94–104. Binghamton: Bilingual Press, 1986.

———. "Myth, Identity and Struggle in Three Chicano Novels: Aztlán . . . Anaya, Méndez and Acosta." *Aztlán: Essays on the Chicano Homeland.* 1989. Edited by Rudolfo A. Anaya and Fransisco Lomeli, 219–29. Albuquerque: New Mexico University Press, 1991.

Alurista, et al., eds. *Festival de Flor y Canto: An Anthology of Chicano Literature.* Los Angeles: University of Southern California Press, 1976.

Alvarez, Rodolfo. "The Psyco-Historical and Socioeconomic Development of the Chicano Community in the United States." *The Mexican American Experience: An Interdiscipli-*

nary Anthology. Edited by Rodolfo O. de la Garza, et al., 33–56. Austin: University of Texas Press, 1985.

Anderson, Benedict. *Imagined Communities: Reflections on the Origin and Spread of Nationalism.* 1983. Rev. ed. London: Verso, 1991.

Anzaldúa, Gloria. *Borderlands/La Frontera: The New Mestiza.* San Francisco: Spinsters/Aunt Lute, 1987.

Anzaldúa, Gloria, ed. *Making Face, Making Soul.* San Francisco: Aunt Lute, 1990.

Arroyo, Luis Leobardo. "Notes on Past, Present and Future Directions of Chicano Labor Studies." *Aztlán* 6, no. 2 (summer, 1975): 137–50.

Bakhtin, M. M. "The Bildungsroman and Its Significance in the History of Realism (Toward a Historical Typology of the Novel)." *Speech Genres and Other Late Essays.* Translated by Vern W. McGee. Edited by Caryl Emerson and Michael Holquist, 10–59. Austin: University of Texas Press, 1986.

———. "The Problem of Speech Genres." *Speech Genres and Other Late Essays.* Translated by Vern W. McGee. Edited by Caryl Emerson and Michael Holquist, 60–102. Austin: University of Texas Press, 1986.

Barrera, Mario. *Race and Class in the Southwest: A Theory of Racial Inequality.* Notre Dame: Notre Dame University Press, 1979.

Berger, John. *Ways of Seeing.* Reprint, New York: Viking, 1995.

Bhattacharjee, Anannya. "Woman, Nation and Identity in the Indian Immigrant Community." *Samar* 1 (winter, 1992): 6–10.

Blau DuPlessis, Rachel. "*f*-words: An Essay on the Essay." *American Literature* 68, no. 1: 15–46.

Bruce-Novoa, Juan. "Homosexuality and the Chicano Novel." *Confluencia* 2, no. 1 (fall, 1986): 69–77.

———. Interview with Tomás Rivera. *Chicano Authors: Inquiry by Interview.* Austin: University of Texas Press, 1980. 137–62.

Brutality Unchecked: Human Rights Abuses Along the U.S. Border with Mexico. New York: Human Rights Watch, 1992.

Bullard, Robert D. *Dumping in Dixie: Race, Class, and Environmental Quality.* Boulder, Colo.: Westview Press, 1990.

———. *Toxic Struggles: The Theory and Practice of Environmental Justice.* Boston: South End Press, 1993.

———. *Unequal Protection: Environmental Justice and Communities of Color.* San Francisco: Sierra Club Books, 1994.

Bustamante, Antonio Rios. *Mexicans in the United States and The National Question: Current Polemics and Organizational Positions.* Santa Barbara: Editorial La Causa, 1978.

Calderón, Héctor. "The Novel and the Community of Readers: Rereading Tomás Rivera's *Y no se lo tragó la tierra.*" *Criticism in the Borderlands: Studies in Chicano Literature, Culture, and Ideology.* Edited by Héctor Calderón and José Saldívar, 97–113. Durham: Duke University Press, 1991.

Calderón, Roberto R., and Emilio Zamora. "Manuela Solis Sager and Emma B. Tenayuca: A Tribute." *Between Borders: Essays on Mexicana/Chicana History.* Edited by Adelaida R. Del Castillo, 269–80. La Mujer Latina Series. Encino, Calif.: Floricanto Press, 1990.

Carrillo, Josie. "Infiltration into the Chicano Movement." *Regeneración* [Los Angeles] 2, no. 2 (1972): 20.

Carrillo, Leonardo, et al. *Canto Al Pueblo: An Anthology of Experiences.* San Antonio: Penca Books, 1978.

Castañeda, Antonia I. "Memory, Language and Voice of Mestiza Women on the Northern Frontier: Historical Documents as Literary Text." *Recovering the U.S. Hispanic Literary Heritage.* Edited by Ramón Gutiérrez and Genaro Padilla, 265–78. Houston: Arte Público Press, 1993.

Castillo, Adelaida R. del, ed. *Between Borders: Essays on Mexicana/Chicana History.* La Mujer Latina Series. Encino, Calif.: Floricanto Press, 1990.

Chabram, Angie. "Conceptualizing Chicano Critical Discourse." *Criticism in the Borderlands: Studies in Chicano Literature, Culture, and Ideology.* Edited by Héctor Calderón and José Saldívar, 127–48. Durham: Duke University Press, 1991.

Chambless, Diane L., and Alan J. Goldstein. *Agoraphobia: Multiple Perspectives on Theory and Treatment.* New York: John Wiley & Sons, 1982.

Chatterjee, Partha. "Nationalism as a Problem in the History of Political Ideas." *Nationalist Thought and the Colonial World: A Derivative Discourse?* London: Zed Books Ltd., 1986.

Cherniavsky, Eva. "Subaltern Studies in a U.S. Frame." *boundary.* 2. 23:2 (1996): 85–110.

"Church vs. Catolicos." *La Raza* [Los Angeles] 1, no. 1 (1969): 19–22.

Cisneros, Sandra. *The House on Mango Street.* Houston: Arte Público Press, 1983.

Cisneros, Victor B. Nelson. "La clase trabajadora en Tejas, 1920–1940." *Aztlán* 6, no. 2 (summer, 1975): 239–66.

Cockcroft, James. *Intellectual Precursors of the Mexican Revolution, 1900–1913.* Latin American Monographs 14. Austin: University of Texas Press, 1976.

———. *Outlaws In the Promised Land: Mexican Immigrant Workers and America's Future.* New York: Grove Press, 1986.

Davis, Natalie Zemon, and Randolph Starn. Introduction. *Representations* 26 (spring, 1989): 1–5.

Díaz, Antonio. "New Developments in Building Regional Networks for Environmental Justice." *Forging the Movement: Environmental Justice from the Grassroots.* ed. Richard Hofrichter. Washington, D.C.: Island Press, 1995.

Díaz, Antonio, and Louis Mendoza. "The FMLN and Revolutionary Change." Unpublished essay, 1990.

Dowling, William C. *Jameson, Althusser, Marx: An Introduction to The Political Unconscious.* Ithaca, N.Y.: Cornell University Press, 1984.

Escobar, Edward J. "The Dialectics of Repression: The Los Angeles Police Department and the Chicano Movement, 1968–1971." *Journal of American History* (March, 1993): 1483–1514.

———. "Mexican Revolutionaries and the Los Angeles Police: Harassment of the Partido Liberal Mexicano, 1907–1910." *Aztlán* 17, no. 1 (1986): 1–46.

Fabre, Genevieve, and Juan Bruce-Novoa. "History and Cultural Production: Introduction." *Aztlán* 18, no. 1 (1987): 1–5.

Fanon, Frantz. "On National Culture." *The Wretched of the Earth.* 1961. Translated by Constance Farrington, 206–48. New York: Grove Press, 1968.

———. "The Pitfalls of National Consciousness." *The Wretched of the Earth.* 1961. Translated by Constance Farrington, 148–205. New York: Grove Press, 1968.

Fernández-Retamar, Roberto. "Caliban: Notes Toward a Discussion of Culture in Our America." *Caliban and Other Essays.* Tr. Edward Baker. Minneapolis: Minnesota University Press, 1989. 3–45.

———. "Caliban Revisited." *Caliban and Other Essays.* Tr. Edward Baker. Minneapolis: Minnesota University Press, 1989. 46–54.

Franco, Jean. *Plottng Women: Gender and Representation in Mexico.* New York: Colombia, 1988.

"Freddie and the L.A.P.D. Conspiracy." *La Raza* [Los Angeles] (January, 1972): 58–59.

Fromm, Erich. *The Sane Society.* New York: Rinehart & Co., 1955.

Galarza, Ernesto. *Barrio Boy.* Notre Dame: University of Notre Dame Press, 1971.

García, Mario T. *Desert Immigrants: The Mexicans of El Paso, 1880–1920.* Yale Western Americana Series 32. New Haven: Yale University Press, 1981.

———. "History, Literature, and the Chicano Working-Class Novel: A Critical Review of Alejandro Morales' *The Brick People.*" *Critica: A Journal of Critical Essays* 2, no. 2 (1990): 189–200.

———. "Mexican Americans and the Politics of Citizenship: The Case of El Paso, 1936." *New Mexico Historical Review* 59 (April, 1984): 187–204.

———. *Mexican Americans: Leadership, Ideology, and Identity, 1930–1960.* New Haven: Yale University Press, 1989.

Garza-Falcón, Leticia. *Gente Decente: A Borderlands Response to the Rhetoric of Dominance.* Austin: University of Texas Press, 1998.

Gómez-Peña, Guillermo. "Death on the Border: A Eulogy to Border Art." *High Performance* 58 (1991).

———. *Warrior for Gringostroika: Essays, Performance Texts, and Poetry.* Saint Paul, Minn.: Graywolf Press, 1993.

Gómez-Quiñones, Juan. *Chicano Politics: Reality and Promise, 1940–1990.* The Calvin P. Horn Lectures in Western History and Culture. Albuquerque: New Mexico University Press, 1990.

———. "The First Steps: Chicano Labor Conflict and Organizing, 1900–1920." *Aztlán* 3, no. 1 (1973): 13–49.

———. *Mexican Students Por La Raza: The Chicano Student Movement in Southern California, 1967–1977.* Santa Barbara: Editorial La Causa, 1978.

———. "On Culture." *Revista Chicano-Riqueña* 5, no. 2 (1977): 26–47.

———. "Plan de San Diego Reviewed." *Aztlán* 1, no. 1 (1970): 124–32.

———. "Research Notes on the Twentieth Century: Notes on Periodization 1900–1965." *Aztlán* 1, no. 1 (1970): 115–18.

———. *Sembradores, Ricardo Flores Magón y El Partido Liberal Mexicano: A Eulogy and Critique.* Los Angeles: Aztlán Publications, 1973. 114–16.

———. "Toward a Perspective on Chicano History." *Aztlán* 2, no. 2 (1971): 2–39.

Gómez-Quiñones, Juan, and Luis Leobardo Arroyo. "On the State of Chicano History: Observations on Its Development, Interpretations, and Theory, 1970–1974." *Western Historical Quarterly* (April, 1976): 155–85.

González, Deena J. *Refusing the Favor: Spanish-Mexican Women of Sant Fe, 1820–1880.* London: Oxford University Press, 1999.

González, Jovita, and Eve Raleigh (Margaret Eimer). *Caballero: A Historical Novel.* College Station: Texas A&M University Press, 1996.

Gossman, Lionel. *Between History and Literature.* Cambridge, Mass.: Harvard University Press, 1990.

Gramsci, Antonio. *An Antonio Gramsci Reader: Selected Writings, 1916–1935.* Edited by David Forgacs. New York: Schocken Books, 1988.

———. *Selections from the Prison Notebooks.* Edited and translated by Quintin Hoare and Geoffrey Nowell Smith. New York: International Publishers, 1971.

Gutiérrez, José Angel. "Chicanos and Mexicans Under Surveillance: 1940–1980." *Renato Rosaldo Lecture Series Monograph* 2 (spring, 1986): 41–58.

———. *The Making of a Chicano Militant: Lessons from Cristal.* Madison: Wisconsin University Press, 1999.

Gutiérrez, Ramón. "Community, Patriarchy, and Individualism: The Politics of Chicano History and the Dream of Equality." *American Quarterly* 45, no. 1 (1993): 44–72.

Gutiérrez-Jones, Carl. *Rethinking the Borderlands: Between Chicano Culture and Legal Discourse.* Berkeley: University of California Press, 1995.

Harlow, Barbara. *Barred: Women, Writing, and Political Detention.* Hanover, N.H.: University Press of New England, 1992.

———. *Resistance Literature.* New York: Metheun Press, 1987.

Harris, Charles H., III, and Louis R. Sadler. *The Border and the Revolution.* Las Cruces: Center for Latin American Studies, New Mexico State University, 1988.

Hart, John M. *Anarchism & The Mexican Working Class, 1860–1931.* Austin: University of Texas Press, 1987.

———. Foreword. "Ricardo Flores Magón in History." *Anarchism and the Mexican Revolution: The Political Trials of Ricardo Flores Magón in the United States.* By Colin M. MacLachlan. Berkeley: University of California Press, 1991.

Hartsock, Nancy. "Rethinking Modernism: Minority vs. Majority Theories." *Cultural Critique* 7: 17–36.

Hernandez, Inés. "Sara Estela Ramirez: Sembradora." *Legacy: A Journal of Nineteenth-Century American Women Writers* 6, no. 1 (1989): 13–26.

Hobsbawm, E. J. *Nations and Nationalism Since 1780: Programme, Myth, Reality.* 1990. 2d ed. Cambridge: Cambridge University Press, 1992.

Islas, Arturo. *Migrant Souls.* New York: Morrow, 1990.

———. *The Rain God: A Desert Tale.* Palo Alto, Calif.: Alexandrian, 1984.

Jameson, Fredric. *The Political Unconscious: Narrative as a Socially Symbolic Act.* Ithaca, N.Y.: Cornell University Press, 1981.

Jussawalla, Feroza, and Reed Way Dasenbrock. Introduction. *Interviews with Writers of the Post-Colonial World.* Edited by Feroza Jussawalla and Reed Way Dasenbrock, 3–23. Jackson: University Press of Mississippi, 1992.

Kanellos, Nocolás. Foreward. *Recovering the U.S. Hispanic Literary Heritage.* Edited by Ramón Gutiérrez and Genaro Padilla, 13–15. Houston: Arte Público Press, 1993.

Kowalczyk, Kimberly. "Oscar Zeta Acosta: The Brown Buffalo and His Search for Identity." *America's Review* 16, nos. 3–4 (1988): 198–209.

La Fuente, Patricia de. "Invisible Women in the Narrative of Tomás Rivera." *International Studies in Honor of Tomás Rivera. Revista Chicano-Riqueña* 13, nos. 3–4 (1985): 81–9.

La Garza, Rodolfo O. de, et al., eds. *The Mexican American Experience: An Interdisciplinary Anthology.* Austin: University of Texas Press, 1985.

Larralde, Carlos. "Emma Tenayuca: La Pasionaria." In *Mexican American Movements and Leaders.* Los Alamos, N.M.: Hwong Publishing Co., 1976.

Lattin, Vernon E., Rolando Hinojosa, and Gary D. Keller, eds. *Tomás Rivera 1935–1984: The Man and His Work.* Tempe, Ariz.: Bilingual Review, 1988.

León, Arnoldo de. *Ethnicity in the Sunbelt: A History of Mexican Americans in Houston.* Mexican American Studies Monograph Series 7. Houston: Mexican American Studies, 1989.

———. *They Called Them Greasers: Anglo Attitudes Toward Mexicans in Texas, 1821–1900.* Austin: University of Texas Press, 1983.

Limón, José. *Dancing with the Devil: Society, Gender, and the Political Unconscious in Mexican-American South Texas.* Wisconsin University Press, 1994.

———. "Dancing with the Devil: Society, Gender, and the Political Unconscious in Mexican-American South Texas." *Criticism in the Borderlands: Studies in Chicano Literature, Culture, and Ideology.* Edited by Héctor Calderón and José Saldívar, 221–35. Durham: Duke University Press, 1991.

———. "Folklore, Gendered Repression, and Cultural Critique: The Case of Jovita González." *Texas Studies in Literature and Language* 35, no. 4 (1993): 453–73.

———. "The Folk Performance of 'Chicano' and the Cultural Limits of Political Ideology." *And Other Neighborly Names: Social Process and Cultural Image in Texas Folklore.* Edited by Richard Bauman and Roger D. Abrahams, 197–225. Austin: University of Texas Press, 1981.

———. "La Llorona, The Third Legend of Greater Mexico: Cultural Symbols, Women, and the Political Unconscious." *Renato Rosaldo Lecture Series Monograph* 2 (1984–85): 59–93.

———. *Mexican Ballads, Chicano Poems: History and Influence in Mexican American Social Poetry.* Berkley: University of California Press, 1992.

———. "El Primer Congreso Mexicanista de 1911: A Precursor to Contemporary Chicanismo." *Aztlán* 5, no. 1–2 (1974): 85–117.

Lizárraga, Sylvia S. "The Patriarchal Ideology in 'La noche que se apagaron las luces." *International Studies in Honor of Tomás Rivera. Revista Chicano-Riqueña* 13, nos. 3–4 (1985): 90–95.

López, Gerald P. *Rebellious Lawyering: One Chicano's Vision of Progressive Law Practice.* Boulder, Colo.: Westview, 1992.

MacLachlan, Colin M. *Anarchism and the Mexican Revolution: The Political Trials of Ricardo Flores Magón in the United States.* Berkeley: California University Press, 1991.

Magón, Ricardo Flores. "A La Mujer (To Women)." *Regeneración* [Los Angeles] September 24, 1910. Rpt. in *Mexican Women in the United States: Struggles past and present.* Edited by Magdalena Mora and Adelaida R. Del Castillo, 159–62. Occasional Paper 2.

Los Angeles: Chicano Studies Research Center Publications, University of California, 1980.

———. "Bread!" Translated by Mary F. Winnen. *Regeneración* [Los Angeles]. (February 28, 1913): 8.

Mann, Coramae Richey. *Unequal Justice: A Question of Color.* Bloomington: Indiana University Press, 1993.

Marable, Manning. *Race, Reform, and Rebellion: The Second Reconstruction in Black America, 1945–1982.* Jackson: Mississippi University Press, 1984.

Márquez, Benjamin. *LULAC: The Evolution of a Mexican American Political Organization.* Austin: University of Texas Press, 1993.

Martínez, Elizabeth. "Beyond Black and White." *Race, Poverty, and the Environment* 4, no. 3 (1993): 1, 21–2.

———. "Chingón Politics Die Hard." *Zeta Magazine* (April, 1990): 46–50.

Martínez, Elizabeth, and Ed McCaughan. "Chicanas and Mexicanas Within a Transnational Working Class." *Between Borders: Essays on Mexicana/Chicana History.* Edited by Adelaida R. Del Castillo, 31–60. La Mujer Latina Series. Encino, Calif.: Floricanto Press, 1990.

Martínez, Oscar J. *Troublesome Border.* Tuscon: Arizona University Press, 1988.

Martínez, Rubén. *The Other Side: Fault Lines, Guerilla Saints, and the True Heart of Rock 'N' Roll.* London: Verso, 1992.

Marx, Karl. *The Marx-Engels Reader.* 2d ed. Edited by Robert C. Tucker. New York: Norton, 1978.

Maynard, Dana Maya. "A Leader of His People and Two Survivors: Chicano Subjectivity in Paredes, Islas, and Moraga." Unpublished essay, 1993.

McLemore, Dale S., and Ricardo Romo. "The Origins and Development of the Mexican American People." *The Mexican American Experience: An Interdisciplinary Anthology.* Edited by Rodolfo O. de la Garza, et al., 3–32. Austin: University of Texas Press, 1985.

Mendoza, Louis G. "Confronting *la Frontera,* Identity, and Gender: Poetry and Politics in *La Crónica* and *El Demócrata Fronterizo." Recovering the U.S. Hispanic Literary Heritage, Volume III.* Eds. María Herrera Sobek & Virginia Sánchez Korrol. Houston: Arte Público Press, 2000. 103–23.

———. "On Buffaloes, Body Snatching, and Bandidismo: Ilan Stavans' Appropriation of Oscar Acosta and the Chicano Experience." (forthcoming in *Bilingual Review*).

Mesa-Bains, Amalia. "El Mundo Femenino: Chicano Artists of the Movement—A Commentary on Development and Production." *Chicano Art: Resistance and Affirmation, 1965–1985.* Los Angeles: UCLA Wight Art Gallery, 1990. 131–40.

Mirandé, Alfredo, and Evangelina Enríquez. *La Chicana: The Mexican American Woman.* Chicago: University of Chicago Press, 1977.

Miyoshi, Masao. "A Borderless World?: From Colonialism to Transnationalism and the Decline of the Nation-State." *Critical Inquiry* 19, no. 4 (summer, 1993): 726–51.

———. "Sites of Resistance in the Global Economy." *boundary* 2. 22:1 (1995): 61–84.

Montejano, David. *Anglos and Mexicans in the Making of Texas, 1836–1986.* Austin: University of Texas Press, 1987.

———. "Is Texas Bigger than the World System? A Critique From a Provincial Point of View." *Review* 4 (winter, 1981): 620–23.

Moquin, Wayne, and Charles Van Doren, eds. *A Documentary History of the Mexican Americans.* New York: Bantam, 1971.
Moraga, Cherríe. *The Last Generation.* Boston: South End Press, 1993.
———. *Loving in the War Years: lo que nunca pasó por sus labios.* Boston: South End Press, 1983.
Moraga, Cherríe, and Gloria Anzaldúa, eds. *This Bridge Called My Back: Writings by Radical Women of Color.* New York: Kitchen Table, 1981.
Morales, Alejandro. *The Brick People.* Houston: Arte Público Press, 1988.
Mujeres Activas en Letras y Cambio Social. "MALCS Declaration, June 1983." *Resistance and Celebration: La Fuerza de las Mujeres.* [Conference Program] Berkeley: n.p., 1992.
Muñoz, Carlos. *Youth, Identity, and Power: The Chicano Movement.* London: Verso, 1989.
Nairn, Tom. *The Break-Up of Britain: Crisis and New-Nationalism.* 2d ed. London: Verso, 1977.
Nora, Pierre. "Between Memory and History: *Les Lieux de Mémoire.*" *Representations* 26 (spring, 1989): 7–25.
Olivares, Julián, ed. *International Studies in Honor of Tomás Rivera. Revista Chicano-Riqueña* 13, nos. 3–4 (1985).
Olivares, Julián. "Sandra Cisneros' 'The House on Mango Street' and the Poetics of Space." *Chicana Creativity and Criticism: Charting New Frontiers in American Literature.* Edited by María Hererra-Sobek and Helena María Viramontes, 160–69. Houston: Arte Público Press, 1988.
Orozco, Cynthia E. *The Origins of the League of United Latin American Citizens (LULAC) and the Mexican American Civil Rights Movement in Texas with an Analysis of Women's Political Participation in a Gendered Context, 1910–1929.* Dissertation, University of California Los Angeles, 1992. Ann Arbor: University of Michigan Press, 1993.
———. "Sexism in Chicano Studies and the Community." *Chicana Voices: Intersections of Class, Race, and Gender.* Edited by Teresa Córdova, et al. Austin: CMAS Publications, 1986.
Padilla, Genaro M. *My History, Not Yours: The Formation of Mexican American Autobiography.* Madison: University of Wisconsin Press, 1993.
Paredes, Américo. *George Washington Gómez.* Houston: Arte Público Press, 1990.
———. *"With His Pistol in His Hand": A Border Ballad and Its Hero.* Austin: University of Texas Press, 1958.
Pérez, Emma M. "'A La Mujer': A Critique of the Partido Liberal Mexicano's Gender Ideology on Women." *Between Borders: Essays on Mexicana/Chicana History.* Edited by Adelaida R. Del Castillo, 459–82. La Mujer Latina Series. Encino: Floricanto Press, 1990.
———. *The Decolonial Imaginary: Writing Chicanas Into History.* Bloomington: Indiana University Press, 1999.
Pérez, Ramón. *Diary of an Undocumented Immigrant.* Houston: Arte Público Press, 1991.
Pérez-Torres, Rafael. *Movements in Chicano Poetry.* Cambridge: Cambridge University Press, 1995.
Ramírez, Arthur. "Review Essay: *The Autobiography of a Brown Buffalo* and *The Revolt of the Cockroach People.*" *Revista Chicano-Riqueña* 3, no. 3 (1975): 46–53.

Rebolledo, Tey Diana. *Women Singing in the Snow: A Cultural Analysis of Chicana Literature.* Tucson: Arizona University Press, 1995.

"Recalling Women of Achievement." *Laredo Times,* June 14, 1981: 1C.

Rivera, Tomás. Interview. *Chicano Authors: Inquiry by Interview.* By Juan Bruce-Novoa. Austin: University of Texas Press, 1980. 137–62.

———. "Into the Labyrinth: The Chicano in Literature." 1971. *Southwestern American Literature* 11, no. 2 (1972): 90–97.

———. *. . . y no se lo trago la tierra/. . . And the Earth Did Not Devour Him.* Translated by Evangelina Vigil-Piñón. 1987. Houston: Arte Público Press, 1992.

Rodríguez, Juan. "The Problematic in Tomás Rivera's . . . *and the earth did not part,*" *Contemporary Chicano Fiction: A Critical Survey.* Edited by Vernon E. Lattin, 131–40. Binghamton: Bilingual Press, 1986.

Rodriguez, Richard. *Hunger of Memory: The Education of Richard Rodriguez, An Autobiography.* New York: Bantam, 1981.

Romo, Ricardo. *East Los Angeles: History of a Barrio.* Austin: University of Texas Press, 1983.

Rosaldo, Renato. *Culture and Truth: The Remaking of Social Analysis.* Boston: Beacon Press, 1989.

Ruiz, Vicki. *Cannery Women, Cannery Lives: Mexican Women, Unionization, and the California Food Processing Industry, 1930–1950.* Albuquerque: University of New Mexico Press, 1987.

Ruiz de Burton, María Amparo. *The Squatter and the Don.* Edited by Rosaura Sánchez and Beatrice Pita. Houston: Arte Público Press, 1992.

Sagel, Jim. *Túnomas.* Ypsilanti: Bilingual Press, 1983.

Salas, Elizabeth. *Soldaderas in the Mexican Military: Myth and History.* Austin: University of Texas Press, 1990.

Saldívar, José. *Border Matters: Remapping American Cultural Studies.* Berkeley: University of California Press, 1997.

———. *The Dialectics of Our America: Genealogy, Cultural Critique, and Literary History.* Durham: Duke University Press, 1991.

Saldívar, Ramón. "The Borderlands of Culture: Américo Paredes's *George Washington Gómez* and Chicano Literature at the End of the Twentieth Century." *American Literary History* 5, no. 2 (1993): 272–93.

———. *Chicano Narrative: The Dialectics of Difference.* Madison: Wisconsin University Press, 1990.

Salinas, Raúl. "About Invasion and Conquest." *East of the Freeway: Reflections de mi Pueblo.* Austin: Red Salmon Press, 1995.

———. "A Trip through the Mind Jail." *Un Trip through the Mind Jail y Otras Excursions.* San Francisco: Editorial Pocho-Che, 1980. 55–60.

Sánchez, Marta Ester. *Contemporary Chicana Poetry: A Critical Approach to an Emerging Literature.* Berkeley: University of California Press, 1986.

Sánchez, Rosaura. "Ethnicity, Ideology and Academia." *Americas Review* 15, no. 1 (1989): 80–88.

———. "The History of Chicanas: A Proposal for a Materialist Perspective." *Between*

Borders: Essays on Mexicana/Chicana History. Edited by Adelaida R. Del Castillo, 1–30. La Mujer Latina Series. Encino, Calif.: Floricanto Press, 1990.

———. "Postmodernism and Chicano Literature." *Aztlán* 18, no. 2 (fall, 1987): 1–14.

San Miguel, Guadalupe, Jr. *"Let All of Them Take Heed": Mexican Americans and the Campaign for Educational Equality in Texas, 1910–1981.* Mexican American Monograph 11. Austin: University of Texas Press, 1987.

Santiago, Danny. *Famous All Over Town.* New York: Plume, 1983.

Saragoza, Alex M. "The Significance of Recent Chicano-Related Historical Writings: An Appraisal." *Ethnic Affairs* 1 (fall, 1987): 24–62.

Sartre, Jean-Paul. *What is Literature? And Other Essays.* Cambridge: Harvard University Press, 1988.

Schaeffer, Robert. *Warpaths: The Politics of Partition.* New York: Hill and Wang, 1990.

Scott, Joan. "Gender: A Useful Category of Historical Analysis." *Coming to Terms: Feminism, Theory, Politics.* Edited by Elizabeth Weed, 81–100. New York: Routledge, 1989.

Smith, Neil. *Uneven Development: Nature, Capital and the Production of Space.* 1984. New York: Blackwell, 1990.

Sommers, Joseph. "Interpreting Tomás Rivera." *Modern Chicano Writers: A Collection of Critical Essays.* Edited by Joseph Sommers and Tomás Ybarra-Frausto, 94–107. New Jersey: Prentice-Hall, 1979.

Spence, Juliette L. "A Bibliography of Writings About Tomás Rivera and His Works." *Tomás Rivera 1935–1984: The Man and His Work.* Edited by Vernon E. Lattin, Rolando Hinojosa, and Gary D. Keller, 153–58. Tempe, Ariz.: Bilingual Press, 1988.

Spivak, Gayatri Chakravorty. Introduction. *Selected Subaltern Studies.* Edited by Ranajit Guha and Gayatri Chakravorty Spivak, 3–32. New York: Oxford University Press, 1988.

Stavans, Ilan. *Bandido: Oscar "Zeta" Acosta and the Chicano Experience.* New York: HarperCollins, 1995.

———. *Oscar "Zeta" Acosta: The Uncollected Works.* Houston: Arte Público Press, 1996.

Tenayuca, Emma, and Homer Brooks. "The Mexican Question in the Southwest." *Communist* 18, no. 3 (1939): 257–68.

Tovar, Inés Hernandez. "Sara Estela Ramírez: The Early Twentieth Century Texas-Mexican Poet." Dissertation, University of Houston, 1984.

Trambley, Estela Portillo. "Sor Juana." *Sor Juana and Other Plays.* Ypsilanti: Bilingual Press, 1983.

Valle, Victor and Rudy D. Torres. "Enough of the Great Melodrama of Race Relations in Los Angeles." *Race, Poverty and the Environment* 4, no. 3 (1993): 20–21.

Vento, Arnoldo C., et al. *Flor Y Canto II: An Anthology of Chicano Literature.* Austin: Pajarito Publications, 1979.

Villareal, José Antonio. *Pocho.* Garden City, N.Y.: Doubleday, 1959.

Villaseñor, Victor. *Rain Of Gold.* Houston: Arte Público Press, 1991.

Viramontes, Helena María. *The Moths and Other Stories.* Houston: Arte Público Press, 1985.

White, Hayden. "The Historical Text as Literary Artifact." *Tropics of Discourse: Essays in Cultural Criticism.* Baltimore: John Hopkins University Press, 1978.

Zamora, Emilio. "Chicano Socialist Labor Activity in Texas, 1900–1920." *Aztlán* 6, no. 2 (1975): 221–37.

———. "Sara Estela Ramírez: Una Rosa Roja en el Movimiento." *Mexican Women in the United States: Struggles Past and Present.* Edited by Magdalena Mora and Adelaida R. Del Castillo, 163–69. Occasional Paper 2. Los Angeles: Chicano Studies Research Center Publications, University of California, 1980.

Zavella, Patricia. *Women's Work & Chicano Families: Cannery Workers of the Santa Clara Valley.* Ithaca, N.Y.: Cornell University Press, 1987.

INDEX

LOUIS GERARD MENDOZA is an assistant professor in the Department of English, Classics, and Philosophy at the University of Texas at San Antonio. He is the interm director of the Hispanic Research Center. He has published a number of articles on the subject of ethnic identity. He received his Ph.D. from the University of Texas at Austin in 1994.

ISBN 1-58544-150-3
90000
9 781585 441501